Interpreting Ceramics

Selected Essays

WUNDERKAMMER

Editors:
Jo Dahn
Jeffrey Jones

First published in 2013 by:
Wunderkammer Press in association with ICRC
(Interpreting Ceramics Research Collaboration)

Wunderkammer Press
Bath School of Art and Design
Bath Spa University
Sion Hill
Bath BA1 5SF

Printed in the United Kingdom

ISBN: 978-0-9566462-5-5 [paperback]
Interpreting Ceramics: Selected Essays
Dr Jo Dahn and Dr Jeffrey Jones (eds)
147 illustrations

Design@GloryHall.com
Type: Frutiger

WUNDERKAMMER

BATH SPA UNIVERSITY
PRIFYSGOL ABERYSTWYTH UNIVERSITY
Cardiff Metropolitan University
Prifysgol Fetropolitan Caerdydd
UWIC
UWE BRISTOL University of the West of England

This book is dedicated to

Emmanuel Cooper (1938-2012)

Contents

Interpreting Ceramics

Selected Essays

Interpreting Ceramics: The First Ten Years

The Interpreting Ceramics Research Collaboration (ICRC) was set up in 1999 by academics from four British Universities: the University of Wales, Aberystwyth, Bath Spa University College, the University of Wales Institute, Cardiff and the University of the West of England, Bristol. We wanted to explore ways in which collaborative effort can lead to broader and more interdisciplinary research into all those categories of human activity that are indicated by the term 'ceramics'. From studio pottery to industrial design, in historical or contemporary context, we were, and continue to be, committed to promoting interest in any practice or mode of inquiry that brings a social and cultural awareness to bear on the manufacture and consumption of objects made from ceramic materials, however they may be classified.

In the mid 1990s the ceramics research 'landscape' in Britain was very different to what it is today. There were isolated pockets of research activity in a few university departments and colleges of art. There were also a few dedicated freelance researchers and a number of passionate collectors who had gained extensive knowledge of the work of individual makers, particularly studio potters. Public and private archives relating to ceramics proved to be surprisingly rich and extensive for those with a mind to investigate, but they were comparatively underused. Organisations such as the Crafts Council and magazines such as *Ceramic Review* provided potentially invaluable research resources in the form of events and published material but, popular as these were, there was still much talk of the need for a firmer theoretical and critical base for the discipline.

In many ways the ground was well prepared for an initiative such as ICRC but it needed a group of people and a good idea around which it could all cohere. The Ceramic Collection in Aberystwyth had been established between 1920 and 1936; from 1974, under the curatorship of Moira Vincentelli, an active acquisitions policy was adopted, resulting in what is now one of the pre-eminent collections of contemporary ceramics in Britain. Vincentelli set up the Ceramics Archive in the late 1980s. It includes a wide variety of research material, including a unique oral history collection of audio interviews relating to ceramics and studio pottery. Then in 1992 Mike Hughes and Walter Keeler founded another important oral history resource: the National Electronic and Video Archive of the Crafts (NEVAC) at UWE Bristol. NEVAC (now called 'Recording the Crafts') formed a partnership with the Victoria and Albert museum in 1998. The archive includes video interviews with makers, collectors, critics, educationalists, shopkeepers, gallery owners and museum curators.

During the late 1990s Jo Dahn and Jeffrey Jones completed their PhDs in Aberystwyth under the supervision of Moira Vincentelli and went on to secure academic posts (Dahn in Bath and Jones in Cardiff). In 1998 Matthew Partington joined NEVAC as V&A Museum Research Fellow in the Applied Arts. What was to become the core ICRC team was now in place, with the important addition of Michael Hose who was rapidly building a research base in Cardiff, including provision for the first practice-based PhDs in ceramics. As the ICRC steering committee began to meet there was much talk of the potential benefits of an online journal but some disagreement about the scope of such a publication. Mike Hughes argued for a journal focused on oral history and archiving in ceramics and, in contrast, the idea of an electronic journal encompassing all crafts was suggested. In the end 'ceramics', broadly interpreted, would define the scope of the journal and *Interpreting Ceramics* (www.interpretingceramics.com) went live in August 2000, launched with a symposium at the V&A. Sadly Mike Hughes was too ill to attend and he died shortly afterwards.

Interpreting Ceramics has been the principle outcome of ICRC. The journal is peer-reviewed and freely accessible. Publishing online offers some advantages: it means that the articles can be read by anyone with an Internet connection and though still accommodating traditional text-based approaches, it also allows our contributors to exploit the possibilities of digital media.

The first issue of *Interpreting Ceramics* appeared in 2000. Designed by Glory Hall, who continues to give the journal its distinctive look, it featured articles by ICRC founder members and thus reflected their particular interests. Since then there have been a further thirteen issues, dealing with a very wide variety of topics and we would like to thank all the authors who have contributed to the journal over the years. As well as conventional submissions from individuals worldwide, we have published sets of conference papers and the journal has twice been guest edited by Mary Drach McInnes, New York State College of Ceramics, Alfred University. This book presents a collection of essays from the first ten years of the journal. They have been chosen with a view to representing the diversity of subject matter that was covered and are organised according to the original date of publication.

In the twelve years since *Interpreting Ceramics* first went online, the editorial team has remained remarkably stable, although other changes have occurred. Three of the Universities have new names: Aberystwyth University, Bath Spa University and Cardiff Metropolitan University. Kathy Talbot has become an invaluable member of the editorial committee as Secretary and Reviews Editor and Conor Wilson and Natasha Mayo have also contributed to the team. The National Museum Wales recently joined ICRC as the fifth participating institution with Head of Applied Art, Andrew Renton, representing the museum on the editorial committee. We continue to develop innovative projects and at time of writing we have just published the papers from the *Ceramics and Sculpture: Different Disciplines and Shared Concerns* conference held at the museum on 5 July 2012.

Interpreting Ceramics: *Selected Essays* is dedicated to Emmanuel Cooper OBE (1938–2012). Emmanuel was a constant supporter and a member of the *Interpreting Ceramics* advisory board from its inception. Editor of *Ceramic Review* from 1970–2010, in the July/August 2007 issue he called for a more rigorous approach to writing on the crafts. While he noted that *Interpreting Ceramics* was addressing what he saw as a lack of 'written critique', he also thought that 'a computer screen is not conducive to long or serious reading'. He wanted 'a hard copy … that is portable and can be picked up and put down at will, one that can even be annotated with notes in the margin'. Here it is.

This is the first of two chapters dealing with women and ceramics that were originally published in the first issue of *Interpreting Ceramics.* Both chapters pursue a 'material culture' approach. Moira Vincentelli examines the changing role of the Welsh dresser and its display in the construction of Welsh female identity. The account is based on a particular case study and draws on audio and video recordings that reveal how the dresser and the objects on the dresser, especially ceramics, are repositories of personal memory and family history. Moira Vincentelli is Emeritus Professor in Art History at Aberystwyth University (formerly the University of Wales, Aberystwyth) and has been Curator of the significant Ceramics collection there since 1975. She has published extensively; her particular interest in gender and ceramics resulted in two key texts on the subject: *Women and Ceramics: Gendered Vessels* (MUP, 2000) and *Women Potters: Transforming Traditions* (A&C Black, 2003)

The Welsh Dresser: A Case Study

Moira Vincentelli

> Jane was happy; the house shone including the old dresser and clock that her mother had given her … And the food was good. She was glad she had sufficient of the new-fashioned little glass plates for cakes and jam.[1]

Originally written in Welsh, this passage by the novelist Kate Roberts conjures up many of the points raised in this chapter. It suggests the delight in domestic activity, in domestic display, in the production of good food, and the status and satisfaction of owning a family heirloom in the form of 'an old dresser' and at the same time being up-to-date with 'new-fashioned little glass plates'. Roberts wrote about Wales in the first half of the twentieth century – a Wales emerging from its peasant and rural roots into industrial and consumer society. Her novels focus on women and evoke the importance of domestic objects as symbols of identity and change in women's lives.

From a different perspective the burgeoning of consumer society can be connected with 'conspicuous consumption' and the expansion of the middle class of the nineteenth century where the *nouveaux riches* demonstrate their distance from practical activity and the world of work through the display of decorative goods chosen for their 'look' rather than their 'usefulness'.[2] This can be linked with the phenomenon of large shops and department stores where personal choice from a wide range of similar items becomes significant. Remy Saisselin deploys the notion of the 'bibelot' and associates it with the female domain.

> woman herself turns into a most expensive bibelot and yet is, at the same time, a voracious consumer of luxury and accumulator of bibelots.[3]

Women and Welsh identity

Although this notion is based on late nineteenth-century, urban, middle-class culture it makes an interesting comparison with what became one of the most popular icons of Welsh culture: the Welsh tea party, where women in Welsh costume sit at a table with teacups. Such Welsh ladies have been dubbed 'the demure and passive doll of the

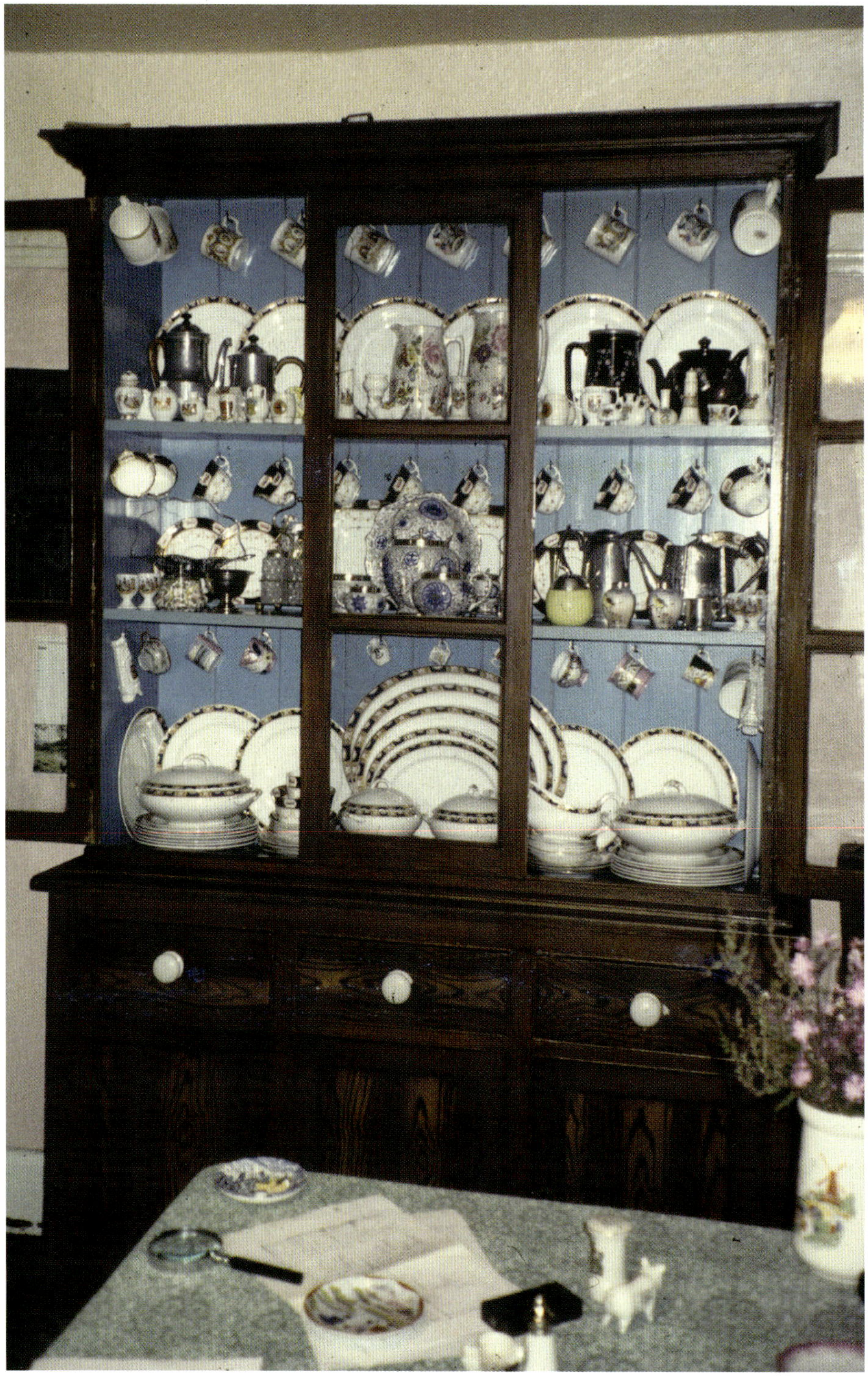

Fig 1. Living-room dresser, 1924, with wedding china.

posters and postcards.[4] The setting is entirely constructed, the costumes taken from the photographer's basket of Welsh costumes – but this is how some Welsh women chose to have themselves photographed. In 1877 an advertisement for Humphreys Fine Art Gallery, Caernavon at the time of the National Eisteddfod reads:

> First Class Photographic Studio …
>
> Public men – including bards, Literary characters, Ministers, Musicians, etc., are respectfully invited to pay a visit to the Studio, as H. H. intends forming a Gallery of WELSH CELEBRITIES.
>
> Welsh Costumes (on hire) for Ladies wishing to be taken in the same.

The photography will record Welsh men as 'great and successful' in public life, whereas women have become the symbols of 'Welshness': the bearers of cultural identity epitomised by the costume, which has its own interesting history as 'an invented tradition'.[5] The teacup also stands as a signifier of respectable feminine identity. In 1847 the Education Report on Wales, the 'Blue Books', had accused the Welsh of barbaric customs and Welsh women of sexual laxity because of the custom of bundling, where couples were allowed to spend the night together before marriage. In part at least, in response to this, and in conjunction with the rise of Welsh Nonconformism, female sexuality was strictly policed.[6] At the same time, in association with the religious revivals, women became leading participants in the Temperance movement. The Welsh tea party became a national icon focused around the respectable activity of drinking tea as opposed to the non-respectable activity of drinking beer. The collecting of china and glass for display on the dresser became interwoven with a Welsh feminine identity. The place where they were displayed – the dresser – became a signifier of both Welshness and female domestic prowess.

An obvious manifestation of conspicuous consumption and luxury would hardly be acceptable in a society where nonconformist values dominated, but what objects would be available to Welsh nineteenth-century society? Jewellery was too strongly associated with worldliness and vanity. Framed pictures were certainly to be found, but mainly in the form of improving texts or portraits – most commonly prints after paintings of famous preachers. The great attraction of ceramics was that such wares as teacups and jugs were ostensibly functional and hence they avoided the worst sin of being merely ornamental.

The dresser in Wales

The particular significance of the dresser in Welsh culture was consolidated at the end of the nineteenth century, precisely the time when Welsh culture was losing its distinctive characteristics, children were punished for speaking Welsh in schools and it was widely believed that the language would disappear quite quickly. Wales could be said to be a colonised country and, with the spread of education, was imbibing negative views of its own culture and values in relation to the dominant culture. But as James Clifford has argued, these processes are both destructive and creative:

> Much has simultaneously been invented and revived in complex, oppositional contexts. If the victims of progress and empire are weak, they are seldom passive.[7]

The response to these processes of change can usefully be examined by focusing around the actuality and the concept of the Welsh dresser. Although some social historians have recognised the social relationships enshrined in the objects displayed on the dresser, it is usually written about and recorded as an item of fine furniture. Furniture historians are most interested in early examples; from the eighteenth century, for example, a time when the dresser was a piece of furniture associated with the gentry. In the nineteenth century it became the prerogative of farmers and artisans in Wales. Originally dressers were made from local materials, in particular oak, but less expensive ones were made of pine, which was increasingly used by the end of the century. By this time the design had been adapted and the open shelving of the upper part was divided up with glass-fronted side cupboards, more appropriate for the display of delicate china. The categorisation of artefacts in design history and furniture history has meant that dressers are invariably discussed, and even photographed, independently of the display, a major factor in their visual impact.

Furniture production is normally assumed to be a male activity, although there are exceptions. Ceramic display, as far as I have found, is largely the province of women. The apparently ephemeral nature of display makes it difficult to record and categorise which, of course, is the way that creative practices gain recognition. Hence the female practice is overlooked in favour of the male practice. The ceramic display is largely formed of material manufactured outside Wales although some of was produced for a Welsh market. But in general, taken individually, these items are neither rare nor finely crafted and consequently not very highly valued as antiques. The whole is undoubtedly greater than the sum of the parts.

There is a vocabulary of display based on symmetrical arrangements, sometimes around a centrepiece such as a clock on the broadest surface with plates standing up on the narrow shelves, the biggest platters on the top. Jugs hang on hooks along the fronts of the shelves. The contrast of blue and white china and lustre jugs is the most typical combination. There are distinct regional variations on this pattern and within that individuals make modifications for their own needs and purposes, whether these are of a social or a sentimental nature or for aesthetic ends.

Welsh dressers took on a particular meaning round the turn of the century, when they became strongly associated with a Welsh identity in response to the threat to Welsh culture and language. This was a period when Welsh people were becoming both more anglicised and more middle class. Dressers are by no means exclusive to Wales but popular parlance often uses the term 'Welsh' dresser even if there is no necessary connection with Wales. Welsh identity became more symbolic and dressers become part of the new mythology.

During the 1990s I conducted a number of interviews with women and some men about their Welsh dresser. Here I want to examine one case study based on an interview with a woman from Fishguard in south-west Wales. From this particular case I hope to tease out issues of gender and Welsh identity and elaborate on some of the points that I have suggested in my more general preamble.[8]

Dresser and *seld*

Firstly it is worth considering language. My interviewee E. was Welsh speaking but her husband was not Welsh speaking so she always spoke English in the family home as well as Welsh. She spoke Welsh to her daughter. When she was young she spoke almost only Welsh in the home and learned English at school. Like many Welsh-speaking people of her generation she read dates and numbers in English even if they occurred in a Welsh context. This was clear when she was reading me inscriptions on commemorative mugs. When her mother wrote her list of wedding presents, which will be discussed below, she wrote in English.[9] Although Welsh was her first language, English was easier to write because that was what she had learned in school. Hence in some of the evidence the tensions between Welsh culture and language overlaid by English are in evidence.

When E. spoke about her dressers, of which she had two, she frequently used the South Walian Welsh word for a dresser, '*seld*'. The word 'dresser' sounded not just English to her but is also close to the North Walian word '*dresel*'. The use of the Welsh and regional word even when speaking English underlines its status as a significant object in her sense of cultural and regional identity.

In the interviewee's house there were two public rooms at the front. On the left as you entered from the entrance corridor was the living room. It had her mother's *seld* on the back wall, a settee, the television and on either side of the fireplace were cupboards and shelves which contained, in one case, more ordinary domestic items, and on the other, bookshelves and a display of the interviewee's collection of ornamental owls. This room was the central focus of the life of the house; the kitchen led off it with a door out to the garden. In the other room on the right of the entrance, the parlour, there was a much more private and personal space where there was another *seld*, a small organ, and a china cabinet with some of E.'s own wedding presents from the late 1940s. The whole room was decorated with popular 'cosmic' designs of suns and moons and table decorations of branches and mosses, which the interviewee collected in the woods.

Her mother's dresser in the living room was made of pine which had been varnished and treated to look like oak although it had a reddish-brown colour. The heavy wood-grain effect from combing was redone, E. remembered, when she was a child but in its original style. It had not been retouched since then, although at some point the background was painted blue. The dresser was given to her parents on their marriage in 1924, by the groom's father. This wedding is particularly well documented because the bride drew up a careful list of all her presents when she was on her honeymoon in Llanwrtyd Wells. The honeymoon to a Welsh spa town was itself a modern custom. The list had been preserved and the dresser appeared on the list of wedding presents as the major piece of furniture along with six chairs, two tables and a sofa.

> There's a replica of this, the original is next door with my grandparents – or it was then – and they decided on a copy for their son Tom. It was made by a local firm, a shop called Nicholls – the younger generation is there now.

Although this was a new piece of furniture there was clearly a strong sense of maintaining a tradition of dresser design even within the family.

The wedding presents

On the list it appeared that the furniture was mainly given by male members of the family: the two fathers and the bride's older brother for whom she had kept house. The groom's mother gave a washstand and dressing table.

What kinds of meanings can we draw from this list? The list was made when the couple were on their honeymoon and it conveyed a sense of satisfaction in what the couple had accumulated. It was headed 'Our list of wedding presents'. According to my interviewee:

> It was customary to make a list of all your wedding presents and you handed it out to show people what you had.

Around 1900 it was not unusual for newspapers to publish lists of presents with their givers and the practice survived in some parts of Britain into the second half of the century. However the accounting for presents has a particular resonance within Welsh culture in the custom known as 'bidding'. A bidder went round before a wedding to invite people to the festivities and to make a contribution to the young couple's needs. It was a formalised system of exchange where marriage was the moment of major inheritance when children were given their due. The presents, money or food gifts were recorded by a clerk and in some cases the food could then be auctioned off to raise further cash. The records would then oblige the recipient at some future date to repay equivalent amounts to the giver or members of their family. The remnants of this custom were still maintained at the beginning of this century.[10] This wedding list, from 1924, seems to have been a public account of what had been received, thus not unrelated to the earlier tradition of bidding.

Although modelled on an earlier example owned by E.'s grandparents, the dresser was of relatively modern design. Two glass doors with a fixed glass panel in the middle enclosed the entire upper part, shielding the contents from the grime and soot exuded from coal fires, important if things were not really for use but only display. When it was created there was nothing on this dresser that had any pretensions of being antique or even traditional and in 1924 it would probably have represented modernity and prosperity, but for all that in this family it had become a very important symbolic object that was carefully preserved by mother and then daughter. E.'s mother had died quite young, just before E. herself married, so E. had stayed on in the family home and had kept house for her father as well as her own husband and children. The dresser had undoubtedly assumed a special importance for her father as a memory of his wife. Nothing in this dresser was ever used: the interviewee had never used any of it herself and did not recall her mother ever doing so. It was from the start an object of display but had taken on additional meaning because of particular family circumstances.

An interest in ceramic collecting and display became very important to women at this time. The wedding present list indicates that the givers are predominantly women: forty-seven women, fifteen men and ten couples. This could be explained by the fact that the bride was one of ten of whom six were girls, and the groom one of three with two sisters, but I doubt if this could account for it entirely and it seems that what is demonstrated here is an elaborate system of gift exchange focused around decorative ceramic and glass objects.

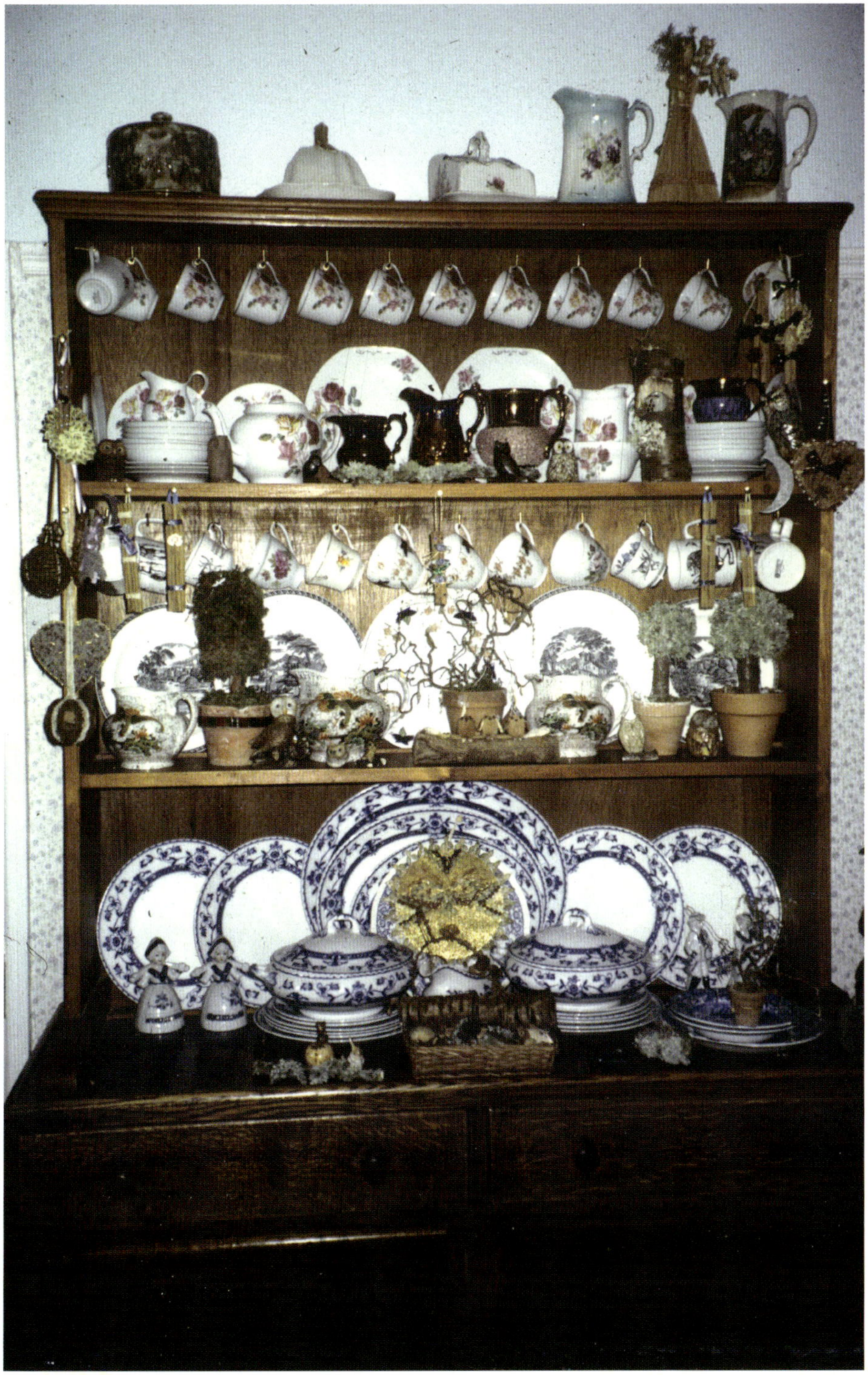

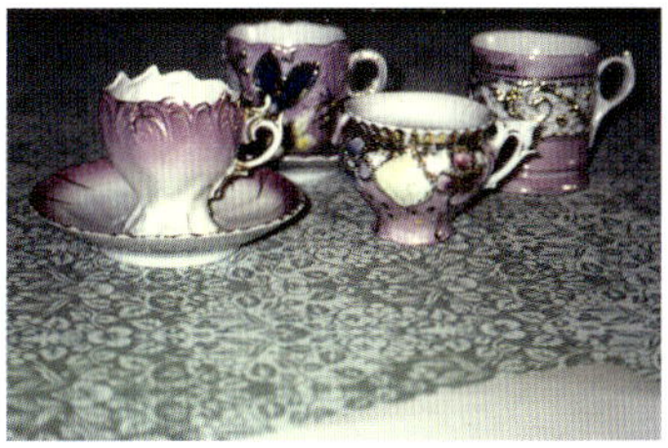

Fig 2. above, Decorative pink china, 1920s.

Fig 3. left, Parlour dresser, assembled 1990s, with china display and modern decorations.

All photos: Moira Vincentelli.

This is further substantiated by other items kept on display on the dresser, including a collection of souvenir china, miniature vases stamped with place names avidly collected and exchanged between women as they began to travel more. There were also examples of pink cups and saucers, which seemed to have been specifically gift china and are particularly characteristic of the period. All of these were delicate and would have been difficult to use but in the case of one of them, quite impossible as the cup had a frilled rim: a sure sign of its display and symbolic nature. This is what the interviewee said about them:

> It was common practice to give these. I had several given to me. Mum's sisters now – going away – they'd bring back a cup and saucer. I remember I had some and I remember thinking why couldn't they bring back a stick of rock or something. I don't particularly like them. They are very ornate. It's too garish for my liking.

Objects and stories

But she was very fond of a little pair of pearlised miniature vases with a print of a 'Welsh spinners party' applied to the side. This is the story she told in relation to these.

> Now it was customary when a man married he was given a present of the Bible and Dad was given a present from his Sunday school class. We lived here and it used to be the Methodist manse next door but one. And Mr and Mrs J. they weren't just our minister and his wife they were great friends of ours … Well anyway Mrs J. was very fond of my mother and felt it wasn't fair that Daddy had a present but not Mum so she gave those out of her own *seld* to my mother. From her own *seld* … On condition that they weren't put down with her list of wedding presents because as minister's wife she could offend other young couples getting married.

This story has preserved a number of points. Firstly it was a personal gift 'from her own *seld*', the more personal because it was not bought from a shop directly. Secondly the dresser was a place where women could have a surplus of disposable goods which could, on appropriate occasions, be used as presents. The story also underlines the public nature of this gift giving. She did not want her present to be recorded on the wedding list because, as a minister's wife, it would immediately put her under obligation to every young bride. Lastly it allows me to consider the form and decoration of these vases. The fineness and iridescent effect, like mother-of-pearl, was particularly admired by E. They were made in Czechoslovakia and decorated with a transfer print (a relatively inexpensive technique) of the 'Welsh spinners party' appropriate for a Welsh market. This motif is a variation of the Welsh tea party discussed earlier and it indicates clearly that the Welsh were consuming this image of themselves; it was not just created for tourists. The cultural traditions and language that were undoubtedly disappearing under the impact of the dominant anglophile culture were being substituted by this kind of picturesque Welshness. In fact E. had a number of photographs of her mother and her sisters in Welsh costume, which they hired from the photographer. She was sure her mother had never worn or owned Welsh costume. Clearly in 1924 this was still prevalent, but by 1949, when the interviewee was married, there were no examples of this kind of china and the photographic tradition of women in Welsh costume had died out.

Such imagery has not entirely lost its appeal although it is now mainly for the consumption of the 'outsider'. Among the wedding presents was a set of eggcups, also with a 'Welsh lady' design, given by nieces and nephews of the bride as children. When one of them who had emigrated to Canada came back to visit she had chosen an eggcup to take back to Canada as a memento. It had additional significance because it came from the '*seld*'.

In another case was a little Japanese cup and saucer of a kind widely imported into Britain, which had been given to the bride not as a wedding present but as a souvenir, by the fiancé of one of her sisters, a sailor on an oil tanker. This was an unusual example of a male giver. When, soon after, the oil tanker was lost with all its crew, the cup and saucer was placed in the dresser, and took on a special significance as a memory of the young man who had died.

Although many of these things were given as gifts and were not strictly 'collected' there were some stories that suggest such an impulse. One concerned a teaset bought with wedding money on their honeymoon, to match a cake-stand and cruet set that had been given. When they got home it was found not to be an exact match. But in the telling of this story one senses the excitement of shopping, selecting and finding matching sets.

Another aspect of collecting which is intimately connected with Welsh dressers is the lustre jug. It seems that these were not given as wedding presents in 1924, probably because they were not seen as 'modern'. However they were collected with great enthusiasm in Wales; their shiny metallic quality contrasts well with blue and white china and they could be found in sets with different designs and in different sizes, which makes them eminently collectable.

E. recounted that her mother and all her sisters received a lustre jug in return for collecting horsehair. Once a year the horsehair merchant visited Fishguard, on Fishguard Fair Day, and offered different-sized lustre jugs in exchange for quantities of horsehair. Their father worked with horses and each year one of his daughters was given the task or the opportunity to collect the horsehair. Clearly lustre jugs were seen as an appropriate and desirable object for a young girl to collect in the second decade of the twentieth century.

In another tale of lustre jugs E. recorded how her aunt had a wonderful collection bought at auction sales in the 1930s, when crockery from house clearances was piled together in big baskets and sold as job lots. She had then given her nieces and nephews one each in her lifetime thus handing on a tradition and creating a memento whereby she herself might be remembered.

When asked to compare her own wedding presents with those of her mother she said:

> It was the end of the war and china was scarce. … We got a lot of Pyrex things – we had a horrible lot of Pyrex things which I don't like at all … and lots of bed clothes … but nobody gave us anything to compare with the china in the *seld* at all.

Then she remembered almost as an afterthought:

> We have a china cabinet next door with presents – little silver things that we never use like jam dishes and cottages. We have a lot of those.

She maintained she did not like any of these things much and did not appear to care about them, nor did her daughter. However they were there on display in a cabinet largely hidden by a chair. They did not appear to have taken on any symbolic value.

Tradition and innovation in display

Also in this room was another dresser which was of great significance. The dresser in the living room was preserved as a family shrine but the one in the parlour was *her* dresser. She talked about this one being 'for me'. At sixty-five she had reviewed her life, much of which had been spent looking after other people. At that point her father, who had always lived with her, had recently died and her children had grown up. She felt very strongly that this was her domain and she had lavished her decorative and creative skills and attention on it and on this room. While we were in this room both mother and daughter reminisced about the female line going back to a great-grandmother 'Mami Coed Du Haul' who had been a midwife and herbalist and had passed on the knowledge of plants and potions to her daughter, the grandmother of my interviewee. This knowledge was not really preserved into the last two generations except perhaps in a renewed form of collecting mosses and plants to make decorations.

The dresser itself was a hybrid, made of recently constructed shelves on top of an older sideboard. The quality of the furniture was of no particular importance, it was the display that counted. In some ways this dresser, although created quite recently, drew on older traditions of display including blue and white china and lustre jugs. It also incorporated other aspects of creative expression in the form of arrangements of natural objects, and decorations made from wood, cones and moss.

The evidence strongly suggests that the dresser and the display on the dresser is a site for female creative activity. Sometimes the dresser is preserved as an historic heirloom in a time capsule, as it were, but in other cases considerable modifications can be made. In this case study E. had one of each. Many dressers are very beautiful examples of furniture, but their visual effect is ultimately in the display. Welsh dresser display is created by women and there is a traditional vocabulary of styles and arrangements which are followed; but there is also scope for individual initiative. The dresser display as a dynamic piece of house decoration, offers an opportunity to display excess wealth, i.e. non-functional goods. It is a place around which family memories and histories can accrue and is also a vehicle for creative expression. The stories people tell about objects invariably have the ring of oft-told stories.

Conclusion

In his study of consumer society and material culture, Daniel Miller distinguishes between personal property, private property and communal property, where private property may be seen as a producer of wealth for the owner who may have no personal relationship with the object.[11] The Welsh dresser has become an object of investment and speculation over the last forty years. The value of a nineteenth-century oak dresser increased ten-fold during the 1960s. However it also embodies both the other categories of personal and communal property. The dresser is communal property in so far as it is seen as an heirloom to be passed down within the family if at all possible. At the same time the objects on the dresser can be of a personal nature relevant to one particular owner and can be disposed of by that person. In the case under discussion a second dresser has been created in order to allow for just that personal element.

I have suggested that dressers and the display on them represent an aspect of family wealth or capital. They also function as 'cultural capital' in Bourdieu's sense. In *Distinction* Bourdieu suggested that all kinds of cultural choices or preferences display taste which in turn conveys class position.[12] Antique dressers and displays of very carefully collected ceramics, or even pewter, undoubtedly have potential to convey taste and specialised knowledge. More than one of my interviewees indicated that a daughter-in-law did not really know how to display things properly on her (recently acquired) dresser. In one case it was suggested by an interviewee from West Wales that this was because her daughter-in-law was from South Wales, that is, a very anglicised region. It seemed that her Welsh credentials were being called into question. In another case a highly educated young Welsh woman with a strong sense of national identity had self-consciously decided that she would have a dresser for everyday use and had rejected the dresser as an object of symbolic and 'aspiring middle-class' display. Thus the dresser and its display of ceramics is a signifier; it conveys taste, educational background, regional difference and attitude to Welsh identity. The dresser is an object that preserves histories – Welsh histories, local regional histories and individual histories – but it remains an active symbol and site for the creation of cultural meaning in contemporary Wales.

Notes

1 K. Roberts, *Feet in Chains*, trans. J. I. Jones (London: Corgi Books, 1980).

2 For a discussion of these concepts see T. Veblen, *The Theory of the Leisure Class* (London: Allen and Unwin, 1912); R. Saisselin, *Bricobacomania: The Bourgeois and the Bibelot* (London: Thames and Hudson, 1985); D. Miller, *Material Culture and Mass Consumption* (Oxford: Blackwell, 1987), p. 147.

3 Saisselin, *Bricobracomania*, p. 53.

4 D. Beddoe, 'Images of Welsh women', in T. Curtis (ed.), *Wales: the Imagined Nation* (Bridgend: Poetry Wales Press, 1986), p. 237.

5 For a further discussion of this see Prys Morgan, 'From death to a view: the hunt for the Welsh past in the Romantic period', in E. Hobsbawm and T. Ranger (eds), *The Invention of Tradition* (Cambridge: Cambridge University Press, 1983); and Beddoe, 'Images of Welsh women'.

6 What came to be known as 'The Treason of the Blue Books' was an attempt to deal with problems of political unrest, religious dissent and the Welsh language but was ostensibly an enquiry into the state of education in Wales. The writers went beyond the brief of producing a report on education and manifest little understanding of cultural differences measuring the Welsh against middle-class English norms. See Prys Morgan, 'From death to a view', pp. 92–3.

7 J. Clifford, *The Predicament of Culture* (Cambridge and London: Harvard University Press, 1988), p. 16.

8 Sadly my main informant (E.) has passed away some years ago but I would like to acknowledge my gratitude to a wonderful lady who generously gave of her time to talk to me and allowed me to photograph her home. All the quotations are taken from a transcription of an interview made in 1994.

9 This is a recognised phenomenon. Catrin Stevens notes that: 'Most Welsh lovers, although they spoke the language fluently, because they had little, if any, schooling in its written form, preferred to write in English, however inadequate their command of it might be.' C. Stevens, *Welsh Courting Customs* (Llandysul: Gomer, 1993), p. 158.

10 J. G. Jenkins, *Life and Tradition in Rural Wales* (London: Dent, 1976), p. 137. Published wedding lists can be found in the *Cambrian News* in 1900 but the practice was also prevalent in Lancashire and could still be found as late as the 1970s.

11 Miller, *Material Culture and Mass Consumption*, p. 121.

12 P. Bourdieu, *Distinction: A Social Critique of the Judgement of Taste* (London: Routledge and Kegan Paul, 1984).

This is the second of two chapters dealing with women and ceramics that were originally published in the first issue of *Interpreting Ceramics*. Here Jo Dahn suggests that the component objects of the domestic interior can be usefully considered as forming an 'objectscape' with many social and cultural functions. She discusses the correlation between women and ceramics in the eighteenth century and shows how ceramics featured in the aristocratic lifestyle of Mrs Mary Delany (1700–80), ultimately arguing that they were central to her notion of feminine community. The principal source material is Delany's published correspondence. Jo Dahn is Senior Lecturer in Critical Studies in Art and Design and Course Director for MA Curatorial Practice at Bath Spa University.

Mrs Delany and Ceramics in the Objectscape

Jo Dahn

Until relatively recently notions of class-based behaviour derived from Thorstein Veblen – particularly conspicuous consumption and emulation – were central to accounts that sought to interrogate our relationship with the objects of material culture.[1] However, the motivation to consume is, and always has been, more complex, more variable and more interesting than Veblen believed. Latter-day theorists have shown that object-systems function in a variety of ways to produce meaning(s). Pierre Bourdieu, for example, has demonstrated that consumption activities may not be motivated by emulation, but by differentiation, whereby each class strives to distinguish itself from others. Research that examines particular instances of consumption increasingly reveals its heterogeneity. Moira Vincentelli gives a useful summary of historical and theoretical approaches to the consumption of objects in the domestic arena. In her view (and mine) gender is an important factor:

> Gender affects people's relationship to the material world, hence men and women have different attachments to different objects corresponding to the gender roles 'scripted' by a society.[2]

From whatever theoretical position one proceeds, it is clear that the organisation of sets of objects forms one of the frameworks via which day-to-day life is experienced. I want to argue that within the domestic sphere there exists what might be thought of as a 'landscape' of objects, which I will term an 'objectscape', that has both psychic and practical function(s) and forms part of the multi-layered environment that each individual inhabits. The assembling of the objectscape, and behaviour(s) with regard to it, continues throughout life. This is a complex process. The objectscape can be 'read', providing insight as to (for instance) character, or fiscal status. Moreover, the material properties of some objects within the objectscape can determine behaviour: the porcelain tea service elicits a very different set of actions from its earthenware equivalent.

The accumulated and accumulating objectscape exerts its own pressures on the individual. In *Discipline and Punish*, Michel Foucault discussed the development of the Panopticon method of surveillance whereby prison inmates are 'caught up in a power system of which they are themselves the bearers ... what matters is that he knows himself to be observed'.[3] He argued that the Panopticon principle is manifest in many variations that strengthen 'social forces', the result being 'a society penetrated through and through with disciplinary mechanisms'.[4] Indeed, Foucault referred to 'the panopticisms of every day', and the objectscape can be seen to have an analogous function, as the individual negotiates a set of objects that themselves signify social relationships.[5] Whatever their peculiarities, such objects are constant reminders of social context. Gifts and inherited objects, for example, are both capable of evoking close personal ties. We might conceive of the 'vigilance' of objects in this connection, for within the objectscape there will be many items that stand witness to that network of other people with whom each individual seeks to interact, and whose understanding and approval is an important factor in the process of individual and social self-definition.

In 1982 Neil McKendrick famously declared that emulation was the spur to 'an unprecedented propensity to consume' that gathered force over the course of the eighteenth century.[6] He saw ceramic objects as central to this 'consumer revolution'.[7] Female consumers in particular, were slaves to fashion and experienced 'a compulsive need' to acquire ceramics.[8] Since then, the correlation between women and ceramics during this period has been noted by several writers. Elizabeth Kowaleski-Wallace, for example, argues that china can be regarded 'as a defining trope for femininity'.[9] She has discussed the development of the relationship between women and china as indicative of the '"fictile" process through which gender is constructed'. To situate or 'read' a woman in relation to a set of china objects was to collude in her commodification. She concludes that overall it was the 'frangible condition' of women that china recalled, and that whereas 'the woman at the tea table' could be constructed in many different ways, 'what she could never be was an independent agent, actively creating her own definition of subjectivity'.[10] The association between women and material culture as represented in many novels of the period lends support for her view. But this is a complex issue and we need more 'real' historical evidence detailing the specifics of women's choice and consumption of china. My concern in this essay is to explore the way(s) ceramics featured in the objectscape of Mary Delany (1700–88). I want to propose that it *was* possible for a woman to actively produce her own subjectivity in the cultural arena of the objectscape.

Best known for her flowers worked in cut paper (her 'flora'), throughout her adult life Mrs Delany collected and displayed ceramics. They were key components of the objectscapes she inhabited, and central to her notion of feminine community. What follows is heavily reliant on her voluminous correspondence, which was edited by Lady Llanover and published in six volumes in 1861–62.[11] Mrs Delany was an aristocratic *habitué* of court circles and an arbiter of taste, close to several important and influential patrons and collectors, most notably her best friend the Duchess of Portland (Margaret

Harley). The world evoked in her letters is a world of privilege from the feminine perspective; there are marvellously vivid references to the acquisition and consumption of objects.

Mrs Delany: biography

Born Mary Granville, Mrs Delany, as she is usually known, was first married (against her inclination) in 1718 to Alexander Pendarves, a man of means forty-one years her senior. The marriage had been engineered by her uncle, Lord Lansdowne, in an attempt to resuscitate the family fortunes. However, Alexander Pendarves died suddenly in 1724. Contrary to expectations, he had not made a will in favour of his wife, and the bulk of his estate went to his niece. His widow was left an income amounting to some hundreds (rather than thousands) of pounds per annum. She went to live with her uncle and aunt, Lord and Lady Stanley, at their villa in Fulham. After the requisite period of mourning, she became a popular member of court society whose taste and artistic abilities were much admired. She developed a high level of skill in decorative work of all kinds, such as textiles, japanning, shell work, as well as the famous flora; she was also considered to be highly accomplished at drawing, painting and music.

After Lady Stanley died in 1730, Mary Pendarves went to live at Richmond with her friend Mrs Donellan. The following year the two women made an extended visit to Ireland. It was there that the widow Pendarves met clergyman Dr Patrick Delany (1685–1768). Upon her return to England in the spring of 1733, she set up house in Lower Brook Street, London. Patrick Delany became a widower in 1740, at the age of fifty-five. Three years later he arrived in London and proposed to Mary Pendarves. Despite some family resistance – her brother Bernard disapproved because Delany was the son of a servant – the couple were married in July 1743. Their first year together was spent in England; then in June 1744 they removed to Dr Delany's residence at Delville in Dublin. Their ensuing twenty-five years of happy marriage were mostly spent in Ireland.

Mrs Delany regularly corresponded with many people, the majority of them women. A large proportion of her published letters was written (often on a daily basis) to her sister Ann Granville, who became Mrs Dewes in 1740. These letters are long and detailed; in many ways they appear to have functioned as a diary. After Ann Dewes died in July 1761, Mrs Delany transferred the correspondence to her niece Mary Dewes, although 'her natural elasticity of spirit did not recover its former level for many years'.[12] That 'elasticity' was tested again in 1768 when Patrick Delany died. His widow spent the first months of her mourning at Bulstrode with the Duchess of Portland, herself already a widow. Their friendship revolved around shared interests, including botany and horticulture, as well as those decorative arts already listed for Mrs Delany. The Duchess of Portland was, amongst other things, a proficient wood turner.[13]

Until the Duchess of Portland died in 1785, Mrs Delany spent 'six months of every year, generally from spring to autumn' at Bulstrode.[14] She occupied an elevated position at court where she was much respected. Her style in all things, even (perhaps especially) in old age, was seen as the epitome of good breeding. She spent the last three years of her life in a 'cottage' provided by the King and Queen on the royal estate at Windsor.

Mrs Delany in relation to Wedgwood

It is hardly possible (or reasonable) to discuss ceramics in Britain during the eighteenth century without making reference to Wedgwood, and it may be helpful to further situate Mrs Delany in relation to him. Thanks to the remarkably extensive Wedgwood archive, his prowess in the field of marketing has been well documented, and much has been made of his ability to identify and make use of the emulative impulse.[15] In an often-quoted letter to his partner Bentley he outlined his plan to first establish his vases as '*Ornament for Palaces*' where they would be 'seen and admired by the *Middling Class* of People'. Having thus promoted the desirability of the vases he would reduce their price to make them more widely accessible.[16]

Other letters tell of his efforts to improve the clay body, of his experiments with glazes, and of his application of scientific method to both those ends. He was of course a member of the *Middling Class* himself, and account should also be taken of his intensive interaction with the new museum culture. What one could call the 'museumisation' of the nation was part and parcel of the establishment of a middle class in society. Access to the collections of acknowledged connoisseurs was an important factor in the cultural education of this up-and-coming social group, which saw itself as responsible for elevating the cultural tone of the nation as a whole, and advancing the position of Britain on the world stage.

Wedgwood had access to the collections of many prestigious connoisseurs, and produced versions of the objects therein. Wedgwood's ceramics, made either in close replication of museum objects, or (and perhaps this is the more significant mode) in the style of museum objects but 'updated' to suit the period, enabled the consumer to possess a sign of museum culture. Arguably the most important of his 'updates' was the Portland Vase, an object poised on a symbolic watershed between the established taste of the aristocracy and the new cultural interests of the emergent middle class.

The original Roman glass vase had belonged to the Duchess of Portland, Mrs Delany's closest friend. Following her death in 1785, her extensive collections were sold at auction. The vase was bought by her son and lent to Wedgwood for the purpose of making a copy. This object and its history became very well known, and Wedgwood's reproduction of it was widely regarded as his crowning achievement. Although it stretched his abilities, at the outset he declared with confidence his intention to 'equal, or excell [sic] if permitted' the original.[17] Where the original was worn, the Wedgwood version was perfect.[18] But recreating the vase was not simply a question of reversing the effects of time: the bas-reliefs on the new version would be more accurate than the original had ever been. It is no wonder that Wedgwood's progress was keenly followed. This was a technical challenge that would set British manufacturing skills – the result of middle-class enterprise – on a par with those of the classical world. Public interest was such that 'at least four different sets or single-sheet prints of the Portland Vase were issued in the 1780s'.[19]

In her account of a visit to Etruria, Wedgwood's mansion in Staffordshire, West Midlands diarist Katherine Plymley gave a comprehensive history of the Portland Vase. It had enormous publicity value for Wedgwood, and some of her information came from a promotional pamphlet. Emphasis was laid on the private origins of the vase:

> The Vase was deposited in the library of the Barberini family. This discovery was made sometime between the years 1623 & 1644. – it remained in the Barberini family above a century, after the dispersion of this library it was purchased by Sir William Hamilton & by Sir William disposed of to the late Duchess of Portland, but with so much secrecy at her request, that she was never known, even by her own family, to be the possessor of it. ... I was told by the family at Etruria that the late Duchess gave fifteen hundred pound for the Vase. – it seems to me wonderful that a person cou'd be gratified by having a thing of that kind in possession when not even her nearest friends were permitted to see it.[20]

Clearly Katherine Plymley expected such an extraordinary object to have a social function, as the focus of group contemplation. I want to argue that this was in fact the case, but that it suited Wedgwood's purposes to play on the notion of secrecy. The vase was an object with a remarkable aristocratic pedigree. For him to suggest that a veil of secrecy had hitherto surrounded it was also to suggest that he had rent the veil and exposed it to general view. The circumstances of its acquisition by the Duchess of Portland were described by Sir William Hamilton's niece in her diary of a month spent at Bulstrode with the Duchess and Mrs Delany in 1783. Extracts from her diary are included in the last volume of Mrs Delany's published correspondence, and, as Lady Llanover remarked, 'The record which has … been preserved of a whole month in the life of Mrs Delany … is particularly interesting.'[21]

Miss Hamilton acted as an agent between her uncle and the Duchess. The acquisition was a long drawn-out affair permeated with all the niceties of aristocratic conduct. One gains an impression of hushed voices at private meetings:

> Mrs Delany came and told me she must contrive to speak to me after dinner, for she had a *secret* message to me from the Duchess Dowager Portland. … and then under the color [sic] of getting me to look for a book took me to her bed-room and told me what the Duchess wanted me to do, viz., to purchase the Vase of my uncle William. … I took him down to the parlour under pretence of showing him the pictures, and then told him what the Duchess wish'd about the vase; when we came upstairs again they talk'd upon the subject. My uncle ... told me he would think upon what the Duchess had said.[22]

The negotiations took over two weeks. Finally, on 15 January 1784 Sir William visited the Duchess of Portland without a go-between: 'she shew'd him many of her fine things ... they talk'd over and *settled* the affair of *the vase*'.[23] Although there does seem to have been a certain amount of secrecy about the acquisition, this was probably no more than to be expected. There is no suggestion that the vase could not be viewed by friends of the Duchess. Indeed, a letter from the novelist Fanny Burney to Mrs Delany included a tentative request to see the Portland Vase and suggests that admission to view it was a sought-after mark of social status.[24]

Ceramics and feminine subjectivity

A well-known anecdote has Wedgwood meeting with 'Capability' Brown. To Brown's assertion that 'his life was devoted to lords and gentlemen', Wedgwood is supposed to have responded: 'and mine, to the ladies'.[25] The conjunction of women and ceramics was established before his time: handling and displaying fine china was central to particular constructions of femininity. Women of Mrs Delany's circle were expected to have an affinity with such objects. They typically bequeathed china to their female friends and descendants. Five years before her death, for example, Mrs Delany's sister, Mrs Dewes, wrote a letter for her daughter Mary leaving her the contents of her cabinets. Various objects were mentioned, but her most detailed description was reserved for an 'old china cup' which had been handed down from woman to woman:

> The old china cup with the gilt cover and saucer, that has a setting in gold belonging to it, Mary must have, and give it to *her daughter* if she has one, if not to one of her brother's *daughters*, as it has gone from *daughter* to *daughter* these *three hundred years!* … These trifles I give to renew in her mind whenever she sees them, the constant tenderness of her truly affectionate mother …[26]

Women like Mrs Delany and her sister did not need new china. Their objectscapes were already replete with the significances that circulated around the existing contents. The 'ladies' to whom Wedgwood addressed his efforts were, with some notable exceptions, women of his own up-and-coming middle class.[27] Ultimately these were the women he needed to please and he made a point of trialling new designs on them. Throughout his professional life he relied on his wife's judgement in questions of taste. 'I speak from experience in Female taste,' he wrote to Bentley, 'without which I should have made but a poor figure amongst my Potts; not one of which of any consequence is finished without the Approbation of my Sally.'[28]

In 1772 Mrs Delany was given 'a profile of Captain Edward Hamilton in Wedgewood-ware [sic] in imitation of the antique', which she commended as 'very like'.[29] She also praised Wedgwood's 'ingenuity and industry'. On viewing the Frog Service[30] for Katherine the Great at his London showrooms in 1774 she wrote:

> I am just returned from viewing the Wedgewood-ware that is to be sent to the Empress of Russia. It consists I believe of as many pieces as there are days of the year, if not hours. … there are three rooms below and two above filled with it, laid out on tables, every thing that can be wanted to serve a dinner; the ground the common ware pale brimstone, the drawings in purple, the borders a wreath of flowers, the middle of each piece a particular view of all the remarkable places in the King's dominions neatly executed. I suppose it will come to a princely price; it is well for the manufacturer, which I am glad of, as his ingenuity and industry deserve encouragement …[31]

It was not quite complete – some 150 views were yet to be painted. Wedgwood was worried that potential customers whose property was not featured might be offended, and in this way he could still accept illustrations for inclusion in the service. Characteristically, Mrs Delany spotted an error in one of the 'drawings': 'my indignation was raised when I read the card … I rectified the mistake with the person that had the care of them'. The mistake concerned her niece's home, Ilam house. It had been ascribed to the wrong owner, so her reaction is not really surprising. She continued, 'and [I] hope Ilam will acknowledge its *true master* to her Imperial Majesty', indicating that the significance of the illustrations, which exported a distinct notion of English culture, was not lost on her. It is clear though, that there was a degree of ambivalence in her response to the array of china: 'I am so giddy', she finally declared, 'with looking over such a quantity of crockery ware …'[32]

Mrs Delany's use of the term 'crockery' suggests that she did not rank the Frog Service alongside her own china or that of her acquaintance. Crockery is common-or-garden tableware, and this is her only use of the word in her published correspondence. Yet the collection and display of china loomed very large in her life. A distinctly emulative approach towards it emerges from her earlier correspondence, perhaps supporting McKendrick's argument. As we have seen, after the death of her first husband, Alexander Pendarves, she was living in London with her aunt and uncle, Sir John and Lady Stanley. She sent regular boxes of provisions from the city to her mother and sister who were living near Gloucester:

> In the box with the linnen [sic] there is … French silver saltsellers [sic], and a pair of china ones, which *you* may think old fashion, but it is the *new mode*, and all saltsellers are now made in that manner …[33]

Two years later, china was again perceived in terms of its fashionability:

> I sent a little box last night to the carrier with a set of china as my mama ordered me: I hope they will come safely, I gave great charge about packing them carefully. China is risen mightily within this month. My Aunt Stanley liked them so well for the oddness of them, that she bought a set of cups, bason, sugar-dish and plate cost fourteen shillings.[34]

China continued to interest Mrs Delany throughout her life. She amassed a considerable collection herself, and she noted the presence of china in the objectscapes of other people. Her own was acquired in a number of ways. Some was bought at shops, sales and auctions. Much was given by friends and family; 'our dear Sir John', she wrote to her sister in 1737, 'has given me a pair of pretty white china babies for my cupboard, and a bowl for a ladle in china, in the shape of an Indian leaf …'[35] As I have noted, aristocratic women frequently bequeathed china to one another, and she inherited several pieces from her friends. Mrs Bristow, for example, gave the Duchess of Portland 'a Japan dressing-box, any shells she pleases, and two pieces of china'. To Mrs Delany she left 'the remainder of her shells and two pieces of china'.[36]

Mrs Delany's own will gives some idea of the nature of the china in her objectscape. Specific mention is made of 'a Dresden cup and saucer', 'a pair of white china bottles with raised flowers', 'the scarlet bowls mounted in gilding with china flowers', 'two saucers of old japan china, with the two bottles that used to stand in them with flowers', 'a pair of old japan china bottles', a 'china bottle set in gold', 'a japan box in the shape of a heart', 'a Dresden china cup and saucer with sprigs of flowers', and 'a Dresden china soup basin, cover and plate'.[37] The will begins with a list of individual bequests in which she distributed many of her personal belongings amongst her closest friends. These were often objects with particular resonance for the recipients, and it should be noted that all the china was given to women. Thus: 'To the Countess Gower the blue and white cup and saucer, Dresden, out of which she used to drink her tea, and a pair of white china bottles with raised flowers.'[38]

To her great-niece Georgiana Mary Port, Mrs Delany left 'the contents of her closet at Windsor' as well as 'all her plate, japan and china (not previously disposed of)'.[39]

Like many other women of her time and class, she had deliberately constructed a decorative objectscape within which to situate herself; almost – I want to suggest – like a self-portrait. Many of the things belonging to it – such as embroidery and shell work, paintings and drawings – were of her own or her friends' making. China formed an important part of that environment, and regular (if not constant) redecoration and refurbishment of the 'closet' or 'cabinet' where she kept it was a source of pleasure. The china took its place amongst a series of arrangements of many different sorts of objects, but was most closely associated with shells:

> I am making some little brackets (…) but instead of gilding them *I cover them with shells*; I design to have eight of them for my closet, to hold little pieces of China.[40]

In 1743, as we have seen, she married Patrick Delany, and in 1744 they went to live in Dublin. This was the period when Mrs Delany was most involved in constructing a personal objectscape. She threw herself into redecorating and refurbishing their house (Delville), and made regular reports of her progress in letters to her sister. A display of china was at the core of her most personal rooms:

> I am going to make a very comfortable closet; – to have a dresser, and all manner of working tools, to keep all my stores for *painting*, *carving*, *gilding*, &c.; for my own room is now so clean and pretty that I cannot suffer it to be strewn with litter, only books and work, and the closet belonging to it to be given up to prints, drawings, and my collection of fossils, petrifactions, and minerals. … In the middle of the closet a deep nitch [sic] with shelves, where I shall put whatever china I think too good for common use.[41]

Although men were by no means prohibited, she saw her 'closet' as ideally a private feminine space: 'retired from all interruption and eaves-droppers'.[42]

Mrs Delany took over the education of her great-niece Georgiana Mary Ann Port in 1778 when Georgiana was seven years old. The girl came to live with her in London, and was inculcated into the mysteries of the china service early on, as Mrs Delany reported:

> Mary … made me follow her into the parlour to behold a complete set of *young* Nankeen china which she had just received from the Duchess of Portland: her raptures were prodigious, and indeed they are *very fine* and *pretty* of their kind, not quite so small as for baby things, not large eno' for grown ladies, and she insists on my telling you all this, and that there are twelve teacups and saucers, 6 coffee cups and teapot, sugar dish, milk mug, 2 bread-and-butter plates, and they have been produced for the entertainment of all my company every afternoon.[43]

The child's tea set was imported. The earliest surviving record of a Wedgwood tea set made especially for children is dated 1811. However, although they were not included in the catalogue of readily available wares, it would have been perfectly possible to order such a set before this date.[44] But Georgiana was being trained to take her place in aristocratic society, and the exclusivity of Oriental china was still an important mark of status in those elevated circles. Then as now, playing with toys like this reflected adult activities and established patterns of behaviour in later life. Georgiana was also introduced to the pleasures of the cabinet collection. As Mrs Delany's great-niece she found favour amongst friends of her aunt who were keen to bestow marks of their approval in the form of gifts. After a visit to Lady Stamford, for example, Mrs Delany wrote that she 'brought away shells in abundance; her collection encreases [sic] so fast that you must provide her with a cabinet to keep them, for she promises herself much joy in sorting and entertaining Mr Beresford with them'.[45]

Mr Beresford notwithstanding, boys were not expected to take an interest in, or show respect for, delicate objects. 'I had 20 frights for my china, shells and books: his little fingers seized everything with such impetuosity that I was ready to box him' complained Mrs Delany, after a visit from Lady Meade and her children.[46] And in 1756, when Mr Mason and Viscountess Grandison were staying at Delville in the Delanys' absence, Mrs Delany expressed her anxiety about their son:

> *I hope* the boy won't break and rifle my shell-cabinet! I have taken the liberty to order it to be constantly covered.[47]

Throughout her published correspondence china objects are primarily related to women. And although many men of her acquaintance, including her brother Bernard Granville, had collections that included china, there was a danger that to display excessive enthusiasm for it would tend to classify them as 'effeminate'.[48] Lord G. in Richardson's *Sir Charles Grandison* – Mrs Delany's favourite novel after *Clarissa* by the same author – is ridiculed for displaying just such a behaviour.[49] Charlotte Grandison mocks him for his present of 'old Japan China with brown edges', especially when she sees him 'taking out, and putting in the windows, one at a time, the cups, plates, jars, and saucers, rejoicing and parading over them, and shewing his connoisseurship to his motionless admiring wife, in commending this and the other piece as a beauty…'[50] She rails against his 'gew-gaw japan-china taste',[51] and explains to Lady L., who attempts to mediate between the couple, that, 'If my lord would but be cured of his taste for trifles and nick-nacks, I should, possibly, be induced to consider him as a man of better understanding than I once thought him: but who can forbear, sometimes, to think slightly of a man, who, by effeminacies, and a Shell and China taste, undervalues himself?'[52]

What was derisible in a man was desirable in a woman. In some of her letters it seems almost as if Mrs Delany believed her china went before her. When important guests were expected, she automatically checked its condition. Thus in anticipation of a visit from Lady Caroline Fox, she had, 'set all my best china in order, and prepared everything for their reception'.[53]

Predictably, china was an important element in the display of food. But although Mrs Delany sometimes referred to her tableware, she rarely (if ever) described its appearance. On the occasion of a visit from Lord and Lady Mornington, she reported:

> my dessert was … *very pretty* and much set off by some fine china, part of my dear Bushe's legacy.[54]

The china service was noted here because it evoked female friendship as well as contributing a strong visual aspect to the meal. The presentation of food is a frequent feature of Mrs Delany's correspondence. A letter of 1752 describes a 'grand ball' in Dublin:

> the musicians and singers were dressed like Arcadian shepherds and shepherdesses, and placed among the rocks. If tea, coffee, or chocolate were wanting, you held your cup to a leaf of a tree, and it was filled; and whatever you wanted to eat or drink, was immediately found on a rock, or on a branch, or in the hollow of a tree.[55]

Over the course of her life, she attended innumerable elaborately staged social functions of this sort.[56] As to her own efforts, every so often she sent menus and table lay-outs to her sister:

You love a bill of fare, and here it is.

First Course

Fish

Beef-steaks

Rabbits Soup and Onions

Fillet-Veal

Second Course

Turkey Pout

Salmon Grilde and Quaills

Pick Sal

Little Terrene

Peas

Cream

Mush-rooms

Terrene

Apple Pye

Crab

Leveret

Cheesecakes

Dessert

Blamange

Raspberries and Cream

Almond Cream

Sweetmeats and Jelly

Current and Goose-berries

Cherries Dutch Cheese

Strawberries and Cream

Orange Butter

I have scratched it out very awkwardly, and hope the servants will place my dinner and dessert better on the table than I have on paper.[57]

This was a particularly grand meal, given in honour of the Lord Primate of Ireland. For her close friends Mrs Delany's approach was rather different, although equally impressive:

> We have discovered a new breakfasting place under the shade of nut-trees, impenetrable to the sun's rays, in the midst of a grove of elms, where we shall breakfast this morning; I have ordered cherries, strawberries, and nosegays to be

laid on our breakfast table, and have appointed a harper to be here to play to us during our repast, who is to be hid among the trees. Mrs Hamilton is to breakfast with us, and is to be cunningly led to this place *and surprised*.[58]

Concluding remarks

It is an extraordinary glimpse of stylish living, but sadly, she did not say what china she chose to complete the effect. As we have seen, however, ceramics were significant components of Mrs Delany's objectscape. Early in her life they seemed fashionable and new, and perhaps her interest in them involved emulation. But she did not aspire to the new styles that Wedgwood produced; whatever class-orientated behaviour she engaged in revolved around her membership of a cultural elite that owned and displayed exclusive objects. In my view such materialist interpretations are overshadowed by the wealth of personal meanings that ceramics represented for her. I began this essay by proposing that objects are capable of 'vigilance'; standing witness to that network of other people with whom each individual seeks to interact, and whose understanding and approval is an important factor in the formation of personal and social subjectivity. I have suggested that the objectscape Mrs Delany created can be regarded as a form of self-portrait: a background against which she produced herself. I hope I have shown that within that objectscape particular ceramics were closely related to particular individuals. They stood for her relationships with other women. More than anything, it seems to me, Mrs Delany associated ceramics with cultured feminine community.

Notes

1 See Thorstein Veblen, *The Theory of the Leisure Class*, (New York: Penguin, 1979 [1899]).
2 Moira Vincentelli, *Women and Ceramics, Gendered Vessels* (Manchester: Manchester University Press, 2000), p. 110.
3 Michel Foucault, *Discipline and Punish* (London: Penguin UK, 1977), p. 201.
4 Foucault, *Discipline and Punish*, pp. 208–9.
5 Foucault, *Discipline and Punish*, p. 223.
6 Neil McKendrick, 'The consumer revolution', in Neil McKendrick, John Brewer and J. H. Plumb, *The Birth of a Consumer Society* (London: Europa, 1982), p. 11.
7 McKendrick, 'The consumer revolution', chapter 1.
8 McKendrick, 'The consumer revolution', p. 101.
9 Elizabeth Kowaleski-Wallace, *Consuming Subjects, Women, Shopping and Business in the Eighteenth Century* (New York: Columbia University Press, 1996), pp. 52–8.
10 Kowaleski-Wallace, *Consuming Subjects*, chapter 3: 'China'.
11 *The Autobiography and Correspondence of Mary Granville, Mrs Delany: With Interesting Reminiscences of King George the Third and Queen Charlotte* edited by the Right Honourable Lady Llanover, volumes I-III, London, Richard Bentley, New Burlington Street 1861, and Second Series, volumes IV-VI 1862.
12 Llanover, *The Autobiography and Correspondence*, IV, p. 3. Mary Dewes became Mrs Mary Port on her marriage to John Port of Ilam in 1770. Her marriage had no noticeable effect on her correspondence with her aunt.
13 Bulstrode was near Gerrard's Cross, Buckinghamshire. The house was a hive of cultural activity that circulated around the Duchess of Portland.
14 Ruth Hayden, *Mrs Delany and Her Flower Collages* (London: British Museum, 1992), p. 106.
15 McKendrick's account (see above) draws heavily on the Wedgwood archive.

16 Wedgwood to Bentley, Etruria, 23 August 1772. See Ann Finer and George Savage, *The Selected Letters of Josiah Wedgwood* (London: Cory, Adams & Mackay, 1965), p. 131.
17 Wedgwood to Sir William Hamilton, Etruria, 24 June 1786, in Finer and Savage *The Selected Letters of Josiah Wedgwood*, p. 295.
18 He had consulted with Sir William Hamilton on this point: 'In examining the bas reliefs on the vase there are a few palpable slips of the artist's attention. Would it be advisable in these cases, to make any deviations from the original, or to copy as close as we can its defects as well as its beauties? Most of the figures have their surfaces partly decayed by time. When we mould from these figures, may we venture to restore their original smoothness, with care to preserve the drawing etc. – or let the copies pass deficient as time has left the original.' Wedgwood to Sir William Hamilton, 24 January 1786, in Eliza Meteyard, *The Life of Josiah Wedgwood* (London: Hurst and Blackett, 1865, Vol. II 1861), p. 579. It seems to me that Wedgwood would have been unable to resist improving the vase. Consulting Hamilton may have been polite procedure with the added benefit of promoting interest in the vase and his own activities.
19 Hilary Young (ed.), *The Genius of Wedgwood* (London: V&A, 1995), p. 117.
20 Diaries of Katherine Plymley in Shropshire Research and Records Office. 1066/14 5/12/1792–17/3/1793.
21 Llanover, *The Autobiography and Correspondence*, VI, p. 151.
22 Diary of Miss Hamilton, in Llanover, *The Autobiography and Correspondence*, VI, p. 195–6, 3 January 1784. Miss Hamilton used old-fashioned language, such as 'ye' for 'the', and many abbreviations. I have given modern equivalents.
23 Diary of Miss Hamilton, in Llanover, *The Autobiography and Correspondence*, VI, p. 205. No prices are mentioned in Miss Hamilton's diary.
24 Miss Burney to Mrs Delany, St Martin's Street, 15 January 1784, in Llanover, *The Autobiography and Correspondence*, VI, p. 204.
25 Meteyard, *The Life of Josiah Wedgwood*, xxiv.
26 Mrs Dewes, Welsbourn, 23 March 1756, Llanover, *The Autobiography and Correspondence*, III, p. 633.
27 Notable exceptions included Queen Charlotte and the Empress Katherine of Russia.
28 Wedgwood to Bentley, undated, referable to 1776–77, in Meteyard, *The Life of Josiah Wedgwood*, II, p. 156.
29 Mrs Delany to Mrs Port, of Ilam, St James's Place, 30 December 1772, Llanover, *The Autobiography and Correspondence*, IV, p. 487.
30 The 'Frog Service' is so called because each piece is decorated with a green frog motif referring to the palace of Kekerekeksinen – meaning the 'frog marsh' – where the service was to be used. See Young (ed.), *The Genius of Wedgwood*.
31 Mrs Delany to Mrs Port of Ilam, St James's Place, 7 June 1774, Llanover, *The Autobiography and Correspondence*, IV, pp. 594–5.
32 Mrs Delany to Mrs Port of Ilam, St.James's Place, 7 June 1774, Llanover, *The Autobiography and Correspondence,* IV, pp. 594–5.
33 Mrs Pendarves to Mrs Anne Granville, at Gloucester, 5 October 1727, Llanover, *The Autobiography and Correspondence*, I, p. 135.
34 Mrs Pendarves to Anne Granville n/d (between April and July 1729), Llanover, *The Autobiography and Correspondence*, I, p. 210.
35 Mrs Pendarves to Anne Granville, Northend, 10 October 1737, Llanover, *The Autobiography and Correspondence*, II, p. 5.
36 Mrs Delany to Mrs Port of Ilam, St James's Place, 27 February 1779, Llanover, *The Autobiography and Correspondence*, V, p. 410.
37 Llanover, *The Autobiography and Correspondence*, VI, Appendix, the will of Mrs Delany, 22/02/1778, pp. 483–92.
38 Llanover, *The Autobiography and Correspondence*, VI, Appendix, the will of Mrs Delany, 22/02/1778, pp. 483–92.
39 Llanover, *The Autobiography and Correspondence*, VI, Appendix, the will of Mrs Delany, 22/02/1778, p. 483–92.
40 Mrs Delany to Mrs Dewes, at Gloucester, Delville, 25 January 1745–46, Llanover, *The Autobiography and Correspondence*, II, p. 415.

41 Mrs Delany to Mrs Dewes, Delville, 6 October 1750, Llanover, *The Autobiography and Correspondence,* II, p. 600. Installing her collection had been a communal activity: 'two Mrs Hamilton's, Bushes, Miss Hamilton, Mr Sackville Hamilton, came to breakfast. As soon as that was done, *I set them all to work*; gave each a dusting-cloth, brush, sponge and bowl of water, and set them to cleaning my picture-frames. Bushe undertook cleaning the pictures, and egging them out, whilst the *carpenters and I fixed up the shelves for* my books and china: everybody that popped their head in, was *seized to work*; no idler was admitted; a very merry working morning it was, and my dressing room is very spruce and handsome.' Mrs Delany to Mrs Dewes, Delville, 22 September 1750, Llanover, *The Autobiography and Correspondence*, II, p. 592.

42 Mrs Delany to A. G., Delville, (believed to be) 11 July 1747, Llanover, *The Autobiography and Correspondence*, II, p. 471.

43 Mrs Delany to Mrs Port of Ilam, St James's Place, 1 April 1779, Llanover, *The Autobiography and Correspondence*, V, p. 418.

44 I am grateful to Ms Lynn Miller of the Wedgwood Museum, Barlaston, for this information.

45 Mrs Delany to Mrs Port of Ilam, St James's Place, 17 April 1779, Llanover, *The Autobiography and Correspondence*, V, p. 422. The Beresfords were friends of Georgiana's mother, Mrs Port of Ilam.

46 Mrs Delany to Mrs Dewes, Delville, 28 September 1750, Llanover, *The Autobiography and Correspondence*, II, p. 597.

47 Mrs Delany to Mrs Dewes, Spring Gardens, 2 June 1756, Llanover, *The Autobiography and Correspondence*, III, p. 433.

48 In the eighteenth-century usage 'effeminacy' in a man was opposed to 'manly' qualities, but it did not have the homosexual connotation that is has today.

49 Mrs Delany thought the book 'so excellent, so improving'. Its hero, Sir Charles, 'is as faultless as mortal hero can be … there is grace and dignity in all he says and does'. Mrs Delany to Mrs Dewes, Whitehall, 3 December 1753, Llanover, *The Autobiography and Correspondence*, III, p. 251; and Mrs Delany to Mrs Dewes, Bulstrode, 9 December 1753, Llanover, *The Autobiography and Correspondence*, III, p. 252.

50 Samuel Richardson, *Sir Charles Grandison* (Oxford: Oxford University Press, 1972, [1753–54]), Vol. IV, letter XXXIII, p. 418.

51 Richardson, *Sir Charles Grandison*, p. 509.

52 Richardson, *Sir Charles Grandison*, p. 519. Sir Charles Grandison, Mrs Delany's ideal man, shows no signs of 'gew-gaw japan-china taste'. Instead he interests himself (for example) in making 'accurate observations … on those treasures of antiquity which have been discovered in the ancient Herculaneum.' See Vol. V, letter XXIX, p. 605.

53 Mrs Delany to Mrs Dewes, Delville, 7 July 1750, Llanover, *The Autobiography and Correspondence*, II, p. 1565.

54 Mrs Delany to Mrs Dewes, Delville, 10 March 1759, Llanover, *The Autobiography and Correspondence*, III, p. 540. The friendship between Mrs Delany and Letitia Bushe began in Ireland in 1731. Mrs Delany thought she had 'a fine genius for painting' (Mrs Pendarves to Mrs Ann Granville, Dublin, 3 February 1731–32, Llanover, *The Autobiography and Correspondence*, I, p. 334). Letitia Bushe died in 1757.

55 Mrs Delany to Mrs Dewes, Delville, 7 February 1752, Llanover, *The Autobiography and Correspondence*, III, p. 85.

56 Other letters describe the pandemonium that resulted when, invited company having dined, the poor were let in to consume the leftovers: 'after the dinner is over the common people are let in *to carry off all that remains* both of dinner and dessert; you may imagine what a notable scramblement it occasions'. Mrs Delany to Mrs Dewes, Delville, 28 October 1747, Llanover, *The Autobiography and Correspondence*, II, p. 481.

57 Mrs Delany to Mrs Dewes, at Wellesbourne, Delville, 20 June 1747, Llanover, *The Autobiography and Correspondence*, II, p. 468.

58 Mrs Delany to Mrs Dewes, Delville, 22 June 1750, Llanover, *The Autobiography and Correspondence*, II, p. 558.

Since leaving the Royal College of Art in the mid 1970s, Alison Britton has been in the forefront of developments within British studio ceramics both as a maker and a writer. On 15 January 2001 she presented the following essay as one of the invited speakers at the 'Diversity in the Making: Studio Ceramics Today' conference, which was held at Camberwell College of Arts, London. Intriguingly, as a hand-builder of ceramics and as a leading proponent of the 'New Ceramics', she chose to talk about throwing. With her keen eye she was able to offer an incisive overview of a practice which was so central to debates in ceramics during the last decades of the twentieth century. Her essay has had minimal revision for re-publication here and it retains the remarkable clarity that is a hallmark of her writing. It was originally published in Issue 2 of *Interpreting Ceramics* in 2001.

Overthrowing Tradition

Alison Britton

If you tell a stranger that you're a potter they immediately imagine you bent over a potter's wheel. Throwing is the normal, commonly understood, core of ceramic practice. I have avoided throwing since my student days, and am well aware that I am walking on thin ice in taking on throwing, the ins and outs of it, as the chosen subject of my text. But I am passionate about pots and the suggestions they make, in use or in sight. I am also more broadly interested in all kinds of ceramic practice, and interested above all in the notion of studio ceramics as a complicated culture with different strands that diverge and link in various ways.

The kinds of studio pottery that developed in the 1970s, and became known as 'New Ceramics', never quite displaced the Leach tradition of wheel-thrown, subtly glazed pottery. But the label did give a name to a tendency that had begun even twenty years earlier, which had determinedly, mainly through hand-building, opened up the range of possibilities of form in clay. Leach's persuasive Anglo-Oriental fusion had dominated the pottery world in Britain for some time. In any creative discipline, rules, in the end, are there to be defied. In this essay I will look at the place of throwing in developments in British studio ceramics in the decades through which I have been working.

During this time there has been an expanding discourse about the craft disciplines. This is due, probably in part, to the Crafts Council, which was formed as the Crafts Advisory Committee in the early 1970s, with *Crafts* magazine and numerous publications, catalogues and books. Design History has also developed as a subject, and the academicism of the Dip AD course transforming into a BA course has required articulacy to extend into new territories. Ceramics especially got off to a good start, because Leach and Cardew both wrote supremely well, philosophically as well as technically.

So it is now much more the meanings of artefacts that we talk about, beyond the old discussions of recipes and temperatures and techniques. Arguably, and this may be a personal dilemma rather than a general one, it is a more difficult task to write something original about traditional thrown pottery, than about the wilder forms of clay sculpture and pots that intend to ask new questions of the discipline. Pursuit of the discourse in the critical establishing period of the 1970s and 1980s may indeed have favoured the more sculptural end of the spectrum of ceramic art. But in recent years this lack has been eloquently addressed, in particular by Edmund de Waal.

I have sought out what some earlier studio potters have said about throwing, beyond the how-to-do-it descriptions. Leach and Cardew, unsurprisingly, take the central importance of throwing for granted. Leach, in *A Potters Book* in 1940, says there is nothing quite like it in any other craft, and talks about the clay being 'urged and pulled and coaxed through a series of rhythmic movements, which like those of a dance are all related and interdependent'.[1] Cardew, in *Pioneer Pottery* in 1969, says that 'no potter who has once seen the wheel in operation can resist it'.[2] Henry Hammond, a student of William Staite Murray at the Royal College in the 1930s, recalled the master teaching by throwing a pot in silence when he thought it was the right minute to do so. He also apparently looked on throwing as a procreative symbol, and disliked pots with thin lips. And Dora Billington, in her much less-well-known, but wonderful, book of 1937, *The Art of the Potter*, says:

> The making of pots on the wheel … is by far the most exciting method. In swift directness it can be compared to drawing, and like drawing it must be done and left, for retouching can only spoil it. Once one has realised the difference, a thrown pot can never be mistaken for one made in any other way, unless of course it has been tampered with and its distinctive character lost.[3]

But best of all I think is Bill Newland's definition in a reflective interview with Peter Dormer in 1985 (Newland was a pupil of Billington's shortly after the War):

> Throwing is concerned with inner force – dynamic growth from the wheel, like a triangle on its apex or a crocus from its stem striking its way upwards. The hands make a gesture in space and the clay records the gesture. There is a simple aesthetic concerned with throwing and it is to do with growth and natural form. A good thrown pot is not one which hangs over its ankle straps – it must not appear saggy or look prolapsed. After all, we learn from the cradle that the fully ripe and expanded fruit is the best, apples that look like prunes are rejected. All good thrown pots must express joie-de-vivre, uplift and umph – there are no saggy pots in the British Museum.[4]

In a more metaphysical tone Hans Coper wrote in 1969:

> The wheel imposes its economy, dictates limits, provides momentum and continuity. Concentrating on continuous variations of simple themes I become part of the process; I am learning to operate a sensitive instrument which may be resonant to my experience of existence now – in this fantastic century.[5]

Philip Rawson, a curator and art historian rather than a potter, in his book *Ceramics* of 1971 which reviews the whole history of the medium, writes:

> The ways in which clay has been shaped for ceramics are either direct or indirect … far the most important of the direct methods is hand-modelling. It

> is among modelled ceramics that the most vivid and lively touch-structures can be incorporated. Patted, squeezed, pinched, and pressed clay objects speak a language like no other.[6]

But writing in 1985 in the *Fast Forward* catalogue of Peter Dormer, Rawson is despondent about the kind of objects that my colleagues in the hand-building sorority were producing, complaining of a Coper-ised effect on the fullness of 'ideal' pot forms:

> But not all sexy silhouettes give good central presence and imply strong volumes … So chillingly often we are nowadays given pots that retreat, flattening themselves and huddling back into diagrams.[7]

The critic Peter Fuller, to conclude this string of quotations, puts the boot in even more vigorously to the New Ceramics reform movement when he says in an article taking its title from Cardew 'The proper work of the potter':

> Clay, of course, can legitimately be handled in many ways: modelling, after all, is one of the twin poles of sculptural activity. But … throwing is close to the heart of any living pottery tradition: it bears witness to the best and the finest that can be done in this craft with clay. Coiled or pinched pots may occasionally divert us: but they seem essentially regressive, anal even; whereas piece pots partake of that collaging of given segments so typical of contemporary practice and so inimical to full imaginative transformation.[8]

Returning to my main theme, how the importance of throwing seems to have shifted around in the development of ceramics in the last four decades, I will relate a combination of my experience of the time with subsequent research.

The Central School of Art and Design, in London, was a great place to be studying ceramics in the late 1960s, with a course established in 1925 by Dora Billington. Her background was industrial, from Stoke-on-Trent, but she had embraced the new ideas in the Studio Pottery Movement without losing her identity in the Anglo-Oriental folk-art fusion promoted by Leach. She enthusiastically fostered new talents, and in the 1950s and 1960s the Central School was significant in disseminating an alternative to Leach. The group that were later known as the Picassettes – William Newland, Margaret Hine, and Nicholas Vergette – studied or worked there. They were inspired by Mediterranean art rather than Oriental, and made exuberant, highly decorated thrown and assembled pieces. The Picasso exhibition that was shown in London in 1950 included ceramics and made a great impression on potters with an eye for a change.

As William Newland said: 'It's not that we were anti-Leach, but there were other things to do.'[9] Newland's work was essentially thrown, but in his hand-built pieces, and likewise in the work of Dan Arbeid, Ian Auld, Ruth Duckworth and Gillian Lowndes, there was a desire for other forms – sculpture, ornament, new vitality. Ethnographic collections from Africa were inspirational.[10] Throwing was still a big part of the Central curriculum, but by the time of graduating, if a student had developed stronger interests in surface decoration, slip-casting or hand-building, that was equally encouraged. One of the influential teachers there in my time was Gordon Baldwin, who always brought a large sculpture he was coiling with him in the Land Rover to continue making while he taught.

The interest in more sculptural ceramics, moving away from the wheel but still based on vessel form, was a recognised 'New' phenomenon by the late 1970s. Ceramics was not the only medium to be changing; the upheaving 'bulge' generation of babies, born after the war, was coming of age; art schools were well funded and full of life. Cities were seen to be creative and stimulating environments for potters.

A rural and urban division was already evident in the location of most wheel-throwing potters of the continuing Leach tradition working in barns, with access to timber, and space to build huge kilns and fire their volume production. The New Ceramics potter was probably to be found in a communal workshop in a derelict warehouse, with electric kilns, making fewer one-off pieces. The approach to learning was also different; Leach and Cardew had thought that apprenticeship was definitely the better path for understanding the reality of the potter's life, and were dismissive of what could be learnt at art school.[11] A fierce debate about the opposing merits of the two approaches had been held in 1966 at an evening meeting at Craftsman Potters Association. Lines were harshly drawn between Henry Hammond and Gilbert Harding Green on the one hand, both of whom led burgeoning Dip AD courses at Farnham and the Central School, versus a number of potters including David Leach who believed that there was no true professional path other than 'the slower, radical, disciplined drill of the workshop'.[12]

Now, however, so many years later, to learn about ceramics at art school is the normal route, and it is not easy to find a potter who will take on apprentices. The 'one-off, non-functional vessel form' did seem to be a definite preoccupation by the early 1980s, no doubt in part as a result of the altered training/educational context. I, as one of a group of potters engaged in making such things, was asked to try and define the attractions of such a form by Martina Margetts for *Crafts* magazine in 1983. I included a comment on tradition:

> Another thing the peer group has in common is a strong regard for tradition, but on the whole a quite separate channel of tradition from the Oriental one which has sustained the majority of pots made here in the last forty years. When I was a student at the Central School in the late sixties I remember that part of our sense of corporate pride and college rivalry was expressed in the fact that we made blue and yellow things whereas at Camberwell they were still green and brown. Anti-Orientalism (in our inspiration though not our appreciation), and divergence from the Leach line, is a stance held in common. Useful sources are varied; though great respect for ancient and primitive and very different cultures is a binding factor. Richard Slee lists influences that range from Pre-Columbian vessels to Krazy Kat cartoons through Sèvres porcelain and the Surrealists, and is entirely convincing … The members of this hypothetical group need and recognise tradition, not in order to follow it, as perhaps the Orientalists have been inclined to do, but to mix it all up and try to invent freely on top of it. How else could Krazy Kat and Sèvres contribute to the same piece? Some sort of distortion, or visual deception, and non-symmetry, are other usual features of these new vessels. Even those who throw now muck about with the shapes afterwards. Both my favourite throwers,

> Walter Keeler and Betty Woodman, are expert at this … The tendency to trust spontaneous improvisation, by which I don't mean accepting what chance brings, but rather 'shaping at the point of utterance', is clearly shown in such pots.[13]

Since nothing is ever tidy or simple, although the makers involved in New Ceramics aimed to stretch and vary ideas about ceramic form, as I have implied in that quotation, throwing was not excluded. Walter Keeler, Janice Tchalenko, Colin Pearson (and the American Betty Woodman who inspired the British) are examples of potters using the wheel in a different way; initiating new forms or ideas about surface. But the hand-building of irregular forms characterised the fresh impetus. Peter Dormer's book *The New Ceramics* was published in 1986. I wrote the introduction for it and raised the idea of Prose and Poetry, different ends from equivalent means, to elucidate the relationship between different kinds of pot. Dr Oliver Watson of the Victoria and Albert Museum enhanced the definition of the two opposing camps, and they were adversarial at the outset, with his definition of 'the expressive pot' (New Ceramics) and 'the ethical pot' (Leach and followers).[14]

Hostility from the old masters to the young, frequently female, upstarts was to do with perceived status, prices, what the makers thought was their proper place in the spectrum of art and craft, the culture of ceramics that includes beauty and utility, humility and irony. 'Awkward *and* beautiful' is the phrase Angus Suttie used in 1985 to describe the objects he sought to make, which sums up perhaps the mood of that time.[15] The Crafts Council, while greatly respecting the Leach ethos, also did a lot to promote and exhibit the new ideas of the young urban 'artist/craftsperson'. But the Leach tradition was tired and clichéd for many people by the 1970s. As Takeshi Yasuda has reflected, what the Leach movement needed was a more questioning ensuing generation who re-worked the initial ideas, but what it got was disciples. At this point in the discourse of ceramics there was a commonly held view that skill and art were somehow in opposition, 'mere' skill was thought to exclude imagination, and the status of thrown ware diminished.[16]

But the tables have turned. In 2000 I wrote a leaflet for an exhibition of new young artists that included thrown work by Chun Liao and Daniel Fisher:

> It has been long enough now since the grip of Leach's persuasive, pervasive 'orientalist' version of the best norms in wheel-thrown pottery has loosened … the wheel seems free, again, for some fresh and serious work. The Japanese potter Takeshi Yasuda has been significant for a lot of younger potters, and he has been teaching here for the past twenty years. Another phase of the east/west conversation has been ongoing.[17]

Yasuda arrived in Britain in 1973 after a traditional workshop training in a family-run pottery in Mashiko and ran his own pottery there for a further decade. He came here to rethink his making life. After a few reclusive years, which mixed smallholder farming with some pottery production, Takeshi applied for a job teaching ceramics for three months in Bergen in Norway in 1978, in the Kunsthandwerksskole. Here he re-found the excitement of pot making, and ever since the production and teaching of pottery have, in differing proportions, filled his life. He has been very much appreciated in both his roles. His work and his thinking have never stood still, he has never rested on assumptions. He is now internationally recognised, has a dense programme of exhibitions, and is currently much more making than teaching.

His work has been through several dramatic changes, and there are substantial bodies of work in all the different types. The first works I saw were the celadons of the 1980s, huge flat dishes with pimpled handles like the limbs of an octopus, and the bucket forms, a down-to-earth reversal of the ceramic basket. These were followed by pieces such as the quintessential Takeshi forms 'the sprung bowl' and the 'plateau' raised dish, which are glazed in a dramatic stoneware version of Chinese Tang Dynasty colours. Subsequent work was with creamware, earthenware that refers to refined English eighteenth-century production. His forms are increasingly loose but poised. His use of very soft clay leads him to make shapes that express plasticity, delicate deformation, give, and sensuality. Exhibitions have been inspiring in the way the rhythmic series of different shapes have been installed, as in the 1996 show at Christ's Hospital School.

Takeshi's presence in Britain has represented a liberation of ideas about throwing. His influence is profound. That he is Japanese, rather than inspired by Japan, is important in the British context. Choosing to work here gave him a clean start, his own sphere. He was not born into the crafts, nor art-school educated – his father was a photographer – and he has wide visual interests, having wanted at first to be an engineer. His discovery of the pottery scene in Mashiko and his decision to go and work there in 1963 was the choice of an alternative lifestyle, like the counter-culture thinking of the UK in the same period. Once in Britain, his early encounter with the British Anglo-Japanese potters made him realise that he wasn't part of that tradition. But he cherishes English peculiarity in many forms, and is pleased with the way in which we have retained a use for the pot in the domestic interior.

In Takeshi's view the postgraduate phase of learning is crucial for throwers. There isn't time on a BA course, he thinks, for the fellowship and competition, influence and inspiration of each other, that feeds the understanding of the discipline. At the postgraduate Royal College of Art, where I teach and he is an occasional tutor, it is plain that interest in throwing has greatly revived. We have recently rebuilt the throwing room to give people more space. Another visiting tutor that inspired new energy in the throwing room was Simon Carroll, who threw sometimes against the plaster walls of huge press moulds. He made great vigorous pots that conjoined loose and controlled aspects of thrown form, and made cheerful reference to medieval English slipware.

The Nigerian Lawson Oyekan, who studied ceramics in London, does not distinguish between hand-building and throwing in his expressive and energetic quest for forms that mean something. He uses both techniques, in different series of pots, and his use of the wheel communicates an outstanding kind of vitality.

Clive Bowen and Gwynn Hanssen Pigott are two quite different potters whose work is very well established. Both of them, in my view, have developed strong personal languages, which do not grow stale, out of the tradition of thrown forms that followed Leach. I included groups of work from both, and from Newland and Oyekan, in curating the exhibition *A View of Clay* at Contemporary Applied Arts in 1998.[18] Hanssen Pigott looms, I think, in the background for a number of young potters who in recent years have contributed to what is almost a craze for simple thrown forms in porcelain.

The New White exhibition at the Victoria and Albert Museum in 1999 was curated by Alun Graves, and included Julian Stair and Edmund de Waal. Here was evidence of the high-cool edge of contemporary throwing in Britain, which fitted so beautifully into moves towards minimalism in the interior. Also in that show was Joanna Constantinidis, whose long distinguished career as a thrower of refined modernist forms ended in 2000. Thus far I have avoided talking about function as a decisive issue in the means one chooses to make pots. But it is clearly is of key importance to many who decide to throw. What other conditions, do we suppose, promote the interest in the purity, or is it puritanism, of the New White? Alun Graves in his exhibition leaflet emphasised that use, as well as the special associations and qualities of porcelain, is central to its appeal. For me the table settings, offering the most functional, everyday pleasures, were the best feature of this exhibition, made by five out of the seven contributing potters.

I want to propose in conclusion that striking developments in thrown pots of the past two decades have rebalanced the ceramic scene. Arguably we are still stuck with the art/craft conundrum, but there is no longer a conflict of status between different types of making. It is, as ever, vitality that counts, whether you pull, pinch, roll, pour, or scrape clay to achieve it.

Notes

1 Bernard Leach, *A Potter's Book* (London: Faber and Faber, 1940).
2 Michael Cardew, *Pioneer Pottery* (London: Longman Group, 1969).
3 Dora M. Billington, *The Art of the Potter* (London: Oxford University Press, 1937).
4 Peter Dormer (ed.), *Fast Forward*, exhibition catalogue (London: ICA, 1985).
5 *Collingwood/Coper*, exhibition catalogue (London: V&A Museum, 1969).
6 Philip Rawson, *Ceramics* (London: Oxford University Press, 1971).
7 Dormer (ed.), *Fast Forward*.
8 Peter Fuller in Peter Dormer (ed.), *Fifty Five Pots and Three Opinions,* exhibition catalogue (Londonderry: Orchard Gallery, 1983).
9 Verbal, in conversation with the author.
10 See Tanya Harrod, *The Crafts in Britain in the 20th Century* (New Haven: Yale University Press, 1999).
11 I explored these differences in 1991 in my essay 'The urban potter'. Alison Britton, 'The urban potter', in *Colours of the Earth*, exhibition catalogue (British Council: 1991), exhibition curated by Janice Tchalenko that toured India.
12 Quoted by Harrod, *The Crafts in Britain*, p. 240.
13 Alison Britton, 'Sevres with Krazy Kat', *Crafts Magazine*, 61 (1983).
14 Oliver Watson, *British Studio Pottery, The Victoria and Albert Museum Collection* (London: Phaidon Christie's, 1990).
15 Angus Suttie with pseudonym Aeschylus Orton, *Step we gaily. The pottery of Angus Suttie. British Ceramics*, exhibition catalogue (Netherlands: Museum Het Kruithuis te 's-Hertogenbosch, 1985).
16 Alison Britton, 'The manipulation of skill on the outer limits of function', in Peter Dormer (ed.), *Beyond the Dovetail*, exhibition catalogue (London: Crafts Council, 1991).
17 Alison Britton, *Momentum*, exhibition leaflet (London: Barrett Marsden Gallery, 2000).
18 Alison Britton, 'The open-minded eye', *Crafts Magazine*, 150 (1998).

This article was originally given as a paper at the 'Diversity in the Making: Studio Ceramics Today' conference which was held at Camberwell College of Arts, London, on 15 January 2001. It was published in Issue 2 of *Interpreting Ceramics* later that year, alongside the other papers that were presented at the conference. Inevitably the text is now dated, not only in the sense that twelve years have passed since it was written, but also in the sense that the turn of the millennium framed the writing in a very self-conscious way. Therefore no attempt has been made to update the text; it is presented here as a period piece with all its outdated references intact. Jeffrey Jones is Professor of Ceramics at Cardiff Metropolitan University.

Studio Ceramics: The End of the Story?

Jeffrey Jones

There can surely be no doubt that we have now passed from the twentieth to the twenty-first century and the arguments as to whether the twenty-first century began on 1 January 2000 or 1 January 2001 can be put aside. Whichever date we favour for this significant transition, we might at least all agree that the period of change from one century to another, from one millennium to another, has shown itself (somewhat predictably) to have been a fruitful time for a discussion of the ends of things. It wasn't until I started to prepare this talk that I discovered that there was a name for this phenomenon: endism.[1] And there is also a name for those of us who dwell deeply on finalities, passings, conclusions and the like. It seems that we are endists and that there are a lot of us about.

You need not look far for evidence of this. Try doing a search for 'endism' on the Internet and see what you get. Or consider the titles of the following books published in recent years: *The End of Science*,[2] *The End of Work*,[3] *The End of Utopia*,[4] and perhaps most notably, Francis Fukuyama's *The End of History and the Last Man*.[5] If all these big things really are over, what then are the prospects for the smaller concerns of life and the chances of survival of more localised forms of human activity such as studio ceramics? Is it time to surrender to this gloomy tendency, accept that what we call studio ceramics has run its course and proclaim the end of that as well? Before becoming too downhearted by what can appear to be the inherent pessimism of endist thought it might be useful to explore the phenomenon in general a little further before coming to any premature conclusions about the end of studio ceramics.

Firstly, let's put aside the more sensationalist manifestations of endism, those concerned with doomsday scenarios and the hastening on of the end of the world as we know it. There's plenty of that available if you have a mind to look but I should think it is not to the taste of most of us here. However the prevalence of such apocalyptic thought does tell us something about the mood of the times. Paying attention to it can alert us to the heightened feelings which are engendered when there is the slightest suggestion that what we hold to be continuous, solid and reliable is threatened by closure. We should also note that for some people the prospect of the end of everything is exciting; although the end of everything in that instance usually means the end of everything that is not to such people's particular liking. That kind of endism can provide an opportunity for some to look forward to the victory of very partial worldviews. This is endism as triumphalism.

In 'The end of history?', Francis Fukuyama's much-discussed article published in 1989 and his subsequent book published in 1992,[6] the author talks of the triumph of the West, and the seemingly unstoppable success of the Western idea. He refers to the exhaustion of viable, systematic alternatives to Western, democratic liberalism and says that 'there are powerful reasons for believing that it is the ideal that will govern the material world *in the long run*' (original emphasis).[7] Now, I am here to talk about studio ceramics not political history and theory but Fukuyama's controversial thesis provides an important lesson for us. Fukuyama writes of the triumph of a particular political philosophy but he is hardly a triumphalist, trumpeting the victory of a particular ideology and the end of competing voices. Fukuyama is more concerned to articulate an awkward, dawning truth: that by all accounts, by all reasonable measures of what is going on in the world, Western, democratic liberalism now finds itself with no serious, ideological competitors. To put it simply, Western liberalism has won; it's the end of the story. History, in the sense of events, things happening in the world, will of course continue, but history in the sense of a struggle for a dominant idea has ended.

In this paper I argue that such an insight can usefully, and I think reasonably, be applied to the discourse surrounding studio ceramics and its position within the wider field of ceramics as a whole. I would ask you to consider if we are not justified now in asking the simple question: has studio ceramics won? And, if the answer is yes, is this in any sense good news?

So in framing the title of this paper as 'Studio ceramics: the end of the story?' I am therefore not so much concerned with writing the obituary of studio ceramics as with interpreting studio ceramics as an ideological phenomenon, which has at its core an implicit sense of historical destiny and convergence. Studio ceramics is therefore understood here as having taken on a particular responsibility both for articulating the potential of the medium of ceramics, and for nurturing and protecting ceramics as a discrete category of human activity. If, as Don Cupitt suggests, 'what people call history evolves over the weeks and years as the provisional outcome of a contest of stories'[8] then I would argue that we have good reason for recognising that studio ceramics has in the twentieth century been supremely successful not only in achieving a pre-eminent place for its own story, but also in achieving for itself the role of narrator of the ceramics story as a whole. Studio ceramics is the end of the story in the sense that it has come to see itself as the final chapter in the great book of ceramics.[9]

I must emphasise here that I make no claim and offer no evidence that the work produced under the aegis of studio ceramics is any sense better, technically or aesthetically, than any other kind of ceramics. But there is evidence that the ideology embedded in studio ceramics can now be understood as an unrivalled success. Before looking at some of this evidence I should say that my concerns here are with British studio ceramics although my arguments may also have relevance elsewhere. I should also point out that I shall be taking as examples people who make or have made pottery, although I readily acknowledge that the term 'pottery' by no means accounts for everything covered by the term 'ceramics'. However I think it is fair to say that British studio *ceramics* has its practical and ideological roots anchored firmly in the twentieth-century studio *pottery* movement. There may be some who would fight at all costs to preserve the nice distinctions between these two but I admit I find it difficult to separate them in many, if not most, circumstances. I must risk giving offence by sometimes conflating the two and talking, for instance, of the studio pottery/studio ceramics movement.

Studio ceramics: telling the story

In the figure of Bernard Leach, arguably the foremost polemicist of that movement, we can observe someone whose sense of historical destiny was central to his life's work. But as well as making a claim for his own historical importance, Leach was as ready to make a grand claim for his chosen medium, saying that 'the history of man is written in clay'.[10] Leach was not alone in making this assertion, for example Dora Billington stated that 'the story of pottery is the story of civilisation'[11] and W. B. Dalton, who I believe was principal here at Camberwell at the beginning of the twentieth century, described clay as 'man's oldest, if not greatest friend' and went on to say that 'clay lives in and through all the history of mankind'.[12] All three, Leach, Billington and Dalton, wrote pottery handbooks in which varying degrees of technical information are juxtaposed with references to a range of ceramic artefacts from the past. The authors are all humble in the face of the achievements of potters from previous ages but there is also a recognition of the privileged position from which they are writing. For example, towards the end of Billington's book *The Art of the Potter*, published in 1937, in a chapter entitled 'The pottery of today', the author writes:

> Although a considerable expansion of studio pottery has taken place only during the last twenty years or so in this country, it has its roots in the last century, when pottery collections were formed and written about, and experiments made, resulting in a gradual readjustment of values. For the first time contemporary pottery could be adequately compared with what had been done before and many attempts were made to recover lost 'secrets' and origins.
>
> Thanks to all this spade work the studio potter can survey the whole field of ceramics and, within the limits of his capabilities, make whatever wares he pleases.[13]

Leaving aside the observation that most studio potters proved to be far more circumscribed in the wares that they made than that which Billington might have hoped for and encouraged, there is a sense here of the studio potter moving towards a privileged vantage point from which the whole field of ceramics can be accessed and interpreted. Billington was neither naive nor unique in her approach; C. F. Binns, Dora Lunn, Bernard Leach, Murray Fieldhouse, all of these writers felt it appropriate to provide some kind of historical survey in their pottery handbooks, usually as a preface to the instructions which they provided to their aspiring colleagues, the new breed of individual potter.[14] Leach may have been fussier than most in his choice of exemplary ceramic traditions, limiting himself to Raku, English slipware and Oriental stoneware and porcelain, but the range of ceramic styles and processes covered by the potter-authors referred to above is impressively diverse. The studio potter's inheritance was indeed a significant one, and one that brought with it a good deal of responsibility, as well as a range of possibilities. As the studio potter emerged as a distinct type, so the story of ceramics coalesced as a seemingly coherent field of endeavour with a distinct, historical trajectory.

As the history of twentieth-century studio pottery/studio ceramics itself came to be written, its unique, privileged and seemingly conclusive position within the wider ceramics world became ever more apparent. Studio ceramics became, literally, the final chapter in an increasing number of publications which covered the history of ceramics in far more depth than any of the authors of the pottery handbooks had attempted. One of the most ambitious of these publications to have appeared in recent years is *The Potter's Art* by Garth Clark, which is subtitled *A Complete History of Pottery in Britain*. Clark's book, published in 1995, is divided up into four parts: 'The peasant potter', 'The industrial potter', 'The artist potter' and then 'The studio potter' as the last and longest chapter. In his introduction the author sets out the rationale for this, describing the book as consisting of four overlapping chronologies and he defends this approach by saying:

> This view is perhaps best understood by regarding the narrative as a kind of cultural relay race for leadership in the ceramic arts in which the baton is transferred at certain points from the hands of one potter type to another.[15]

The metaphor of baton passing is a vivid and compelling one, but in its very success as a metaphor there is an uncomfortable reality laid bare at its foundation. This metaphor surely begs some important questions. If we, the studio ceramics community find ourselves carrying the ceramics baton, then where now should we run with it, and perhaps more pertinently, will there ever be any other kind of potter type to whom we can eventually hand it on? It seems as if the race is over but has anyone actually won? Are we really justified in consigning to history those non-studio potters who have played their part, handed on the baton and dutifully stepped aside? There is surely a case for looking more closely at these other ceramics stories and noting, at the very least, that their individual narratives have a life beyond their apportioned stages in the ceramics relay race. I shall briefly look in turn at the stories of these three other potter types as described by Garth Clark, with especial regard to the way that those stories have been positioned within the larger ceramics story. I shall begin by asking, what happened to the peasant potter?

The peasant potter

The extinction of this species has been dated to various points throughout the first half of the twentieth century, their demise hastened by the First World War, or by the Depression, or by the Second World War. Bernard Leach thought he had spotted the last of them in the figure of Edwin Beer Fishley.[16] It is easy to romanticise such a figure; the peasant potter and his story can so easily be assigned to folklore and quaint, British customs rather than to any serious social history. But if we look dispassionately at the fortunes of the places in which these potters worked, what are usually called country potteries, and which I prefer to call small, local potteries, there is a thread of stubborn survival. The stories of two such potteries are extraordinary.

The Curtis family has been associated with Littlethorpe Pottery in North Yorkshire since about 1912 or 1913 when George Curtis started work there as a clayboy. He subsequently became manager and then owner of the pottery through marriage in 1939. George's son Roly Curtis continues to work the pottery although its continued existence as a going concern seems to hinge on plans to reposition it within a heritage context, somewhat in line with other potteries such as Wetheriggs in Cumbria. Littlethorpe has a good claim to be the most intact survivor of this kind of small local pottery, at least in terms of the preservation of the buildings and the continuity of methods of manufacture.[17]

As impressive as Littlethorpe, though in a slightly different sense, is Ewenny Pottery in South Wales. There are records of pottery making in this area since the fifteenth century and there is an oral tradition of a pottery on this site from 1610. For many years the Morgans family worked the pottery and in 1820 Evan Jenkins married into the Morgans and thus was established what surely must be the longest-lasting pottery dynasty in Britain. Caitlin Jenkins, who now works at the pottery with her father Alun, is the seventh generation of the Jenkins family to have worked there.[18] Unlike at Littlethorpe, the original pottery buildings at Ewenny, although they survive, are no longer used for pottery making but as a furniture workshop. A newish building provides working accommodation for the potters who continue to produce a range of thrown earthenware for sale through the attached showroom. Both Alun and Caitlin Jenkins have completed BA degrees in ceramics in Cardiff and so can be said to have trained as studio potters. However, Ewenny Pottery itself resists categorisation as a studio pottery and in terms of its market it still operates very much as a small, local pottery. For example, amongst the most striking aspects of Ewenny is that the potters continue to make a living almost entirely through passing trade. The pottery is situated on the road to the coast a few miles away and this must help, but it is not a well-established tourist area. There is some tourist trade but a livelihood is made easier here through what can only be described as local loyalty; people from a certain catchment area in South Wales buying pottery for their own use or as gifts, from a pottery which they more than likely remember from their childhood. This sense of the pottery being able to satisfy a need in the local community is one that many studio potters have aspired to but hardly, if ever, achieved.

Littlethorpe and Ewenny are both alike survivors against the odds, but that is not enough in itself to guarantee the acknowledgement of a studio ceramics community which has often, in real terms, been indifferent to the fate of such indigenous, long-standing, local enterprises. Oliver Watson pointed out some years ago that 'it is surprising that Bernard Leach and Cardew did not try to seek out more thoroughly the remnants of the tradition whose passing they so deplored'.[19] There are welcome signs of an awakening interest. Andrew McGarva's well-researched book *Country Pottery* is the first real attempt to cover the field since the Peter Brears book published nearly thirty years ago. But McGarva is selective; unlike Littlethorpe, Ewenny is not listed amongst the surviving potteries worthy of extended comment but then it does not fit his criteria. Ewenny is classed alongside Rye Pottery in Sussex as places which continue to produce (and I quote) 'pots of a decorative nature ... developing the "art ware" style rather than country pots' (original emphasis).[20] In referring to the large amount of this kind of pottery produced over the years by potteries such as Ewenny, Mcgarva makes his position clear:

> It is not by this decorative ware that the country potter's work should be judged. For a historian or anthropologist, they may seem more interesting, and a certain rustic charm in this decorative ware is undeniable. But any potter can see what these old potters made best, with skill and spontaneity, were the 'ordinary' pots for everyday use.[21]

But if ordinariness really is a criterion that should be taken seriously, where should we look for it now? Is the taste of the people who have bought the work of Ewenny Pottery over all these years not ordinary enough to count for anything? Applying a studio ceramics sensibility to small, local potteries inevitably results in an interpretation that gives undue weight to a highly refined taste that hardly connects at all with actual patterns of production and consumption that made and, in the case of Ewenny, continue to make such potteries viable. If the story of these small, local potteries continues to be told through a studio ceramics-centred narrative how faithful can that story be to the experiences of the participants within that story?

The industrial potter

It was the relationship between the industrial potter and the studio potter that provided the richest area of debate in the ceramics world during the twentieth century. It is in this area that the idea of a contest between opposing ideological ceramics camps can be most clearly seen. It is also in this area that the 'Britishness' of the debate is most clearly exposed; there are examples readily at hand in other European countries to show that the industrial potter/studio potter contest was not an inevitable historical outcome. Indeed there are examples to be found in Britain which show that at times such a debate was seen as either meaningless or counter-productive. Gordon Forsyth's book *20th Century Ceramics*, published in 1936, gives a good indication of the diversity that can be identified as a prime feature of the inter-war period in Britain. Forsyth saw no need to categorise ceramics and the illustrations in his book reveal an easy acceptance of different ways of making.[22] Similarly, Dora Billington, in an interview published in 1950, was able to say:

> Because I grew up with the industry, I have the feeling that pottery, whether mass-produced or studio pottery, is one thing. I cannot recognise any very clear distinction.[23]

Others, however, did and it was during the middle years of the twentieth century that a contest of a rather undignified kind broke out between those in the ceramics world who, on the one hand, represented the factory and, on the other hand, represented the studio. Strong support for industry came from a perhaps unexpected source, namely, W. B. Honey, curator of ceramics at the Victoria and Albert Museum. Honey's predecessor at the museum Bernard Rackham had been generally supportive of the emerging studio pottery movement in the 1920s through his articles in *The Studio* magazine, but W. B. Honey in his book *The Art of the Potter*, published in 1946, showed himself to be far less convinced of their merits. One of the chapters of Honey's book is entitled 'Traditional and modern design in English pottery' and it consists of the text of a paper which was presented to the National Council of the Pottery Industry on 26 March 1945. Honey compares a jug by Bernard Leach to work designed by Keith Murray for Wedgwood. Honey comments:

> I am now offering no opinion on the relative merits of these two widely different sorts of work. But I must point out in passing that the one preserves or revives artificially, for the satisfaction of a cultivated and leisured class of well-to-do patrons, a style belonging to peasant craftsmanship; while the other looks forward to a time when the potential power of a fully mechanized and wisely directed industrial system will provide leisure and amenities for all. The one has no economic reality; the other belongs to the present day. And between them there is really no bridge at all.[24]

Honey's text gave encouragement to a pottery industry which in the early 1950s confidently believed in its power to see off this upstart called studio pottery. The pages of the industry trade magazines of this period provide interesting reading. They are surprisingly generous in their scope, including reviews of studio pottery books and exhibitions, but not so generous in their comments when studio potters or their supporters overstep the mark and make too grand a claim for their approach to pottery making. When they do then the full force of the pottery industry's wrath descends on their heads. A harsh but effective tactic by a reviewer in the November 1952 edition of *Pottery and Glass* was to dismiss studio pottery as a cult and to go on to claim that:

> The originators of this cult must realise that the Second World War destroyed forever the social conditions necessary for its survival. But the legend they created still stalks the land, deluding the minds of innocent art school students and sophisticated housewives, and setting a halo around the head and hands of the thrower in his corduroys.[25]

It is extraordinary that this extract continues to possess such resonance today, nearly half a century on, even though the reviewer was so strikingly wrong when he/she went on to sound the premature death knell of studio pottery by claiming that this 'fashionable artistic cult … was knocked on the head in 1940, and has been lying on a cold slab in the morgue ever since, awaiting identification'.[26]

Indeed it is studio pottery/studio ceramics that has survived and prospered as the once-mighty industry in Stoke-on-Trent has contracted to a fraction of its size half a century ago. But it is not just manufacturing capacity that has been lost; what has also disappeared is the capacity of the ceramics industry to fight an ideological battle. It is to the studio ceramics journals that we must now turn for discussion of ideas and for the airing of opinions rather than to the trade journals. There surely must still be some apologists for the industry who would point out the continuing importance of Stoke-on-Trent to the field of ceramics, but we now have to look hard for measures of that importance in terms of a confident voicing of its position. The ceramics industry in Britain may well still have a voice, but if it does then it is one that is increasingly not being heard.

The artist potter

What then of the artist potter? Of all potter types this is the one that appears to be most historically circumscribed. The terms 'art potter' or 'artist potter' are now understood as referring to a type of maker who was active for just a few decades straddling the changeover from the nineteenth to the twentieth centuries. Such a potter was a product of very specific historical conditions and it may be that the story of the artist potter is best left as a brief but colourful episode in the long history of ceramics. To go back to the relay race metaphor, they did their bit, ran their stage and then handed the baton on to the studio potter who had the privilege of running the final leg. But there are some interesting aspects of the story of the artist potter which are relevant today.

For example, the original representatives of this potter type, in spite of the fact that they were often associated with an Arts and Crafts ideology, were generally unhindered by any qualms about the division of labour. They would frequently employ others to complete parts of the manufacturing process which they were either unable or unwilling to complete themselves. The emphasis was clearly on Art rather than Craft and there was little if any investment in the idea of any particular skill having an intrinsic value within the overall ideology of making. For example the elevation of throwing to mystical heights would have to wait for the emergence of the studio potter a couple of decades later for its realisation.

It is extraordinary to reflect on the way that the completion of every task by the maker themselves has become endemic to the practice of studio ceramics. So much so, that when this code of practice is breached it can seem scandalous to the studio ceramics sensibility. Handing on responsibility for a part of the making is seen as something that artists might do but that studio ceramists should not. There are examples of contemporary fine artists who use clay but are not identified as studio ceramists, at least by themselves, and a strongly defining indicator of this distinction is the willingness of the artist to delegate key tasks. One of the most intriguing examples of this is Cecile Jonhson-Soliz who in strictly descriptive terms is both an artist and a potter.

For Johnson-Soliz craft skills are fundamental to her art; it is important that her work is as well made as it is well thought out. She has, however, no qualms about enlisting help when she needs it and she retains control of all the making processes. It is with considerable skill and sensitivity that she marshals the labour of herself and others as well as the conditions under which her work is shown. She is clear about her intentions and will hand on to others crucial tasks such as firing as long as she is confident that she will get the results she wants. There is no investment on her part in that attenuated self-sufficiency which has become a hallmark of studio ceramics, and in abandoning such orthodoxies she creates considerable creative space for herself; space in which the appropriateness of the context in which her work is presented is as crucial as the quality of the artefacts themselves. Johnson-Soliz clearly makes pottery, but has succeeded in avoiding classification as a maker of studio ceramics. There are other examples (Andrew Lord is one such) of fine artists who exclusively use clay as their medium, but who have taken great pains to avoid being called studio ceramists. However they have not escaped the often-envious gaze of the studio ceramics community and such work is increasingly incorporated into the studio ceramics debate and into the studio ceramics consciousness. However much artists such as Cecile Johnson-Soliz and Andrew Lord would like to distance themselves from the ideology of studio ceramics, it is an ideology that has an increasing capacity for gathering such makers to itself.

Conclusion

To conclude, I would argue that studio ceramics has been the great ceramics success story of the twentieth century. Studio potters/studio ceramists have established themselves as (to use Garth Clark's phrase) the 'potter type' against which all other potter types are measured. Also, the story of studio pottery/studio ceramics has in the twentieth century been central to the wider story of ceramics, and has offered a paradigm for the telling of stories of other potter types. These other potter types have survived, and cling on to separate identities, but their stories have to a large extent been told through a narrative that has placed studio ceramics as the end point.

To some extent, at least, the stories of the peasant potter, the industrial potter and the artist potter have been told by different kinds of narrators and have been heard by different kinds of audiences. For example, archaeologists and ethnographers are taking an increasing interest in country pottery, the design historian already pays a good deal of attention to industrial pottery, and even the art critic occasionally casts an eye on fine artists who use clay. It is, however, only studio ceramics as a category that enjoys the privilege and responsibility of being able to draw on the diversity of ceramics practice in order to inflect and enlarge not only its own area of practice but also the general discourse around ceramics, over which it has a largely unacknowledged measure of control.

I have limited myself in this paper to a discussion of pottery making in Britain, but if there were time to extend my arguments to other branches of ceramics and to other countries then I believe that my argument would be strengthened further. For example, through coming into contact with some of the overseas students in my work at the Centre for Ceramics Studies in Cardiff, I have begun to realise that in very many parts of the world what might be called the studio ceramicisation of ceramic practice is accelerating. In many cultures it seems that the baton is being passed quickly now from peasant potter to studio potter without going through any intervening stages.

To go back to Garth Clark's metaphor of a relay race, I would argue that it is unimaginable, at least in the foreseeable future, that we as a studio ceramics community will have either the inclination or the opportunity to pass the baton on; there is no other kind of potter type on the horizon to whom the baton can conceivably be passed. Perhaps that metaphor itself is now obsolete, that kind of race is over, that kind of history making no longer holds good.

Of course people will continue to use clay to make pots and to make art, and the diversity in the making heralded in the title of this conference will, I hope, be a continuing reality. But I also hope that when the story of ceramics is told in future years, the central role of studio ceramics in the narration of the story will be seen to have been discharged with fairness and with due regard for all the actors within that story.

In his article 'The end of history?' Francis Fukuyama wrote: 'the victory of liberalism has occurred primarily in the realm of ideas or consciousness and is as yet incomplete in the real or material world'. I suggest that, similarly, the victory of studio ceramics can now be observed as having occurred in the realm of ideas or consciousness. I am left wondering whether the completion of that victory in the real or material world would be good news for all makers in clay, both within and beyond the studio.

Acknowledgements

I am grateful to Richard Carlton of the University of Newcastle-Upon-Tyne for material relating to Littlethorpe Pottery and to Caitlin Jenkins of Ewenny Pottery, Bridgend, South Wales for material relating to Ewenny Pottery.

Notes

1 A useful, short introduction to the notion of endism is to be found in Stuart Sim, *Derrida and the End of History* (Cambridge: Icon Books, 1999), pp. 12–16.
2 John Horgan, *The End of Science: Facing the Limits of Knowledge in the Twilight of the Scientific Age* (Reading, Massachusetts: Addison-Wesley, 1996).
3 Jeremy Rifkin, *The End of Work: The Decline of the Global Labor Force and the Dawn of the Post-Market Era* (New York: G. P. Putnam's Sons, 1995).
4 Russell Jacoby, *The End of Utopia: Politics and Culture in an Age of Apathy* (New York: Basic Books, 1999).
5 Francis Fukuyama, *The End of History and the Last Man* (London: H. Hamilton, 1992).
6 Fukuyama's article entitled 'The end of history?' was published in *The National Interest*, Summer 1989, pp. 3–18, and was subsequently expanded into the book entitled *The End of History and the Last Man*.
7 Fukuyama, 'The end of history?', p. 4.
8 Don Cupitt, *What is a Story* (London: SCM Press, 1991), p. 20.
9 I am using the phrase 'studio ceramics' here as a kind of shorthand for a body of people and ideas much as 'the West' might be used to stand for both a group of countries and an ideology. Exhibitions, conferences, journals, books, courses in further and higher education all testify to the fact that studio ceramics can be identified as a particular ideological phenomenon.
10 Annotation by Bernard Leach on the cover of the Summer 1950 edition of a magazine entitled *Far and Wide*. On the front of the magazine Leach has written: 'Write article for this Quarterly this winter: 1000–1500 words. The modern potter – what makes a pot good – The first international conference of artist potters. The history of man is written in clay.' Bernard Leach archive, Crafts Study Centre, catalogue no. 538. (At the time of writing the Craft Study Centre is in transit from The Holburne Museum, Bath, to Farnham Campus, Surrey Institute of Art and Design.) Leach's article was published in 1952 as 'The modern craftsman potter', *Far and Wide*, the magazine of the Guest Keen and Nettlefolds group of companies, 20 (Spring 1952), pp. 17–21.
11 Dora Billington, *The Art of the Potter* (London: Oxford University Press, 1937), p. 6.
12 W. B. Dalton, 'Just clay', printed for private circulation, 1962, p. 87.
13 Billington, *The Art of the Potter*, p. 108.
14 See C. F. Binns, *The Potter's Craft*, second edition (New York: D. Van Nostrand Company, 1922, [first published 1910]); Dora Lunn, *Pottery in the Making* (Leicester and London: Dryad Press, 1931); Bernard Leach, *A Potter's Book* (London: Faber and Faber, 1940); Murray Fieldhouse, *Pottery* (London: W. & G. Foyle Ltd, 1952).
15 Garth Clark, *The Potter's Art: A Complete History of Pottery in Britain* (London: Phaidon Press, 1995), p. 7.

16 See Bernard Leach, *Beyond East and West: Memoirs, Portraits and Essays* (London: Faber and Faber, 1978), p. 148.
17 See R. J. Carlton, 'Littlethorpe Potteries, Ripon, North Yorkshire', a report prepared for Harrogate Borough Council and North Yorkshire County Council by the Littlethorpe Potteries Project.
18 Information provided by Caitlin Jenkins, Ewenny Pottery.
19 Oliver Watson, *Studio Pottery: Twentieth Century British Ceramics in the Victoria and Albert Museum Collection* (London: Phaidon Press, 1993), p. 41, n. 11.
20 Andrew McGarva, *Country Pottery: Traditional Earthenware of Britain* (London: A. & C. Black, 2000), p. 112.
21 McGarva, *Country Pottery*, p. 12.
22 Gordon Forsyth, *20th Century Ceramics* (London: The Studio, 1936).
23 Dora Billington in John Farleigh, *The Creative Craftsman* (London: John Bell and Sons, 1950), p. 189.
24 William Bowyer Honey, *The Art of The Potter* (London: Faber and Faber, 1946), p. 96.
25 'The not-so-modern potter' (book review), *Pottery and Glass*, 30:11 (November 1952), p. 72. The book under review was by George Wingfield Digby, *The Work of the Modern Potter in England* (London: John Murray, 1952).
26 'The not-so-modern potter', p. 72.

Author of more than sixty books, Garth Clark has been a significant force in the ceramics world for over thirty years; his first book, *Potters of Southern Africa*, was published in 1974. Amongst his many subsequent publications are two anthologies that reflect his longstanding quest to establish a critical context for ceramics: *Ceramic Art: Comment and Review* (1977) and *Ceramic Millennium: Critical Writings on Ceramic History, Theory and Art* (2005). *Shards: Garth Clark on Ceramic Art* (2003) features a selection of his own essays, written over a twenty-five-year period. Clark's *Michael Cardew: A Portrait* was published by Kodansha Press, Tokyo in 1976 and subsequently by Faber and Faber, Oxford in 1978. This account of 'Michael Cardew in America' offers a very immediate, sometimes intimate, sense of Cardew the man. It was given as a conference paper at the ICRC 'Michael Cardew Centenary Symposium', held at the University of Wales, Aberystwyth, UK (27–28 June 2001), and was originally published with other papers from the Symposium in Issue 3 of *Interpreting Ceramics*.

Cardew in America

Garth Clark

Cardew in America is a somewhat more ephemeral concept than Cardew in England, Africa or even Australia. He did not make pots in America (aside from workshop demonstrations). He did not teach the Native Americans how to make stoneware. He did not set up schools, nor did he search the American wilderness for raw materials. However, he did have six North American apprentices who now run active potteries and a grandson potting in Vermont. They are the most tangible aspect of the Cardew legacy in America. By virtue of the fact that they have run country potteries in Cardew's spirit, focusing on making functional work rather than teaching and exhibiting in art galleries, they have not played an influential role in the power structures in American ceramics.

Nonetheless, Cardew in America, the patchwork of visits and contacts, represents a very special part of his life. His frequent appearances as featured or keynote speaker at American conferences encouraged him to write, and much of his thoughtful analysis on the role of the functional potter in the twentieth century was initiated by his trips across the Atlantic.

Unlike Leach, who made his first visit to this continent in 1949, Cardew arrived much later in 1967, nearly two decades after Leach. However, he was known and his work had been already seen in America from time to time. His first exhibition was a four-person show (Bernard Leach, Cardew, Katherine Pleydell-Bouverie and Shoji Hamada) at the Harvard Society for Contemporary Art, Boston in 1927, curated by Lincoln Kirstein. His work appeared in various survey exhibitions over the following years, but he did not have any solo shows of his ceramics in America until the 1980s.

Cardew's first visit lasted from June to October. He worked with Kent Benson in Hollywood on a film that was never completed and taught summer school at the University of Wisconsin. He went to America because:

> I had a burning desire to visit that country. Why? I wanted to be stimulated. I was finding the close society of British potters just a little suffocating. And stimulated I

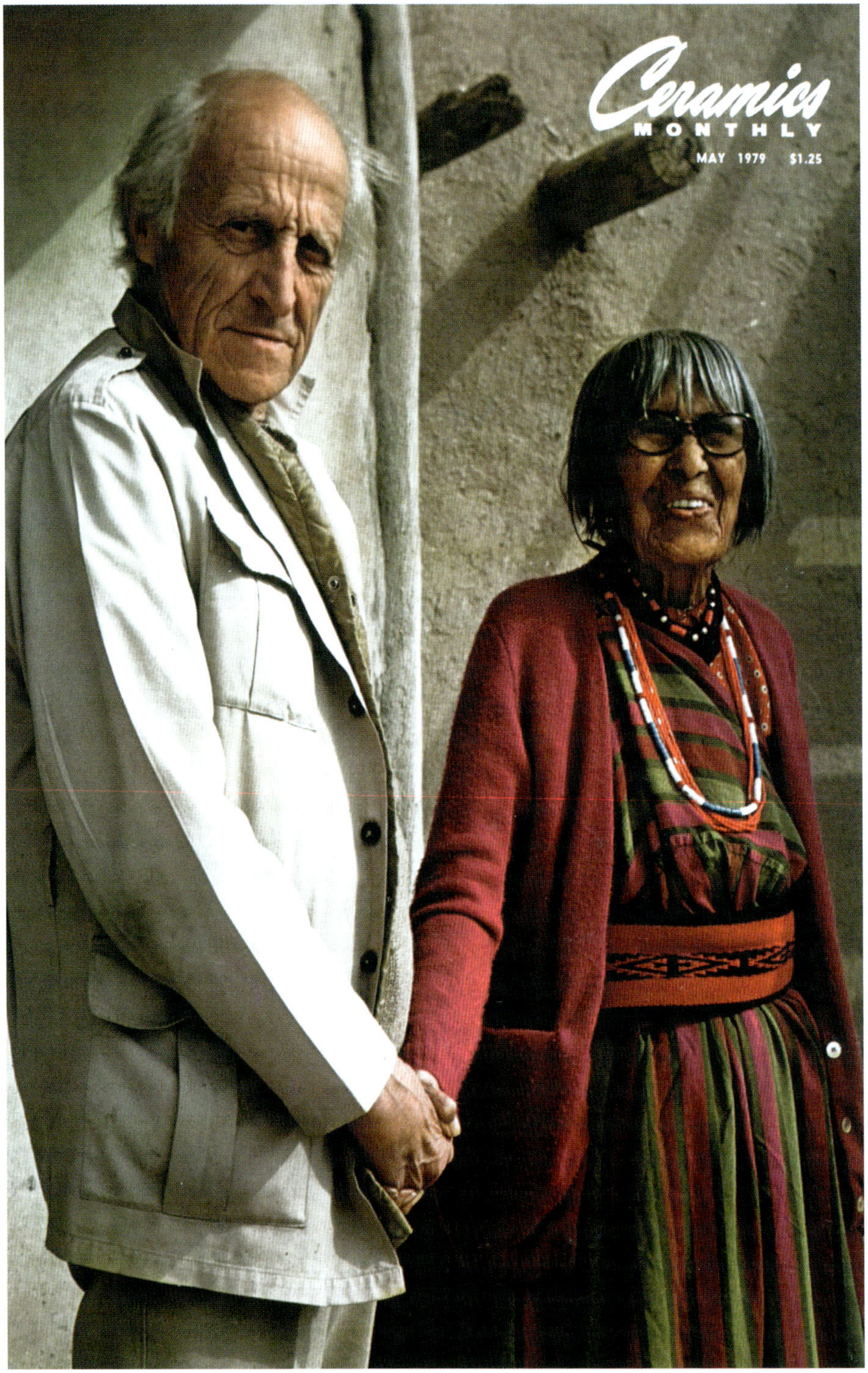

Fig 1. Michael Cardew and Maria Martinez on the cover of Ceramics Monthly, May 1979. Photo: courtesy of Ceramics Monthly.

> was. America is a country that contradicts any and everything that one has heard about it. It is so diverse it defies generalization.[1]

He was somewhat over-stimulated and returned a physical wreck, postponing a planned trip to New Zealand.

Cardew returned in 1971, to teach at the Arrowmont School of Crafts in Gatlinburg, Tennessee, but by then he was an anointed celebrity. His book, *Pioneer Pottery*, published in 1967, was a hit amongst the USA's workshop potters. As one reviewer summarised its impact:

> For some years potters have felt the need for a book that could act as a sequel to Leach's book both freeing them from perhaps too great a dependence upon Japanese techniques and usage and at the same time enabling them to progress further in the development of pottery that lives and grows out of its own environment. This is such a book.[2]

American potters found its technical approach more practical, more productive and reliable than Leach's *A Potter's Book*. Also they admired his pots much more than they did those of Bernard Leach because Michael's were more from the clay and less from the mind. Moreover, Cardew was a true believer in the workshop concept, unlike Leach who paid lip-service but was really more of an artist-potter at heart.

Cardew loved being in America. He felt free and celebrated. His 'infectious humanity', as Charles Counts described his big and extrovert personality, meshed perfectly with the American sensibility. He never felt defensive on American soil as he did in England, where he was always defending his decision to leave the isle of Britain for Africa. 'The British pottery community never accepted that,' Cardew told me, 'not even Bernard [Leach]'. Nor did he have to correct the constant challenges over his misunderstood role in Africa. American potters also loved and identified with his pioneer spirit. Here was a man who became an amateur geologist to find the materials he needed, who defied civil war and malaria to make his pots and make them true. Americans, despite their usually determined anti-intellectualism (and potters are even more so) appreciated his wide, sharp intellect because he wrapped it around concerns that were practical and real.

In 1971, before returning to England, he presented a lecture 'Potters and Amateur Potters' at the Smithsonian Institution, Washington DC, his most succinct and impassioned credo to date. Those who came to the Smithsonian expected a talk about making a living from pottery and instead were drawn into the deeper implications of making pots by hand. An article by Thelma McComrick of York University, Toronto entitled, 'Folk culture and the mass media' sparked the lecture's theme. She proposed that 'folk' in its pre-Modern sense had ceased to exist, and that this role had been taken over by a new category that she called 'amateur culture', declaring hand-made ceramics as one of its products. Cardew responded angrily:

> Amateur, Professional – how I hate these rigid categories. Amateur just means that you love it; professional merely means you are good enough at it to earn your living that way. But a good professional, if he stays alive, will never lose the spark and the freshness, even some of the clumsiness, coming from his probably amateur

> beginnings. And the amateur is always being drawn on by glimpses of things that at the beginning he never thought would be within his range.[3]

He also used the occasion to warn against 'art' pots, a genre he particularly disliked. He felt that these pots were rendered eccentric by 'deliberately willed injections of personality'. At a time when the tide was just beginning to turn against traditional craft values, Cardew argued that learning craft was the access point to true character in pottery:

> Learning to make pots is like learning to write. When as children we were being taught to write they didn't tell us the great thing to aim at was to make writing 'express our personality'; personality is something too big and too mysterious to be treated that way. They taught us skill, or craftsmanship, that is, to make our writing legible. But while you are learning to write legibly, your handwriting becomes yours and yours only. Legibility is not going to rob it of its personality; on the contrary, it makes it possible for your personality to flower and be seen; your handwriting is you and nobody else can imitate it exactly.[4]

Cardew was back the next year for what I have dubbed the 1972 Cardew-Kwali Road Show, accompanied by his African companion, Kofi Attey, and the Nigerian diva, Ladi Kwali. This trio stormed through the United States and Canada on a staggering two-and-a-half-month whistle-stop tour in which they presented forty-five sold-out official workshops and several others that were not scheduled. Those who attended these workshops speak of them today with the same reverence that is usually reserved for sightings of the Virgin Mary. It was quite an act with the regal Ladi Kwali in her brightly coloured, African-print fabric and Michael alongside in his bush uniform of khaki shorts and shirt. This was Cardew at his most selfless, proudly showing off his most talented African student before large audiences who were mesmerised by this handsome threesome; Ladi Kwali effortlessly coiled elegant, large water pots while Kofi quietly lent support and Michael contributed a witty running commentary that often had his audience convulsed with laughter.

In 1976, Kodansha and Faber and Faber published my modest biography, *Michael Cardew a Portrait*, and in that year I also moved from London to Los Angeles. The book was a great success in America where Cardew was now established as the grand old man of functional pottery, a reputation based more on his writings than first-hand access to his pots. The book partially bridged this gap but I felt that it was important for America to see his art in the flesh so to speak and so began to make plans for a retrospective of his work

We managed to pull this off in 1981 in conjunction with the National Council on Education for the Ceramic Arts (NCECA) conference in Wichita, Kansas, a rather barren mid-Western city in the heart of the Bible Belt. Through a small organisation I had formed, the Institute for Ceramic History, we gathered just enough money to assemble a mini-retrospective for this meeting that drew a national audience of two thousand potters, teachers and students. Most of the work came from lenders in Britain as little existed in American collections at that time.

Cardew's celebrity had now reached the ceramic equivalent of a rock star. The combination of Alistair Hallum's film *Mud and Water Man*, his tours, the biography, and other exposure had made him widely known and admired. Droves of young potters saw the show, responded warmly to his honest, direct pottery, followed him around and hung on his every word. Cardew was never happier than when surrounded by adoring, handsome young potters and so Wichita was a kind of nirvana for him. For most, this was their first opportunity to see Cardew's work. They were not disappointed, admiring both the *élan* of his fluid slip decoration and the vigour and vibrancy of glazed African stonewares.

Cardew spoke at various venues, satisfying his audiences' every Anglophilic fantasy, appearing as the arrogant aristocrat of clay and dispensing one-liners with his perfect diction and rich, resonant and cultured voice. 'Ah yes, my very good friend Hamada who makes such horrrrible pots' or 'Whose work do I admire? Quite frankly, only my own.'[5]

Michael returned to London and for a while I was his golden boy. He even gave me the first and only praise for my book. Looking puzzled he said, 'I really do owe much of my current popularity to your book. It's had a remarkable effect, thank you.'[6] Which in Cardew-speak can be reinterpreted into, 'Isn't it amazing that your little book could have such an impact.' But the honeymoon did not last. The venerable British firm of H. Lock was responsible for returning the pots to their various owners in Britain. We sent them off, beautifully packed, and wired the money for this service. Unfortunately the money was accidentally credited to another account by Lock. The firm then told the lenders that we had defaulted on payment and they could only have their pots back if they paid their share of the delinquent shipping costs.

Then came the missive from Michael. He ignored Katherine 'Beano' Pleydell-Bouverie's warning not to fly off the handle. She instinctively believed that it was Lock and not myself who had made the error (God bless her ash-glazed soul). 'I consider it infamous that they wrote to you and received no reply' his letter began, the ominous drum roll of anger beginning to be heard in the background. One could see his face reddening and foot beating that telltale tattoo that presaged rage. (We never received any communication from the company.) Speaking of the lenders as 'victims' he thundered on: 'It is an intolerable thing you have allowed to happen and will effectively strangle any future enterprises your "Institute" [the word always in jagged, sceptical quotation marks] may embark on once the facts are made public property; viz. that collectors were conned into sending some of their treasures, and were blackmailed into paying considerable fines to ensure the return of their own property.'

This was property, he added, that had been left 'to the tender mercies of your tissue paper "Institute"'. The letter went on in this vein for four pages with Michael's distinctive chicken-scratch handwriting showing more agitation that usual. I contacted the firm and the error was discovered. They promised to refund all the monies and write sincere letters of apology to all the lenders. I replied with remarkable calm to Michael because the game had begun: Michael was going to have to do that thing he most hated, admit he was wrong and apologise.

The first letter was hardly an apology. It began:

> Since reading your professions of injured innocence, I can see that there MAY have been some substance in Beano's first assumption that the real villains are H. Lock Limited. IF that is so, then I do owe you an apology.

I had explained to Michael that the person who was out of pocket was myself. There was a shortfall in revenues for the exhibition that I had to make up personally, which he dismissed blithely as 'the price you paid for fun and games'. Then the letter of apology from Lock arrived at Wenford Bridge.

I read quickly through three pages of general chatter in Michael's next without a word about our recent disturbances until the last paragraph in which, in what must have been a Herculean grasp for humility, he wrote: 'And my dear, beloved, devoted, slow-to-anger long suffering, overflowing with loving kindness GARTH, I live in the hope of being forgiven'. I was rather chuffed until I realised that even at that point he did not apologise but adroitly transferred to me the responsibility for forgiveness and restoring the relationship to its previous warm status quo. Former apprentice Mark Hewitt claims that I did better than most. He never received an apology from Cardew no matter how unfairly he behaved. But occasionally, when Michael obviously felt some guilt, Hewitt would find a bag of greengages on his wheel in lieu of apology. And just for the record, the tissue-paper Institute, now renamed the Ceramic Arts Foundation, held its eighth international conference on ceramic scholarship, a massive one-million-dollar event in 1999 in Amsterdam, attended by three thousand delegates from sixty-three countries.

Cardew and my exchange is not reported out of any meanness or buried resentment, for I feel none. It is shared as a picture of the double-edged sword that friendship with this volatile, complex, contradictory, often misanthropic man involved. Michael could be generous and supportive to a fault. He certainly was when I worked on his book, taking a young, callow, inexperienced yet stubbornly opinionated man into his life, and frequently, his home. He put up with my visits, my disruption of his life and my challenging of his principles with an almost saint-like reserve and patience. These letters are interesting for two reasons. One shows his growing anger that I had had the effrontery to actually found an Institute! The extent to which this offended his respect for institutional protocols revealed a surprising conventionality and respect for authority buried deep within what I had always considered to be a thoroughly unrepentant anti-establishment figure. The other touches on Cardew's vulnerability. When I read the letter through more carefully I realised that, touchingly, it was the anger of one who felt betrayed and, as he wrote, I had hurt 'one who has always called himself your friend'.

His apology-resistant letters compared interestingly to another note that arrived later from the kind and generous collector, Bill Ismay, who had lent to pots the exhibition and received the same letters from Lock. After all the dust had settled and refund checks had arrived, a letter was delivered from Ismay. It was short and to the point: 'I am writing to you dear Garth,' Ismay wrote in measured terms, 'to apologise most sincerely for the fact that for a few months I did not have very nice thoughts about you. Please forgive me, Bill Ismay.'

Cardew was soon back in America and our friendship returned to its mixture of affection and spirited, sometimes testy, debate. His trips were not just to speak at pottery gatherings. On one of his visits he had a Quixotic mission. He had read Bill Perzig's *Zen and the Art of Motorcycle Maintenance* and had decided that Alastair Hallum should make a film of this moving and singular book. So he set off to try and meet with Perzig and obtain the film rights. He came back empty-handed but his interest reveals something else about Michael.

For all his railing against industry and his sternly traditional view of pottery he was a surprisingly modern man, another reason he meshed so well with the American culture.

I remember his speaking at another NCECA gathering at the University of Michigan, elegantly and unhesitatingly without notes to an entranced, overflow audience in the Great Hall. In his final summing-up of his discourse on the mystery of creativity he cited the difficult and opaque films of Pier Paulo Pasolini as demonstrating the ultimate expression of this elusive act:

> Pasolini was trying to give back to reality its original, sacred significance. He was concerned with the magic of a moment, the sanctity of a moment. The real holiness in life is when you walk out in the month of February and the sun is shining and suddenly you look around and, for a second, it is all there.[7]

We saw Michael several times in Los Angeles in his last years. He would stay with Isakae Meksin, in one of her cluster of cottage-like apartments that ascended a steep hill in the Silver Lake district. Several of the residents of this enclave were Mexican transvestites and Isakae's home was their community centre. They were actively involved in creating weekly drag shows for the local gay bar and it was charming to see the Mud and Water Man, a glass of red wine in his hand, presiding over a court of queens who paraded immense quantities of tulle and lace through Isakae's living room, dropping sequins at every step while the hum of busy sewing machines could be heard throughout the complex. I had never seen him happier or more at ease, laughing and trading witticisms with these creative and vital young men who had no concept that he was one of the great potters of the twentieth century. It would probably not have mattered much to them anyway and Michael found a certain sanctuary in this anonymity.

During the last LA visit I remember one evening, when over the traditional glass of red wine, he railed against those who kept pushing him to make pots and how unpleasant the process had become for him, how he hated and resisted his infrequent returns to the wheel. It made me a little guilty that I had earlier put pressure on him to make me a Gwari casserole. He made two, one for me and one for the Smithsonian Institution. Mine is better. But then I remembered those letters about the shipping mishap and the guilt melted away thinking, 'fine, that is the price you pay for fun and games'.

A few days later while *en route* to visit Susan Peterson he said much the same thing, but this time more chillingly because it was about life itself. 'I am very tired', he complained, 'this body has become a surly, miserable servant [he suffered from acute, painful sciatica amongst other ailments] and I have reached a time where I have really done everything I want except for completing my autobiography. I want rest.' So when the news came through eighteen months later that he had died from a stroke, the sorrow was softened by a sense of relief that he had been allowed an exit, more or less on his terms.

So what does his American legacy add up to? In Mark Hewitt's opinion, as one of his most active former apprentices, not very much, having little to point to that is concrete and perhaps, in his admiration of Michael, hoping for more. But influence, even profound influence, is not always visible. Sometimes it is at its most effective when it is woven almost invisibly into the cultural fabric. Certainly, Hewitt has a point in that Cardew is less of a presence than Bernard Leach. Cardew never had his disciples placed in the university art schools. Warren McKenzie, for decades a professor at the University of Minnesota, the home of the so-called 'Mingei-sota' potters, and Leach's first American apprentice, has proselytised the Leach viewpoint for nearly forty years. McKenzie's ceramic department produced many excellent potters, most of whom in turn became teachers and to varying degrees furthered the Leach mystique.

Cardew has only four apprentices working in the United States: Hewitt, Todd Piker, Jane Herold and Miranda Thomas. There is even the beginning of an American dynasty with a grandson, Ara Cardew who works with Thomas in Maine. Ara's sister while not a potter herself is married to one, Mark Skudlarek from Cambridge, Wisconsin. There are two more ex-apprentices in Canada: Sam Uhlick in Edmonton and Tom Roberts in Winnipeg.

In saying this I do not want to in any way diminish the considerable achievement of Cardew's apprentices. They just took a different path from most mainstream American ceramists. Each of the USA potters works in the Cardew tradition of the country potter, making useful wares and selling them primarily in their local market: Mark Hewitt's studio is in Pittsboro, North Carolina, in the heart of traditional American folk pottery country; Jane Herold's is in Palisades, New York; Todd Piker's in Cornwall Bridge, Connecticut; and Miranda Thomas' in Bridgewater, Vermont. Only Herold's work is in the style of Michael Cardew, the rest have evolved their own aesthetic with traces of Michael's influence in handles, spouts or other distinctive touches from his work, but influences from Shigaraki, Sung, provincial French stoneware and other styles have transformed the aesthetic they inherited in Wenford Bridge.

All are commercially self-supporting. Hewitt and Herold sell most of their ware at studio sales held three to four times a year after firings. Thomas and Piker both employ a number of potters in their pottery and have their own retail outlets, sophisticated shops that sell other pottery and crafts besides. Piker's store is in historic West Cornwall whereas Thomas has two shops, one attached to the workshop in Bridgewater and another in Woodstock, also in Vermont. This gives them a strong regional presence, but except for Hewitt, little by way of a national profile. However Thomas and Piker have ambitious, handsome websites where their pots are also sold and this will expand their reach.

If this thing called 'the Cardew influence' has failed in any sense, it is that it has not become institutionalised in the same way that Leach's influence has, something that I believe would have made Michael quite happy. He never liked art schools, saying that they were the equivalent of hospitals for art and the more schools that existed, the sicker the arts must be. But Hewitt's scepticism still rang in my ears, much as I doubted it, and so I decided to test my belief that Cardew had actually left a legacy behind, albeit ephemeral. A few days ago I was in Helena, Montana taking part in the fiftieth anniversary festivities of a ceramics workshop, The Archie Bray Foundation, attended by six hundred ceramists, mostly potters.

I deliberately and frequently turned the conversations to this up-coming conference celebrating the hundredth anniversary of Michael's birth. Almost every potter I spoke to responded with surprising knowledge and enthusiasm about Cardew. Some of the older ceramists spoke of attending Cardew's NCECA keynote addresses, or even the Cardew-

Kwali Road Show of 1972. Others spoke enthusiastically of his book *Pioneer Pottery* or of meeting him at various workshops. Others owned pieces of his work that they treasured.

Many had made the pilgrimage to see an exhibition 'Cardew in Africa' that I had organised in my New York gallery in May. Even twenty year olds knew who he was and they surprised me with their knowledge and respect. Admittedly, those who made sculpture rather than pots often received the name with a blank stare, but that is a different world. One of the most enthusiastic endorsements of Cardew's impact came from John Ballestreri, a brilliant young ceramic sculptor who now throws the pots for Peter Voulkos.

This informal survey amongst a few score of makers from three generations and across the length and breadth of the United States is hardly a scientific sampling, but it was more positive than I had expected. It was clear that Cardew's contribution is indeed woven into the identity, self-respect, ethical standards and imagination of the American potter. So I left the Rockies for the Welsh shores of Aberystwyth warmed by the knowledge that to one degree or another, the intelligence, passion and principles of this grey-haired eagle of a man had left an indelible mark in American ceramics, and with the republication of Cardew's *Pioneer Pottery* in the United States, after having been out of print for over a decade, his legacy is set to be revived and renewed.

Website links

Todd Piker: www.cbpots.com
Mark Hewitt: www.markhewittpottery.com
Miranda Thomas: www.shackletonthomas.com/pottery
Jane Herold: www.ece.utexas.edu/~perry/fun/pots/

Notes

1 Garth Clark, *Michael Cardew: A Portrait* (Tokyo: Kodansha Press, 1976), p. 85.
2 McMeekin, Ivan, 'Book review: *Pioneer Pottery*', *Pottery in Australia*, 8:2 (1969), p. 43.
3 Michael Cardew, 'Potters and amateur potters' (1971), in Garth Clark (ed.), *Ceramic Art, Comment and Review* (New York: E. P. Dutton, 1978), p. 103.
4 Cardew, 'Potters and amateur potters'.
5 From lecture notes made on the occasion by Garth Clark.
6 Personal communication (letter from Cardew to Clark).
7 Cardew speaking at NCECA annual conference, University of Michigan, 1980. Notes by Garth Clark.

Emmanuel Cooper OBE (1938–2012) was amongst the most influential figures in British Ceramics. As editor of *Ceramic Review* magazine (jointly with Eileen Lewenstein from 1970 and sole editor from 1997–2010) he encouraged many fledgling writers and developed the magazine from a glorified newsletter into an internationally recognised journal. This chapter draws on Cooper's extensive research for his definitive biography of Bernard Leach, *Bernard Leach, Life and Work* (Yale University Press, London, 2003). In an account that paints Cardew's years at St Ives in the 1920s in great detail, Cooper argues that this was his formative period. Although he had studied at Oxford, and was seen as a capable scholar, Cardew left with a third-class degree and no intention of continuing his studies. His vocation lay elsewhere, and he had already learnt potting skills by the time he arrived at St Ives. There was a 'meeting of minds' between Leach and Cardew, who described his three years at St Ives as 'the most important part of my education as a potter'. Like the essay by Garth Clark which precedes it, this chapter was originally delivered as a conference paper at the 'Michael Cardew Centenary Symposium', organised by ICRC at the University of Wales, Aberystwyth (27–28 June 2001) and published with other papers from the Symposium in Issue 3 of *Interpreting Ceramics*. We would like to thank David Horbury for his support in publishing this chapter.

Leach and Cardew – The Early Years

Emmanuel Cooper

Beginnings

In January 1923 the Leach Pottery at St Ives was visited by Michael Cardew,[1] then aged twenty-two, an eager would-be potter in search of a training. Flashingly good looking, he was described by Leach as a 'young Apollo', a 'young man … as handsome as a Greek god, with forehead and nose all in a straight line, vivid eyes, golden curly hair, and a strong good jaw'.[2] Cardew was then reading Humanities at Exeter College, Oxford, but having been introduced to traditional country pottery by W. Fishley Holland at Braunton Pottery he was determined to become a potter. Despite having won a scholarship, an academic career held no interest, and he had been bitten by the pottery bug, in particular by English country pottery.

Perhaps not surprisingly, given the privileges of their class, their backgrounds were very similar. Like Leach, Cardew was born of a highly respectable, middle-class family involved in public service. One of six, he was born in Wimbledon, his father was a high-ranking civil servant. Leach, an only child, was brought up in Hong Kong and China. Their routes to potting were very different. After studying at the Slade and the London School of Art under Brangwyn, Leach had gone to Japan at the age of twenty-two to teach etching. Introduced to pottery at a raku party in 1911, he was seized by a desire to learn the craft and studied for two years with a traditional teacher, Urano Shigekichi, who held the title the sixth Kenzan. The court tradition in which Kenzan worked involved more decoration than making, and though Leach learnt to throw, he never claimed to be highly proficient. Cardew was later to say that Leach was one of the few studio potters less able to throw than himself.

In 1920 Leach returned to England where, sponsored by Frances Horne, a local philanthropist who had established the St Ives Guild of Handicraft, he set up a studio pottery in the town. By contrast, as a child Cardew had become totally enamoured of the deep earth colours and shiny lead-glazed earthenware pots made in north Devon, quantities of which filled the family holiday home at Saunton. As a child he visited the old potteries with his family, when his father purchased pots for everyday use. Later as a young man he visited the Fishley Pottery and here he paid a £1 a week for throwing lessons and had a wheel built. While still a reluctant student, his attention was caught by an article, 'An art pottery in Cornwall',[3] in *Pottery Gazette and Glass Trade Review*. This described the work of the Leach Pottery, which somewhat confusingly was illustrated by photographs of Leach and his pottery assistants in Japan and an image of a jug with a painted armorial design that had also been made in Japan. During a visit to relatives in Cornwall, Cardew decided to pay a visit to see Leach, arriving in the town in the evening. At the edge of the town he found 'a sign board with a curly inscription just legible in the dusk "The Leach Pottery"'.[4] He was greeted by the short, stocky figure of George Dunn, the ex-builder, fisherman and smuggler who prepared the clay, helped fire the kiln and carried out any other odd jobs. He introduced him to Hamada, who was living in a room in the pottery. Knowing that he soon intended to return to Japan, Hamada thought Leach could do with some help from an energetic and enthusiastic young man and walked with him to Carbis Bay to meet Leach, both enthusing *en route* about Ethel Mairet's weaving.

The previous year Leach had moved into the Court House, a large property where Leach, his wife Muriel and five children plus *au pair* were still settling in. No doubt intimidated by meeting the great man, Cardew found the house 'vast, cold and empty'. There seemed to be only a few pots around, and as far as he could see these were from the orient and very different to the warm, generous, lead-glazed shapes he admired. 'They looked very strange to me',[5] was Cardew's verdict.

Fifteen years his senior, Leach appeared to Cardew as 'a perfectly preserved example of an English Edwardian',[6] formal in manner, favouring collar and tie, plus fours, tweed jackets and brogues rather than casual dress, to all intents and purposes a gentleman potter. A meal was served on 'grey stoneware, with decoration in a reserved blue'.[7] Wasting little time in testing the enthusiastic young student's sensibility to pots, Leach soon started to quiz his guest, asking his opinion on an eleventh or twelfth-century Chinese bowl. Completely at a loss, wisely Cardew said little. The testing ceremony also included discussion about other wares and when Cardew spoke enthusiastically about English slipware and revealed that he had learnt to throw reasonable-sized pots, his place was secured. Writing to offer the position, Leach was alarmingly frank. 'I want someone like yourself, young, strong and enthusiastic', he said, adding 'I cannot afford to pay a salary we are pretty well at the end of our capital invested and must from now on depend on sales'.[8] Undeterred Cardew accepted.

Early days

After scraping a third at Oxford, Cardew arrived at the pottery in the summer to begin work, finding the pottery full of visitors.[9] In addition to Leach, Hamada, George Dunn and the general bookkeeper/manager Edgar Skinner who arranged his lodgings at two shillings (ten pence) a night, there was Old Basset, a retired fisherman, and the potter William Staite Murray. Another visitor was the architect and collector Sidney Greenslade, who had a close relationship with the University of Wales at Aberystwyth,[10] who took Cardew to one side and told him how delighted he was that he was starting with a group 'so full of enthusiasm'.[11] As Cardew soon discovered, enthusiasm was not in short supply, though any professional or workmanlike approach to business was in his view severely absent.

After hearing Cardew enthuse so much about the north Devon wares, Leach went with him to visit his family house in Saunton to admire their collection of Edward Beer Fishley's pots. They travelled in Leach's recently acquired Martinside motorcycle and sidecar,[12] on which, in George Dunn's phrase, Leach used to roar up the Stennack 'like a ball of fire'.[13] The journey took two days. While quietly appreciative of the green-glazed pitchers and vases, in the kitchen Leach discovered plain water pitchers and a couple of old oven dishes decorated with slip-trailing, which he preferred, cheerfully pointing out that they were part of the true English heritage.

Aware of Cardew's growing ambivalence to the qualities of Oriental pots and what he saw as his lack of understanding, Leach lent him his copy of Kakuzo Okakura's *The Book of Tea*. Although Cardew responded to the quietness and contemplative nature of the rituals, the actual objects left him cold. To him they remained alien, and though twenty years later he eventually saw the advantages of the tougher, more hard-wearing stonewares, he was drawn far more to the softer, earthier qualities of earthenware and its association with function rather than ornament.

During a visit to the Paterson Gallery, where Leach's pots were on show, Cardew was introduced to another would-be student, Katharine Pleydell-Bouverie, whom he found 'very beautiful and also very big, with a large frame like a French peasant's; and yet at the same time somehow petite, because her features were so curiously fine'.[14] She had been highly impressed by their 'dignity of shape, depth of colour, and quality of surface'.[15]

When Pleydell-Bouverie met Leach at the gallery, whom she described as 'a long spidery man, giving a curious impression of shagginess in a Norfolk jacket and an extensive moustache',[16] she immediately asked to become a private pupil. Although at first reluctant, in the face of her enthusiasm and tempted also by her readiness to pay a £26 fee for six months,[17] Leach relented. Just as he had written to Cardew, in his letter offering to take her Leach was brutally honest about the life of a potter, giving some idea of both the physically tough work involved and the idealism of the venture.

> It is hard work of any woman not to say man and she would have to be prepared to take the rough with the smooth. We do everything with our hands from the wood splitting and mixing of clays to throwing and packing. That is to say the techniques of the East where no machinery is employed; we get dirty and tired, hot and cold, and unusual enthusiasm is the sole panacea.[18]

Undeterred, Beano, as she came to be known, joined the Pottery in January 1924.

Following Hamada's return to Japan, Cardew gladly moved into his old room, slept in the curious bed Hamada had built and relished the spartan surroundings, even making a cult of them by taking a daily bath in the cold water of the Stennack. Living without pay, Cardew was more than happy with what he called holy poverty, with its blend of idealism, austerity and minimal creature comforts. All went well until, in the middle of winter, he was stricken with pneumonia and spent six weeks in the St Ives cottage hospital. During his convalescence Leach brought him books of early Chinese paintings of landscapes inscribed with Chinese characters that Cardew thought were as wonderful as the images themselves.

The Leach Pottery

Here it might be useful to look briefly at the background to the Leach pottery. With no model on which to base their work, Leach and Hamada had opted to set up a smallish building that was more studio than workshop. On a patch of pasture on the main Lands End road out of St Ives, which had a busy stream running down its side, they constructed granite buildings and designed the wood-fired kiln. This was built largely by Hamada using home-made refractories from material that could be obtained locally. Neither potter had much experience in building or firing kilns and by 1923, when Cardew arrived, it was literally on its last legs, having developed giant splits and cracks. Only about ten per cent of the ware was thought to be up to exhibition standards, the remainder was sold as seconds or thrown into the Stennack. A small, round, updraught wood-fired kiln was used for earthenware. This had a domed top in which raku could be fired, and is illustrated in *A Potter's Book*. With no set pattern of work, or what today would be called a business plan, the two potters produced individual pots in stoneware, decorated dishes in earthenware, and a quantity of small raku that, because it was more colourful, was easier to market.

Financially the pottery was in poor shape. Reflecting on its finances in 1924 Leach noted, 'We have but little cash in hand & this year there is my income to meet as well as the usual running expenses.'[19] In the first four years of operation the Pottery lost £2,534.[20] Much of his inheritance had been swallowed up and Muriel continued to invest her capital with little hope of return. In an effort to raise funds in 1925 some sort of 'shares' were sold in the Pottery, which among other benefits gave purchasers discounts on pots. Bankruptcy seemed a real possibility again two years later and Leach was forced to mortgage the property. As a business the Pottery reeled shakily from one financial crisis to the next with Leach often writing to Yanagi in Japan about 'his multitudinous pottery problems'.[21]

Industry or Studio?

With two young potters to supervise, plus others sent on from the Central School in London or the Royal College of Art, after the relatively relaxed disorder of the early days when Leach had to do his own throwing, Cardew was seen as a godsend, able to make shapes for Leach to decorate, and Leach was keen to develop tableware with slip decoration to go alongside the individual pots. The casual studio atmosphere gave way to a more established routine and a more organised air of industry imbued the workshop.

The erratic progress of the Pottery was greatly improved by the arrival in 1923 of Matsubayashi Tsurunoske from Japan. He was described as 'a precise little man',[22] who was an engineer, chemist and craftsman potter of a well-known Nara pottery family. Known to all as Matsu he was generally credited as 'thoroughly practical', knowing as much about the theoretical basis of high-fired ceramics as any Western ceramist at that time.

Horrified by the state of the kiln Matsu insisted it should be pulled down and be replaced with a professionally designed and built wood-firing structure that had three chambers. Cardew was roped in to help make firebricks for the new kiln, a tough process that involved ramming crude kaolin into wooden moulds and throwing saggars from coarse clay whilst trying to avoid losing too much skin. Recognising Cardew's more practical understanding, before returning to Japan Matsubayashi led him aside saying 'I hope you will stay here with Mr Leach, and always help him with his work, because – ah – I think – ah – Mr Leach – ah – rather poetical.'[23]

As far as organisation and business management was concerned, little had really changed to make the Pottery more financially viable. Cardew thought it highly disorganised, particularly the clay-making arrangements, which he found 'chaotic and always inadequate for our needs'.[24] The treadle wheel he had had built at Braunton Pottery was installed, which he found easier and more efficient than the Japanese wheel used by Leach that could only be turned clockwise and was propelled by a stick.

Nevertheless, the team were bound by shared goals and a passionate commitment to pots. A strong sense of community, jovial and club-like pervaded the Pottery. Practical jokes involved buckets balanced over doorways, and endless ribbing. Nicknames were freely given, Leach gaining the name Rik, Riketty or Rickety because of the shaky state of his Martinside motorbike. Norah Braden, a student from the RCA, was known as Lise; Ada Mason, another student, as Peter.

Break and meal times at the pottery were not only functional but instructive. Leach talked about pots, waved his arms about, drew on the blackboard, described shapes in the air in a great miming act, sometimes made pieces on his Japanese wheel and smoked endless cigarettes. Cooking was a collective activity and food was prepared with enthusiasm, good appetites making up for limited culinary skills. Cardew confessed to having no culinary skills and had to learn fast. Leach and Matsubayashi insisted on using chopsticks but Cardew claimed he was too hungry to learn the technique.

Although Cardew had mastered basic throwing techniques, these were far from the professional skills required, and he quickly realised there was still much to learn. This involved the Oriental method of spiral wedging, a process of working the clay by hand to remove air bubbles and strengthen the clay prior to throwing. He also had to learn to throw small pots off a clay hump so speeding up production. Watching Cardew throwing pots one day, Leach said that while he saw that he still had problems controlling the material, he 'liked his forms' – a huge compliment in Cardew's eyes.

Cardew's principle making tasks involved throwing earthenware and pieces for raku. Slipware included souvenir mugs, jugs and tankards in earthenware that were sold in the pottery showroom and locally. While Leach was sceptical of the rightness of such objects, he also realised they tempted buyers who were unlikely to purchase his much more expensive individual pieces. These were often embellished with traditional rhymes or quotations from William Blake scratched through a layer of white slip. Later Cardew made teapots and recalled Leach rejecting the shape he made, explaining again what he required. With not very good grace Cardew tried again, and showed Leach the result, asking 'Will this do?' 'Well it will do', Leach replied, in a tone that was quite kind, but distinctly rebuking. That was all he said, but it made a great impression on the young student, concluding that in pottery, as in art, it is a case of All or Nothing.[25]

By far the most significant earthenware pieces produced were the large, individually decorated slipware dishes and chargers based on seventeenth and eighteenth-century pots produced by Toft and others. The powerful, simplified designs gave scope for Leach's graphic skills, and employed a limited range of earth colours such as yellow ochre, black, brown and white under a clear glaze. Some dishes were produced in a mould, others thrown on the wheel. More modest-sized dishes were made by shaping a slab of clay over a hump mould, and for these Leach devised simple decorative motifs. Cardew made many of these dishes for Leach to decorate.

Raku

The other main group of pots that Cardew had to throw were for raku firings. These were made from a white firing, heavily grogged body that would withstand the thermal shock. As a way of increasing sales and alerting public interest, on Thursday afternoons Leach instituted raku sessions at the Pottery, based on the model of the Japanese raku party, when visitors were invited to have a go. Standing by the kiln Leach first explained the history and technique before encouraging visitors to buy biscuit-fired pots at prices from half-crown (twelve pence) to a shilling (five pence) and decorate them with ready-prepared pigments.

Recognising the unique qualities of raku, which I think I am correct in saying that Leach introduced to the West, and its possible use in schools, he made notes in preparation for 'a potter's notebook on the making of the simplest kind of Oriental pottery',[26] which described the processes as well as its history. Support for this came from Henry Bergen,[27] an American-born Classical and Oriental scholar, collector, Marxist, amateur potter and enthusiastic supporter of artist potters with whom Leach had become friendly in the early 1920s. Cardew described Bergen as 'a tall, powerful man with a rather square head and an athletic build'.[28] Offering sound advice Bergen urged Leach to 'write just as simply as you can and where there are many choices of expression ... choose the clearest and leave nothing open to doubt',[29] advice that both Leach and Cardew took to heart, though Leach found such directness far more difficult than the more pragmatic Cardew.

Idealism versus Industry

At St Ives both potters firmly adhered to the view that hand-work ruled supreme, believing that technique should follow idea. This was graphically illustrated when Matsubayashi gave technical talks on ceramic materials, kiln construction, plasticity of clay and chemical formulae. Diligently, Pleydell-Bouverie took copious notes, but Cardew, unsure of the value of Matsubayashi's knowledge or more particularly its relevance to his work, took virtually none. Leach was even more dismissive; attending 'rather as a critic posing questions', always 'interrupting with philosophical questionings such as whether all this theoretical stuff was really relevant to the quality of what you produced',[30] was how Pleydell-Bouverie recalled it.

Both Leach and Cardew felt that there was no substitution for handwork, no matter how tedious and labour intensive. Their unwillingness to consider the benefits of mechanical help, and remain 'poetical', was tellingly brought home when Leach and Cardew travelled by motorbike to Gordon Russell's[31] furniture workshop at Broadway in the Cotswolds in the spring of 1926. They were to take part in an Easter exhibition of rural crafts and industries, where Cardew was to demonstrate throwing. The journey took three days and two nights, with the motorbike and sidecar, packed full of luggage, constantly breaking down.

It was a tense occasion as the two potters found themselves out of sympathy with Russell's move towards greater mechanisation. Talking specifically of furniture and architecture Russell argued that the intelligent use of machines, together with sensitive design, could provide a satisfactory means of removing much of the donkey work, increasing production and reducing costs without loss of quality. Such impersonal mechanical processes had little appeal for purists such as Leach and Cardew who saw the machine as no substitute for individual skill and the fine judgement of hand-work.

Traditionalists or Modernists

Cardew as a Westerner thought it inappropriate to base his work on Oriental forms, and was drawn almost instinctively to the softness of English earthenwares. The question of tradition was one with which he was acutely concerned. It was a topic very much in the air, and was written about with great insight by notable writers such as T. S. Eliot who debated the value and importance of tradition to contemporary artists. In his essay 'Tradition and the individual talent', written in 1919, Eliot argues that tradition cannot be inherited but can only be obtained by great labour. Tradition, he believed, 'involves a perception, not only of the pastness of the past, but of its presence'. He went on to argue that almost inevitably our understanding of the past is altered by the present as much as the present is shaped by the past. For Eliot, acquiring a meaningful understanding of 'the pastness of the past' is hard won and something that few achieve. It was something Cardew sought and many would argue did achieve.[32]

Leach's attitude to the past was more ambiguous, for while he was fond of quoting William Blake's aphorism to ride your coach and horses over the bones of the dead, the forms and decoration of the past were a constant presence in his work, though rarely a subject of reproduction. Equally important is the fact that his model lay not in English or European culture, but in the Chinese Sung Dynasty. This was eloquently sketched out in 'Towards a standard', his seminal essay published in *A Potter's Book* in 1940. Here he wrote about the importance of adopting the Sung standard, though this, he was at pains to point out, was not about aping historical styles, but the practice that informed the work, whether it be through the use of local materials, appropriate making methods, or design that exemplified fitness for purpose – all crucial aspects of the modernist canon.

For Cardew tradition was a living force. When, for instance, he was on one occasion asked if he was going to make new shapes he reacted in horror, arguing that he wanted sound, living shapes. To critics of traditionalism he replied that 'the artist who is an innovator is also the only true traditionalist artist', adding that practitioners who call themselves traditionalists, are really traitors to tradition.[33]

Conclusion

To conclude, despite the lack of business acumen, the endless technical problems of bloating bodies and over-fired or over-stoked kilns, Cardew was adamant that his three years at St Ives with Leach were 'the most important part of my education as a potter'.[34] There were many issues over which these two highly opinionated, strong, powerful personalities did not agree, such as the merits of Oriental versus English country pottery, the importance of technical understanding, and the value and role of industrial production. They were also of vastly different temperaments. Leach, by nature, was a socialite who loved nothing more than an admiring audience, and when crossed tended to be quiet, withdrawing into hurt silence. Cardew, by contrast, had a rapid and flamboyant temper that was easily aroused, and could be terrifying to witness. However, it soon subsided, and he quickly returned to his usual equitable but excitable self. Leach's art lay at the centre of his life to the exclusion of other activities; like Pirandello, he could claim that he had no life outside his art, whilst Cardew had many interests, including playing music, country dancing, and practising Latin.

On one fundamental point their differences seemed insurmountable. For Leach, pottery was an art, and he saw his individual pots as belonging in the gallery alongside painting and sculpture. Price was determined by what the market would stand. For Cardew, pots were about use, and he declined to make individual pots, though his rose bowls come dangerously close. A pot for Cardew was a functional object, and he tried to price them accordingly, often at great cost to himself. Both, in their own way, were romantic idealists in the William Morris, Arts and Crafts tradition, rooted in, but not quite of, the world in which they lived. They carved out new and little-understood paths, pioneered new ways of working that often overlapped, ran side-by-side, but rarely ever merged.

Notes

(LA refers to the Leach Archive held at the Craft Study Centre, West Surrey, University College of Art and Design, Farnham; DA refers to the Dartington Archive held at High Cross House, Dartington.)

1 1901–83.
2 Bernard Leach, *Hamada: Potter* (London: Thames and Hudson, 1976), p. 62.
3 *The Pottery Gazette and Glass Trade Review*, no date, LA1629.
4 Michael Cardew, *A Pioneer Potter: Autobiography* (London: Collins, 1988), p. 24.
5 Cardew, *A Pioneer Potter*, p. 25.
6 Michael Cardew, 'Bernard Leach, essays in appreciation', in Terry Barlow (ed.), *New Zealand Potter* (Wellington: New Zealand, 1961).
7 Bernard Leach, *Beyond East and West* (London: Faber and Faber, 1979), p. 147.
8 Bernard Leach, letter to Michael Cardew, 24 January 1923, LA 6540.
9 The Pottery had a series of distinguished visitors in the early years, including the artists John Piper, Edward Bawden and Eric Ravillious, and the writer Angela Brazil, all of whom signed the visitors book. LA2047.
10 1866–1955. Sidney Kyffin Greenslade, architect and designer of the National Library of Wales; an enthusiastic and knowledgeable collector, he had met the Martin brothers in 1898. In the 1920s and 1930s he selected contemporary art, including studio ceramics, for the University of Wales at Aberystwyth University, now in the Arts Centre. The collection includes early pots by Bernard Leach.

11 Leach, *Hamada*, p. 31.
12 Acquired July 1922; a 1921 6hp machine, registration number N7C 4498.
13 Quoted in Michael Cardew, 'Bernard Leach – recollections', in T Barrow (ed.), *Bernard Leach Essays in Appreciation* (Wellington, New Zealand: Editorial Committee of the NZ Potter, 1960), p. 23.
14 Cardew, *A Pioneer Potter*, p. 34.
15 Unidentified cutting, LA1385.
16 Leach, *Beyond East and West*, p. 150.
17 The actual terms were a short trial period, a £26 premium to cover six months at £1 a week, followed by six months without pay, and one year at a salary of £1 a week. If the agreement was for a shorter period than two years, the premium would have to be higher or the pay less. Letter to Katharine Pleydell-Bouverie, 20 January 1923, LA6540.
18 LA6540.
19 Quoted in Oliver Watson, *Bernard Leach: Potter and Artist* (London: Crafts Council, 1997), p. 19.
20 'Summary of Leach Pottery Balance Sheets 1921–31', DA.
21 Quoted in a letter to Bernard Leach from Margarita C. Lucas, 8 August 1926, LA2421.
22 Leach, *Beyond East and West*, p. 151.
23 Cardew, *A Pioneer Potter*, p. 43.
24 Cardew, *A Pioneer Potter*, p. 35.
25 Michael Cardew, 'Pioneer pottery at Abuja', LA1762.
26 Bernard Leach, manuscript, a notebook 'on the making of simplest Oriental pottery', 1923, LA514.
27 Bergen was a great admirer and loyal friend of potters, working with Leach at St Ives, Cardew at Winchcombe (opened in 1926) and Murray in London. At St Ives Bergen laboriously carved lettering through slip-covered surfaces and helped fire the kiln, including the first firing of the new kiln.
28 Cardew, *A Pioneer Potter*, p. 94.
29 Bergen, letter to Bernard Leach, 7 March 1924, LA2386.
30 Cardew, *A Pioneer Potter*, p. 36.
31 Russell was later made Director of the Council of Industrial Design.
32 Thomas Stearns Eliot, The Sacred Wood (New York: Alfred A. Knopf, 1921; Bartleby.com, 1996), www.bartleby.com/200/.
33 Garth Clark, *Michael Cardew A Portrait* (London: Faber and Faber, 1978), p. 96.
34 Cardew, *A Pioneer* Potter, p. 29.

We introduced Issue 5 of *Interpreting Ceramics* in 2004 by saying that readers may agree or disagree with Edmund De Waal's comment that 'ceramics is an art whose practitioners have become peculiarly suited to silence'. This theme was taken up by various authors, including Geraint Roberts whose essay focuses on the silence at the heart of the work of Claudi Casanovas. Through looking closely at the work shown in the exhibition *Twenty Blocks*, Roberts examines Casanovas' claim that 'each piece is a silence'. His essay implicitly raises questions about the extent to which the writer can speak on behalf of the maker, especially the silent maker and their silent work.

Filling the Silence: Towards an Understanding of Claudi Casanovas' Blocks

Geraint Roberts

Each piece is a silence
If I were a poet, I would inscribe words there
to bring us closer to the truth
which urges us on from within

If I were a philosopher, or writer, I would inscribe words so
that the heart would overflow with knowledge
and the meaning of clarity
If I were a monk I would inscribe prayers in which all spirit might find repose
and glory in the same Being
Only I am a simple mortal

surrounded by simple obscurity
and unfailing silences

Each piece is a silence
that is filled with the sounds of your gaze

Claudi Casanovas' statement for the exhibition *Twenty Blocks*
(Translated from the Catalan by Marilyn McCully)

Galerie Besson, London, 17 October – 16 November 2001[1]

In this article I want to examine the ceramic work of Claudi Casanovas (Spain, 1956–), giving special attention to the body of work *Blocks*.[2] I want to begin to understand how he has arrived at these objects, objects that arguably look as though they were found rather than made, naturally occurring phenomena rather than intelligently directed products. The intrigue aroused by the objects themselves is added to by Casanovas' statement about this work, a statement that I find complex and challenging, a statement that raises more questions than it answers.

In his statement, Casanovas refers to several kinds of silence: the silence of the pieces themselves and the 'unfailing silences' that surround him. But there is an additional silence implicit in his words and that is his own silence, that as a 'simple mortal' he cannot explain himself through words.

It seems, then, given the silence of the maker, that it is up to us as viewers to make sense of the work. How are we to approach the work, to begin to gain an understanding and appreciation of it? But in saying what he is not able to say, in indicating the direction of the thoughts he says he cannot express ('If I were … I would …') he is nevertheless establishing a kind of framework that might bring us closer to his intentions as a maker.

In the first section of this article, I want to look at some aspects of ceramics and silence – since it appears that this is by no means a unique instance of a relationship existing between them – and to consider some of the reasons for and implications of the various kinds of silence alluded to. This will also provide some insights into Casanovas' methods and philosophical intentions.

There are various established methodologies for – in the language of the poem – 'filling' works of art. Given the scale of this article, however, there is not space either to outline, or to consider the merits of, all the different approaches. I intend, therefore, in the second section, to consider briefly factors affecting our perception of works of art and to look in more detail at Casanovas' *Blocks* in relation to his life and previous work.

Silence

In his statement, Claudi Casanovas refers directly to different kinds of silence: the silence of the pieces themselves and the 'unfailing silences' that surround him.

To begin with, what does he mean in saying that 'each piece is a silence'? Can he be referring to the literal interpretation of 'absence of sound' for surely that is a given with inanimate objects? Are we then dealing with an 'abstention from sounding, speech, mention or communication':[3] a refusal, failure or inability to speak? He intimates as much in his litany of 'If I were …' statements and his claim to be 'only a … simple mortal'. If we take him at face value then we can understand his silence as an inability to speak. And so there is another kind of silence at work here and that is his own silence, the silence of the 'simple mortal', the silence of the maker.

But already we seem to have these two kinds of silence, which may or may not be distinct, entangled: the silence of the maker and the silence of the object. Moreover, the silence of makers, as well as the silence of objects, seems to be a commonplace in the field of ceramics. Jeffrey Jones comments:

> Ceramics is not only a site where silence happens, it is somewhere where different silences happen and, in particular, it is a place where the relationship between the silence of people and the silence of things can be apprehended and explored.[4]

It is perhaps impossible to disentangle these different kinds of silence, since, as Jones says, they are in relationship. However there are some things that can be said separately about them.

The silence of makers

One of the commonest ways of accounting for the silence of makers is that the work 'speaks for itself'.[5] True, Casanovas isn't claiming that his does – he is expressly inviting *us* to do so – but the upshot is similar. As he has said himself: 'Everything is registered there, and everything is to be read there.'[6] The responsibility for interpreting the work is ours alone and requires no explanation on the part of the maker. And why should it? Why, after all, should someone who has spent countless hours, days, weeks, years, of practical exploration and material production have then to explain themselves again in words? Surely the work should 'speak for itself'. If makers, having spent hours in the studio, have then to explain themselves in words, they've been wasting their time, haven't they? Surely making has its own language, with its own vocabulary and syntax? But is it impossible for this language to be translated into the language we read and write?

Peter Dormer seems to think so. In describing craft as a 'practical philosophy', he adapts an Aristotelian definition of moral philosophy as 'an exercise in self-clarification on the part of individuals who seek to live excellently',[7] whereby 'the thinking is in the making'. Because of the practical nature of this quest, very little about it can be verbalised or theorised.

> whatever clarification of motives and values the craftsperson achieves can be inferred from the work and what he or she does but cannot, with any depth, be put into words.[8]

The only way (according to Dormer) of judging such work is through connoisseurship – knowledge accumulated through experience – whereby quality is assessed by comparison with this body of knowledge, and this cannot be adequately described, only shown.

One of the values Dormer talks about is 'honest work'. He distinguishes between rules of procedure and rules of making. The latter are 'how to' rules and once learnt can be forgotten or broken with impunity. Rules of procedure on the other hand are self-defined and form the basis on which the maker builds his/her criteria of success. Integrity in the work relies on the craftsperson adhering to their rules of procedure and not cheating.

In the case of Casanovas, this is evidenced by the demanding technical means that he develops in order to overcome the obstacles between him and the realisation of his final goal. Which is not to say that he necessarily knows beforehand what that goal might be: the process is intuitive. It also involves reflection, and the difficult task of editing, as the journey unfolds.

> There comes a moment when I have nothing left but the certainty of what I do not want … And one after another I start to break up weeks of work … I say to myself,

> 'You're at the beginning, this has already happened to you many times before, you can manage.' And I carry on breaking them, scared as I am ...[9]

The certainty he speaks about applies equally to knowing when the work is finished. British ceramicist Gordon Baldwin (1932–) echoes the sentiment:

> I work at a thing until it means something to me. I may not be able to define what it is, but I know when I've got there and I know when I haven't got there. They keep going into the kiln until that happens. It has to be done without thinking about it, that I do know.[10]

These are vague descriptions of actually quite a precise procedure – there is certainty and knowledge – that highlight the difficulty of articulating knowledge that is intuitive.

One view of artists distinguishes between two types: the teacher and the researcher. The teacher, conscious of an audience, seeks to some extent to persuade. The researcher, on the other hand, is chiefly engaged in defining her/his problem and seeking a solution, and would rather be silent. Cezanne, Klee, Brancusi and many of the Abstract Expressionists are examples. 'The end he is working towards may be unattainable and he probably knows it.'[11]

Casanovas himself has said (in a statement that recalls Picasso's claim: 'I do not seek, I find'):

> I realise that I will never succeed in making a piece from inside its own self. But for the moment I am going to pretend that it is possible for me. Some pieces I search for; others come to meet me. The first may be interesting, but the others are better.[12]

Such a level of engagement with process and material is a modern artistic response to the conditions of modernity that persists to this day. Alienation caused by, amongst other things, mass production, the division of labour, the replacement of natural cycles by clock time and by a consumer culture that (apparently) demands such things as ready-peeled fruit, means that makers are potentially some of the few people able to create a bridge back to the real. Fully engaged with the stuff of this world, the artist is able

> to see and sense more than we see and sense, and to build out of this experience works that lead us towards his more comprehensive experience ... He is the least alienated worker, his labour being a natural part of his life as a whole, self-directed, self-assessed and self-satisfying.[13]

Bruce Metcalf perceives in his students the joy that comes from being engaged body, mind and soul in creative (craft) work, and feels that that the popularity of craft disciplines is in direct response to feelings of alienation. M. Anna Fariello, a maker who calls herself a 'romantic materialist', backs him up:

> Craftsmen have a privileged relationship with their material. We are connected through material to nature, which helps us cope with a society increasingly removed from nature.[14]

Including, perhaps, our own nature, for according to Metcalf the intuitive knowledge of the craftsperson has a biological basis. He describes different kinds of biological intelligences that to him mark the distinction between contemporary art (which embodies meaning independently of a medium or object) and craft (where objecthood and commitment to medium are essential). Whilst verbal and logical cognitive abilities seem to be privileged in Western society, craftspeople, on the other hand, rely chiefly on their bodily-kinaesthetic intelligence: 'It's the mind speaking through the body.'[15] Western intellectual tradition is distrustful of the body; the crafts act as a counterbalance to this attitude.

> In their loyalty to medium, process and skill, the individuals who comprise craft culture elevate the bodily and spatial intelligences to a position of primary importance.[16]

The process of making is, then, a different way of thinking and of expressing thought. Making precedes meaning (and indeed can have its own meaning). There is a danger in talking or theorising about art: talking can lead to paralysis of intuitive creation and understanding, and to formulaic production.

However, there remains the difficulty of how to approach and assess the work of a silent maker, and a further danger in the competition established between ways of thinking.

> The delicate balance of all a person's powers – which alone permits him to live fully and to work well – is upset not only when the intellect interferes with intuition, but equally when sensation dislodges reasoning … Unchecked self-analysis can be harmful, but so can the artificial primitivism of the person who refuses to understand how and why he works.[17]

In his article entitled 'Speak for yourself' Edmund de Waal takes ceramicists to task for their lack of discourse above the level of 'potchat' (his term for technical discussion). He argues that the reason for, and the attraction of, silence to makers is that it confers authenticity and seriousness to them and their work. However, it also allows an 'interpretive vacuum' to open up, one that is commonly filled using an 'ethnographic' methodology.

> The truly authentic and serious potter is the one who unknowingly makes pots, whose artistic journey is unmapped, whose silence allows a critical space to open up into which the critic, the curator and collector can step …[18]

Thus (according to de Waal), the 'authentic' potter is perceived as Yanagi's (and Leach's) 'Unknown Craftsman', not only unknown but unknowing, his work predetermined by tradition, produced in quantity and recognisably 'other' in the eyes of collectors and critics, for it is they who assign aesthetic value to the work.

De Waal wants makers to contextualise their work because an object's meaning is contingent on how it relates to other objects and ideas. His argument, however, seems self-defeating in the end because he later says 'it is often the things that remain unsaid that are most revealing'.[19]

Jeffrey Jones discusses the silences of Hans Coper (Germany, 1920–81) and Lucie Rie (Austria, 1902–95). These can partly be accounted for by personal biography, but Jones suggests that their personal experiences (as émigrés) mean that their individual silences have a wider significance, not least within the broader world of the arts (e.g. Samuel Beckett in literature, John Cage in music).

> Silence not only surrounds them and defends them, it reveals and locates them too. That silence which hides them from us also shows us where they are.[20]

Perhaps this is what de Waal means about 'things unsaid'.

The silence of objects

Jones identifies the silence of objects as being located in their 'inexhaustible nature'.[21] He refers specifically to everyday domestic ware: things that tend to go unnoticed but are likely to outlast us; things that don't demand our attention and thus are not drained of interest through overexposure.

But can Casanovas' work be located in the category of 'everyday'? Obviously his work is raised above this, is made special, if only because it is displayed in galleries and museums, is bought and sold by collectors. The disparity is bridged perhaps by Casanovas' own observation of the process of firing as:

> a quiet moment of enduring change. Maybe the sensation of silence and peace which emanates from ceramics are rooted in this phenomenon.[22]

The effect of firing on ceramic is to produce a chemical change that is irreversible and that gives strength to the material such that it will endure for millennia. The hitherto reliance by archaeologists on ceramic artefacts for information about our earliest ancestors is testament to this. And it might be speculated that the long history of ceramics' use in funerary and mortuary rites hints at a more intuitive and profound understanding of the nature and implications of clay's endurance.

Philip Rawson describes how the 'transformation image'[23] that the firing of clay gives rise to acts upon maker and user alike, functioning both as a witness to an individual's existence in the world, and to the reality of the world as a material capable of transformation by that individual.

> A pot thus 'contains' both the reality of materials and process, and the inner realities of man's sense of identity in relation to his own world of meaning.[24]

Gordon Baldwin reiterates this reading of ceramics in talking about his own work:

> They sit in my studio and solemnly, silently, produce events which seem to have meaning and seem to give me a *raison d'être*. I am because I do: they are very existentialist.
>
> The pieces don't make any noise, yet, when I look at their silences, there are lots of different sorts, almost as if they are making noises. I don't know how to describe it but we all know that you can go into a place and it's silent, but it's a different sort of silence in one place than another. Maybe the silence is made up of tiny noises; I

> don't know. There is a true silence about the pieces, but they may speak to you just as a stone may speak to you, out of a true physical silence.[25]

Claudi Casanovas has described his practice as 'like trying to give life to a stone'[26] and, of course, clay and stone are closely related, both geologically and in appearance. But it is worth remembering that it is not just objects made from fired clay that enable us to locate ourselves in the world. The entire material world is capable of communicating to us in the way suggested by Rawson. Casanovas wants his work to act on us

> like stones on the road, like wood on the beach, or pieces of machinery in a scrap-yard. We pick them up so that they accompany us with their silent presence and reflect to us what we cannot see in ourselves.[27]

So why does Casanovas attempt to make pieces that echo the effect of found objects? One reason might be that direct creative engagement with material is necessary in order to understand more profoundly how that communication operates. To learn any language requires study and practice, to become as fluent as a native speaker requires deep and lengthy immersion. Furthermore, as each individual is unique, so is each individual's communication with the material unique and therefore the conversation that Casanovas has with his material is a conversation only Casanovas could have.

> The artist's activity begins with an attempt to understand, to penetrate 'reality', including in this 'reality' the fact itself of our attempt. All that I learn in ceramics seems to me something that I forget completely. With each new piece either this comes back or it does not. One thing I do know: once a finished piece disappears, in time or place, it is always a surprise when I see it again.[28]

The conversation that happens is of the moment, and when we – and even Casanovas himself – look at that object again, a different conversation will occur. Perhaps this is what Jones' description 'inexhaustible nature' means.

The contemplation of nature and natural objects, and stones in particular, has a long history in Oriental cultures. In China this stretches from Neolithic times (7000–1600 BC) – carved stones have been found in tombs dating from this period – to the present day. By the time of the Han dynasty (206 BC – AD 220) the Chinese were adorning their gardens with found stones and by the late Tang (AD 618–907) or Song (AD 960–1279) dynasties Scholars' Rocks were being collected by the literati for display and appreciation in their studios.

Although apparently natural found objects, rocks were often shaped by craftsmen or submerged in river beds for several years 'so that the stone may be scoured by wind and rain and its patterns restored to a living appearance', to better capture the essence of 'the universe in microcosm'.[29] Scholars' Rocks can be dated because they embody styles apparent in other works of art (especially landscape painting) of the same period. A particular idea and ideal of nature is being expressed through the rocks, whether natural or shaped. There are complex cultural codes governing their selection by collectors, who nevertheless have the final say on what does or does not make it into the studio.

> There is a kind of control thus asserted over nature itself, at the point when the rock quite literally enters into culture as it passes through the doors of the

> scholar's study … these objects serve as 'beacons' which chart the shifting terrain of culture.[30]

In Japan, a similar culture of aestheticised nature is found in the tea ceremony. The teabowls used in these ceremonies were valued for their apparent naturalness and their closeness to the making process. The wood firing of pots, such as Bizen ware, and the accidental outcomes that are part of the process, was seen as a way of incorporating nature into the work; porous or cracked pots were equally valued.

A Victorian collector, Captain F. Brinkley, had this to say about Bizen wares:

> A connoisseur must have been specially educated when he consents to pay ten or twenty guineas for a water holder that might easily be mistaken for a drain pipe, partially blackened by fire and ornamented by patches and streaks of brick colour.[31]

In the same century, John Ruskin's views on architecture were inextricably linked to his appreciation of and beliefs about nature, which strongly resemble Oriental ones. He abhorred contemporary science's reductionism of nature to empirical data, and felt like the Chinese that visual idioms could be found to convey the essence of nature; a boulder expressed geological processes as well as any mountain. These processes were at the core of what he called naturalist religion.[32]

This may be a key to the meaning of the 'unfailing silences' in Casanovas' statement. The 'silent presence' of the natural elements (stones, etc.) expands to include the mountainous, volcanic landscape in which he lives and works, and perhaps even to nature as a whole. The solitary pursuits of philosopher, writer and monk that he refers to in his statement hint at an inner silence; religion is perhaps the primary arena where silence happens on a regular basis; and of course the ultimate silence of death is of spiritual and philosophical concern.

Oriental spiritual traditions have always had a particular reverence for mountains:

> places from which to survey not the panorama of the earth but the mysterious immaterial essence of its spirit …
>
> staircases to the celestial, or crumbly aerial platforms on which to concentrate on the dissolution of the bodily self [33]

However in the West, mountains have more often been the focus of human conquest. However there have always been those, whether Christian ascetics, poets, philosophers or mountaineers, on whom mountains have had a profound effect. Petrarch, Dante, Shelley, writer and translator Ramond de Carbonnieres, nineteenth-century Alpinist Edward Whymper, Himalayan mountaineer Francis Younghusband, 'for all of them, the panorama showed nothing so clearly as the scenery of their inner selves'.[34]

> Spend any time in their company … and you will be robbed of your conventional grip on time. Human history, human *revolutions*, will suddenly seem a momentary blink against the immense scroll of eternity embedded in the rock. At a particular geological fault line, 'one world ends; another begins, governed by laws of a wholly other existence … traversing the mountain one travels from life to death.'[35]

Casanovas' 'unfailing silences' may be an expression of the sublime and it is possible that his work too allows us access to that experience.

Filling the silence

There are various approaches that can be taken to understanding and appreciating works of art. Foremost amongst these should perhaps be the direct appreciation of the work itself. The visual and other sensual properties of scale, texture, colour, etc., and the way these properties interact should create some sort of impression, even if only on the level of 'I like it'/'I don't like it'.

However, very rarely are we able to separate the object itself from other factors affecting our perception, i.e. purely to apprehend the thing itself (although phenomenology is one approach that seeks to do this). Factors that affect our perception include what we know, or think, or are told about the person who made it, under what conditions and with what intention; the processes used and the materials employed. Where and how an object is displayed – whether in a public museum or private gallery or consumer outlet, a corporate or domestic or natural environment – might also affect our perception.

One way of deepening our understanding of a maker's work is to place that work in some kind of context. Claudi Casanovas' *Blocks* can be placed in the context of his life and previous work, in the context of ceramics as a field of artistic endeavour and within the visual and tactile arts as a whole. They might equally be located within Catalonian and Spanish and European culture. Casanovas himself has said:

> If I had to make a choice, I would choose our own tradition, interpreted from that originated by this century's avant-garde.[36]

Claudi Casanovas: the maker, the making and the made

Claudi Casanovas was born in Barcelona in 1956. His family moved to Olot (near Girona, Catalonia), and he returned to Barcelona at eighteen to study theatre and ceramics. He was apprenticed to a ceramic studio there, producing wheel-thrown domestic stoneware. He returned to Olot in 1978 and helped found a co-operative (*La Cooperativa de Ceramistes Coure*) of seven potters, who while working independently, shared the responsibility of a shop and organising ceramics-related events in the region.

With the assistance of a local authority scholarship in 1980, he was able to begin exploring his interest in the effects of fire as a shaping force, causing distortions by firing the clay body above the appropriate temperature. He went beyond this to the point of 'boiling' clays and creating artificial magmas. In his attempts to solve the technical problems arising from such experiments, he found himself naturally adopting the traditional Japanese technique of *neriage* (the laminating together of different clay bodies).

By the late 1980s his sculptural ceramics had completely taken over from the production of domestic pottery. Support from his wife and her family has freed him from the constraints of commercial pressures and allowed him to fully devote himself to his ceramic work.

His earliest works recall traditional Mediterranean forms: amphorae, storage jars, and large plates. Decoration and form are integrated in the making and often recall the geometric patterns on old Iberian pieces. Strong contrasts of light and dark reflect the lighting conditions of his home country.

In working alone and on a large scale, he often relies on industrial machinery and is ingenious in his use of this equipment and other materials in creating his forms. He often includes a variety of combustible materials into the making, and sometimes sandblasts fired pieces, processes that create alternating depths of surface and make apparent the different qualities of the dozen or so clay bodies he uses, sometimes all in the same piece.

It was his first experiments with high firing that led him to make the connection between his material and the volcanic landscape in which Olot is set, and to begin using material from that landscape. Casanovas has said that 'Nature in all its forms'[37] is his chief inspiration and, for reviewers of his work, aspects of the natural world are what they primarily evoke. However, he 'is at pains to indicate that he has no special interest in geology, and that any resemblance between his fired work and rocks and land forms is coincidental'.[38] He is not aiming to create a representation of the landscape, but he is mimicking some of the processes that brought that landscape into being.

There are other ceramicists whose work bears at least a superficial resemblance to Casanovas', most notably Ewen Henderson (1934–2000). However, Tony Birks says that Ryoji Koie (Japan 1938–) is 'the only ceramic artist seriously to have influenced Casanovas'.[39]

Casanovas and Koie have worked together both in Japan and Spain. Koie's major influence on Casanovas was his encouragement of the younger artist to discover his own voice. Casanovas is affected by the exuberance of Koie's personality.

> Ryoji Koie taught me another way with the wheel … the spinning clay of fun, mischief-making, joy, mistakes, lightness, surprise and freedom. The living, not the ideal.[40]

Ryoji Koie grew up in Tokoname – one of the six ancient clay sites – and makes everything from traditional Japanese wares, through spontaneous expressive and experimental pieces, to installations. He is a prolific maker and tireless experimenter who has said that all he needs to make him happy is a source of clay.

His background in the Japanese art world in the post-war period of the 1960s and 1970s introduced him to American and European innovations in art. He was particularly drawn to European *art informel* (of which Catalonian Antonio Tapies was a major figure) and American Abstract Expressionism, which are linked by their spontaneous approach to material and process.

Koie explores and interrogates the elements of earth, fire, air and water.

> In the process of probing the nature of pottery, as many modernists and postmodernists have probed the nature of sculpture and painting, Koie is led time and again to experiences of intimacy, delight, uncertainty, bewilderment and revelation. He has grappled with the human talent for destruction and discovered

> paths into nature's imagination. As light and fast moving as his pottery may appear to be, his work carries considerable existential and metaphysical weight.[41]

Although his work often evokes natural forms and textures, the marks of his hands are everywhere to be seen, constant reminders of the making process and the maker's involvement. Casanovas' work, however, is much more self-effacing. He has talked about the imperative to touch clay as little as possible during the making process; every potter knows that overworking clay 'deadens' it, but Casanovas takes the imperative to the extreme.

In 1996, Anita Besson (proprietor of Galerie Besson) asked Casanovas to produce some smaller pieces. He went back to the wheel and brought to it all that he had been assimilating in his large-scale pieces and what he had learnt from Ryoji Koie, making a series of 'teabowls', that archetypal Zen form, 'pieces almost found rather than thrown'.[42]

I think that working on these forms and on this scale may have influenced the production of *Blocks*. They seem to me to be more concentrated pieces, perhaps because they are substantially smaller than much of his previous output. However, if we are to detect in *Blocks* any reference to traditional ceramic forms it is surely the teabowl, albeit a giant one.

It seems appropriate that the work to which Claudi Casanovas' statement refers, given the difficulties raised by their 'silence', is *Blocks*, suggestive as this is of some kind of obstacle. But it also describes their appearance. These are heavy, solid lumps of clay, contradicting totally the ceramic imperative not to build too thickly or unevenly.

Miquel Jimenez believes that it is Casanovas' purpose

> to open the material to sight, to enlighten what is in the dark, to organise the primordial chaos of the constant transformations … Casanovas makes explicit a new way to express the inner side of the material penetrating as far inside as it is possible to understand and see without destroying its own identity.[43]

To me, they seem like small boulders that have been found and harvested like the Scholars' Rocks. Some have internal spaces or openings created and blackened by the burning up of combustible materials: caves; others seem to have erupted from the internal pressures caused by firing, to have undergone tremendous, earth-shattering violence, and bear the scars; others are quieter, slowly yielding to the effects of time; some seem like fragments from ruined buildings, detritus accreting palimpsests. The eye travels like a mountaineer, searching for the next foothold and never stopping for long: the journey is restless, endless; and yet there is a sense of peace that comes from being thus engaged, a sense of being outside of time, where activity and stillness are the same thing.

Conclusion

The silent maker can be a practical philosopher and making can be as valid a way of understanding oneself and the world as academic philosophy. However, to pit one against the other seems to me to be mistaken. Academic philosophy undoubtedly relies on imagination and intuition, just as reason is an essential part of making. An uncritical attitude towards making can lead to barren technique, empty style and false claims to authenticity. Nevertheless the difficulty of translating intuitive, body-centred discourse into words remains.

The silence of makers can also be understood because of course the work should be appreciated for itself and words are no substitute for direct experience of it. Words do, though, afford an additional way of engaging with the work and with other people about the work, becoming a dynamic part of culture and society, transforming and being transformed. Engagement with other people, as much as with material, is an antidote to alienation.

There is a need to contextualise the work of silent makers, although their very silence can itself provide a context. Casanovas' work could be considered in relation to Catalonian and Spanish art. It would be interesting to consider his affinities with artists such as Tapies and Miro, both Catalonians. It is worth remembering how recently Spain was a military dictatorship and the implications of this to the topic of silence, as well as the Catalonian struggle for autonomy and linguistic identity.

Tapies, incidentally, was very interested in Eastern philosophy, as were very many modern artists. In ceramics, the nature of the artistic and philosophical communication between East and West is often presented simplistically. Casanovas and Koie are perhaps a means to explore the complexity of the exchange. As with Scholars' Rocks, a contemplative relationship with the work can, for some, be a way to connect with the ultimate ground of being, whereby the particular is a portal to the all. But this too is as much a matter of culture as individual experience. It also raises the complex relationship between nature and culture. Some critics have made connections between the Romantic notion of the sublime and Abstract Expressionism and I think this is also worth further consideration in relation to Casanovas.

My attempt to fill the silence only goes to show how vast and varied the silence is.

Notes

1 *Twenty Blocks*, exhibition pamphlet (London: Galerie Besson, 17 October – 16 November 2001). (Can be viewed at www.galeriebesson.co.uk/cas2exhib2.html.)
2 Galerie Heller, Heidelberg, Germany and Galerie Besson, London, UK in 2001.
3 Chambers English Dictionary's definition of 'silence' (1990), p. 1368.
4 Jeffrey Jones, 'Keeping quiet and finding a voice: ceramics and the art of silence', *Interpreting Ceramics*, 5 (2004).
5 Bernard Leach used this phrase in a Lucie Rie exhibition catalogue in 1967.
6 Tony Birks, *Claudi Casanovas* (Somerset: Marston House, 1996), (no page no.).
7 Peter Dormer, 'The language and practical philosophy of craft', in Peter Dormer (ed.), *The Culture of Craft* (Manchester: Manchester University Press, 1997), p. 219.
8 *Ibid.*
9 Birks, *Claudi Casanovas*, (no page no.).
10 Gordon Baldwin in Hannah Wingrave, 'Gordon Baldwin: modernist inspiration', *Ceramics in Society*, Winter (2001–2), pp. 13–17, p.16.
11 Norbert Lynton, *The Story of Modern Art*, second edition (Oxford: Phaidon, 1989), p. 362.
12 Claudi Casanovas in Eileen Lewenstein, 'Claudi Casanovas: individual potter – ingenious engineer', *Ceramic Review*, 132 (1991), p. 31.
13 Lynton, *The Story of Modern Art*, p. 356.
14 M. Anna Fariello, 'Material meaning', *The Studio Potter*, 25:1 (1996), pp. 28–30, p. 30.
15 Bruce Metcalf, 'Craft and art, culture and biology', in Dormer (ed.), *The Culture of Craft*, p. 77.

16 Metcalf, 'Craft and art, culture and biology', pp. 79–80.
17 Rudolf Arnheim, *Art and Visual Perception*, new version, (Berkeley and Los Angeles: University of California Press, 1974), p. 3.
18 Edmund de Waal, 'Speak for yourself', *Ceramic Review*, 182 (2000), pp. 32–4, p. 32. Republished in *Interpreting Ceramics*, 5 (2004).
19 de Waal, 'Speak for yourself', p. 34.
20 Jones, 'Keeping quiet and finding a voice'.
21 *Ibid*.
22 Birks, *Claudi Casanovas*, (no page no.).
23 Philip Rawson, *Ceramics* (Philadelphia: University of Pennsylvania Press, 1984), p. 6.
24 *Ibid*., p. 8.
25 Gordon Baldwin, quoted in Peter Saunders, 'Gordon Baldwin's silent clay', *Ceramics Art and Perception*, 39 (2000), p. 40.
26 Claudi Casanovas in Elspeth Owen, 'Forms for the time being: International Potters Festival Aberystwyth 1991', *Ceramic Review*, 131 (1991), pp. 8–9, p. 9.
27 Casanovas in Lewenstein, 'Claudi Casanovas', p. 31.
28 *Ibid*.
29 Twelth-century connoisseur Du Wan in Robert D. Mowry, 'Chinese Scholars' Rocks: an overview', *Oriental Art*, 44:1 (1988), pp. 2–10, p. 4.
30 Laurie J. Monahan, 'Finessing the found: 20th century encounters with the "natural" object', *Oriental Art*, 44:1 (1988), pp. 39–45, p. 45.
31 F. Brinkley quoted in Edmund de Waal, 'Scorched earth', *Ceramic Review*, 172 (1998), pp. 19–22, p. 19.
32 See Simon Schama, *Landscape and Memory* (London: Harper Collins, 1995), p. 509.
33 *Ibid*., p. 407 and p. 411.
34 *Ibid*., p. 422.
35 *Ibid*., p. 488 (inc. Ramond de Carbonnieres quote from *Voyages au Mont-Perdu*, Paris, 1802).
36 Claudi Casanovas, 'Catalan roots', *Ceramics Monthly*, 34 (1986), pp. 28–31, p. 28.
37 Claudi Casanovas, *A Mini Retrospective*, exhibition pamphlet (London: Galerie Besson, 2000).
38 Birks, *Claudi Casanovas*, (no page no.).
39 *Ibid*.
40 Claudi Casanovas, *Teabowls*, exhibition pamphlet (London: Galerie Besson, 1996).
41 Michael Brenson, 'Ryoji Koie: the energy of fire', *American Ceramics*, 12:3 (1996), pp. 36–8, p. 36.
42 Casanovas, *Teabowls*.
43 Miquel Jimenez, 'Claudi Casanovas' blocks', *Ceramics Art and Perception*, 49 (2002), pp. 45–7, p. 46.

Matthew Partington's chapter charts the birth of coffee bars in Britain during the 1950s and explores the design influences upon them. His principle focus is the work of three artist potters who made ceramics for a number of the coffee bars and whose work represented a unique meeting of art, design and commerce. Drawing on oral history interviews with the artists and previously unpublished photographs, Partington discusses how those who worked on the coffee bar interiors operated: how the commissions came about, how the overall design schemes worked and what the finished interiors were meant to do. First published in Issue 6 of *Interpreting Ceramics*, in its original digital form this chapter included several audio clips from oral history interviews, which readers could listen to. Matthew Partington is Senior Lecturer at the University of the West of England, Bristol (UWE), Visiting Fellow in Twentieth-Century Crafts at the Victoria and Albert Museum, London and Director of Recording the Crafts, based at the UWE Department of Creative Industries. Recording the Crafts is a long-standing project that gathers and archives resources for researching the nature of the crafts. These usually take the form of digital video and sound recordings of individuals who have been intimately associated with the development of the crafts in Britain.

Espresso, Exoticism and Earthenware: The London Coffee Bar Ceramics of the Picassoettes

(William Newland, Margaret Hine and Nicholas Vergette) 1952–1966

Matthew Partington

The birth of the coffee bars

In 1952 a new phenomenon hit London that was to make an enormous impact on the British high street: the coffee bar. To Londoners used to cafés ranging from the 'greasy-spoon' and American-style snack bar to the ubiquitous Lyons Corner Houses and Fuller's tea-rooms, the coffee bars were a revelation. By 1960 there were more than five hundred in the Greater London area alone.[1] Evocative of all corners of the world, they bore names such as Mocamba, Moka-Ris, La Ronde, El Cubano, Negresco, Il Latino, Sphinx, Aloha and Las Vegas.

In Don Sharp's 1958 film, *The Golden Disc*, the heroine helps her aunt brighten up her newly acquired and extremely dowdy café. The old, dark-wooden tables and bar, the net curtains and the bentwood chairs give way to a horseshoe-shaped bar, a jukebox, painted metal chairs, high bar stools, 'mad line drawings' on the walls and striped curtains. Most telling is the ceremonial arrival of the Gaggia espresso machine and the juxtaposition of the old man amongst the modern surroundings and the recently arrived young people. Just as the owners of the fictitious bar in the *Golden Disc* are two singers and a retired lady, the proprietors of the real coffee bars had little to do with the catering trade. As Edward Bramah points out in his 1972 book *Tea and Coffee*, the catering trade rejected the Gaggia machine and those who opened coffee bars included 'a wine merchant, an interior decorator, an antique dealer, a milliner, not to mention furriers, tailors, dentists,

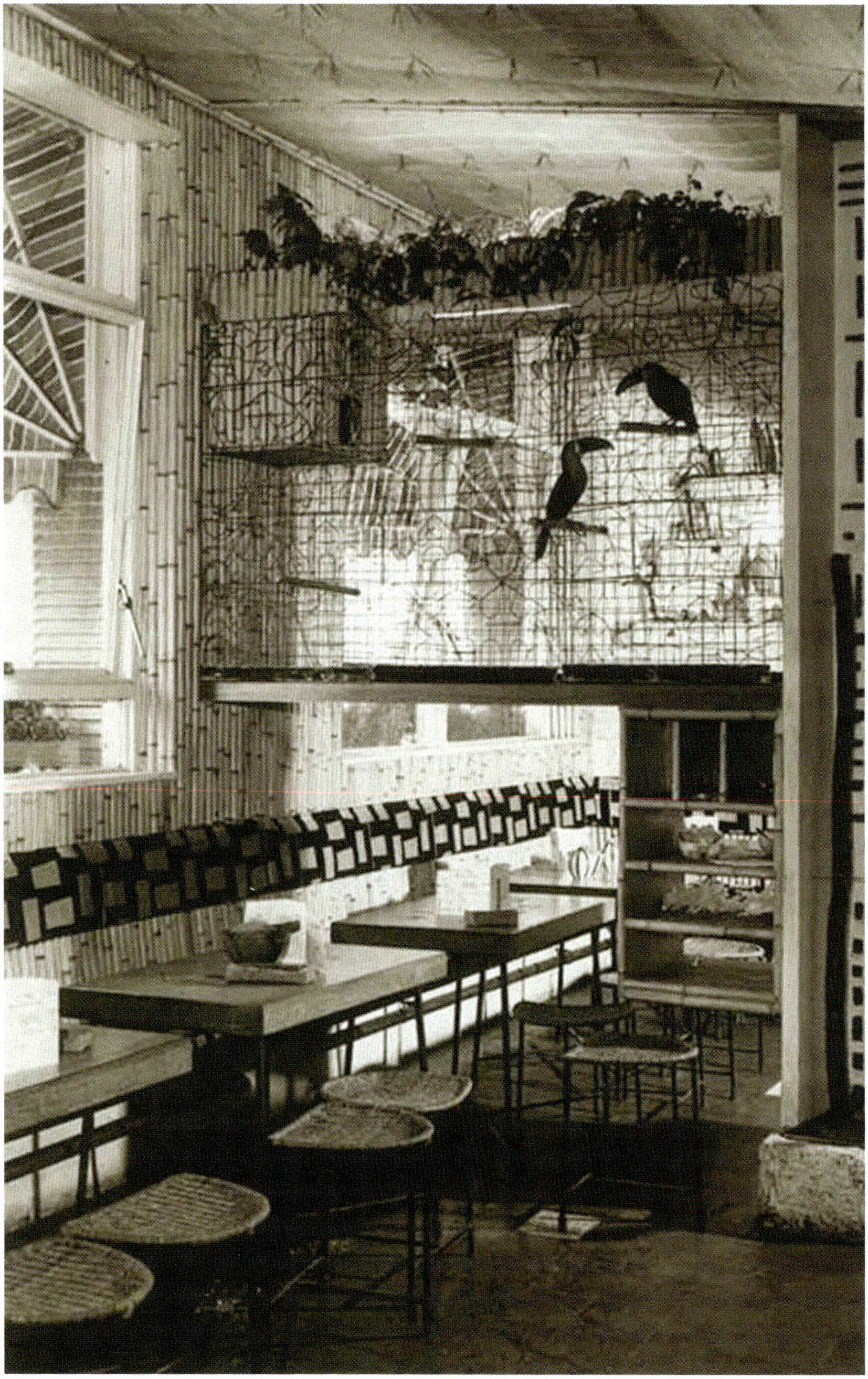

Fig 1. Interior of the El Cubano Coffee Bar, 1954, designed by Douglas Fisher. Photo: the Design History Research Centre, University of Brighton.

sculptors, psychiatrists and film stars'. Bramah's conclusion was that 'Perhaps it was a good thing that caterers had refused to use this machine, for had they done so it might well have been lost amid the conventional and uninteresting decor of an English café.'[2] From the beginning the coffee bars represented a new phenomenon: a place that anyone could go to but that had interesting and unusual interiors and consciously aimed at attracting a young clientele.

It was the machine that made the coffee, which spawned the first coffee bars. Invented in Milan in 1946 by Achille Gaggia, the Gaggia espresso machine made coffee with a concentrated flavour that could be diluted with steamed milk to make a cappuccino. Pino Riservato, an Italian dental technician, brought the first espresso machine to London, apparently in response to the poor quality of the coffee on offer in England's cafes. Riservato and Partners Ltd was set up to import Gaggia machines from Milan. However, there were no takers for the first machines, so Riservato opened his own coffee bar in Frith Street, Soho, to show potential buyers what the machine could do in a café setting. The Moka Bar was fairly restrained with lots of Formica and a Gaggia machine taking centre stage. Although traditional machines made equally good coffee, Riservato succeeded in making the Gaggia *de rigueur* for any aspiring coffee bar proprietor. Despite being stylistically at odds with most of the interiors, the chrome, art deco Gaggia acted as the focal point and dominant visual element of many of the bars.

As the number of coffee bars grew in central London, the battle began to make each one even more distinctive. Some had jukeboxes and attracted young people; others had large menus, attracting diners in the evenings and shoppers and workers during the day; but most had a mixture of coffee, food and music and aimed to appeal to a wide spectrum of Londoners with money to spend. Whilst the Moka Bar only needed the Gaggia to make its mark, the bars that followed had to try much harder to attract customers. As a result, they began to lose their early restraint and sought to stand out from the crowd.

What set the coffee bars apart from other interior design of the period was the range of styles and influences at work. Edward Bramah describes the El Cubano in Knightsbridge (Fig 1) designed by its proprietor Douglas Fisher:

> Not only was there vegetation added to matting, stucco, marble and bamboo, there was an imitation of the parrot house at London Zoo and wild-life was provided to entertain the customers. The coffee was good. The menus were enormous and graded to suit every purse. There were Spanish guitars and air-conditioning and brightly dressed girls to serve the food. Downstairs there was a Roman room, and if there were not exactly orgies, there was certainly an orgy-like atmosphere.[3]

Whilst fairly restrained interiors were designed by the likes of Misha Black, Humphrey Spender and Terence Conran, more still were by less-well-known designers, such as Fisher, whose aim as proprietor *and* designer was to entice people in, appeal to popular taste and make money. In a 1955 *Architectural Design* article, the Piazza coffee bar is featured. The walls were covered with large photo-murals of Italian piazzas and the architects, John and Sylvia Reid, included their own furniture alongside furniture by Arne Jacobsen and ceramics by Rörstrand.[4] Despite the much more restrained overall design of the Piazza coffee bar, the accessories (metal-legged chairs, Formica-topped tables and Scandinavian ceramics) are indistinguishable from those in the exotic wonderland that was Fisher's El Cubano.

The decorative eclecticism and inconsistency of some of the coffeebar interiors was a strange mix of modernist furniture and accessories, alongside proto post-modernist flourishes. This made it a problematic area for the modernist design establishment to deal with.

The design establishment

The interior design of the coffee bars represented the meeting of popular taste and 'official' taste, as defined by the design establishment. The journal articles of the 1950s that I have found relating to the coffee bars are from *Architecture and Building*, *Design*, *Architectural Design* and *Architectural Review*. The articles concentrate on the exotically named bars of South Kensington and Chelsea. Soho bars such as the famous Two I's (the home of British rock 'n' roll), and numerous others with jukeboxes, a coffee machine and less exotic names (such as Sam Widges and the Coffee Pot) were not covered as they only began to appear in 1956, following the birth of rock 'n' roll. The journal articles ceased to publish substantial articles on the coffee bars after 1955.

The journal articles represent the attitude of the design establishment to the coffee bars. Under the directorship of Gordon Russell, the Council of Industrial Design (responsible for *Design* journal) saw itself as the arbiter of good taste in design. This meant that a clear distinction was made between popular/commercial taste and the designers' taste as championed by the Council of Industrial Design. As a result the articles give a very narrow view of the coffee bar phenomenon and the images we are left with are mainly from the journals and could easily be used to paint the story from one particular point of view. I have used oral history interviews, magazine articles and unpublished images to present a more balanced view.

This is perhaps best illustrated with reference to a 1955 *Picture Post* article about the coffee bars.[5] Despite essentially being social and commercial spaces, not one of the journal articles includes an image of a coffee bar with customers in it. The *Picture Post* article has several images, all including people, and another that wasn't used shows people enjoying themselves in the Mocamba. However, the images of the Mocamba used in an article by Paul Reilly in *Architecture and Building*[6] concentrate on the décor. Whilst one may not expect a design-oriented journal to concentrate on people, it does have the effect of de-contextualising and de-personalising the interiors.

By looking at the hand-crafted ceramics made for coffee bars during the 1950s by a small group of artists we can begin to re-contextualise the interiors and find a more rounded image of the coffee bars than that available in the journal articles.

The ceramics of the Picassoettes for the coffee bars

William Newland, Margaret Hine and Nicholas Vergette worked on ceramic tiles, sculpture and decorative items for a number of coffee bars in central London in the mid 1950s. Known in retrospect as the Picassoettes (a reference to their stylistic debt to the colourful ceramic sculpture being made by Picasso at this time), these three artists typified a style of work that grew out of the Central School of Art and Design and were renowned for the use of brightly coloured, tin-glazed earthenwares. Seen as the antithesis of the Bernard Leach 'school' of Orientally inspired stoneware, the work of these artists quickly went out of fashion and until Tanya Harrod's 1989 article 'The forgotten fifties'[7] they were largely overlooked in writing about twentieth-century ceramics.

Whilst Bernard Leach looked to the cool simplicity and 'timeless elegance' of Far Eastern ceramics as a source of inspiration, Newland, Hine and Vergette were the post-modernists to Leach's modernism. Fun, irreverent, colourful and ephemeral, their work was perfectly suited to the coffee bar interiors. Their stylistic borrowings ranged from African tribal carvings and Mexican pottery to Picasso, Scandinavian ceramics and Italian maiolica (incidentally, described by Leach in *A Potter's Book* as 'generally weak, ornate and closely allied to third-rate Renaissance painting').[8]

Kenneth Clark, a friend and colleague of William Newland, described their work in a 1997 interview:

> I think they were very influenced by what Picasso had just been doing in Vallauris. So this was the very strong counter element to the Leach tradition ... Very much to do with stoneware, muted colours and you know, nobody would dare dream of using colour in stoneware such as a bright blue glaze or a turquoise glaze you know it was all delightful, subtle, muted, rich tenmokus or celadons and that was the ideal. So this was a completely different field, a different approach: still ceramics.[9]

This 'different approach' is clear in the images of Pino Riservato's second coffee bar: the Moka-Ris Experimental Bar (Fig 3). It was the venue for an August 1955 interview in *Picture Post*, an immensely popular publication during the 1950s. The feature, headlined 'A red-head in search of black coffee',[10] followed the actress Adrienne Corri,[11] touring a number of coffee bars. The Moka-Ris had no particular theme, geographical or otherwise, but was intended by Riservato to be an example, to those wanting to open a coffee bar, of what could be achieved (provided of course the Gaggia occupied centre stage).

Newland, Hine and Vergette made brightly coloured plates that were decorated with Picassoesque imagery and placed on the wall to diffuse the lights behind them. The *Picture Post* described the Moka-Ris as 'fantastically decorated' and to readers who were only just beginning to see adverts for Spanish holidays in the small ads, the new coffee bars, inspired by the Mediterranean, Africa and Latin America, were a sophisticated and colourful addition to the British high street. The *Picture Post* (representative of a populist view of the coffee bars, as opposed to the more esoteric outlook of the design journals) saw the bars as fun places and concentrated on the Gaggia machine, the commercial growth of the bars and the rise of the coffee bar as *the* place to be seen.

William Newland was interviewed in 1994 and in this excerpt he discusses why their work fitted the coffee bars so well:

> Yeah well, coffee bar design. Of course one of the first essentials was it had to be attractive, it had to be jolly, for want of a better word, gay. And fairly large scale and fortunately going back to all the hand-building we'd done and press-moulding

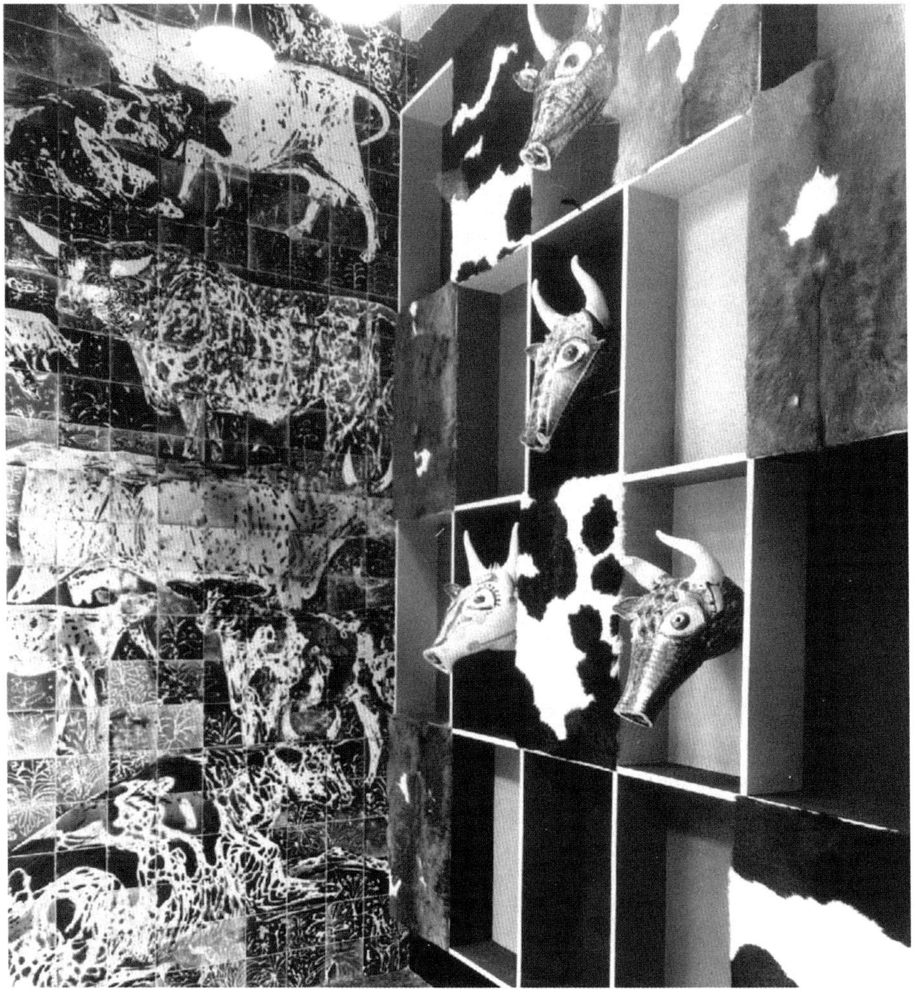

it was within our sort of repertoire. And we could do six-foot press-moulded figures, standing, and size was no limitation. Colour, because of our tin-glaze, we had, yeah? ... and design was no problem because we'd been through so-called art school.[12]

As Kenneth Clark put it:

> They did lots of decorative pieces: figures on horses, animals, birds, plaques, plates, all put on the walls round these coffee houses ... they were designing for an interior and they made you a whole lot of plates to go on a particular wall ... I remember one of Bill's donkeys with panniers on them and someone sitting on the donkey. All these things went in almost as entertainment, into these coffee houses.[13]

Fig 2. Interior of Moo Cow Milk Bar, Victoria Street, London, c.1952, (architect, Geoffrey Crockett). The entrance area includes thrown earthenware cow heads by William Newland and tiles by Marcus Vergette. Photo: Marcus Vergette.

The Picassoettes made Spanish ceramics for a Spanish interior and African ceramics for an African interior. Their primary concern was pleasing the patron who paid their wages and

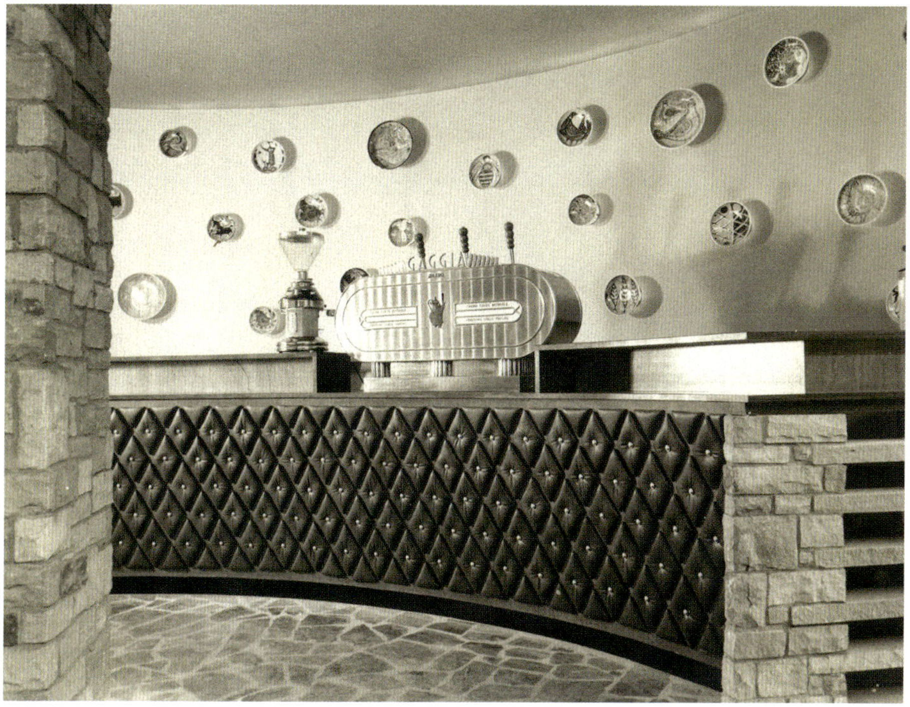

Fig 3. Moka-Ris Experimental Bar, Dean Street, Soho with wall-hung plates by William Newland, Margaret Hine and Marcus Vergette, (architect, Geoffrey Crockett). Photo: Marcus Vergette.

so they fitted their style to the theme they were presented with. The context defined the work (at a time when most ceramics were not site specific).

The interior of the 1953 Moo Cow Milk Bar is clean, tasteful and modern (Fig 4). The architect, Geoffrey Crockett, used over 2500 square feet of Formica. However, this modernist image of acres of wipe-clean Formica is rather compromised by the entrance featuring a huge multi-coloured tile panel of cows by Vergette, alongside a wall of cubby-holes bearing ceramic cows' heads by Newland and lined with real cowhide (Fig 2). Whilst milk bars were soon to disappear amidst the onslaught of the coffee bars, the Moo Cow was a good example of what made the coffee bars so different. The milk bars were formal, clean and uncluttered. Coffee bars had individual touches, often reminiscent of foreign holidays; they opened late and they sold coffee (a much more sophisticated drink than milk). The entrance area of the Moo Cow Milk Bar was meant to entice the visitor in to the traditional milk bar interior, whilst coffee bars sought to make the *whole* of the interior exciting and welcoming.

Newland was a member of the Studio Club in Soho and said that his membership led to commissions from the Kaye brothers (businessmen who owned a number of coffee bars):

> because we were at the Studio Club and because we were doing Italian tin-glaze as it were, the architect walked down and said you must come and do the first, you know come and work on the coffee bar with these Italianate sort of designs. Which we did, and there were two Jewish brothers who financed the thing called, not Kray, Kaye, and they started building one every two to three months and it was marvellous: very, very lucrative ...[14]

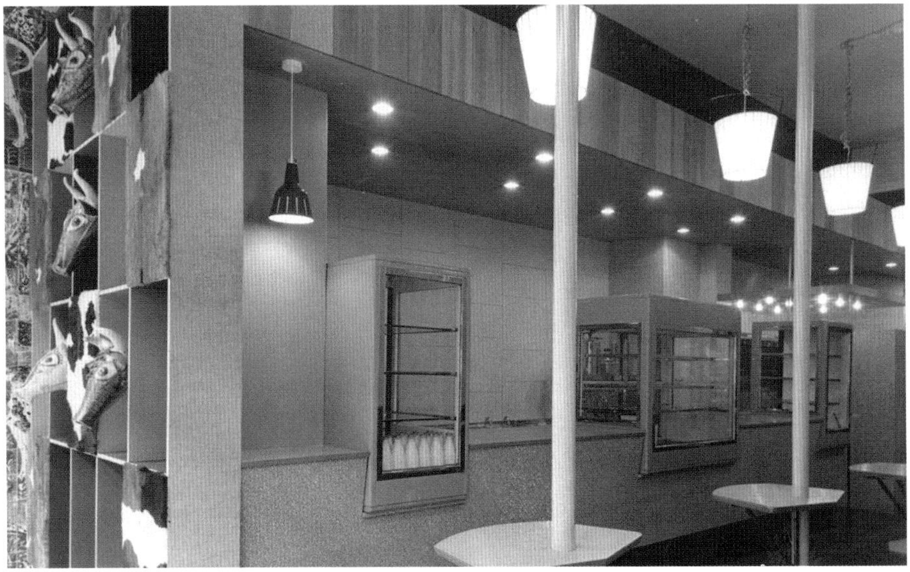

Like the milliners, furriers and film stars who were also starting coffee bars, the Kayes were new to the business and as a result they didn't go to a recognised designer and ask for what had gone before. They wanted something that would stand out. Interviewed in 1965 for Malcolm Newell's book, *Mood and Atmosphere in Restaurants*, Philip Kaye described a 'ghastly eight-foot-high ceramic mask' by William Newland in the 'window of the Edgware Road branch [of the Golden Egg restaurant]: people stopped to look: they were horrified, they were mystified, but it intrigued them and they went in to the restaurant'.[15] Uninterested in discreet design, the Kaye's wanted to attract attention. The Picassoettes were making ceramics that made people stop and stare: the very antithesis of the understated Leach ideal, but exactly what the coffee bar owners wanted.

Newland explained the rather informal nature of the commissioning process:

> Well, the normal way we were commissioned was that if we had to do a job we'd take along drawings and meet the patron, the Kayes, and the architect and show them our drawing and the main thing of course, we were always paid but of course you looked after the guy who was going to pay you: if he approved it was alright and of course the architects were so hungry for bloody work that if the patron wanted something, they agreed too. So we more or less had a free, absolutely free hand. And we did some really crazy ones you know, and got away with it ...[16]

Having built up a reputation for making brightly coloured sculptural ceramics, they were in the right place at the right time to decorate coffee bar interiors. Not being part of the ceramic establishment and eager to make a living, they were happy to make objects to fit a patron's scheme. They were not making art for galleries or private clients: they were to decorate coffee bars, enhance the overall design scheme and give a hand-made quality to the surroundings. As Newland said, 'we did some really crazy ones ... and got away with it'.[17]

Fig 4. Interior of Moo Cow Milk Bar, Victoria Street, London, c.1952, (architect, Geoffrey Crockett). Photo: Marcus Vergette.

Conclusion

The work of Newland, Hine and Vergette was very much 'of its time' and as a result it quickly went out of fashion. In this way the work of the Picassoettes echoed the end of the coffee bar phenomenon. Although many of the bars survived throughout the 1950s and well into the1960s, the majority did not. Whilst many simply ceased trading as the custom could not support the ever-increasing number of bars, many became cafes and restaurants, concentrating on serving food. Running a restaurant, whilst having higher overheads, had a greatly increased revenue per customer and as a result it was easier to make a living.

Very little survives of the ceramics made by the Picassoettes for the coffee bars. Newland, Hine and Vergette are no longer with us: we are left with interviews with Bill Newland, which include discussions of the 1950s. It is only with these oral history interviews that we gain some depth of understanding of the day-to-day mechanics of the coffee bar interiors, allowing us to go beyond the rather dry, de-personalised approach of the journal article.

The ceramics were defined by their context: they were made to decorate a design scheme and liven up interiors and when those interiors ceased to entice enough customers through the door, they closed. Perhaps it is fitting that these ceramics, which were so of their time and so site specific, should have gone when the coffee bars went: victims of the very commercial imperative that led to their creation.

Notes

1 Edward Bramah, *Tea and Coffee: A Modern View of Three Hundred Years of Tradition* (London: Hutchinson, 1972), p. 70.
2 *Ibid.*, p. 72.
3 *Ibid.*
4 'Three restaurants', *Architectural Design*, December 1955, p. 391.
5 P. Graham, *Picture Post*, 21 August 1954, pp. 38–9.
6 Paul Reilly and Helen Low, 'London coffee bars', *Architecture and Building*, March 1955, pp. 83–95.
7 Tanya Harrod, 'The forgotten fifties', *Crafts*, 98 (1989), pp. 30–3.
8 Bernard Leach, *A Potter's Book* (London: Faber and Faber, 1957), p. 120.
9 NEVAC (National Electronic and Video Archive of the Crafts), interview with Kenneth Clark, MD 171, 00:35:17.
10 Graham, *Picture Post*, pp. 38–9.
11 Adrienne Corri (1933–) was a Scottish actress promoting her latest film, *Make me an Offer*. The article includes two photos of her and one of customers in the Moulin Rouge coffee bar. The fact that Adrienne was a Glaswegian was not mentioned as perhaps it was not conducive to the rendering of the exotic tone desired by the writer.
12 NEVAC, AC118 (side 1), 00:35:00 onwards, audio recording of William Newland, 1994.
13 NEVAC, interview with Kenneth Clark, MD 171, 00:35:17.
14 NEVAC, William Newland, AC118 (side 1), 00:31:37 onwards.
15 Malcolm Newell, *Mood and Atmosphere in Restaurants* (London: Barrie and Rockliff, 1965), p. 34.
16 NEVAC, AC118 (side 1), 00:31:37 onwards.
17 *Ibid.*

First published in Issue 6 of *Interpreting Ceramics*, this chapter was written when Christine Longworth was Curator of British and European Antiquities at National Museums Liverpool; she is now a freelance consultant. Here she draws on a range of sources to discuss Buckley potters in the light of general cultural developments. The Buckley area in North Wales has been associated with pottery making from the medieval period to the mid twentieth century, but its most productive period was the late seventeenth and early eighteenth centuries. Buckley potters at this time were low in the social scale; they often eked out a living and are unmentioned in contemporary sources. After a general historical overview, the account focuses on ways in which the Buckley potters began to respond to consumer interests. Changes in taste led to a desire to copy fashionable imported ceramics, metal wares and other materials, and the pottery at Brookhill, Buckley produced a wide range of vessels, including some intriguing sgraffito dishes that appear to have been influenced by medieval bestiary texts. Christine Longworth would welcome any reports of Buckley sgraffito ware finds and can be reached at: christinelongworth47@gmail.com.

Buckley Ceramics in the Seventeenth Century: Socio-Economic Status of the Potters and Possible Design Influences

Christine Longworth

Status of medieval potters in Britain

There are few documentary references to potters and pottery production in the medieval period that provide information about the lives of the people. The evidence that exists demonstrates that their social status was extremely low compared to other craftspeople and that they only just managed to eke out a living. Pottery was a relatively cheap commodity, made by peasants to supply the local middle and lower ranks of society.[1] The richer sections of medieval society were not interested in this type of pottery, preferring sophisticated vessels of other materials and imported pottery for their tables.

In the towns, documentary evidence shows that potters were at the bottom end of the social scale and were also too poor or insufficiently numerous to form a guild until almost the end of the medieval period.[2] Terminology in relation to the various craftspeople making table and kitchenware makes it difficult to determine their trade. This is because wares could be made in various materials such as wood, metal or clay. Words such as *pottarius*, *ollarius* or *ollator* are used equally for metal and clay. Le Patourel suggests that, when consulting documentary sources, the trade 'potter' should be considered a metalworker if located in a town unless there is additional information to indicate a clay potter. In a village, one can assume that he is a clay-worker.[3] On consulting printed records for larger towns, Le Patourel has been unable to find any potters' guilds. The guilds referred to as potters proved to be metalworkers.[4]

Much of late medieval potting was located in the countryside where potters often combined potting with growing crops and keeping animals.[5] This dual occupation was also characteristic of other rural industries such as mining, cloth making and various woodland crafts.[6] It provided some form of financial security, ensuring that they were not totally dependent on their craft for an income. The pattern of work allowed the potter to fit his production into the slack periods of the agricultural year. Ethnographic literature gives examples that show a similar pattern. The combination of both pottery making and agriculture by ethnographic groups living in marginal agricultural areas maximises their economic productivity.[7]

Potters in the medieval period were economically obscure, but an indication of the distribution of the medieval potting industry can be found by examining taxation returns and other records and looking at fieldnames containing potter or crocker elements. However, this information is scattered partly due to a lack of organisation within the medieval industry and partly to the relative poverty and insignificance of its individual members.[8] Late fourteenth-century poll-tax returns studied by Le Patourel for the counties of Somerset, Sussex and West Riding of Yorkshire do not have any clay potters mentioned, although there are a large number of other trades listed. Information about potters on other documents shows that they were assessed at the lowest rate for a man and wife, the fourpence rate paid by the mass of the peasantry compared to sixpence rate paid by most small craftsmen.[9] The family was the basic unit of production, including the children. Any larger-scale operations would include the employment of three or four men.[10]

Pottery was distributed in the local market and would have been bought largely by the peasantry and the smaller landowners. The demands of the consumers would have had a direct influence on the quantity and type of pottery produced. The lack of change in items produced over a number of generations implies a conservatism in the taste of consumers.[11]

End of the medieval period

In the late fifteenth and early sixteenth centuries, there was a change in the structure of domestic life in the British Isles. This was partly caused by the final collapse of demesne farming, the break up of great feudal households and the waning power of the guilds.[12] More influential was a series of economic and cultural trends developing throughout north-west Europe.[13] Expanded trade with the continent brought in imported pottery and new ideas in eating and drinking. The traditional medieval domestic wares of wood, leather and metal were replaced by pottery, and the simple ceramic forms which had continued throughout the medieval period expanded into many new wares to supply a growing domestic market in all levels of society.

This change in fashion led to a sudden increase in the number of potteries all over the country. Small potting communities established themselves in areas which had suitable raw materials; clay, fuel, water and lead.[14] Their activities, such as clay digging or firing smoky kilns were unpopular, as was the fire hazard, therefore they were not encouraged to work near the larger towns and villages. They were commonly situated on wasteland close to the source of their raw materials.[15] An example of this is at Potovens, in West Yorkshire, where a group of potters settled immediately outside the enclosed fields of Wakefield in the Out-wood, a waste area supplied with clay, fireclay, coal, stone and water, all used by the potters in their craft.[16] In the Merseyside area, suitable clays and fuels existed on the coalfields of South Lancashire and in North Wales. These were exploited by cottage potters, who built domestic kilns to serve the local markets around Liverpool and Chester. Documentary evidence shows that by the middle of the seventeenth century many farmers in the St Helens district were producing pottery and clay tobacco pipes as part of their livelihood and excavation has revealed evidence of pottery production.[17]

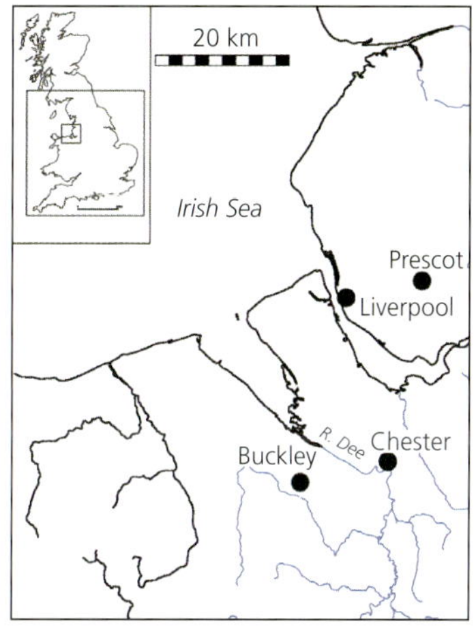

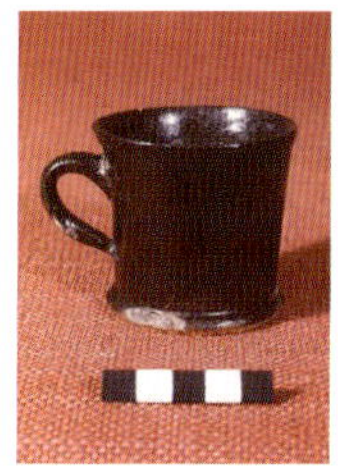

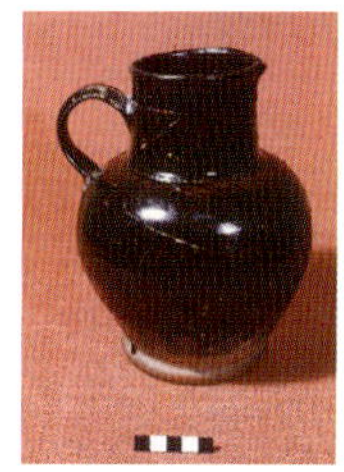

Buckley in the seventeenth century

By the early seventeenth century, a group of cottage potters had settled on encroachments on the common in Buckley, North Wales. Buckley is situated 12 km west of Chester at a height of 140 m above sea level overlooking the River Dee estuary (Fig 1). The area is rich in natural resources, Buckley itself lying on top of coal measures and clays. There is a major geological fault line north/south through Buckley and associated smaller faults that have exposed the range of clays and coal. The faulting caused mineralisation to take place, producing lead sulphide, the source of lead for glazing the pots.[18] The potters exploited the suitable supplies of clay, fireclay, open-cast coal and nearby sources of lead. Water transport was available on the Dee Estuary, down the hill from Buckley. They utilised the wide range of clays found in the region. Red boulder clay, the most common raw material, was often mixed with a lighter, buff-coloured clay to produce the domestic pottery. White clays were used in the production of clay tobacco pipes and pottery. Cooking pots and saggars were made from fireclays.

The earliest map evidence dates from the eighteenth century. An estate map entitled *The Lordship of Ewlow* dated 1757 gives acreages, land values, names of occupiers and buildings drawn in perspective. This map clearly illustrates the location of kilns on Buckley Common.[19] Other maps from the Gwysaney Estate covering the years 1750–81 provide information about names of occupiers, encroachments on Buckley Mountain (another name for Buckley Common) and the location of pottery kilns.[20] A survey carried out in 1976 identified nineteen pottery production sites in and around Buckley Common, dating from the medieval period up to 1946, when the last pottery closed.[21]

Some of the earliest documentary references to potters come from clay accounts, which provide a window on the extent of the industry. The potter had to pay for a licence to dig clay. This was usually on the moor, waste or common land.[22] The earliest records for Buckley date from 1759, 'For cash received from Benjamin Codrell and others for clay raised in the Ewloe Lordship in the year 1759: £5.2s.6d.'[23]

A typical Buckley pottery was small, tenanted and worked by a master potter who employed three or four men and boys.[24] Messham researched the clay accounts between 1783–1810 and the available estate maps and was able to produce a table to show the extent of the Buckley industry.[25] Very few of the families managed to make much of a success out of their potting, most being in production for only a few generations. The craft was passed on from father to son and there was much marrying within potting families. When there was no male heir to carry on the business, it passed to the widow or daughter. Messham lists three women responsible for running potteries in the late eighteenth century.[26] This ensured the continuity for some time. The Hayes family is the

Fig 1. top, North Wales and Merseyside. Photo: National Museums Liverpool.

Fig 2. bottom left, Dark-glazed cup, excavated from the kiln site at Brookhill Pottery. Photo: Peter Davey.

Fig 3. bottom right, Dark-glazed jug, excavated from the kiln site at Brookhill Pottery. Photo: Peter Davey.

most notable for its continuity. They were producing clay tobacco pipes in 1695 and the family continued making pots until 1942. After the flourishing in the seventeenth and eighteenth centuries, the two families of Catherall and Hancock became the leading producers, making large quantities of utilitarian wares.

Unlike most country potters, in Buckley they worked full time at their potting. This was also the situation in Potovens in Yorkshire. Both these groups of potters fit into the low socio-economic group of rural potters found throughout the country who lived on marginal land, eked out a living using the raw materials around them and supplied their local markets.

Brookhill Pottery, Buckley

Brookhill Pottery was situated on the north side of Buckley Common, close to an exposure of clays and coal. It was in production from c.1640–1720.[27]

In medieval England, the cooking pot, jug and bowl were almost the sole products of the potter,[28] but by the time Brookhill was in production an extremely wide range of wares, largely modelled on Continental originals, were being made. This was the same for most potteries throughout the country. The desire to copy fashionable imported wares, metal wares, and also other materials such as wood and leather, led to the changes in pottery forms and decoration. Potters could then supply an existing demand, especially among people who aspired to more expensive items, such as metal vessels, but could not afford them.[29]

One change was in the production of ceramic drinking vessels to replace wooden ones. This was partly as a result of the increase in the drinking of ale.[30] Brookhill potters met this demand by producing a range of dark-glazed and slip-trailed mugs, cups and jugs (Figs 2 and 3).

Seventeenth-century plates imitated pewter forms and edged out wooden boards and trenchers.[31] In Brookhill these influences can be seen in the range of vessels that copy metal prototypes (Figs 4 and 5) and the large quantity of slipware and press-moulded dishes that replaced wooden boards (Figs 6 and 7). The standard of wares produced in seventeenth-century Buckley is low compared to the wares found, for example, in Chester at the same date, where a variety of high-quality English and imported ceramics have been found in excavations. These include Saintonge and Beauvais wares, lustrewares, Italian and Spanish wares.[32] The Buckley potters continued to provide for the lower and middle ranks of society.

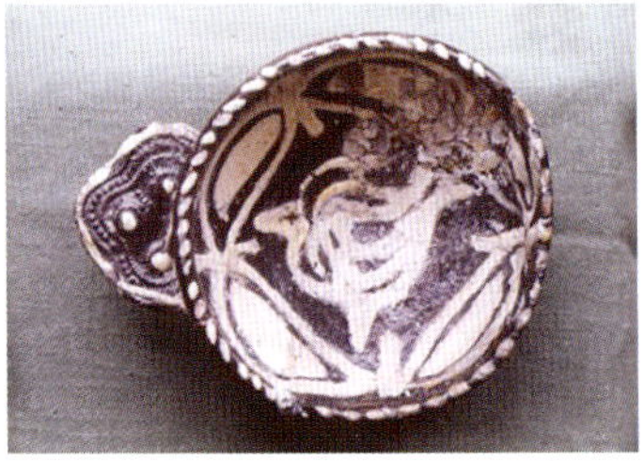

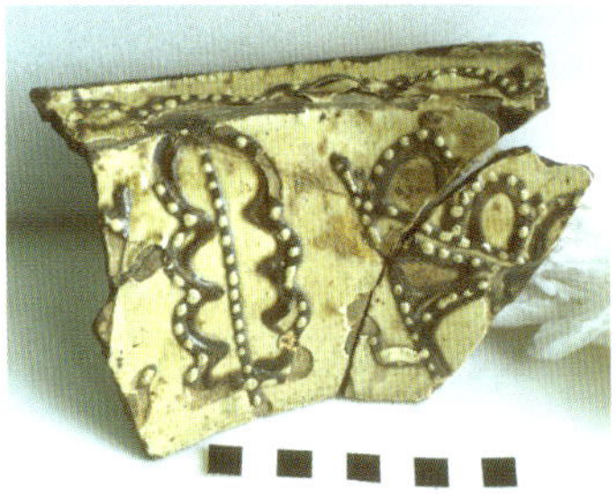

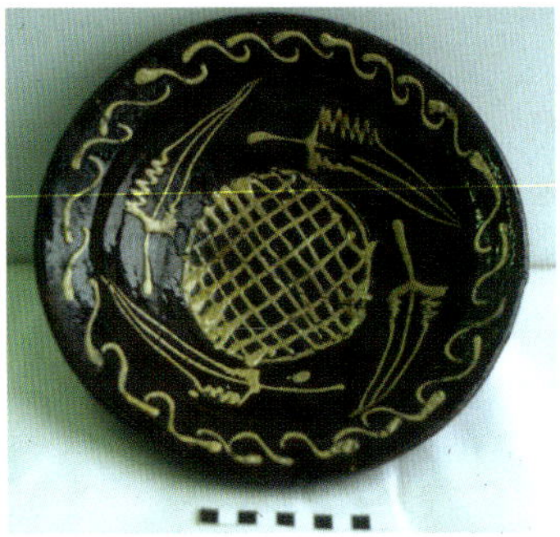

Fig 4. Slip-trailed porringer with press-moulded handle, excavated from the kiln site at Brookhill Pottery. Photo: Peter Davey.

Fig 5. Fragment of a deep bowl, white slip-coated with trailed brown slip design and white slip jewelling. Excavated from the kiln site at Brookhill Pottery. Photo: Christine Longworth.

Fig 6. Slip-trailed plate in characteristic leaf design. Excavated from the kiln site at Brookhill Pottery. Photo: Christine Longworth.

Designs and influences

The most common method of decoration in Buckley is by slip trailing in a contrasting colour directly on to the earthenware body of the pot. There are also some pieces that have been decorated in the sgraffito technique. This is produced by applying a slip coat over the whole of the pot and scratching a design through the leather-hard slip to reveal the contrasting body beneath. The decorated pieces of trailed slipware and sgraffito ware from Brookhill give us an insight into the minds of the seventeenth-century potters. Everything is crudely drawn by hand (Fig 8) but it is possible to suggest outside influences in these pieces. The potters took their wares to Chester market where they would have had the opportunity to see everything available for sale, including wares imported from the Continent. One sherd of Beauvais sgraffito has been found on the production site at Brookhill.

Influences in decorative styles on slipwares spread from east to west. In northern Italy they were copying Middle-Eastern and Eastern-Mediterranean prototypes in the medieval period. The main centres were the Po Valley and Liguria.[33] In the Saintonge region of south-west France, very fine jugs were produced which were exported along the French coast, to other parts of Europe and to the British Isles.[34] By the fifteenth century, the Beauvais region of northern France was producing slipwares and sgraffito ware in large quantities. These have been found throughout Britain and the Low Countries.[35] By the late sixteenth and early seventeenth centuries an extensive slipware industry had developed in northern Germany. These wares were exported through the port of Bremen in large quantities to the Low Countries, Scandinavia and Britain.[36]

The earliest slipwares in Britain using the sgraffito technique were made at Nether Stowey in Somerset in the late sixteenth century.[37] By the early seventeenth century, 'Metropolitan slipware' with slip-trailed decoration was manufactured in Essex with its principal market being London and southern and eastern England. Another production centre was based at Wrotham in Kent.[38] By the 1640s, slipware was being produced in Staffordshire and North Wales and by the 1650s there were a number of centres of production, including West Yorkshire and South Lancashire.

The technique of sgraffito decoration had been adopted in North Devon by the early seventeenth century, heavily influenced by its trading links with the Low Countries. The North Devon industry was directed principally to export, the major routes being to Ireland, America and the coastal trade around the Irish Sea.[39] Donyatt in Somerset was also producing sgraffito ware by the early seventeenth century and slip-trailed designs from the mid seventeenth century, but it had a limited export market.[40] The only known site to produce early sgraffito wares in northern Britain is Buckley.

The slipware reaching Britain from Northern Europe clearly had an influence on the choice of decorative style in the British production centres. The most common themes are botanical, zoomorphic and geometric. For example, pieces produced in Donyatt in Somerset frequently show bird and tulip motifs. These design themes also appear on pieces produced in Buckley.[41]

Two sherds of North Devon sgraffito pottery were found on the Brookhill site. There is considerable documentary and artefactual evidence of North Devon sgraffito pottery reaching Chester and Liverpool,[42] so it is likely that the pieces found in Buckley were traded through Chester market. The designs on North Devon ware come in two main categories, geometric and floral. The central motif often combines compass-drawn petals and geometric patterns and can be quite intricate.[43] Watkins considers that there is much circumstantial evidence to make a connection between North Devon sgraffito ware manufacture and design and the influx of Huguenot and Netherlands Protestant artisans into south and south-west England. Although some motifs seen on North Devon pieces are also found on Buckley pottery, the North Devon designs are not as crude as those

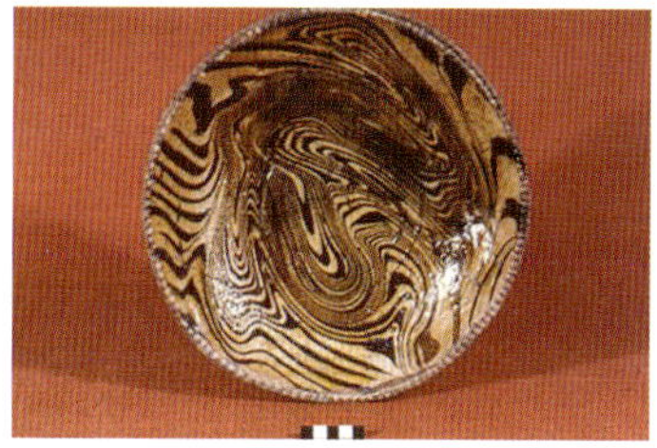

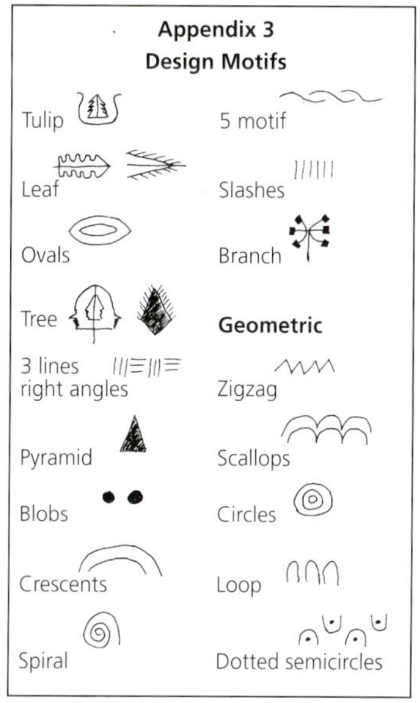

Fig 7. Press-moulded dish with two concentric circles in relief near the centre and a dentelle rim. Interior surface has dark-brown slip-trailed lines joggled on a white ground. Excavated from the kiln site at Brookhill Pottery. Photo: Peter Davey.

Fig 8. Common design motifs on seventeenth-century Buckley pottery. Photo: Christine Longworth.

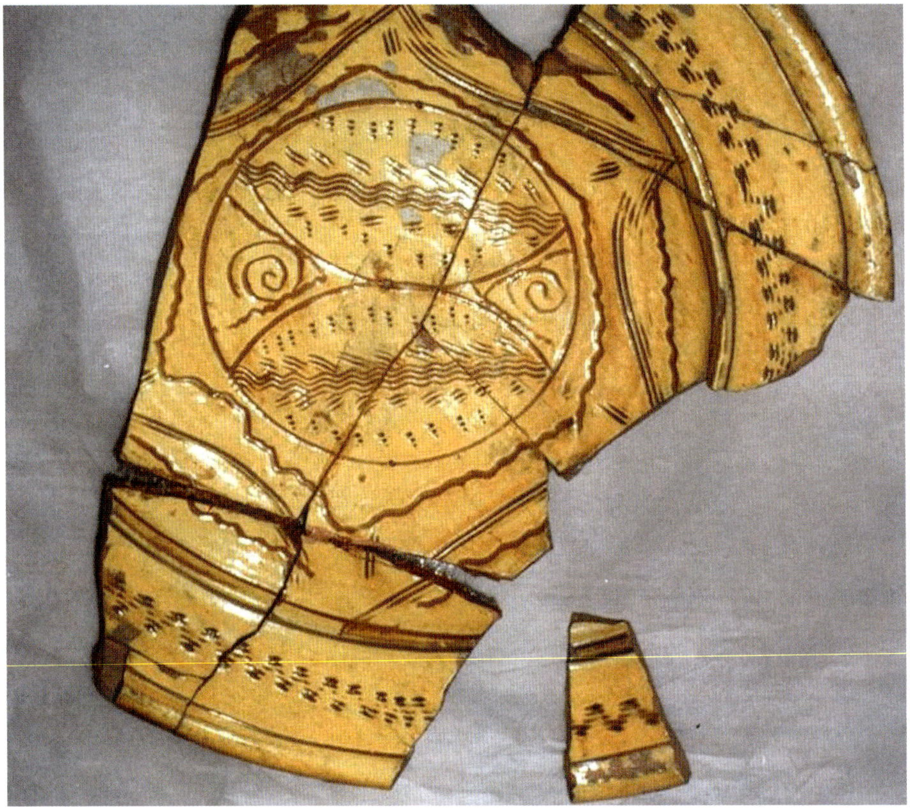

from Buckley. Possibly the Welsh potters gained some inspiration for their decoration from North Devon pieces but they chose to interpret them in their own way (Fig 9).[44]

Other types of influences should not be ignored. The sophisticated designs and styles of the time were intended for the town and country house. There was a growing library of information available for anyone looking for design ideas. The pattern books produced for the silk-weaving industry and for needlework provided a range of plant and animal designs. There were also pattern books for furniture decoration and for use in the kitchen. The range of motifs included flowers, tulips, leaves and birds. As well as the pattern books, objects themselves featuring popular designs would have been available in a place like Chester, with its thriving market and affluent society. Fine silks and embroidery, other textiles, furniture and household goods would have been accessible for anyone to see and purchase. Buckley pottery was traded regularly in the city, providing ample opportunity for Buckley folk to browse and possibly purchase items to take home.

During the mid seventeenth century, the regional furniture of Lancashire and Cheshire features, in particular, designs of tulips, leaves and dragons, very similar to the Buckley images. Furniture craftsmen travelled around the country and could possibly have had some contact with Buckley. Documentary evidence suggests that potters moved between potting centres,[45] so it is more than likely that craftspeople in different trades had contact

Fig 9. North Devon sgraffito plate found during excavation at Sefton Old Hall, Merseyside. Photo: Christine Longworth.

with each other. It is suggested that some of the floral motifs seen on Lancashire chairs are related to needlework designs.[46] Various needlework pattern books were published in the early seventeenth century detailing naturalistic motifs and other related designs.[47]

Bestiary influence

There is an intriguing small group of sgraffito dishes from Brookhill Pottery that contain images of birds, worms, fish and elephants. Some of these dishes also contain a motto around the rim (Fig 10).

The source for these images and texts cannot be determined precisely, but it is possible that they derive from the medieval bestiary texts and illustrations.[48] In the sixteenth and seventeenth centuries there was a resurgence of interest in the bestiaries and the earlier Latin texts were translated into English. The bestiaries are a collection of morality tales of animals, plants and fishes written to convey an understanding of the scriptures and the conduct of a good Christian.[49] They were a popular source for sermon writers. Good and evil were embodied in nature and all natural elements were segregated into those that had good properties and those that had bad properties.[50]

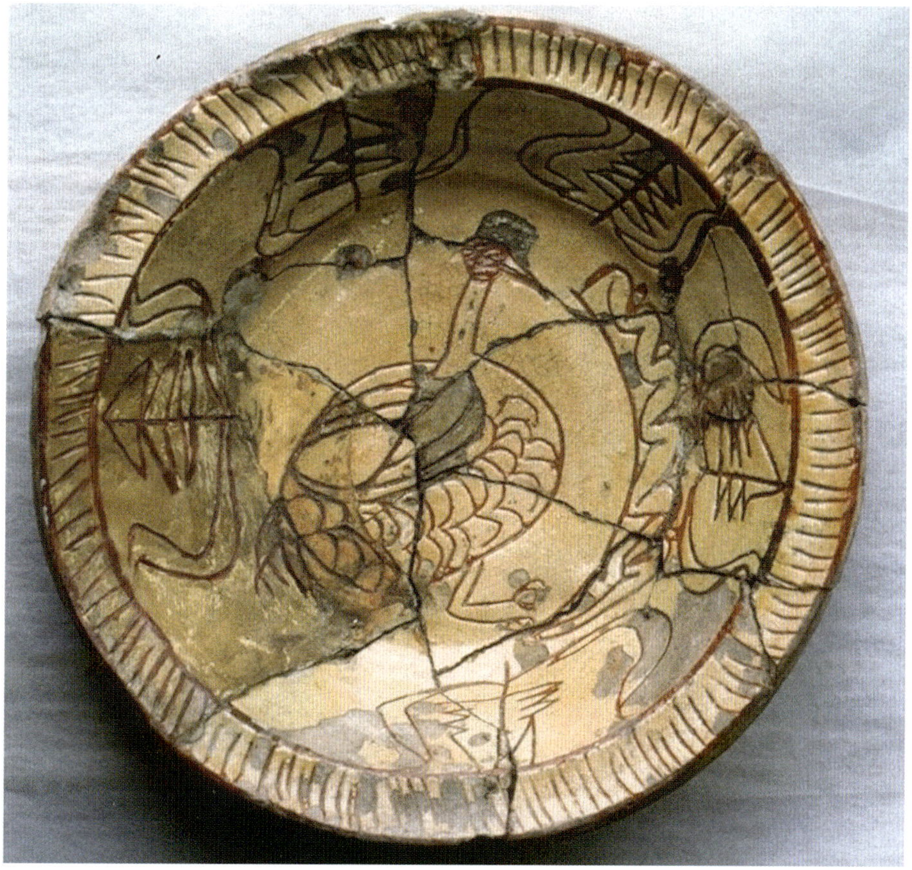

Fig 10. White slip-coated dish with sgraffito design showing a bird and worm. Excavated from the kiln site at Brookhill Pottery. Photo: Christine Longworth.

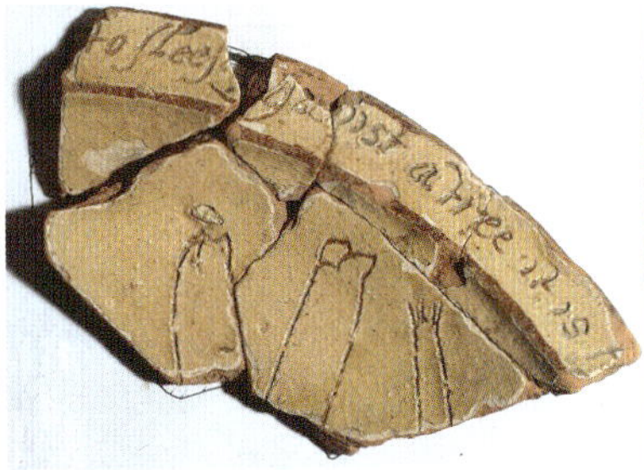

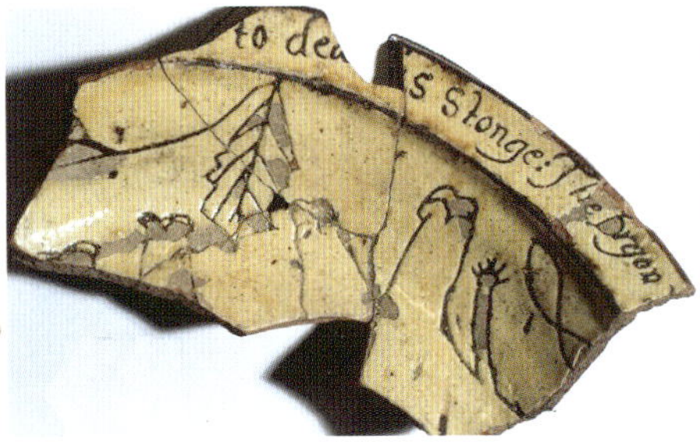

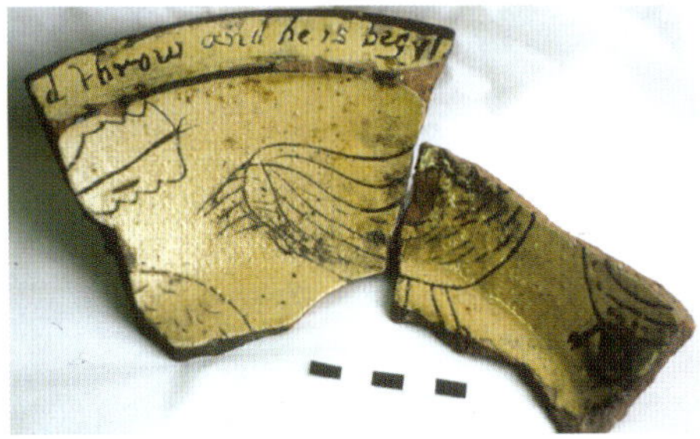

In the medieval period, much of the population was illiterate so the use of images and icons were forms of a visual parable which created a direct means of communication.[51] By the sixteenth and seventeenth centuries more people could read and translations into English led to a wider contact with the bestiary tradition. This coincided with the growth of Puritanism in the country. It is not possible, within the scope of this paper, to research the bestiaries and sermons produced from them. However, it is likely that the religious leaders in the sixteenth and seventeenth centuries taught the Christian doctrine using the symbolism of good and evil contained in the bestiaries, as had been done in previous centuries. The entire text of a bestiary is heavy with biblical quotations. The first, literal, section tends to include passages from the Old Testament, and the second section relates to the New Testament.[52]

There are at least two vessels from Buckley depicting elephants, two that state 'elephant' in the motto and at least one mentioning a dragon in the text. Although no direct quote can be found for the mottoes, there are links to elephants and dragons in the bestiary texts. In the Christian moralisations, the elephant and the dragon symbolised good and evil. Illustrated is part of a dish that depicts the two legs and tail of an elephant with the text 'to sleep .gainst a tree ·it is t' (Fig 11). A twelfth-century manuscript, now in the Cambridge University Library, translated by White, reads as follows:

> The elephant's nature is that if he tumbles down he cannot get up again. Hence it comes that he leans against a tree when he wants to go to sleep, for he has no joints in his knees.[53]

Another Buckley dish fragment shows four legs and tail of an elephant with the text 'to dea..s stonge: The Drgon' (Fig 12). White's translation is as follows:

> The dragon has a crest, a small mouth and a narrow gullet through which it draws breath or puts out its tongue. Moreover, its strength is not in its teeth but in its tail, and it inflicts injury by blows rather than by stinging. Even the elephant is not protected from it by the size of its body; for the dragon, lying in wait near the paths along which the elephants usually saunter, lassoes their legs in a knot with its tail and destroys them by suffocation.[54]

Illuminated bestiaries are a peculiarly English phenomenon, reaching their peak at the beginning of the thirteenth century. A very fine illustration of an elephant and dragon appears in a manuscript (Bodley 764) discussed by Barber.[55] This shows clearly the dragon entwining itself around the elephant.

Fig 11. left, Fragment of white slip-coated dish with sgraffito design depicting an elephant with the motto 'to sleep .gainst a tree .it is t'. Excavated from the kiln site at Brookhill Pottery. Photo: Christine Longworth.

Fig 12. middle, Fragment of white slip-coated dish with sgraffito design depicting an elephant with the motto 'to dea..s stonge: The Drgon'. Excavated from the kiln site at Brookhill Pottery. Photo: Christine Longworth.

Fig 13. right, Fragment of white slip-coated dish with sgraffito design depicting a bird with the motto 'd throw and he is begyl'. Excavated from the kiln site at Brookhill Pottery. Photo: Christine Longworth.

The author gratefully acknowledges that all the pots illustrated in this chapter are part of the Regional Archaeology Collection, Museum of Liverpool.

There may be as many as fourteen vessels from Buckley depicting birds, only one of which has a motto, which reads 'd throw and he is begyl' (Fig 13). There are many birds featured in the bestiaries but it is quite impossible to link any particular one to the Buckley images.

An examination of the text around the rim of these dishes shows inconsistencies. Capital letters have been used for Dragon and Elephant on one dish. On another dish, elephant is written in lower case. The spelling of elephant appears in two different forms, one with and one without an 'h'. There are two versions of the word he – 'he' and 'hee'. It appears as if this text has been copied and not necessarily copied correctly. What was it copied from? It is almost certain that the source for these is the bestiary texts. To copy text does not necessarily mean that the potter was literate, which could explain the inconsistencies. Another possibility is that some texts were heard and repeated many times in church, much as we recite The Lord's Prayer today, and that the potters reiterated those parts they could remember, but how literate were they in Buckley at this date?

Another possibility is that these dishes were part of a special order, the details for the decoration being supplied for copying. To date, no pieces of these dishes have been found beyond the production site itself. This suggests that there was a very limited production, probably by one potter. All the pieces are from one kiln, the earliest kiln on the site, dated between 1640–70. It is even possible that these dishes are the result of one firing by one potter.

Conclusion

Buckley potteries, just like other rural pottery industries in the seventeenth century, developed because of the availability of natural resources and the changes in cooking, eating and drinking fashions of the time. The local market in Chester is the likely source of many of their design ideas, both from the sophisticated ceramics available for the wealthy citizens of Chester, including imported wares from the Continent, but also from other materials such as furniture and textiles and the availability of pattern books.

The potters created their own versions of what they had seen to supply their local market. Although the designs appear crude, they are appealing and follow the fashions of the time to serve the peasant population. The market for their wares was very local and at the lower end of the social scale, therefore the need to provide highly sophisticated designs was not necessary. The fact that some pieces were decorated would be sufficient to satisfy the demand for more expensive-looking items from their customers who wished to follow the latest fashions but could not afford to purchase high quality goods.

The sgraffito pieces with mottoes and bestiary images appear to be unique. These images only appear on Buckley dishes. The closest parallels to the Buckley pieces are the North Devon sgraffito wares but their designs are distinctively different from the Buckley pieces. North Devon wares have no images or text that relate to the bestiaries. Most North Devon pieces at this time are without text and their designs are carefully executed. The few that do contain text have either something in verse or simple initials on commemorative pieces.

The early-established potting centres such as Donyatt, North Devon and Buckley maintained their own distinctive styles of coarse earthenware production throughout the eighteenth and nineteenth centuries.[56] Buckley focussed on producing plain earthenwares for use in the kitchen and dairy and also made industrial products.[57] The continued use of birds, animals, plants and inscriptions is seen in particular on the harvest jugs of North Devon, which are often very elaborate and inscribed with the recipient's name.[58]

Notes

1 Christopher Dyer, 'The social and economic changes of the later Middle Ages and the pottery of the period', *Medieval Ceramics*, 6 (1982), pp. 33–42, p. 37.
2 Jean Le Patourel, ' Potters and pots', *Medieval Ceramics*, 10 (1986), pp. 3–16, p. 3.
3 Jean Le Patourel, 'Documentary evidence and the medieval pottery industry', *Medieval Archaeology*, 12 (1968), pp. 101–26, p. 102.
4 *Ibid.*, p. 103.
5 Dyer, 'The social and economic changes of the later Middle Ages', p. 37.
6 J. Birrell, 'Peasant craftsmen in the medieval forest', *Agricultural History Review*, 17 (1969), pp. 91–107.
7 Dean E. Arnold, *Ceramic Theory and Cultural Process* (Cambridge: Cambridge University Press, 1985), p. 199.
8 Le Patourel, 'Documentary evidence and the medieval pottery industry', p. 103.
9 *Ibid.*
10 Dyer, 'The social and economic changes of the later Middle Ages', p. 37.
11 Michael McCarthy and Catherine Brooks, *Medieval Pottery in Britain AD 900–1600*, (Leicester: Leicester University Press, 1988), p. 55.
12 Peter Brears, *The English Country Pottery* (Newton Abbot: David and Charles, 1971), p. 13.
13 D. Gaimster and B. Nenk, 'English households in transition c1450–1550: the ceramic evidence', in *The Age of Transition: the Archaeology of English Culture 1400-1600* (Oxford: Oxbow Books, 1997), p. 171.
14 Andrew McGarva, *Country Pottery: Traditional Earthenware of Britain* (London, A. & C. Black, 2000), p. 9.
15 Brears, *The English Country Pottery*, p. 14.
16 *Ibid.* p. 14; Stephen Moorhouse and Ian Roberts, *Wrenthorpe Potteries* (Bradford: West Yorkshire Archaeology Service, 1992), p. 4.
17 Peter Davey, 'Merseyside: the post-Roman pottery', *Journal of the Merseyside Archaeological Society*, 7 (1991), pp. 121–42, p. 127.
18 B. Smith and T. N. George, *British Regional Geology: North Wales* (London, HMSO, 1961), p. 73.
19 Flintshire Record Office, Gwysaney, 96/3.
20 J. E. Messham, 'The Buckley potteries', *Flintshire Historical Society Publications*, 16 (1956), pp. 58–9.
21 Peter Davey, 'Recent fieldwork in the Buckley potteries', *Journal of the Buckley Society*, 4 (1976), pp. 16–29.
22 Le Patourel, 'Documentary evidence and the medieval pottery industry', p. 113.
23 Messham, 'The Buckley potteries', p. 32.
24 *Ibid.*, p. 33.
25 *Ibid.*, pp. 56–9.
26 *Ibid.*, p. 56.
27 A. Amery and P. J. Davey, 'Post-medieval pottery from Brookhill, Buckley, Clwyd (site 1)', *Medieval and Later Pottery in Wales*, 2 (1979), pp. 49–85; K. Lloyd Gruffydd, 'Seventeenth-century bestiary ware from Buckley, Clwyd', *Archaeologia Cambrensis*, 129 (1980), pp. 160–3; D. A. Higgins, 'Clay tobacco pipes from Brookhill, Buckley', *Medieval and Later Pottery in Wales*, 6 (1983), pp. 50–64;

D. A. Higgins, 'More pipes from the Bentley Collection, Buckley, Clwyd', *Society of Clay Pipe Research Newsletter*, 46 (1995), pp. 9–13; Christine Longworth, 'Buckley sgraffito: a study of a 17th century pottery industry in North Wales, its production techniques and design influences', *Internet Archaeology*, 16 (2004) http://intarch.ac.uk/journal/issue16/longworth_toc.html.

28 Brears, *The English Country Pottery*, p. 13.

29 McCarthy and Brooks, *Medieval Pottery in Britain AD 900–1600*, p. 56.

30 Dyer, 'The social and economic changes of the later Middle Ages', p. 40.

31 McCarthy and Brooks, *Medieval Pottery in Britain AD 900–1600*, p. 90.

32 Pers. com. Julie Edwards, Chester Archaeology.

33 J. G. H. Hurst, D. S. Neal and H. J. E. van Beuningen, *Pottery Produced and Traded in North-West Europe 1350–1650* (Rotterdam: Rotterdam Papers VII, Museum Boymans-van Beuningen, Rotterdam, 1986), p. 30.

34 Jean Chapelot, 'The Saintonge pottery industry in the later Middle Ages', in P. J. Davey and R. Hodges *Ceramics and Trade* (Sheffield: Department of Prehistory and Archaeology, University of Sheffield, 1983), p. 51.

35 Hurst *et al*, *Pottery Produced and Traded in North-West Europe 1350–1650*, p. 108.

36 *Ibid*., p. 242.

37 David Barker, *Slipware* (Aylesbury: Shire Publications, 1993), p. 8.

38 *Ibid*., pp. 11–13.

39 A. Grant, *North Devon Pottery: The Seventeenth Century* (Exeter: University of Exeter, 1983), p. 93; C. M. Watkins, 'North Devon pottery and its export to America in the 17th century', *Contributions from the Museum of History and Technology, United States National Museum Bulletin*, 225 (Washington DC: Smithsonian Institute, 1960), p. 53.

40 R. Coleman-Smith and T. Pearson, *Excavations in the Donyatt Potteries* (Chichester: Phillimore & Co Ltd, 1982).

41 Longworth, 'Buckley sgraffito', 6.3 History of the development of designs and patterns – designs using plants and animals. http://intarch.ac.uk/journal/issue16/1/ch6.31.html.

42 P. J. Davey, 'Slipwares', in 'Excavations in South Castle Street, Liverpool 1976 and 1977', *Journal of the Merseyside Archaeological Society*, 4 (1985), p. 33; Davey, 'Merseyside: the post-Roman pottery', p.1 36; P. J. Davey and J. A. Rutter, 'A note on Continental imports in the North-West 800–1700 AD', *Medieval Ceramics,* 1 (1977), p. 28; Grant, *North Devon Pottery*, p. 93.

43 Watkins, 'North Devon pottery and its export to America in the 17th century', p. 43.

44 Longworth, 'Buckley Sgraffito', 7.4 Spread of influences – decorative styles and vessel forms. http://intarch.ac.uk/journal/issue16/1/ch7.43.html.

45 Moorhouse and Roberts, *Wrenthorpe Potteries*, p. 110.

46 Temple Newsam House (compiled by Anthony Wells-Coles), *Oak Furniture from Lancashire and the Lake District*, exhibition catalogue (Leeds: Halton, 1973), Figs 21 and 22.

47 Ralph Edwards, *The Connoisseur Period Guides to the Houses, Decoration, Furnishing, and Chattels of the Classic Periods: The Stuart period, 1603–1714* (London: The Connoisseur, 1957), p. 127.

48 Lloyd Gruffydd, 'Seventeenth-century bestiary ware from Buckley, Clwyd', p. 160; Longworth, 'Buckley sgraffito', 6.3 History of the development of designs and patterns – bestiaries. http://intarch.ac.uk/journal/issue16/1/ch6.34.html.

49 John Williamson, *The Oak King, the Holly King and the Unicorn*, (New York: Harper and Row, 1986), p. 49.

50 *Ibid*., p. 41.

51 *Ibid*., p. 42.

52 R. Baxter, *Bestiaries and their Users in the Middle Ages* (Stroud: Sutton Publishing Limited, 1998), p. 33.

53 T. H. White, *The Book of Beasts* (London: Jonathan Cape, 1969), p. 26.

54 *Ibid*., p. 166.

55 Richard Barber, *Bestiary* (Woodbridge: Boydell Press, 1999), p. 182.

56 Barker, *Slipware*, p. 20.

57 Peter Davey, *Buckley Pottery* (Buckley Clay Industries Research Committee, 1975), p. 2.

58 Mary Wondrausch, *Mary Wondrausch on Slipware* (London, A. & C. Black, 1986), p. 61.

One of the highlights of the International Potters Festival, Aberystwyth, in 1999 was a slide lecture by Michael Casson, which he repeated by popular request later during that weekend. What follows is an edited transcription. Looking back over the century, he articulated a continuing commitment to the values of the Leach tradition. The enthusiasm with which it was received suggests how, at that time, the Leach tradition still had its place in the culture of contemporary ceramics in Britain in spite of many competing philosophies. This transcript was first published on the website of the Ceramic Collection and Archive, University of Wales, Aberystwyth. It was published in Issue 6 of *Interpreting Ceramics* in 2005 in a special supplement dedicated to the life and work of Michael, or 'Mick', Casson, one of Britain's best-loved studio potters, who died in December 2003.

Michael Casson at Aberystwyth 1999

Michael Casson

I've got a sort of subtitle – 'one potter's point of view of the twentieth century'. So, it is my own point of view. I am going to try and make no value judgements but I know I am going to fail. But, as far as I can I am going to be as factual as possible but that's relative isn't it? I know that at times I am not going to be up to the task and I am going to have to say what I really feel, especially as we get nearer to today.

Another subtitle to this talk would be 'diversification and polarisation' and as I go along I'll mention those two words again. It is quite evident being here today that diversification is here to stay. The biggest change in twentieth-century ceramics has been the inclusion into the canon of pottery of aspects of using clay, which until the 1950s were the concern of sculpture. There has always been modelling with the human figure, modelling of animals etc., etc., but it was called sculpture. And now, as you look around the arena today at the various people throwing and building, it's obvious this all comes under one umbrella. It is an interesting question to say why that happened. I believe that as Fine Arts have gone more and more esoteric, more and more conceptual, they have become less acceptable to ordinary people – whatever they are. But at least people can appreciate more of what people are doing in clay than some of the conceptual work being done today. I hope conceptual work will go on – I am sure it will – but it is limiting and I think the response to a more broad use of clay, in part, came about because of that.

I want to look back over this century and I see this century as a sort of landscape with hills, dips and hollows, and for me two mountain ranges. One of the hills which is, I think, particularly interesting and important but not vital to the understanding of twentieth-century ceramics is labelled Lucie Rie and Hans Coper. You can leave now if you want to. I am not saying they didn't do the most interesting and unique work this century – they did. But in terms of the influences, direction, and the condition of ceramics, I don't think that they are as important as the two mountain ranges I see when I look back over the century – the hundred years, or seventy-five that is my age. So I see two mountain ranges. One mountain range is concerned with everything to do with that name Bernard Leach.

The other mountain range, looking back, is a mountain range of education. And I think these two aspects of using clay – the Leach phenomenon and education, especially what's happened in education since the fifties, post-the Second World War – have changed the condition of our work today. And I think both of them point to the future.

Now – Bernard Leach and all his name implies. So much has been written about Bernard and so much has been written by Bernard that I would like to clarify what his message means to me and probably to some of you too. I list four aspects of the Bernard Leach scenario.

Number one, he said it on the first page of *A Potter's Book*, 'We are all some kind of Artist Potter now'. I can't remember whether it was capital A or small A. It is an interesting point. He called his book *A Potter's Book* not *The Potter's Book*. Written in 1939, read by most people after 1945. Implicit in his writing and his work and his talks and everything else is the use and understanding of materials: in many cases natural materials and processes. You can tell a Staite Murray pot before he met Hamada and after it; turn it up and look at the clay. Before Staite Murray met Hamada through Leach he was using what most potters at that time were using: industrial clay. They used to call it paste – there's a word for you. Leach introduced clay dug from the earth or at least, if not that, clay that had iron and other impurities in it. So, one: we are all some kind of Artist Potter. Two: know about materials and about processes. Go out on the kiln site today. All those firings out there are about process.

I remember twenty years ago the Crafts Council people came to me 'now we're not going to talk about how, we're going to talk about why'. I remember in America once hearing Richard De Stabler, a conceptual clay worker – he said to NCECA [National Council on Education for the Ceramic Arts], 'I only want to know about why' and he got a fantastic round of applause and then Daniel Rhodes stood up and said a little bit later 'I only want to know how I do things – and how I do things changes my life'. He got a round of applause too.

Right, number three of the Leach philosophy. He looked to the anonymous, the humble, and the vernacular peasant tradition of the East and the West. He looked at English slipware. Before that, he looked at English and European medieval jugs and pots. So he – and all the people connected with him, at the time and since – made us look at those sort of traditions.

So that's three things. And the fourth one, probably the most difficult, is the moral issue, the moral pot. The idea that Leach said that if you make a thing in a certain way you are altered and if you use the pot that's being made in that way the user is affected. I often say to students I don't care if you go into Woolworths and buy a Mickey Mouse mug – good luck. All I ask is that if you are using a Mickey Mouse mug and you're using one which has been made with – what did Bernard say, 'head, heart and hand' – that you know the difference! If you can't tell the difference you've got a problem.

So, four things: we are all some kind of Artist Potter; understanding the use of materials and processes; the humble, the vernacular, the anonymous, the peasant tradition; the way of life and the moral issue. These can get bogged down in dogma. They can foster intolerance and end up in pots without life or they can produce work which is significant, timeless – for all time. So that's the Bernard Leach one. I see that as a mountain range which has affected us all ever since. Whether we accept it or reject it – we can't ignore it. Although at times ambiguous, even contradictory, the message is flexible – capable of endless interpretation.

Now the other thing is education. Just briefly about education, it can embrace and include the Leach ideology and I give you two schools – that's the Harrow course in 1963, and the Farnham course about the same time with Henry Hammond and John Reeve.

Education is open ended – a quest for the original. Put the original in brackets … because I know some of you have heard me say before 'I don't believe in the original unless you come from Mars'. I believe in innovation and, incidentally, I believe in change and development. But anyway education suits the 'original' through a search for ideas. Is this a common goal for all art education, whether you're working in clay or paint or metal or whatever? It's to bring out the best of the person – the uniqueness that we all have in us. This can result in tortuous materials and fashionable trivia but it can also result in what I said about the other thing. I'd better say them again – timeless work, open up new vistas. So there's not one good way and one bad way. What is certain is that from now on most potters will come from education.

Right, we start the century. The century begins with Art ware – pottery for the clients that were eager to buy Arts and Craft Movement pottery. But they were using industrial techniques and industrial materials. They used pastes. They were set up as individual studios by people like Lord Elgin, Ruskin Pottery, and Moorcroft especially. Or they were set up as independent departments inside the factories like at Pilkington's and Doulton's. That ended more or less with the end of the First World War. But there were a few potters beginning to look at different aspects of using clay: Reginald Wells, Bernard Moore, some others' names escape me, but in 1911 somebody called William Staite Murray. William Staite Murray only really worked for a short space of time – 1925 to 1939 – in a significant way. His philosophy was very simple, very interesting and significantly picked up again in the early seventies. It was, to sum it up, 'Today I make a painting, tomorrow I make a pot. There is no difference.'

Murray in his own way was an inspired teacher. He would appear in a cloak with a walking stick. He would walk past your pots and if he noticed them he would slash them to pieces with his walking stick. I said to Henry Hammond, 'Weren't you offended by this?' and he said, 'We were delighted. He might have ignored us.' What Staite Murray did produce was a series of excellent teachers imbued with the same ideology. There was a time after the Second World War, shall we say the early fifties, where you could start in Scotland and go right from Katy Horseman in Scotland, right the way down the country to places like Falmouth and there would be a Staite Murray pupil, ex-pupil, in charge of a ceramic course, if not the whole art college. That meant that from post war onwards that idea that pottery would equal to painting was there as something to gradually go into the art-school system.

He had some wonderful pupils – the one we've lost, he would have changed the course of history, I'm sure. Sam Haile. He went to America, came back to this country and was killed tragically in 1948 just when things were starting to happen.

Bernard Leach – let's have a look at Bernard – earthenware, stoneware, porcelain, pots, function? I should have entered that word function when it came to looking back on the vernacular, the peasant tradition. Of course, it brought in function and of course many people who have read, and looked, and met Bernard took up the ideal of function as being something that could alter their lives – I, for one, certainly. Also, remember that 'we are all some kind of Artist Potter now'. Bernard was not a good technician. He was an artist, whatever that word implies, but he worked around people like David, his son, who is a precision merchant. This is why I quote this whole syndrome of Leach, not just Bernard himself but all the people who were around him. People often said – oh yes, Bernard, great writer, great ideologist. I think some of them should look at the pots. They're wonderful pots, OK they're heavy – so what. It's a pot that has life.

He brought back Hamada didn't he? And Hamada is on that mountain – no doubt about it. Looking at today, and I mean 1999, whether they know it or not people owe a great debt to Hamada. I remember somebody asking him about the crawling on the neck and he said, 'I chose the pot because of the crawling'. Everyone went – 'Aaah'. I need a year to think about that! But he made us see that faults are acts of God, acts of kiln. You judge a pot not by its technical perfection but by something else. And Hamada did that as well as many other things.

Another man who came on the scene in 1923 – of course, Michael Cardew. Leach seemed to gather round him these people who had giant personalities and there was one if ever there was – Michael Cardew. And he looked, in particular, at that aspect of Bernard Leach's ideology, the philosophy of the vernacular, of the peasant and, just for a moment in time, he recreated that slipware tradition – which is no mean feat.

Right, another aspect of Leach – function. Repetition throwing. Use them for everyday life. Back to the kitchen, back to the stove, to cooking. This aspect of his work was not particularly taken up by Bernard. Bernard was not a repetition man, but he could judge and he could evaluate and David and the team there in the post-war period developed a range of pots. I remember when we started at Harrow in 1963 we looked at that particular range and that particular clay and those particular firing and making methods. You just could not equal, if not beat it.

Potter or craftperson, a designer-maker, a ceramicist or a clay artist – the words change and those words mean something. In particular they mean diversification and I am all for that. But it is significant if those words have changed. I remember a very well-known designer first seeing a Walter Keeler pot. And he fell hook line and sinker. 'What wonderful pots', he said, 'can I see your drawing?' Pinned up around the workshop were various notes and back-of-envelope drawings and Wally said, 'I don't really do that'. The visitor said, 'But you obviously designed these first'. To this day I cannot get across to some people that the design is vital to making anything, but it needn't be the first thing you do. Perhaps you go on to the wheel first of all. Perhaps you play with coiling first of all and the whole thing is – what's the word – 'holistic'. It grows in a flash till you make and you think of the firing and all of it at once. So you're designing and making, making and designing. It's not a stepping-stone, one, two, three. So I think that when they started to change the name from Arts and Craft to Art and Design, I think it was a significant turn of events.

From the early sixties when the Coldstream Report came out it said that all artists should be literate and numerate. Well, I knew that with literate we would be in with a chance – but numerate I thought … Anyway, Dip AD gave way to BA, a bachelor of arts (honours) in a particular craft subject. Great, wonderful, and in the fullness of time the MA, and just recently the MA has burgeoned and is a growth area. One of the few growth areas and I am not worried by it so much, but I want to bring your attention to the fact that an MA is usually two years long. So if you're coming from another discipline – you can now come from Textiles or Glass and do an MA in Ceramics – you won't throw. But learning to throw in two years is possible but you will need very specialist teachers and a very specialist environment. Some will hand-build or many of you will go in for some form of sculpture. Now I think there is a danger of too many people going into ceramics and going into the sculptural side and making an imbalance over the whole course of pottery.

The managerial revolution in the eighties, I suppose. It took place in business, took place in the National Health Service and it took place in education. I said that I wouldn't make value judgements, well I damn well will make one now. I believe that was the wrong move and I believed it has resulted in the education in this country becoming top heavy. So when Alan Barrett Danes – with all that knowledge stuffed in that brain of his about glaze technology – when he leaves he is not replaced. When Walter Keeler leaves, as he is, he will not be replaced. There may be another sub-Dean but you will not get anybody else eyeballing the student and saying, 'what about this, what about that?' You won't get people sharing things. What's wrong with sharing things? I remember being told in the eighties – sharing – you might contaminate their souls.

Well I do think that is a worry and I only wish that when some of us went to the Houses of Parliament just before the Labour government got in and we were asked to say our piece and I said exactly what I say to you now – restructure your education and you will have a better system. They wrote it down, some of them wrote it down, I saw him writing. He might have been writing 'not on your life', I don't know. But it hasn't happened.

Right, the last thing I want to write and end on a happy note is about revival. Talking to Peter Dworok about the Anagama kiln they have built at Rufford – I really do think that those people like those sort of middle forties to early fifties are very important people now. They hold a lot in their hands. They can go forwards with techniques and with understanding of materials and processes and make sure that all that Leach way does not die out, and there will be a balanced spectrum for ceramics.

Ending on a happy note – 1979 and I was pretty pessimistic – 1999 I am full of hope. Thank you very much.

In 2005–6 ICRC organised the 'Speak for Yourself' competition, to encourage makers to write about their own work. With no competition rules as such, the call for entries simply invited submissions of any length that 'deal with any aspect of the process of making ceramics or that explore, analyse or reflect on any issues that the work raises. The focus may be on something particular to the work or something of more general concern.' Submissions were received from ceramists in Canada, Nigeria, the USA, Mexico and France as well as the United Kingdom. This chapter is the first of two that began life as competition entries; it was the outright winner in the open category and was originally published in Issue 7 of *Interpreting Ceramics* (2007). 'A collection of small miseries' is a considered and sophisticated account of the thought processes that inform Carole Epp's activities as a ceramicist. She argues for a notion of the artist-maker as 'presenter of critical dialogue', capable of initiating social change, whose work can 'situate the viewer in a position of self-reflection'. The discussion covers a wide intellectual territory, weaving together personal concerns and socio-political issues. Epp has a light yet incisive touch with so-called 'heavy' theory and never loses sight of 'my own practical production of objects and attempts to imbue singular objects with the content and context that I desired'.

Interpreting Ceramics

Selected Essays

A Collection of Small Miseries: Studio Philosophy and Project Research

Carole Epp

The aim of my studio practice has been to analyse social reality through the creation of work dealing with issues of a political and humanitarian nature. Through an ethically sound methodology I aim to adequately represent the issues investigated in a manner that might also work towards social change. I chose to work in ceramics for numerous reasons, but primarily because I feel that the medium, its historical and contemporary contexts, aesthetics, and domestic associations offer the potential to speak about controversial and politically charged subject matter in a manner that is not limited by, but involves, theories of art, craft and political activism. The main connection that I am trying to make through the work is that the role of objects and ethics are central to an understanding of the social life of a culture.

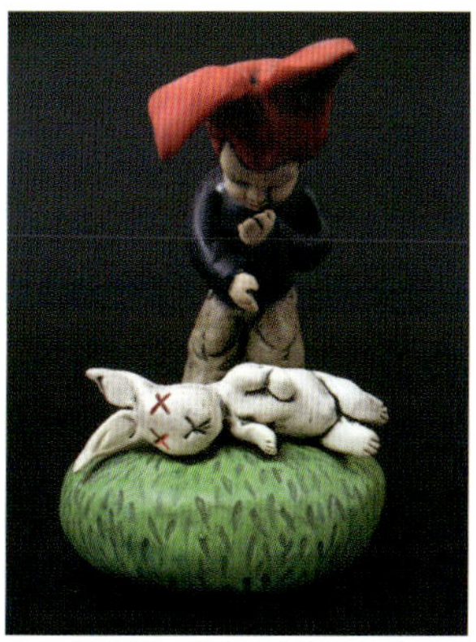

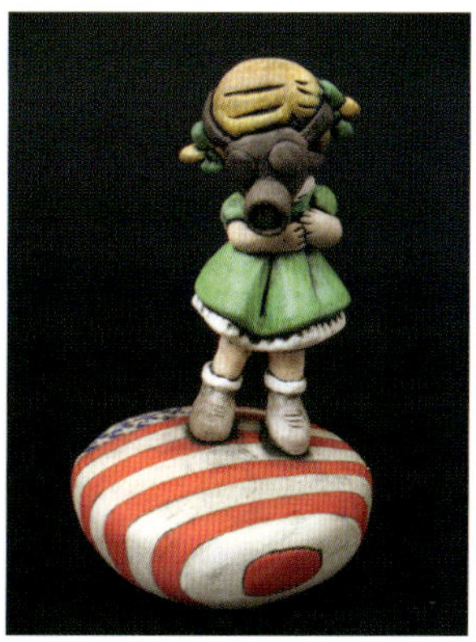

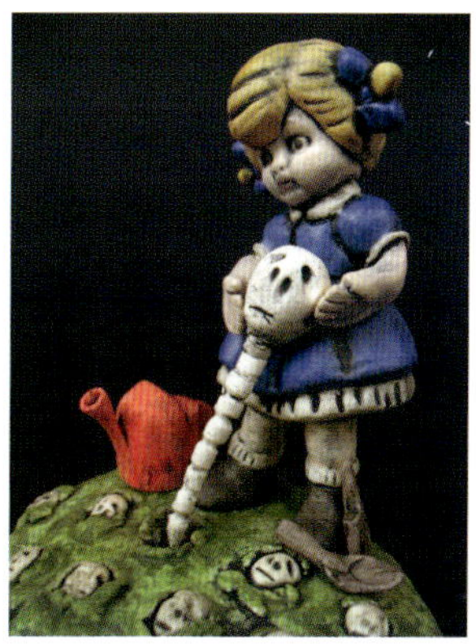

Fig 1. left, *Little did he know he would soon be next* (2005).

Fig 2. middle, *Such things brought tears to her eyes* (2005).

Fig 3. right, *The seeds would terminate them all* (2005).

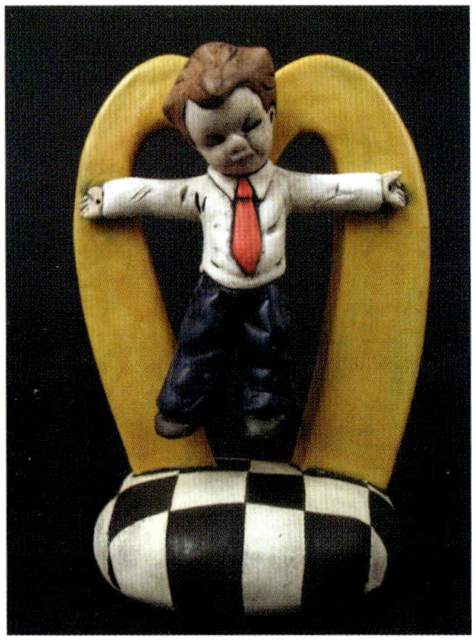

Fig 4. *He was dying for a hamburger* (2005).

Interestingly my investigation into the role of objects in our everyday lives and the life of society began through my desire to move away from my past practice of installation-based ceramics art and move towards an investigation focusing on the individual crafted object. Little did I know at that point in time that the next few years would develop this incentive into a body of research centring around the role, proliferation and context of objects within an economic discourse. In the beginning my struggles were based in my own practical production of objects and attempts to imbue singular objects with the content and context that I desired.

The body of work discussed is entitled *A Collection of Small Miseries*. It is a body of work that subverts and manipulates the traditional genre of collectible figurines by revealing an alternative representation of behaviour and morality in contemporary society. An analysis of consumer culture is unveiled and dialogue is presented regarding the personal relationship one has with global events and politics.

I have always had a firm belief in the ability of art to present individual and collective perspectives on life, as a source of documentation for an alternative writing of history and as a means of inciting change in the world. As Leon Trotsky saw it art was not a mirror but 'a hammer; it does not reflect, it shapes'.[1] I see my practice as both the mirror and the hammer, based on the belief that the time and space for contemplation is required before one can possess the incentive to change.

But to base an investigation of the social reality of consumer culture in politics, economics, humanitarian and ecological concerns, I have had to first evaluate my position relative to the issues. As artists establish themselves as presenters of critical dialogue, as witnesses to cultural/political/humanitarian events and as conscious social activists, they must work with awareness that their role is both precious and precarious when held in relation to appropriation and questions of identity. I have had to question what limits or rules, if any, are placed on artists who, through their work, present statements on such charged and controversial events as war or economic inequality. As media and journalism move towards an era of the abuse of personal narrative, exploiting individuals in times of crisis, manipulating them into signs to be associated with an event, artists must, rather than follow suit, establish an ethical code towards the subjects and topics they will re-interpret and re-present.

Our postmodern world is quickly becoming a 'globalised' world: one in which media and the internet provide us with access to information and perspectives that were previously unattainable from the comfort of our living rooms. This information provided needs much deciphering if one is to gain access to the central issues and events. We may have more access to information, however that information has never been so manipulated.

A focus on the awareness of my personal position and context was the starting point for the works created. I knew I had to acknowledge that my position was one of privilege. I knew that I did not want to attack the issues through a sympathetic or authoritarian framework that ran the risk of further victimisation or misrepresentation. I was also aware of the distance, geographically, emotionally and intellectually, from the issues, and that this directly impacted my understanding, response and reading of the events. So what was my participation with the issues I felt passionate to speak about? Where was I as an individual within the framework of the event? It became clearer and clearer to me that it was easy to say that one's life had little impact on such circumstances, yet this was a tactic used to defer responsibility when in fact my way of life, my ideals and actions were directly involved. And this is not in any way an attempt to set up a sort of us-versus-them mentality, but rather to see the enormity of the interconnectedness of our world, at a community level and at a global level. Through that understanding I chose to take the approach of consciously working from my personal standpoint and through a visual language of signs and metaphors that were a part of my culture and identity: which is part of the reason for the emphasis on consumer society in the work. But while the work developed as some of the most personal work I have made to date, it did not rely on my individual narrative at the expense of a larger dialogue, for as Rosalind Krauss stated, 'The privacy of our memories is what is most trivial about them; rather than our uniquely personal memories, it is those we share that form the "touchstone of humanity".' [2]

In 2004 I ran across an article in an issue of critical writing on the concept of 'resistance' in art practice published by *Parachute* magazine, which reinforced the position I had chosen to take in relation to these bodies of work. In the article, writer Elisabeth Wetterwald describes the position of artists towards global, political or social events as 'distant participation' and encourages a chameleon-like re-situating of the artist through the dissolution of the authority of the artist as author by recontextualising their standpoint and placing themselves not in opposition but in a state of awareness of the diverse perspectives and arguments for a given dialogue.[3] This situated the artist not as a contrasting force, presenting the opposing side, the underdog outlook, upon the world, but rather through an acute awareness of the artist's personal position, which allows for their context and the diverse context of others to be assimilated into a more elaborate dialogue.

The notion of resistance seems central to my practice as well as my life in that it offers a form of action that does not have to be directly linked to solutions. The questions and problems presented in my work are questions to which I have no solutions, yet I want to actively engage in the process of questioning in the hope that it might foster awareness and change. My understanding of Michel Foucault's theory of resistance positions power as disassociated from such central sources as 'the Law, the State, the institutions and forms of domination', instead locating it within the framework of the interconnection of all relations.[4] So if power is located throughout all relations, then the potential for resistance is not centralised at one level of society. But through presenting a form of resistance to critiqued ideologies one risks setting themselves up as oppositional to a defined source of power, in this case what we might term 'the Utopian ideology of the marketplace' and thus creates the potential for a replacement source of power. This in turn contradicts Foucault's theory of power situated not centrally but within a 'network of "power relations" that traverse the entirety of our relations'.[5] My challenge became to structure the critique within a framework of acknowledgment of my own complicity in the power structures.

Above all the aim was to create a body of work that did not focus too closely on individual narrative, but that did find its voice through personal context. I wanted to speak locally and globally at the same time, offer reflection and opportunity for change in the same

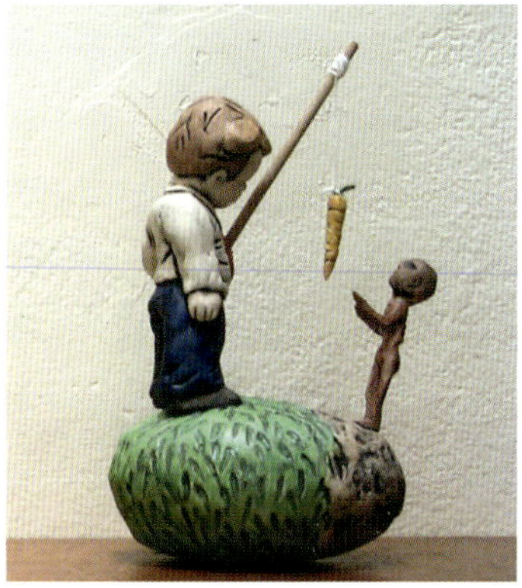

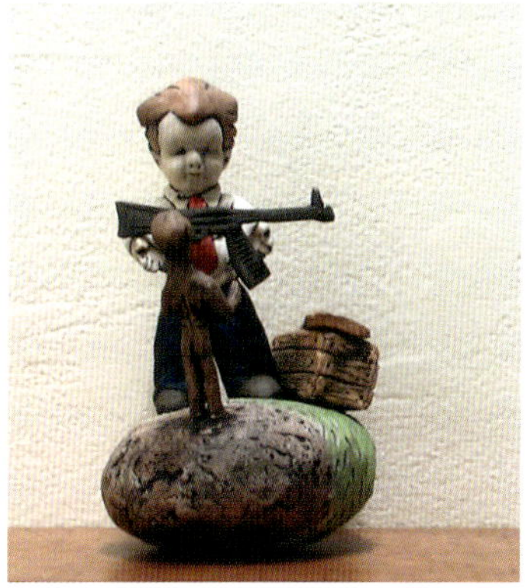

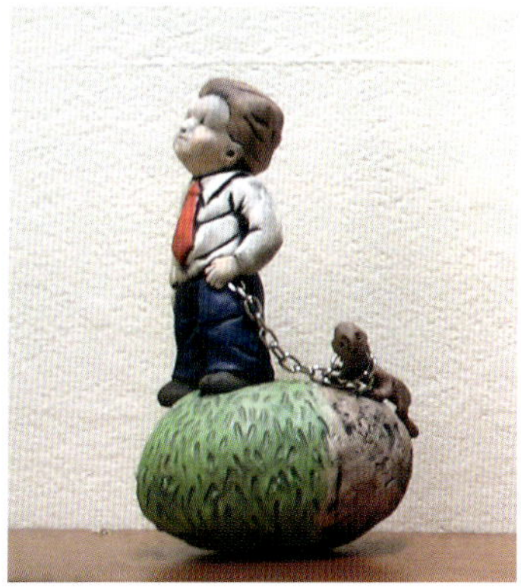

Fig 5. *He figured he was doing his part* (2005).

Fig 6. *He could think of a million ways for them to repay their debt* (2005).

Fig 7. *His great power was their great weakness* (2005).

breath and to bring to light Wetterwald's idea that 'what is at stake is to see the world not as a monster alien to oneself but as something in which one fully participates'.[6]

The Spectacle

A central investigation of my project is consumer culture, its commodified objects, and the impact of excessive consumption on particular dialogues of a social, political and humanitarian nature. Part of my aim was to establish the role of consumerism in the alienation of the individual in society and in creating gaps between different cultures. This led to writings by Guy Debord and the Situationist International on their presentation of similar ideas, and notions of the 'Spectacle'. I was particularly interested in their argument that consumption had taken such a hold on the individual and society that it was through such consumption that one would define their happiness.[7] Consumption, as they had come to realise, acted not only to define but also to suppress the individual and any form of personal freedom.[8] In Debord's words the Situationist project encompassed 'a systematic questioning of all the diversion and works of a society, a total critique of its idea of happiness … In societies where modern conditions of production prevail, all of life presents itself as an immense accumulation of spectacles. Everything that was lived has moved away into a representation.'[9]

I became interested in developing the means of presenting ideas of the Spectacle through analysis of our relationship to it, through the objects of mass production, but knew that there would be various problems along the way. What I set out to accomplish was the development of a body of work presenting the argument that it is through the objects that we consume that we have a direct impact on the surrounding world and its political, environmental, and humanitarian problems. But how then could I present these ideas of the Spectacle with direct relation to this thesis? The manner in which the Situationists attacked the issues was through attempts at the creation of anti-art or anti-situations, through the 'critical reflection of the "society of the spectacle", [which was] characterized by an absence of all authentic communication'.[10] In their pursuit of an adequate methodology of commentary, it seemed imperative to develop the means of working outside of that critiqued system, creating situations that offered different means of awareness for a desensitised populace.

What I had set out to accomplish with my work and research was to analyse my reading of the Spectacles presented to me in the media, critique my own culturally accepted indifference, which is a product of the systematic desensitisation of the Spectacle, and to locate a source of resistance within that dialogue. Trying to locate the work in the idea of the Spectacle was difficult but important as the Spectacle represents how we depict the world to ourselves, the interpretation of events that is totalitarian in essence and which, according to Debord, 'induces passivity rather than thinking, and a degradation of life into materialism'.[11]

When it came time to develop the means of presenting my own commentary of the Spectacle in my work I moved away from the Situationist methodology of working with the critique, instead siding with the approach that Marshall McLuhan addresses, locating the message within the medium.[12] This locating of the dialogue through the critiqued medium and its context unified the conceptual nature of the work with its physical manifestation

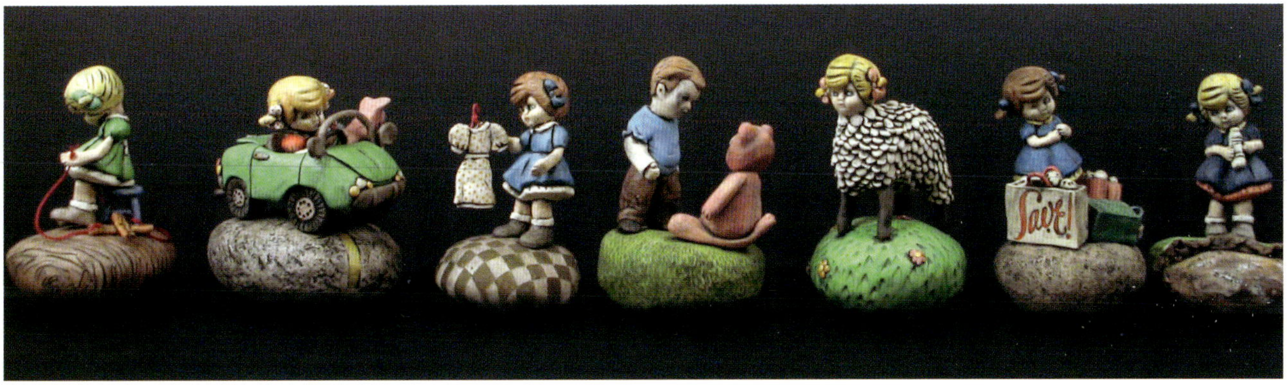

in such a way that it attempted to remove itself from the mere representation of the 'real' towards a more equivalent reproduction of a form of lived reality.

The development of *A Collection of Small Miseries*

A Collection of Small Miseries presents a narrative dialogue recalling my personal readings of the local and global events that I encounter daily. This series became my first to incorporate the figure. I began working on this project during the summer of 2004. I had for a time been interested in working with the figure and its history and context within ceramic art. I think in the past I had avoided this genre as I felt that there were too many strong associations with traditional representations of the figure that would have to be addressed within the work, and until this point I had not found a manner of using this context appropriately or to my advantage.

It seemed fitting that an investigation into personal narratives and humanitarian concerns should use the figure as a vehicle to transpose emotion and meaning. The figure could work on many levels, but primarily as a tool for projection. The initial reason that I turned towards figurative ceramics was to help situate myself, and my personal narrative, into the work. Previously I had always addressed the subject matter through a distancing from personal narrative; a methodology that I began to see as lacking in its ability to address its audience in a manner that would emphasise their own narrative in relation to the work. I knew that if I wanted to push my practice to the next level I had to start putting something on the line; I had to make a more consciously self-exposing stance in relation to the subject matter.

Needing to have the work directly linked with the world of the commodity, I began by looking for found pieces to use in moulds for the work, rather than begin by working with a modelled figure of my own making. Figurines such as the cheap knock-offs I used and their original counterparts, the closest link being the German Hummel figurines, were products created to represent a form of historical interpretation and ideology. Through subverting them I hoped to find a way of presenting more personal and reflective interpretations of history and society. I felt that these figurines acted as references and as readable signifiers highlighting my background and upbringing, as well as being a medium that contained a direct link to commodities in the market. Three figurines were chosen to

Fig 8. *Gluttony series* (2005).

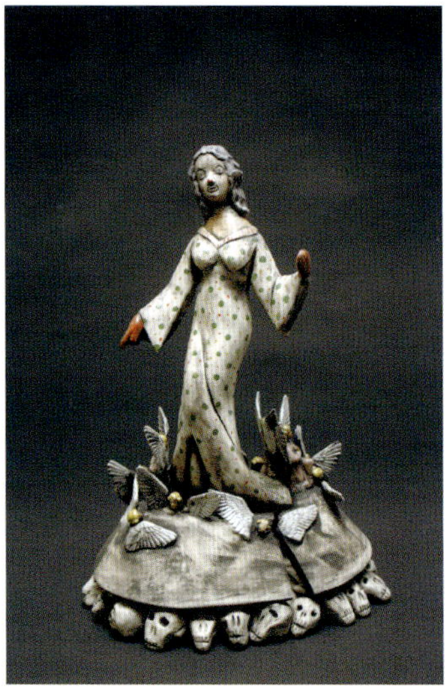

Fig 9. *She felt like a joke and was falling apart at the seams* (2011).

act as the models for the scenes to be produced; they consisted of two females and one male, bought at markets or second-hand shops.

The use of the traditional figurine was of course heavily laden with this context and history, some of which I was pleased to use to my advantage to manipulate and subvert. In particular the Utopian ideologies presented in the narrative scenes would be essential to a questioning of contemporary political and social ideologies. I was also interested in the development of the Hummel figurine as a form of visual propaganda during war times and how I might make connections with contemporary media, visual and consumer culture.

The nostalgic associations of the miniature figurines I felt could be used in an analysis of childhood as a source of identity development in which innocence and faith are determinates alongside curiosity and questioning. I felt a need with the work to have a strong link with narratives of childhood and innocence in order to juxtapose them with identity and behaviour development in adulthood and indifference taking the place of faith and innocence. I found it interesting to work with images that were nostalgic in nature, in that the past is often revered as being ideal, a strange concept in light of the fact that we've lived through it and know it to be otherwise. And it seemed ironic that it is in the nostalgic past as well as in the present that these issues exist, whereas, on the other hand, it is in the future that we might find the solutions to the problems.

The Collection and the consumer object

I was never under the impression that I would be able to present my research through a singular or limited number of objects and thus The Collection was born. This project I have come to realise has no end, as there is little hope for resolution to the issues that are investigated in the work. But the idea of The Collection was not an arbitrary one, as it also fed into the content of the work. In the beginning I had played around with the idea of the seven deadly sins as a Collection, an idea that I have since returned to, to unify the pieces selected for the exhibition of the work. This Collection of sins or bad habits comprises the morals and attitudes you inherit from the world and people around you as you grow and mature, all of which become an intricate part of your identity.

I was interested in the idea of collecting these bad habits in relation to the idea of how we define ourselves via the objects we collect and surround ourselves with. The following, taken from an Art Theory paper entitled 'Arguing the necessity of handcrafted ceramic objects', which I wrote in 2004, further describes this interaction with objects.

> Beginning early in life and cognitive development, the relationship that a child develops with objects precurses the development of language through an attachment to objects as a means of negotiating the world.[13] Objects aid in the negotiation of the world around us by supplying substantiated examples helping to represent intangibles in life and by acting as intermediaries between a person and the world.[14] While arguably this negotiation and relationship is an interaction between cognitive beings and inanimate objects, it is still an interaction that directs, motivates and impacts our daily lives in subtle and unconscious ways. Objects contain signifiers of each owner's ideals, attitudes, and morals. By looking at objects as signs we can analyze

> and determine the role of objects in a greater context than that of daily life; that is in their role as historical markers, social commentary, and political instruments, inciting change in our negotiation of the world around us privately, publicly and globally.

The searching out, coveting and hoarding of objects incorporates an act of projection. Objects are chosen based upon their function as signifiers of wealth, values, taste, and priorities.[15] But it is not the objects themselves that contain these intrinsic values; culture and economy place the objects within a system, and we as consumers buy into those value systems because we believe that the objects will project desirable values about our identity outwardly for us. As James Deetz points out 'material culture is that segment of man's physical environment which is purposely shaped by him according to a culturally dictated plan'.[16] The reality becomes, as a result, that the objects often project divergent representations than those we desire. Take, for example, the modern four-wheel-drive family sedan or jeep which is consumed based on the notion that it implies a return to nature, an outdoorsy spirit and respect, a valuing of technology and crafted design, when in reality it functions as a symbol of greed, over-consumption and environmental degradation. We seek to define ourselves through our objects, yet those objects are more powerful in their defining than we intend. It is a case of master being dependant upon slave, not slave to master. Baudrillard defines this relationship in terms of the seducer and the object; wherein the seducer becomes seduced thereby giving up control of the situation.[17] We must let go of the notion that the objects are there to be ordered, controlled and used, instead we must bring to light the reciprocal relationship between object and owner in terms of defining.

The reason for the importance of referencing The Collection and the consumer object was to directly link them to the consumer mentality/obsession of the first-world culture I am a part of. This is done with the aim of highlighting the role of consumerism in the perpetual cycle of destruction of natural resources, the proliferation of war, the imposed dependence created by mishandled foreign policy and the progress of science and technology towards monetary gain over sustainable practices. The reference to the collectable figurine was to purposely place the viewer in the position of consumer to highlight their personal role and impact upon the issues.

The Collection also brings about the idea of pride. Collectors pride themselves on the acquisition of rare, precious or unique pieces. But I also wanted to look at pride in the sense of our society and what it prides itself upon, what it is that we chose to celebrate and relish. Contemporary first-world culture can hardly hide behind the fact that it takes a sick form of pride in behaviour that is morally corrupt. But the media perpetuates this and the economy proves that we buy into it. This Collection highlights the societal pride that is taken in technological advancements regardless of their consequences, the glory of war and conquering terrorism, and the pride in the proliferation of media that promotes violence and aggression. But that pride is a thin veil that hides the truth of the disturbing nature of society, but it is a veil that politicians, scientists, marketing and advertising executives, corporate CEOs and a majority of the population cling to rather than face the overwhelming problems of our world.

Michel Foucault spoke of the collection of objects as a means of acquiring knowledge, and based on the idea that knowledge was power, and vice versa power was

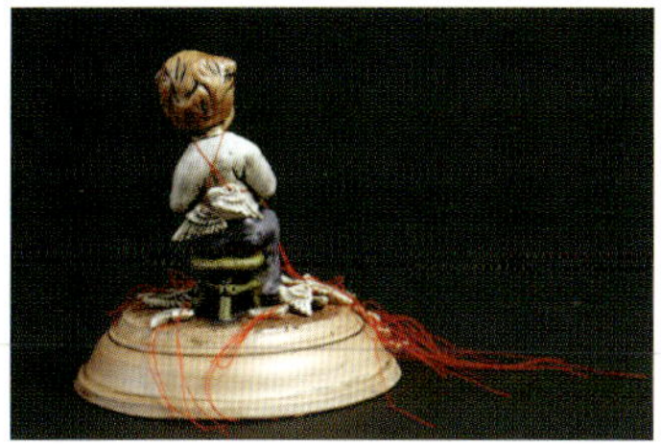

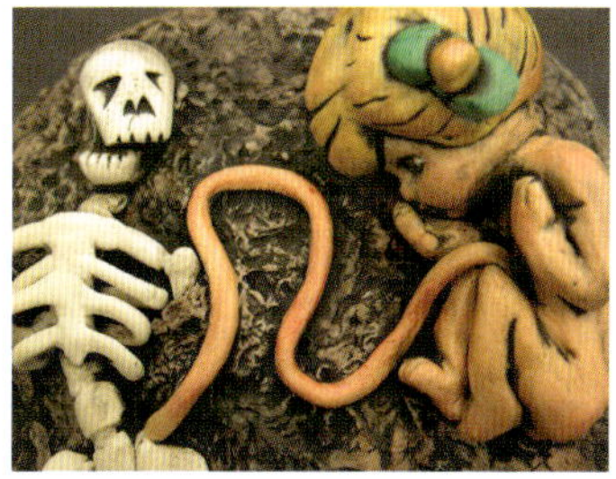

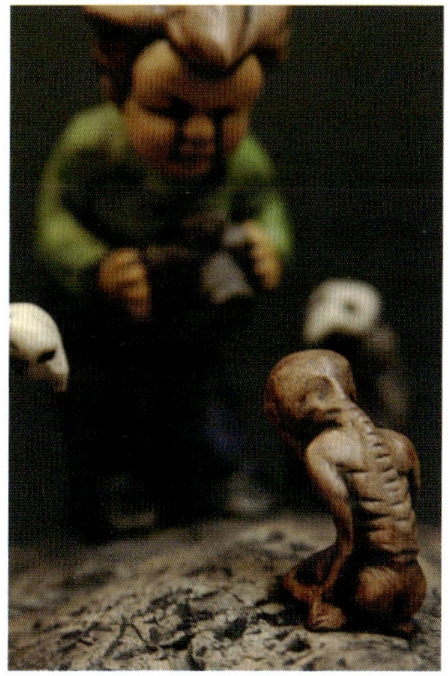

Fig 10. *Faking it as best he could* (2009).

Fig 11. *Nature/Nurture* (detail) (2008).

Fig 12. *He maintained an ethical distance (detail)* (2008).

All photos: Carole Epp.

knowledge, then the objects possessed could be used as tools of comparison between the power and knowledge of one individual and the next.[18] Through this work I am aiming to present alternative perspectives and to increase knowledge of the issues so that the knowledge gained might truly be used as power, that being the power to create change.

Whereas The Collection implies a form of classification and order, the work seems to deny the possibility of this through its unsystematic attack on the issues presented, and the ultimate difficulty of controlling, dismantling or deconstructing the structures that create the problems. The work offers limited possibilities for change in the face of overwhelmingly negative situations. The open-ended aspect of The Collection, its change and growth over time, parallels my own interaction with the subject matter and my relational readings of the events over time. The growth and change of The Collection reflects my incentive to change upon attaining greater knowledge of the issues, which fosters a proactive change of behaviour.

But the irony of the object is ever present in the work. To critique consumerism through its commodified objects becomes problematic and runs the risk of having the work turn back upon itself and become an element of the critique rather than a space for the presentation of the critique. While I have been consciously aware of that risk, it has been in the hope that the objects would bring light to the condition of their context through a distance produced by the introduction of other readings and context present in the work.[19]

Beauty, kitsch and ideology

The refined beauty often associated with the ceramic medium is to me a perfect tool to manipulate audience expectations. To use beauty as a carrier for such subject matter creates an accessible entry point into the work for the viewer, one that allows them to interact with controversial and emotionally charged subject matter through means that are easily digested and comfortable.[20] Beauty, decoration and kitsch are used as entry points and context for the work, but once the viewer is actively engaged with the work and decoding the layers of subject matter, the aim is to create a less positive emotional response which moves beyond a reliance upon formal aesthetic readings. Susan Best discusses the affect of art on an audience in an article entitled, 'What is affect? Considering the affective dimension of contemporary installation art', in which she looks to Freud and his analysis of the Ego and the Id. In this analysis the argument is presented that 'sensations of pleasurable nature have not anything impelling about them, whereas unpleasurable ones have it in the highest degree ... The latter impel towards change, towards discharge and that is why we interpret unpleasurable as implying a heightening and pleasure as a lowering of energic cathexis.'[21]

While we tend to respond unfavourably to subject matter if it is presented through confrontational means, 'positive affects have a limited call on our psyche'.[22] Thus I have consciously worked to maintain a relationship between both the positive and negative in the work; one to entice, the other to motivate. This manipulation of beauty and horror within the object lies parallel with the thin line between beauty and the grotesque in life, which directly impacts our compulsion towards and our rejection of events of a disturbing nature. Similarly Charles Baudelaire stated, 'beauty as encompassing the morbid and the perverse as well as the strangely familiar'.[23]

From the beginning I was fully aware that the vehicle I have chosen to work with was inescapably kitsch, and I went into the investigation of its context with the aim of using this essential nature of the chosen figurine objects to my advantage, similar to the use of beauty. But the use of kitsch, I was to discover, was also highly problematic and limited in its reading to relativist theories and particular cultural contexts.[24] But since the work was using my personal context as a beginning, it was essential that the pieces speak of that context through the mass-produced kitsch objects of my upbringing. Contemporary Western art analyses kitsch through theory and critical analysis, and many artists have made elitist, esoteric or aesthetic works based on the historic, anthropological and social context of kitsch. My initial and main interest was in the proliferation of kitsch objects in the global economy, as accurately stated by Jacques Sternberg, 'Kitsch is everywhere. Even more pervasive and indestructible now that it is fused to a civilization based on excess consumption.'[25]

I was also intrigued by the use of kitsch in the political realm, in particular totalitarian politics, and the morally uneasy relationship between political leaders whose images are turned into mass-produced/consumed kitsch objects, and the realities of their regimes. According to Tomas Kulka's writing on kitsch, in which he references both Milan Kundera and Saul Friedlander, kitsch has been used 'as a main instrument for the manipulation of the masses by communist regimes' and it has been shown 'how central a role it played in the mobilization of the masses in Hitler's Germany'.[26] This use of kitsch as propaganda became interesting to me as a display of the pervasiveness of kitsch throughout a variety of arenas of visual culture, its diverse readings in historical and in contemporary contexts as a means of disseminating ideology, and most interestingly as a tool of manipulation. Kitsch downplays the complexity of everyday life and the individual through the creation of generalised and stereotyped ideologies, which the majority of culture falls prey to on some level. I would argue that the reach of contemporary kitsch is far greater than we care to acknowledge, infiltrating all levels of media and visual culture, and the majority of contemporary art has a conscious or unconscious relationship with it.

But my main interest was in the associations of kitsch figurine as the ultimate lie, the presenter of Utopian ideology: that ideology being that the world is perfect, an ideology that puts us at ease with our situation through a false identification with others, an ideology that sits at an uneasy distance from most notions of 'reality' and which does not compel us towards any sort of personal re-evaluation or change. Clement Greenberg exemplified the critique of kitsch ideology when he stated that kitsch was 'the epitome of all that is spurious in the life of our times'.[27] The analysis of ideology and the resulting hegemony mark one of the central dialogues of the work. The particular ideologies questioned are not simply those presented by the kitsch objects, but rather those that perpetuate the proliferation of kitsch objects. It is the ideologies I am most familiar with, those of a capitalist society that I am aiming to question. I wanted to use objects that directly referenced those sorts of ideological beliefs that are proliferated through the Spectacle and which contribute to the system of social/cultural lies that individuals perpetually fall back upon in their everyday lives as a means of escaping responsibility for their actions, or for their inaction relative to the actions of others. The notion of ideology is itself problematic within the work, in that trying to represent an analysis of ideology risks creating a polemic dialogue that assumes another ideology to replace the one analysed. And I was also aware that by using kitsch, an instrument associated with conformative and stereotypical ideologies of behaviour, I would have to create proper balance when referencing personal, idiosyncratic narratives so that they would not become a part of a larger universal and simplified commentary. I knew this would be working counter to the prescribed aims of kitsch. Yet I maintain that I wanted to use aspects of kitsch such as our attitudes, reading of, and emotional response towards them to drive certain elements of the subject matter. I knew that my challenge would be to rework the reading of the objects so that although they came across as kitsch, they would still situate the viewer in a position of self-reflection, beyond simple self-identification in a larger narrative.

The analysis of political and social ideologies and similarly the investigation of the theory of 'resistance' are both aspects of the work that remain open-ended, in that they offer more questions than answers. But if conclusions could not be reached then at least I wanted to develop the means or tools for destabilising the hegemony of the Spectacle and offer possibilities for the creation of resistance and change in one's personal life in relation to the actual events at the centre of the Spectacle. As stated by Greil Marcus in the article, 'The long walk of the Situationist International', 'if capitalism had shifted its organization from production to consumption and its means of control from economic misery to false consciousness, then the task of would-be revolutionaries was to bring about a recognition of the life already lived by almost everyone'.[28]

The miniature

The challenge for myself at the beginning of this project was to investigate different manners of presentation with the aim of developing work that would be more cohesive in its scale, production and presentation in relation to subject matter; I then chose to move away from my past of working in installation and to reinvest in the object. The move away from large-scale, physical presence and the interaction of objects in space towards focus upon the object became a more fruitful investigation than I had intended. But I quickly realised that scale still played a crucial function in the work, however now at the other end of the spectrum.

The figurines quickly evolved into figures on a base that acted as a platform for the narrative. The bases began to play a part in the narrative as well as to contain the subject matter in small hermetic scenes, miniature in scale. And although each varied in its execution, they deliberately maintained a reference to the originals. The formal nature of the scenes create a world of arrested time through the isolation of singular events commonly associated with and presented by the spectacle of the media, reinterpreted and removed from that speed of information via the medium of ceramics.[29] This allows for pause and a space for reflection and contemplation. This introspective and interior nature of the miniature object relates the subject matter back to the viewer via relational analysis of the subject matter to their own daily lives.[30] The ability of a small object to offer layers of unfolding information within a small container reflects the unfolding nature of our lives and creation of identity.

The miniature has an interesting past in art history and I was intrigued about using its scale as a way of presenting controversial subject matter in the work. Small works tend to be read as timid, fragile, private and inconsequential, whereas a larger scale can evoke the monument and authoritarian readings.[31] I wanted the work to exist on a scale that referenced the domestic sphere, the body and the commodity.[32] The miniature offered this while also breaking from a reading of the artist's authoritative stance.[33] While the work was highly personal and subjective, it was also presented and grounded in research. I wanted to make sure that its reading would not be viewed as moralistic, authoritative, filled with hierarchical or oppositional didactic readings. The use of miniature also allowed a move away from the grandiose spectacle of larger work, and therefore allowing the work to adequately focus on the grandiose spectacle of the subject matter.

The formal nature of the miniature commands a certain degree of investigation. The closer scrutiny required in reading the objects directly relates to the level of inquiry commanded by the subject matter.[34] Scale is used to bring the viewer into a more intimate relationship with the object, presenting an agreeable position in which to investigate the confrontational subject matter.[35] Were the work to be confrontational in its presence as well as in its subject matter I felt that viewers would be tempted to turn away and not invest in the layered dialogue presented. The only way for the work to be successful was for the message to get across, the dialogue to be activated in the viewer; aesthetics, process and craftsmanship became secondary to this exchange between viewer and content. As stated by Paul Ardenne in *Contemporary Practices: Art as Experience*, 'artistic expression [is] the gesture of introspection, of punctual questioning, of encounter taking precedence over form'.[36] I wanted to create objects that would be appealing and accessible, inviting in scale, decoration and aesthetics, but which would unveil themselves as to their true nature upon closer inspection. To trick the viewer into investing in the objects before being repelled by them would be a fine line to walk between beauty, fetish and disgust, but one that I felt offered the possibility of a greater exchange between object and viewer. The miniature offered the possibility of presenting the subject matter in a way that was controllable, non-aggressive and potentially humorous.[37] The creation of objects that would require contemplative visual and intellectual analysis, would also allow for a slower pace of discovery for the viewer. In this manner the controversial subject matter could be digested at a pace determined by the viewer.

In direct reference to particular narratives in the subject matter I wanted to place the viewer in a position where their scale in relation to the object 'worlds' could potentially be conceived of in terms of a god-like scale.[38] The small scale of the figurine worlds render the viewer gigantic and in a position of control. This sense of control relates directly back to the control individuals have in relation to the world around them through active participation or indifference. The overseeing of the smaller world from the position of control is also reflected back to the narratives presented about scientists, corporations and tyrannical governments acting without moral reflection on their control and manipulation of the environment, the economy, the global population, technology and industry.
The scale of the viewer's body in relation to the object also creates a sense of isolation which mirrors the manners in which we can socially justify and isolate ourselves from responsibility towards what is happening in the local, national and global arenas. The

pieces do, however, run the risk of disconnecting the viewer from the subject matter both physically and emotionally as a result of their scale. This is perhaps similar to the separation we create for ourselves from a more meaningful engagement in the world around us. And I felt that if that disconnection were present it might parallel that distance created by media culture and the Spectacle.

It is my intent that the emotional intensity of the miniature scenes and the complexity of the messages they carry will befit the work, in that they may still manage to create a sense of overwhelming frustration in the viewer that is linked directly to this emotion and not the presence of the overbearing physical objects, which are often seen as monumental and authoritative.[39] Most importantly the miniature, in contrast to the gigantic, references more so our failing rather than our victories.[40] They become non-monuments to our shortcomings, rather than the glorification of our successes.

The exhibition

The installation of *A Collection of Small Miseries* was based upon the idea, and the importance, of the collection as a representation of the mass proliferation of objects in consumer culture. My aim was to intentionally position the viewer in a space that would emphasise their role as a consumer through an environment reminiscent of the domestic sphere, wherein one might display their prized collection. I chose to highlight the changing subject matter of the series through installing the work in thematic groupings, each on a separate wooden shelf attached to the walls of the space. These shelves where fabricated to resemble a mantelpiece or a decorative trophy shelf. This more ornate finish to the shelves brought them into dialogue with the context of the work, rather than simply serving their functional purpose, through emphasising our glorification of the immoral behaviour that the pieces portray. Brass plates were also used as title cards for the works, again referencing trophies and collections but also because of their reflective quality which confronted the viewer with their own image when engaging with the work, which assisted in emphasising their personal interaction with the subject matter. The titles were important as a device highlighting specific references, and to introduce humour or nostalgic references.

Notes

1 LeonTrotsky, *Literature and Revolution* (Ann Abor, Michigan: University of Michigan Press, 1968), pp. 136–61.
2 Susan Stewart and Ralph Rugoff, *At The Threshold of the Visible, Miniscule and Small-Scale Art, 1964–1996* (New York: Independent Curators Inc., 1997), p. 25.
3 Elisabeth Wetterwald, 'La rivoluzione non siamo noi: Pierre Joseph and Francis Alys', *Parachute*, 115:07,08,09 (2004), p. 86.
4 Jean-Ernest Joos, 'Making resistance work: on Alicia Framis' interventions', *Parachute*, 115:07,08,09 (2004), p. 50; L. Hubert Dreyfus, 'Being and power: Heidegger and Foucault', from the website http://ist-socrates.berkeley.edu/~hdreyfus/html/paper_being.html (June 2005), for the Department of Philosophy at the University of California, Berkeley.
5 *Ibid*., pp. 50–1.
6 Wetterwald , 'La rivoluzione non siamo noi', p. 90.
7 Greil Marcus, 'The long walk of the Situationist International', in Tom McDonough (ed.), *Guy Debord and the Situationist International Text and Documents* (Cambridge, Massachusetts: October Books, The MIT Press, 2004), p. 3.

8 *Ibid.*
9 *Ibid.*, p. 7.
10 Vincent Kauffman, 'Angels of purity', trans. John Goodman, in McDonough (ed.), *Guy Debord and the Situationist International Text and Documents*, p. 285.
11 Marcus, 'The long walk of the Situationist International', p. 8.
12 Jean Baudrillard, www.csun.edu/~hfspc002/baud/ (January 2005), referencing Jean Baudrillard, Simulations, trans. Paul Foss, Paul Patton and Philip Beitchman (New York: Semiotext(e), 1981, 1983). [SIM] (January 2005).
13 Pamela Johnson, 'Out of touch: the meaning of making in the digital age', in Tanya Harrod (ed.), *Obscure Objects of Desire: Reviewing the Crafts in the Twentieth Century* (London: Crafts Council, 1997), p. 295.
14 Margaret West, 'Touching hands and other values – the social implications of craft', Craft Australia: 1995 National Crafts Conference Papers, *Making Culture: Crafts, Communication and Commerce* (New South Wales: Craft Australia, 1996), p. 62.
15 Sandra Flood, 'The lives of objects', in Paula Gustafson (ed.), *Craft Perception and Practice: A Canadian Discourse* (Vancouver: Ronsdale Press, 2002), p. 101.
16 Susan M. Pearce, *Museums, Objects and Collection: A Cultural Study* (Leicester and London, Leicester University Press, 1992), p. 5.
17 Jean Baudrillard, *Fatal Strategies* (New York: Semiotexte(e), 1990), p. 111.
18 Eilean Hooper-Greenhill (ed.) 'Museum communication: an introductory essay', in *The Educational Role of the Museum* (London: Routledge, 1994), p. 21; Sandra Alfoldy, 'Buy me and become me', in Harrod (ed.), *Obscure Objects of Desire*, p. 334.
19 Paul Wood, 'Commodity', in Robert S. Nelson and Richard Shiff (eds), *Critical Terms for Art History* (Chicago and London: The University of Chicago Press, 1996), p. 273.
20 Johnson, 'Out of touch', p. 293. Neal Benezra and Olga M. Viso, *Distemper: Dissonant Themes in the Art of the 1990s* (New York: Distributed Art Publishers, 1996), p. 17.
21 Susan Best, 'What is affect? Considering the affective dimension of contemporary installation art', *Australian and New Zealand Journal of Art*, 2:2 (2001) and 3:1 (2002), pp. 207–8.
22 *Ibid.*
23 Benezra and Viso, *Distemper*, p. 15.
24 Thomas Kulka, *Kitsch and Art* (University Park, Pennsylvania: Pennsylvania State University Press, 1996), p. 2.
25 *Ibid.*, p. 13.
26 *Ibid.*, p. 17. See Milan Kundera, *The Unbearable Lightness of Being* (New York: Harper and Row, 1984), p. 251; Saul Friedlander, *Reflections of Nazism: Essay on Kitsch and Death* (New York: Harper and Row, 1984).
27 Greenberg.
28 Marcus, 'The long walk', p. 10.
29 Susan Stewart, *On Longing. Narratives of the Miniature, the Gigantic, the Souvenir, the Collection* (Durham, North Carolina and London: Duke University Press, 1993), p. 67.
30 *Ibid.*, p. 68.
31 Stewart and Rugoff, *At The Threshold of the Visible*, p. 11.
32 *Ibid.*, p. 69.
33 *Ibid.*, p. 11.
34 *Ibid.*, p. 12.
35 *Ibid.*, p. 69.
36 Paul Ardenne 'Experimenting with the real: Art and reality at the end of the twentieth century', trans. Stephen Wright, in Pascal Becusse and Laurent Goumarre, *Contemporary Practices: Art as Experience* (Paris: Editions Dis Voir, 1999), p. 14.
37 Stewart and Rugoff, *At The Threshold of the Visible*, p. 14.
38 Stewart, *On Longing*, p. 56 and p. 75.
39 Stewart and Rugoff, *At The Threshold of the Visible*, p. 27.
40 *Ibid.*, p. 11 and p. 83.

The Casualties Project' was a 'Highly Commended' entry in the 'Speak for Yourself' competition and was first published in Issue 7 of *Interpreting Ceramics*. A relatively short piece of writing, it conveys a very immediate sense of Ozioma Onuzulike's experience as a ceramist in contemporary Nigeria. His father had been a military police officer in Biafra and both parents were caught up in the civil war: 'I was first exposed to the horrors of war through tales told by them. … I grew up worried over how men can inflict so much pain on fellow men.' This chapter describes the artist's studio project in which clay transgressed its traditional boundaries by playing strategic roles in the examination of the perennial violence and conflicts around the world. Onuzulike's main influences and motivation for the project are described, along with a list of ceramics studio processes and gestures upon which he has drawn as creative sources. A moving section subtitled 'Casualties Idiom' lists horrifying practices, drawing metaphorical connections with the actions involved in making ceramics. Percussive, at moments frantic, this is an innovative account that gathers in pace, rises to a crescendo and mutates into poetry. Ozioma Onuzulike was awarded a PhD in Art History (2007) by the University of Nigeria, Nsukka, where he lectures in the Department of Fine and Applied Arts.

My Hands in Clay and Other Media: The 'CASUALTIES' Project

Ozioma Onuzulike

Up until recently, the clay medium has not been taken very 'seriously' within the mainstream art historical and critical circuit. This is perhaps because clay appears to be a 'traditional' medium that has been tagged with the limiting badge of 'utility'. Works in clay have for so long suffered critical invisibility because of the high academic partition walls by which they have been marginalised as 'craft' or 'applied art' or 'low art'.

For me, however, clay holds a natural sensibility, and persuasive power, capable of activating the creative idioms inherent in other materials or media found around my immediate Nsukka environment (Nsukka is the location of the University of Nigeria). I have sought to tap into the idioms and metaphors locked into clay and its working processes, as well as those locked into a range of other materials around me. I brought these together for the sake of expanding the horsepower of clay for my 'CASUALTIES' project, spanning 2001–2005.

CASUALTIES: Why 'casualties'?

My country Nigeria fought a devastating civil war, which ended just two years before I was born in 1972. While growing up under my father (a veteran Biafran military police officer) and my mother, who took active part in the *Oso agha* (literally, 'war race' or 'running from war') episode of the 1967–70 era, I was first exposed to the horrors of war through tales told by them. My parents would often shake their heads in pain and sob bitterly at the thought of close friends and family members who were 'eaten' by the avoidable war. Particularly, my mother's recitation of the dirges usually sung by hungry and betrayed Biafran soldiers during the war, often in honour of their slain colleagues, drew tears to her eyes. And mine too. These stories have eventually found their way back to my pet studio project ...

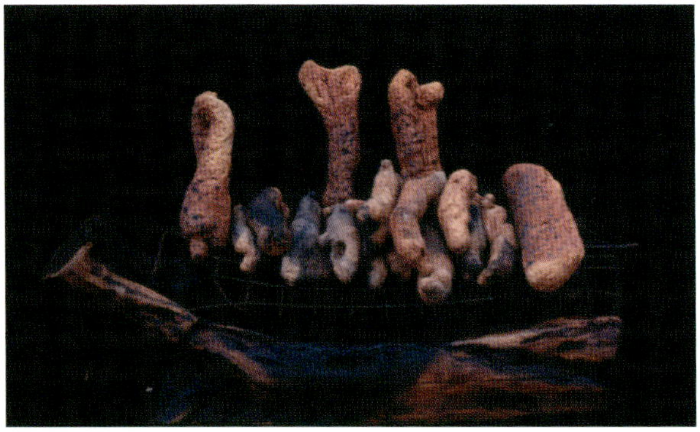

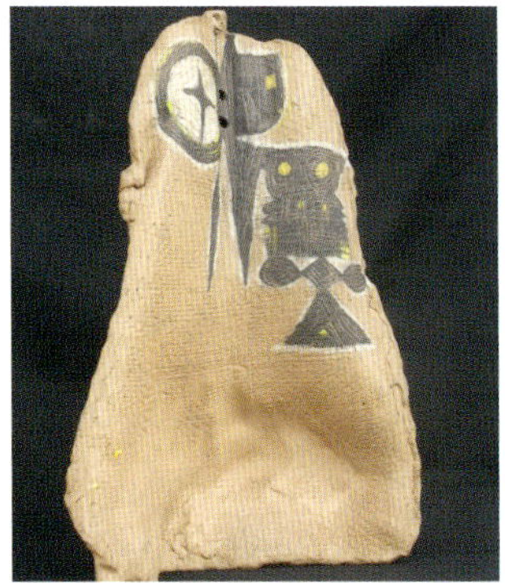

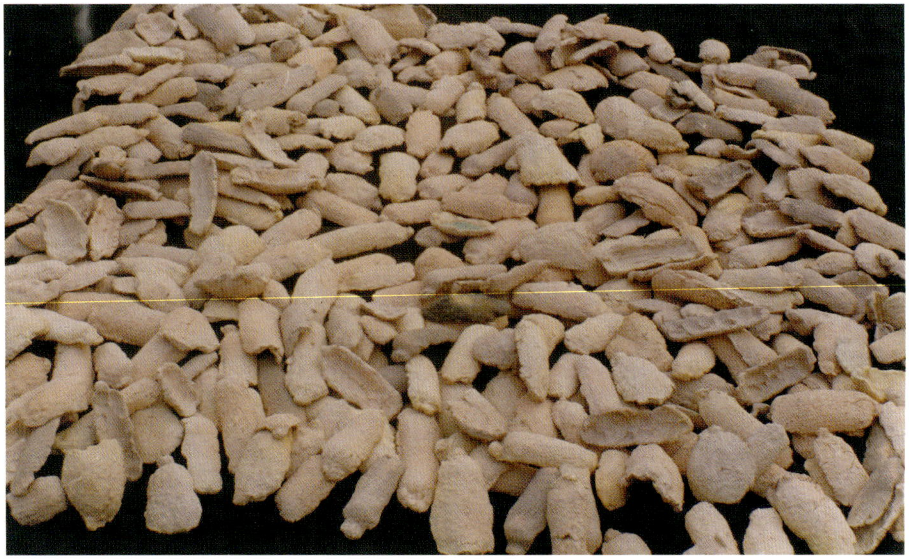

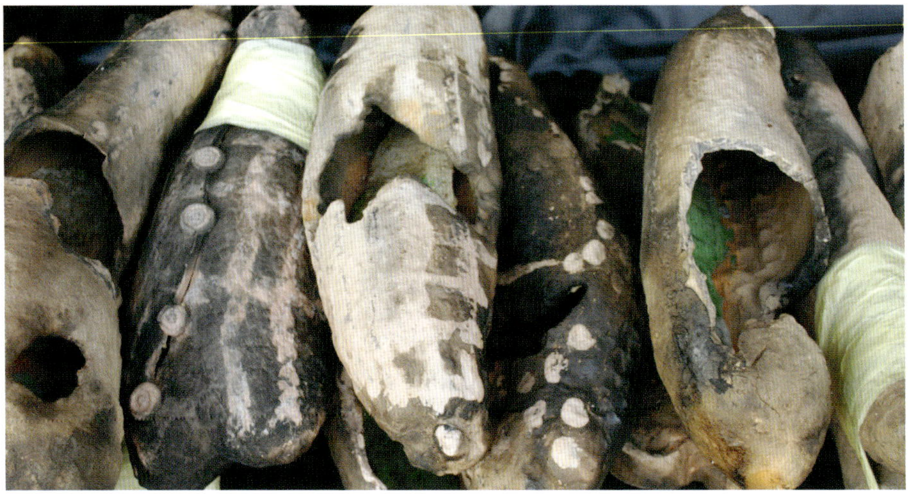

Clockwise from top left

Fig 1. *Yam Bodies I.*

Fig 2. *Politician I.*

Fig 3. *Mass Burial I.*

Fig 4. *Orthopedic Hospital III.*

I grew up worried over how men can inflict so much pain on fellow men. I read about armed conflicts in books, journals and magazines. I saw the horrors of war on the television. I was shocked by the brutal conflicts and horrors going on around the world – Angola, Burundi, Sierra Leone, Liberia, Kosovo, Bosnia, Kuwait, Iraq, Iran, Israel, Palestine, Cote d' Ivoire, the Congo, Pakistan, India, Rwanda ... terrorist bombing in different parts of the world is already a recurring decimal!

Beyond physical wars and terrorism, I also began to see the idea of 'casualties' in a new light. For instance, the bad roads across Africa generate lots of uncounted casualties on a daily basis. Victims or casualties usually end up in mass graves or some ill-equipped orthopaedic hospitals. There are also lots of political casualties – those who are rigged out of elections or eliminated entirely by assassination. I also see African leaders causing the masses of Africa to fall victim to hunger, starvation, disease and death through bad economic policies, the looting of the communal treasury and other forms of corruption.

These are the issues being raised and interrogated by the works in my 'CASUALTIES' project. They include titles such as *Refugees I*, *Genocide*, *Suyascape*, *Victim*, *Yam Bodies I* (Fig 1), *Burial Arrangements*, *Calendar II: Explosives Market*, *Ejigbo and Oke Afa Canal Disaster*, *Politician I* (Fig 2), *Politician II*, *Mass Burial I* (Fig 3) and *Orthopedic Hospital III* (Fig 4). They draw upon the long list of metaphors identified below for their signification.

The 'casualties' idiom

For me, every technical gesture in the ceramics studio relates directly to the causes and effects of 'casualties'. In such works as *Politician I*, *Politician II*, *Mass Burial I* and *Orthopedic Hospital II*, I make direct and indirect references to metaphors relating to clay winning, working and firing processes such as hammering, kneading, wedging, pinching, crushing, slaking, stabbing, cutting, mixing, loading, bundling, scourging, scorching, crumpling, rupturing, locking, burning, roasting, ramming, choking ...

When in such works as *Refugees I* (Fig 5), *Burial Arrangements* (Fig 6), *More Casualties* (Fig 7) and *Amputees* (Fig 8) you find pinched terracotta figures conjoined with household *garri* and *akpu* colanders, cassava graters and gravel sieves crafted by local tinkers from off-cuts of aluminium roofing sheets, then ruminate over elimination, relocation, demarcation, division, separation, sorting, distancing, scourging, isolation, extermination, exclusion, marginalisation, screening, besieging, amputation, hammering, crushing, maiming, slashing, hacking, disfiguring, perforating, shooting, terrorising, sawing, handicapping, harassing, horrifying, emasculating, demobilising, paralysing, damaging, violating, afflicting, annihilating, assaulting, destroying, battling, bombarding, bastardising, battering, beating, flogging, slapping, kicking, bruising, wounding, beheading, blowing, exploding, blistering, buffeting, breaking, bulldozing, butchering, splitting, squeezing ...

When, as in *Suyascape* (Fig 9) and *Ejigbo and Oke Afa Canal Disaster* (Fig 10), I pass nails and rods through slabs of clay before they dry and are fired, I strive to raise questions relating to nailing, screwing, killing, shooting, collision, raping, indicting, violating ...

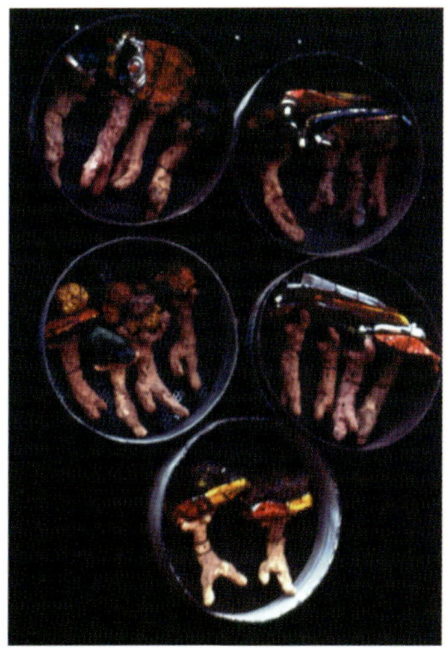

Fig 5. *Refugees I.*

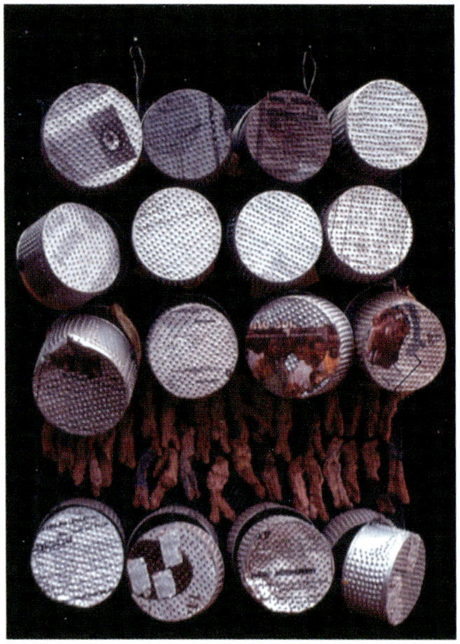

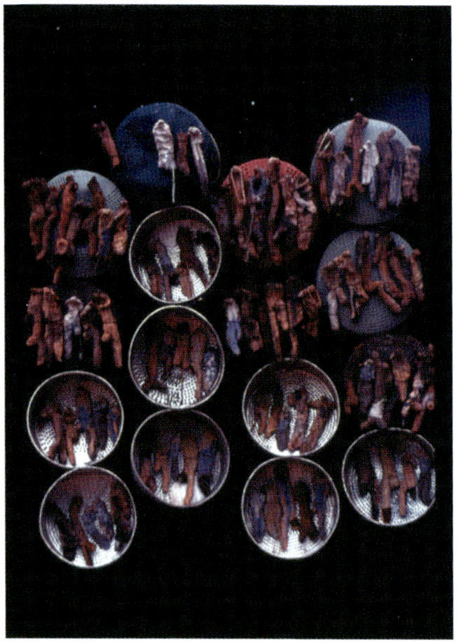

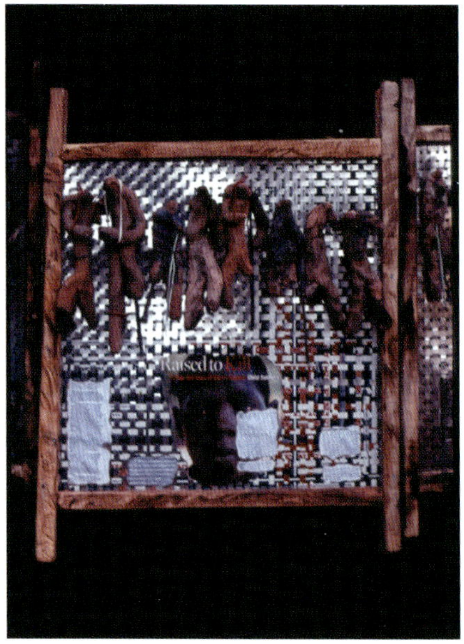

When, as in *Refugees II*, you find the pinched-out figures installed on chicken mesh used widely in poultry farms and market stalls, then think deeply about separation, partitioning, caging, capturing, monitoring, spying, demarcating, restricting, blockading, restraining, excluding, hindering, handcuffing, hijacking, clamping, arraigning, barring … When I make the fleeing refugee figures carry loads of iron slag sourced from old iron-smelting sites at Nsukka I am simply drawing attention to exploitation, abandonment, trampling, rejection, littering, bloodletting … When I tie the figures with the cobbler's twine and wire I am drawing attention to binding, gathering, bandaging, healing, rehabilitating …

Conclusion

I have looked through
the sharp eyes
of cassava graters and nails;
the bulging eyes of hammered cans;
the magnifying lenses of garri colanders;
gravel sieves, chicken mesh, garri graters …

I have looked through
the spy holes
of the potters' furnace
I have seen casualties
casualties, casualties
everywhere
casualties.

Fig 6. left, *Burial Arrangements.*

Fig 7. middle, *More Casualties.*

Fig 8. right, *Amputees.*

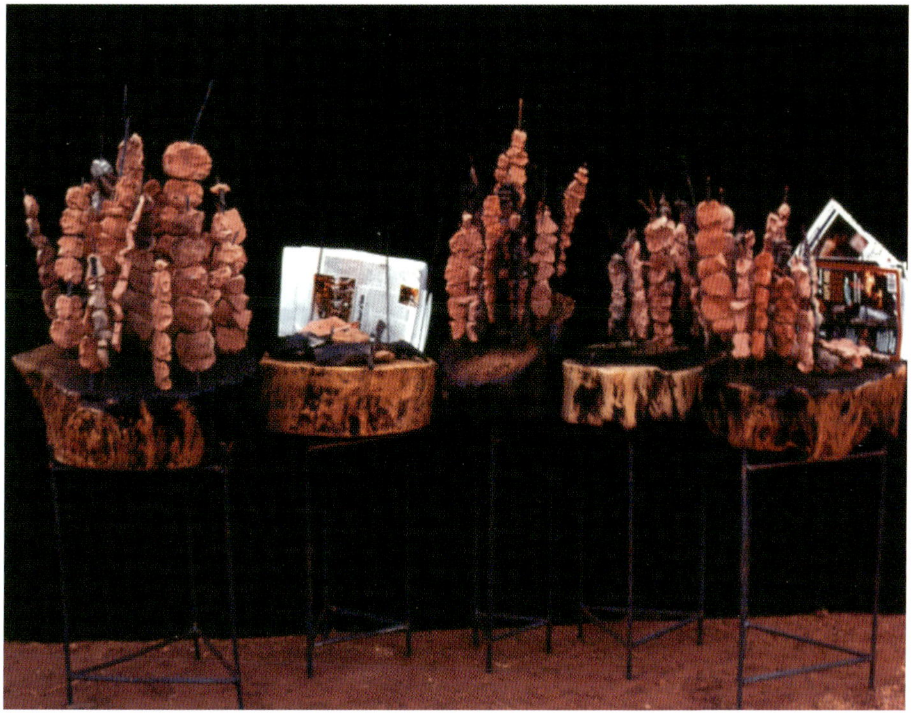

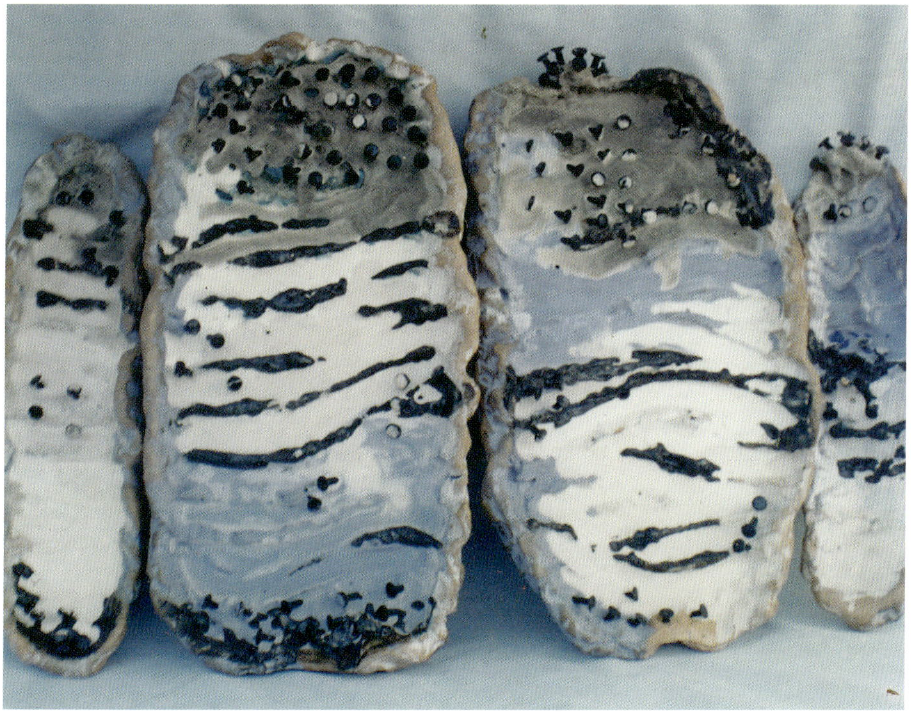

Fig 9. *Suyascape.*

Fig 10. *Ejigbo and Oke Afa Canal Disaster.*

All photos: Ozioma Onuzulike.

The ‘Fragmented Figure’ conference was held at Cardiff School of Art and Design, Wales, UK, on Wednesday 29 and Thursday 30 June 2005. Key issues related to the figure were identified and debated by researchers, by those writing critically on the subject, and by practitioners. In total there were twenty-one presentations and the South African representation was particularly strong, with three speakers present. Unusually, conference delegates were given the opportunity to hear the artist Wilma Cruise talk about her work and also to hear Professor Brenda Schmahmann of Rhodes University, Grahamstown, discussing Cruise’s work in the light of the differentiation that Norman Bryson makes between those forms of viewing termed the ‘gaze’ and the ‘glance’. All the papers from the conference are still available to read online in Issue 8 of *Interpreting Ceramics,* originally published in 2006. Wilma Cruise is an independent artist and writer. She is currently a doctoral student at the University of Stellenbosch.

Partial Figures and Psychic Unease: an Artist's Perspective

Wilma Cruise

I have used the partial figure consistently throughout my *œuvre* as a cipher for unease/(dis)ease. However, here, I reserve my focus for two bodies of work, made nearly a decade apart – the cycle *Nicholas – October 1990* (1991–93) and the *Claybody* series (2002–3). These two bodies of work interrogate the experience of trauma, that which lies beyond the reach of words to encapsulate or describe.

Theoretically I have aligned myself with the approach of the French literary theorist Hélène Cixous. Cixous asserts a

> reformulated relationship between language and the body [which] counters the discourse of … critiques which persist in a logocentric Cartesian discourse that posits the mind as the source of writing.[1]

She speaks of an oppositional language, *écriture feminine*, that nevertheless 'is impossible [to define] except through subjects that break automatic functions, border runners never subjugated by any authority'.[2] The body as text functions in the area of the subliminal and the subconscious, resisting order and structure. It is this approach that I find empathetic to my work – one in which the reach for meaning lies beyond the rational means to apprehend.

Via the *Nicholas* and *Claybody* sculptures and their accompanying writings, I offer the proposition that (logocentric) language fails to capture realities that function beneath the surface of conscious apprehension. Through the partial and incomplete bodies of the figures in these two cycles, I attempt to access the unconscious and the psychical, that reality which lies beyond language. In addition I show that the public writings and the news reports that surrounded the events that prompted the two bodies of work fail to capture the nature of private reality.

Nicholas – October 1990

Statement from notebook, 1993:

> This cycle of works revolves around the event of the murder of Nicholas Cruise on the morning of October 2, 1990. On that particular morning Nicholas Cruise was telephoned and asked to receive a computer that would be sent to him for repair. Nicholas worked for a computer company, which was managed by a group of young South Africans. These concerned young men had been active in the End Conscription Campaign. They also did work for the [then banned] ANC on a contractual basis. However, the motivation for sending a bomb hidden in a computer to this company and Nicholas in particular still remains obscure. Nicholas was blown away as he opened the computer and triggered the bomb. This event abounds with ironies. Nicholas had worked for the company for less than two months. He was a concerned Christian and active in the welfare of his fellow man. But he was not a political activist. Nicholas's killers were three members of the [extreme right-wing organisation] *Orde Boerevolk*. These men were apprehended after this event and charged with Nicholas's murder amongst other crimes. In an attempt to obtain their freedom while awaiting trial the three harnessed their 'cause' to the political amnesty agreement, which was in effect at that time. Political prisoners were granted indemnity for their crimes under this agreement. Ironically they had not yet been tried or convicted for the crimes from which they were demanding pardon. The murderers' initial demands for release were not met and the three embarked on a highly publicized hunger strike. During the media hype that surrounded this strike no less a personage than Nelson Mandela visited the ailing three and pleaded to the then president of South Africa, F. W. de Klerk, for their release on 'humanitarian' grounds! In the months of publicity that followed, screaming headlines made the names of Henry Martin, Adrian Maritz, and Lood van Schalkwyk household words. Nicholas was forgotten. His name not mentioned while arguments raged on about whether the three strikers had or had not been eating chocolates while on strike [they had].
>
> Nicholas had effectively been negated; reduced to yet another forgotten number in the litany of mysterious political murders that makes up the South African experience. The cycle of works is an act of mourning. It is also an attempt to redress the balance; to refute the negation of Nicholas. The works explore the ironies involved in these events – the juxtaposition of good men with evil. The link between the murderers and the murdered – a bizarre dance of death – a link that stretches into eternity. The cycle has to do with power, threat, death, and the absence of God/god. These ideas encompass all the bizarre inexplicable killings that have littered the South African landscape in the past years. Thus the works while they have to do with Nicholas are also beyond Nicholas. The works are neither portraits nor indeed illustrations. They are a shout against the silence.

The exhibition was held at a particularly sensitive time in the history of South Africa. Chris Hani, the ANC (African National Congress) leader, had been assassinated. His funeral was held on the day that the exhibition opened. Johannesburg was under siege and emotions

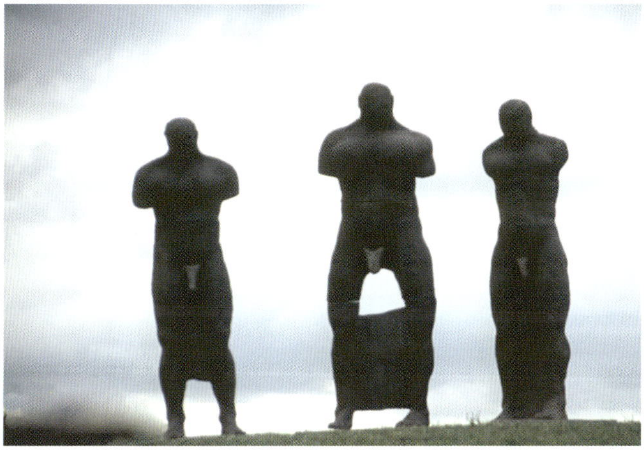

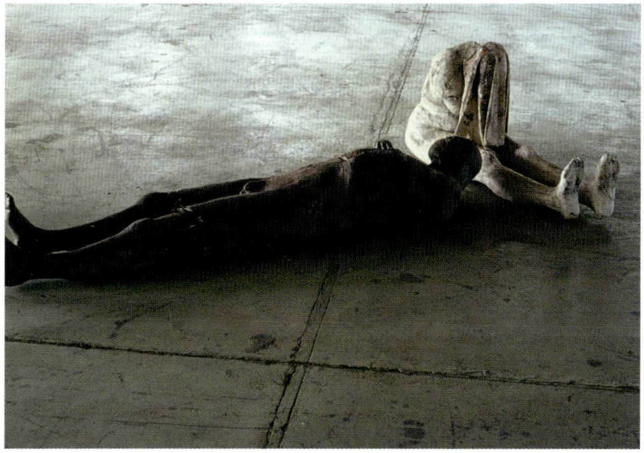

were running high. If violent revolution was going to happen, it was now. The day before the opening and Hani's funeral (Friday 16 April) *The Star* newspaper implicated the *Orde Boerevolk* in the Hani murder.[3] Those who braved the police cordons and attended the exhibition were highly emotional – a mood picked up by the press. 'A mother's shout against the silence' was one such headline.[4] M. Witthaus, assuming I was Nicholas's mother, wrote, 'As I walked into Wilma Cruise's exhibition … I felt an overwhelming urge to weep.'[5] Johannes Bruwer thought that Nicholas was my husband and wrote about 'the widow next to the broken body of her man'.[6] Anthea Bristowe in turn wrote: 'This body of work seeks to … deal with the *anger, grief and guilt*' (my italics).[7]

Nicholas had in fact been murdered three years before the exhibition and two years before the first works in the cycle made their appearance. Further, I did not know him well; he was the son of my husband's brother. Nicholas's murder interested me inasmuch as it posed a moral dilemma. If I felt anger, it was abstracted towards all the senseless killings typified by Nicholas's murder; grief was not of the wild sort that tears and rips at the soul. Of guilt I felt none. One critic was able to pick up on the difference. In a small review Michael Coulson commented on 'a key statement' in my annotated sketches, 'Art has nothing to do with reality. It is … only is.'[8]

This statement encapsulates the necessary disengagement between the observer and the experiencing subject. The journalists had committed an affective fallacy – confusion between the emotions evoked by the artwork with the emotion felt by the creator of the work. I, on the other hand, was dispassionate and, like Simone de Beauvoir, I felt that 'The *I* that speaks stands at a distance from the *I* that has experienced.'[9]

This is not to say that I did not want to evoke emotion on the part of the viewers. I did. It was important for me to ring a true emotional note, free of easy sensationalism and overstatement. In a critique of my 1990 exhibition, *Untitled (Everlasting Nothingness Made Visible)*, Kendell Geers had noted the 'cliché' of the 'silent gaping mouth'.[10] I negated the scream (and the possibility of further criticism) by constructing the figures for the 1993 exhibition without mouths. In an age bombarded by violent images whose shock value has numbed sensibilities I felt that the only resort was silence.

Fig 1. left, *Three shades (the bully boys I, II and III)* (1992–93), ceramic and cast metal on concrete bases, *I* 175 x 80 x 40 cm; *II* 184 x 76 x 65 cm; *III* 172 x 70 x 76 cm. Collection: Durban Art Museum.

Fig 2. right, *Durban Pieta* (1991–93), two ceramic figures, fired metal and cloth, 54 x 244 x 244 cm. Collection: University of South Africa, Pretoria.

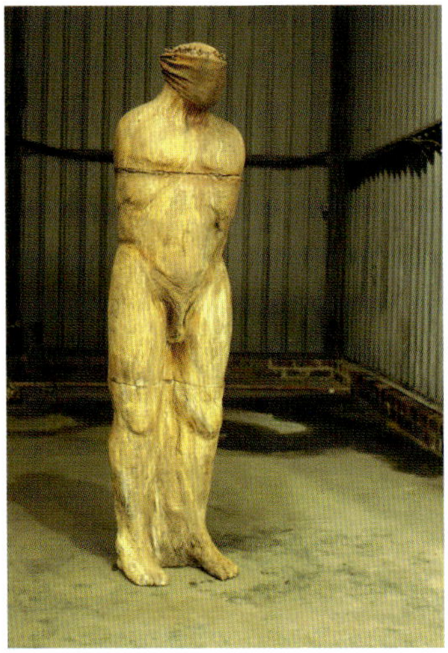

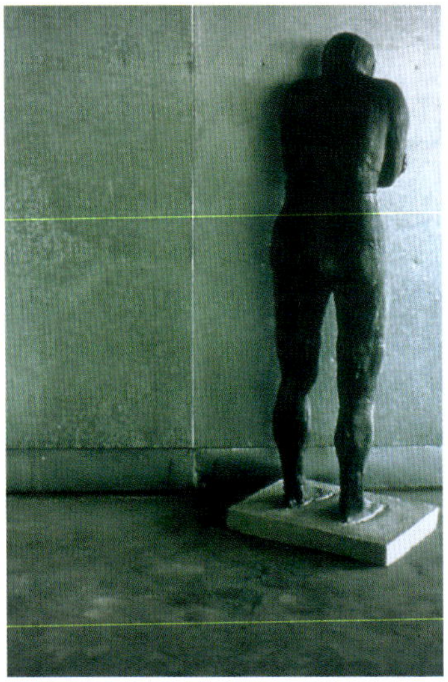

Fig 3. *Yellow Christ* (1992–93), ceramic with cast-bronze face and mask on concrete base, 173 cm. Private collection.

Fig 4. *Self-portrait* (1992), ceramic on concrete base, 173 x 62 x 45 cm. Private collection.

The central work in the cycle of eleven life-size figures is *Three Shades (the Bully Boys I, II and III)* (1992–93) (Fig 1). The figures are incomplete and naked with only their organs 'sheathed in cast metal, turning their maleness into a weapon'.[11]

Three Shades (the Bully Boys I, II and III) represent the collective shadow that hangs over nations when inexplicable murders and disappearances are committed. In both the metaphysical sense and in actuality the bully boys are seldom seen. They are the malevolent shades that hover just off the edge of consciousness. They are featureless and armless. The erasure of their primary means of expression, face, arms and hands, renders them mute. They are helpless, caught up by the web of their own violence. Only their darkness, their massiveness and their sheathed organs reveal their power.

The tragic event in 1990 brought vividly to the fore the moral paradox that revolved around the existence of God as the fount of good. I had perceived Nicholas's murder in terms of a war between good and evil, where evil triumphs. In evoking these absolutist concepts, I was adopting a fixed ethical position, albeit from an ironic and a rhetorical position.[12] I saw tragic irony in the failure of Nicholas's God to save him or to intervene in any way to validate his death. Working notes for the exhibition explored this theme.

god and the absence of god
light and the absence of light
a dialectic
like silence and
a scream
if there is hell must heaven exist?

Nicholas Cruise was a concerned Christian. His right-wing murderers claimed the same position. Yet it was evil and the forces of darkness that had prevailed. Thus, while *Durban Pieta* (1991–93) (Fig 2) suggests the grieving mother of Christ, it offers no possibility of redemption. The madonna is hidden beneath and blinded by a cloth; bands of steel bind the figure of Christ/Nicholas. Both are armless and faceless; rendered mute and powerless.

Yellow Christ (1992–93) (Fig 3) is the last work in the cycle. In the face of the unremitting darkness of the other figures, I had felt the need to use colour. Yellow is the colour of affirmation and of rebirth both in a biblical and natural sense.[13] But while *Yellow Christ* was the natural end point and may have signalled personal closure, it should not (necessarily) be read as an affirmation of Christian redemption. A note made at the time of the construction of the work acts as a reminder of my position of atheistic disillusionment:[14] 'christ has a cock / why then is he impotent?'

Atheists, paradoxically, are more concerned with the existence of God than those who accept his being unquestionably. It is a position marked by the 'wild grief that God is dead'.[15] Woman and man are alone in a world that is mute as to its meaning. Reality is permanently in question.

The penultimate sculpture is *Self-portrait* (1992) (Fig 4). *Self-portrait* stands in relation to *Yellow Christ* as marking the end of the cycle. But while *Yellow Christ* is rendered impotent by his armlessness and silenced by his mask, *Self-portrait* is whole, indicating the power of the artist to make sense of her world.

the artist has power
she has arms
she controls
she is god
(for a small while)
but like god
she confronts evil
only in a place where
chaos reigns[16]

By investigating Nicholas's choice of a fixed moral order and how it failed him I was exploring the nature of moral choice. My freedom from God and the implied ethical order lay in contrast to his. In taking responsibility for my own values I have adopted what A. G. Rooks has called an 'anguished position'.[17] It is this anguish that motivated the cycle of works and the physical and moral silence they provoked. This was drowned by the more literal interpretation of the sculptures by the press who chose to confront the actual event rather than the metaphysical questions provoked by it.

The *Claybody* series

While the relationship between the artwork and reportage in *Nicholas – October 1990* revolved around intentional and affective errors, the *Claybody* series explored the slippage of language in another sense altogether. The series takes as its topic initiation and circumcision practices in South Africa.

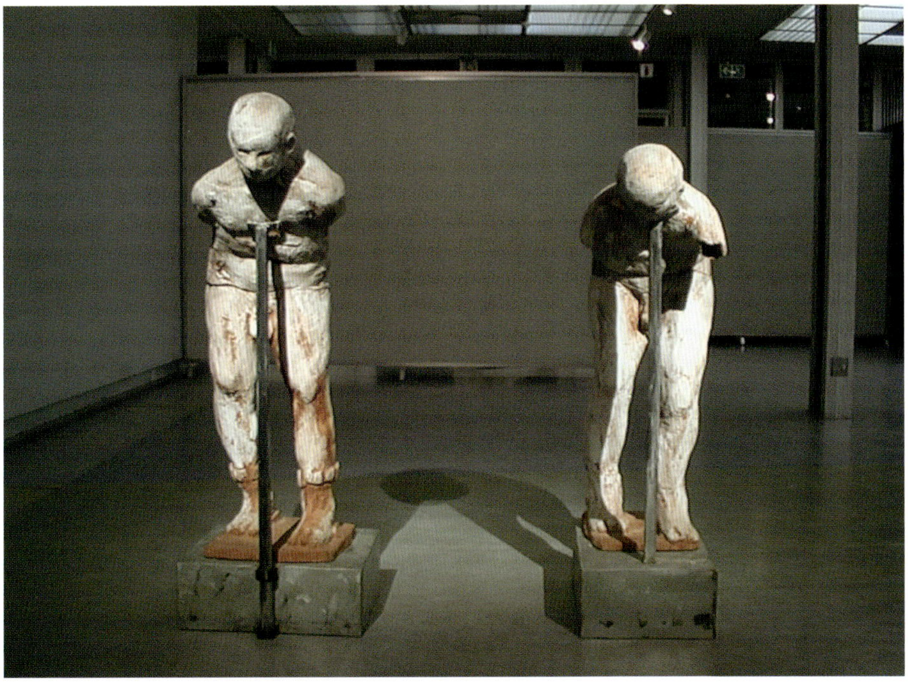

Fig 5. *Claybodies #4 and #5* (2002), ceramic on steel base, 157 cm and 124 cm. Private collection.

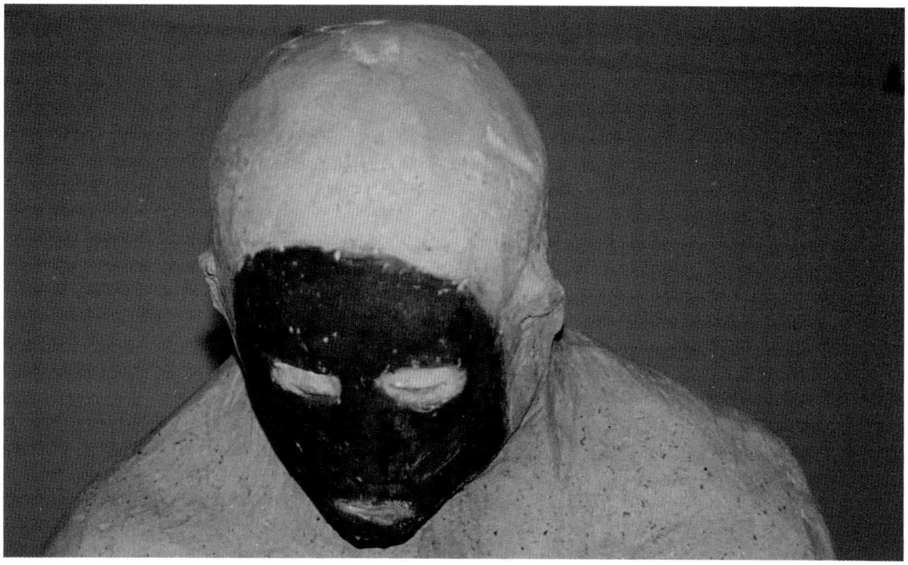

Circumcision is practised by certain tribal groups in South Africa, notably by the Xhosa and Sotho. In the ritual, which lasts weeks or months, boys make the transition from boyhood to manhood. A part of the ritual involves circumcision, which is done by a traditional surgeon, the *incibi*, usually without anaesthetic or sterilisation.[18] Circumcision is frequently done with a spear, and the same blade is used from one initiate to the next. In addition, during the weeks of secret initiation, the young men[19] suffer extreme physical privation. They are removed from their homes and villages, live in rudimentary shelters, wear only a blanket against the winter cold, and are given little nutrition. As one reporter put it, initiates 'are not supposed to drink any liquids for a week after the procedure'.[20] The *abakhweta,* as they are known, are seldom seen. They are identified by their reclusiveness, their blankets, and the white clay with which they are daubed as a sign of purity.

The title of the series, *Claybodies*, refers to the practice of covering the body with clay as well as an ironic reference to the substance from which the figures are made. By drawing attention to the clayness of the sculptures I am insisting on an axiomatic truth-to-material position, even though I consistently defy this dictum by using non-ceramic materials and techniques in my ceramic sculptures.

During every circumcision season, usually in the winter months of June and July, many initiates become ill, suffer penile amputations, and, in some cases, die. These events become the topic of numerous press reports.

> They had staggered from the hills saying that scores more were in agony from infected wounds after a surgeon used the same rusty spear on 80 initiates. 'The stench of rotting flesh was unbearable.'[21]
>
> The mutilations and deaths that followed the inevitable slips of the hand were traditionally dismissed as a sign that the victim had not been destined to reach manhood.[22]

Fig 6. *Claybody #3* (2002), ceramic (Corobrik Agate White), 150 cm. Artist's collection.

For white South Africans the subject of circumcision and initiation is generally remote. In the comfort of our couches we can shake our heads at the barbaric practice and once the topic has slipped from the news, as it inevitably does, we can forget about circumcision, penile amputation and death altogether. The situation was the same in 2002. 'Five teenage boys have died and 51 others have been injured during initiation rituals in South Africa', read one report.[23]

However, in that winter I was confronted with the question of circumcision in a personal way. My ward, Themba Mahlangu, a young man of Zulu descent, said that his grandmother wanted him to undergo initiation.[24] Themba, then eighteen, was ambivalent, swinging between a desire to follow in his elder brother's footsteps and achieve a ritual recognition of his manhood, and a fear of it. A war, perhaps also, between his Westernised upbringing and his heritage. During the family debates that followed, I came to understand that my attitude to circumcision could not be a simple condemnation of the practice, however desirable such an absolutist position would be. My personal confrontation of the process of initiation forced me to a relativist position. The information that filled the papers for a short while entertained and titillated the readers who could feel shock and outrage. I, on the other hand, experienced reality in a way that was at odds with the reportage. The word had failed and emotional knowledge had seeped away between the interstices of word and image. I wrote,

text
is
vision
is
(re)vision
text
is
the in-between-ness of
things
a
vector of inspiration

'In-between-ness' is the place in which I found myself – one of a moral unease. I felt I had to respect a cultural practice, for which I simultaneously felt abhorrence. Nevertheless a simple condemnation of a cultural practice from my Western perspective would not suffice. The territory had to be negotiated with care. The *Claybodies* became a vehicle for this state of unease. Yet to discount other readings would be unnecessarily reductive. As Brenda Schmahmann has pointed out, 'in-between-ness' is an intermediary zone between one paradigm and another. It refers to the transition from boyhood to manhood, a place between Western and traditional modes of being, and perhaps Themba's emergence from the care of his mothers to independence in the world.[25]

The five bodies in the *Claybody* series adopt postures of vulnerability:

> [they] are hunched and armless, … appear to be shivering and are, not only physically but also psychologically, turned in on themselves. Also, jagged marks scored across the figures defy an understanding of the skin as a definitive boundary

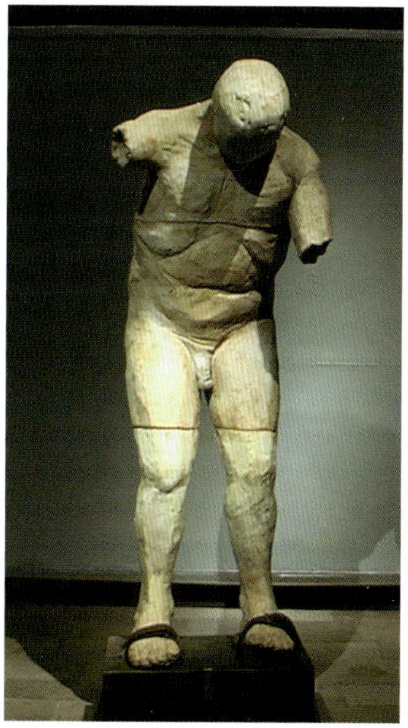

Fig 7. *Claybody #1* (2002), ceramic on wooden base, 160 cm. Collection: Pretoria Art Museum.

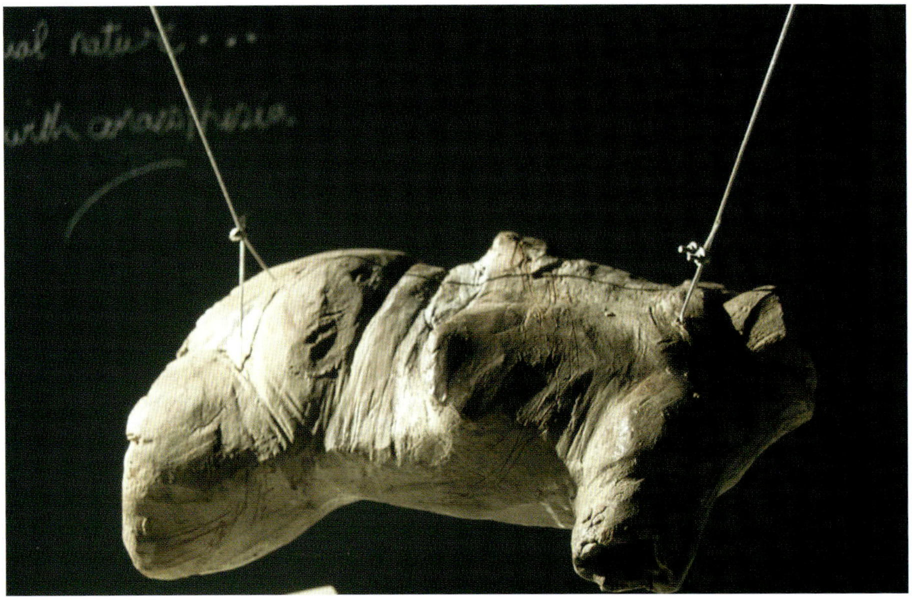

> for the body: what appear to be slashes or wounds to skin and flesh create a sense that these figures are ruptured … [they are] in a condition of susceptibility, of flesh that is violable and permeable.[26]

The fragmented figure and the partial figure

Schmahmann argues that the suspended torsos in *Hysteria Suspended* are abject not only in the conventional sense of being debased, but also in the Kristevean sense of resisting the imposition of systems of order.[27]

She is led to this interpretation by the scored and disrupted skin of the figures, which interrupt and break a look that, following Bryson, she has termed the glance. The glance is itself episodic and fragmented. The suspended torsos in *Hysteria Suspended* speak of fragmentation and disintegration that emanates from a state of hysteria. Yet they are not only *about* fragmentation – they are made *from* fragments and are *read* in fragmented form.

The surface of the figures in *Nicholas – October 1990* and the *Claybody* series, like those in *Hysteria Suspended*, are also scored and disrupted, and in this sense Schmahmann's interpretation of fragmentation holds true. However, there is one difference. The works in *Nicholas – October 1990* and the *Claybody* series were never whole in the first place. Their incompleteness speaks of impotence and helplessness signalled by the lack of arms and faces – the means of expression. It is also an impotence experienced by the artist in the failure of language in word and image to convey the true nature of experience.

Cixous sees the role of text and the act of writing as transformative. In much the same way the sculpture in these two cycles of work have, in their act of becoming, functioned as sites of meaning. They reflect, as she would put it, 'a question of writing today's pain and making it heard without betraying it'.[28]

Fig 8. Detail: *Hysteria Suspended* (2001), installation with three ceramic torsos, table, text and soundtrack, size variable. Artist's collection.

All photos: Doreen Hemp.

Notes

1 Julia Dobson, 'Hélène Cixous (1937–)', in Jon Simons (ed.), *Contemporary Critical Theorists* (Edinburgh: Edinburgh University Press, 2004), p. 130.
2 Cixous quoted in Dobson, 'Hélène Cixous', p. 127.
3 J. Pauw, 'Waluz Linked to Three SA Neo-Nazi Groups', *The Star* (16 April 1993).
4 M. Witthaus, 'A Mother's Shout Against the Silence', *Weekly Mail*, (23–9 April 1993), p. 27.
5 Witthaus, 'A Mother's Shout', p. 27.
6 Translated from Afrikaans: 'Die weduwee naas die gebroke lyk van haar man.' Bruwer was referring to the tableau *Durban Pieta*. J. Bruwer, 'Die vergete slagoffer', *Vrye Weekblad* (23 April 1993), p. 21.
7 Anthea Bristowe, 'Power in Personal Works', *Business Day* (28 April 1993).
8 Michael Coulson, 'A Woman's Life in Art', *Financial Mail* (23 April 1993).
9 Simone de Beauvoir, *All Said and Done*, trans. Patrick O'Brian (London: Penguin Books, 1972), p. 130.
10 Kendell Geers, 'Gallery's Crucial Role in Showcasing Art', *Star Tonight* (17 October 1990), p. 10.
11 Gavin Younge, 'Representing Global Conflict and Transnational Trauma – the Case of the Legacy Project and its Visual Arts Archive', keynote address, 20th meeting of the South African Art and Architectural Association, University of Natal, 23–5 September 2004.
12 Rooks has pointed out that Sartre too, on occasions, referred to 'fixed Values – the one unforgivable sin in [his] eyes'; A. G. Rooks, *Jean-Paul Sartre's Concepts of Freedom and Value* (Natal: University of Natal Press, 1959), p. 14.
13 Nicholas's brother, Christopher Cruise, pointed out this interpretation to me during a conversation at the opening of the exhibition.
14 This was later published in *Book 1, The Negative Aspects of God*, one of seven artist's books produced for the 1996 exhibition, *John's Wife. Book 1, The Negative Aspects of God* (1995–96), poetry and altered photomechanical prints, in metal cover, 14 pages, edition 5, one page a coloured print, 26×20.3×2.4 cm, private collection.
15 H. J. Blackham, *Six Existentialist Thinkers* (London: Routledge and Kegan Paul, 1961), p. 155.
16 Book 3, The Artist (1995–96), artist's book, poetry and altered mechanical prints in colour, in metal cover, 6 pages, 33×43.7×0.8 cm, private collection.
17 Rooks, *Jean-Paul Sartre's Concepts of Freedom and Value*, p. 12.
18 There have been moves in recent years to formalise the practice of circumcision by training the traditional surgeons in Western modes of medicine. 'Doctors have tried to encourage initiation schools to adopt more hygienic techniques, but these are often rejected by village elders as contrary to traditional teachings.' *BBC News* (Friday 30 June 2000).
19 Women do not have access to initiation schools.
20 Mike Cohen, 'A Noble Custom? South Africa's Xhosas Ponder Changes for Ritual Circumcision', *Associated Press* (27 February 2000).
21 Alec Russell, *Daily Telegraph*, London (23 January 1997), p. 17.
22 Russell, *Daily Telegraph*, p. 17.
23 'South Africa Youths Die During Rituals', *BBC*, London (Wednesday 26 June 2002).
24 This request was especially odd since it is not customary for Zulus to practice initiation.
25 Brenda Schmahmann, 'Initiating in-between-ness: Wilma Cruise's "Claybody" sculptures', in catalogue for the exhibition *Earthworks/Claybodies*, Pretoria Art Museum, 16 March – 26 May 2003; Standard Bank Corporate Gallery, 8 July – 30 August 2003; Sasol Museum Stellenbosch, 15 September – 24 October 2004, p. 16. Note that Themba has two mothers – the author and his biological mother (who have shared duties comfortably for twenty-one years).
26 Schmahmann, 'Initiating in-between-ness', p. 17.
27 Brenda Schmahmann, 'The Sculptures of Wilma Cruise: Fragments and Feminist Transgressions', paper presented at the Fragmented Figure Conference, Cardiff School of Art and Design, UWIC, 29–30 June 2005.
28 Quoted in Dobson, 'Hélène Cixous', p. 131.

Professor Christie Brown is a member of the Ceramics Research Centre and a supervisor on the graduate programme at the University of Westminster, UK. Her figurative work makes references to both archaeology and psychoanalysis and she has commented that 'archaeology presents a fragmented narrative of past lives and holds parallels with the practice of psychoanalysis where layers are carefully stripped away to reveal hidden information'. As such, her work and ideas fitted well into the theme of the 'Fragmented Figure' conference held at Cardiff School of Art and Design in July 2005. We are pleased to be able to publish in print form her essay, which was first published alongside all the other papers from the 'Fragmented Figure' conference in Issue 8 of *Interpreting Ceramics*, originally published in 2006.

Embodying Transformation

Christie Brown

In 1997 I was commissioned by the Women's Playhouse Trust to make a body of work for the Wapping Hydraulic Power Station in London. This exhibition eventually emerged in the year 2000 after some delays, due to the very ambitious project the WPT was engaged in to transform this derelict industrial building into an art space. The exhibition was the most challenging body of work I had ever produced and the overall title of the show was *Fragments of Narrative*. This title encapsulates many of the ideas and themes that I continue to address in my ceramic practice.

My figurative practice relates to discourses from archaeology and psychoanalysis and the symbolic parallel between these disciplines. The archaeological process can be compared to psychoanalysis, in which layer after layer is carefully stripped away in search of a fragmented truth, which can offer insight and knowledge or transformation and healing. Fragments of statuary and pottery shards provide us with information about the past. From the academies of the early Renaissance to contemporary museology, the study of these archaic scraps offers knowledge, a way of learning, and provides us with stories about our ancestors, however incomplete these narratives may be.

Inspired by narratives that make reference to myths of creation, and objects from burial sites that embody rites of passage, my work connects to the viewer through the overlap between the personal and the universal. While exploring the transformative qualities of clay and the metaphorical associations of the casting process, it exploits the material's capacity to receive an imprint, connecting to ideas about mimesis and the patterns of repetition in human life.

In many ways I view my practice as embodiments of transition from one state to another, of transformation and individuation, and I would like to present two series of work made between 1999 and 2005 which illustrate these ideas.

After many years of making single decorative objects I found myself drawn to the idea of working within a themed series which began with *The Cast of Characters* between

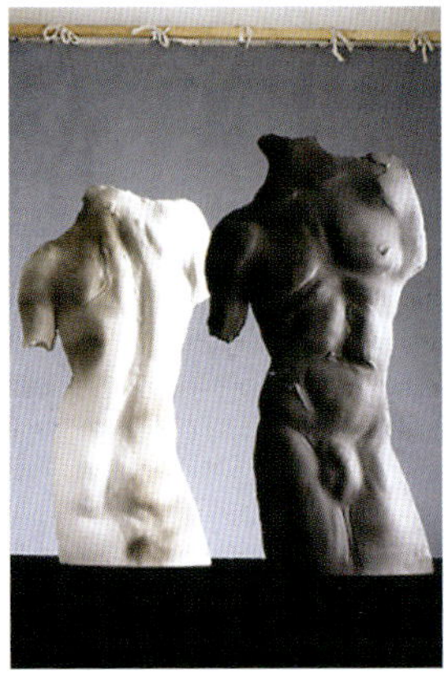

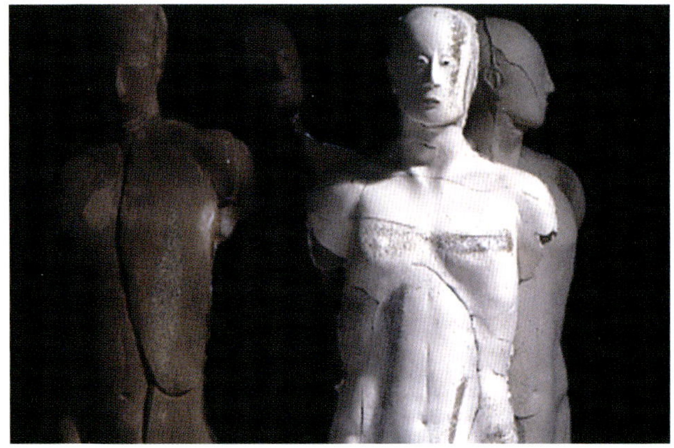

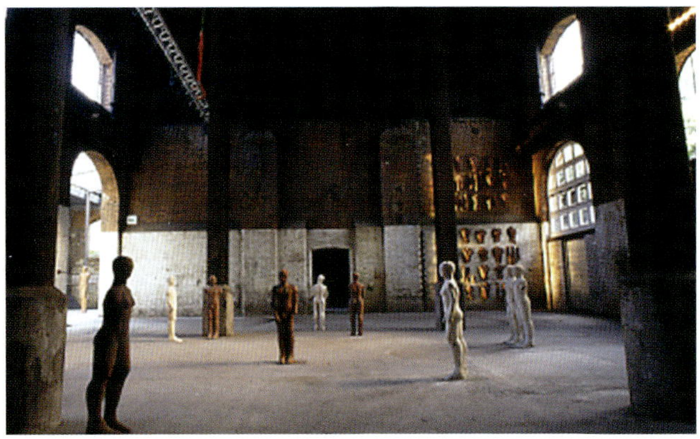

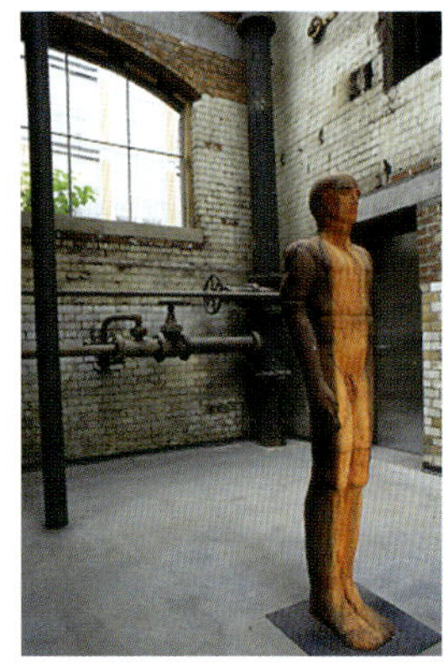

Fig 1. top left, *The Philadelphia Twins* (1991), 79 × 43 × 10 cm each figure. Photo: Brendan Macneil. Owner of work/ location: Collection of Adrian Sassoon, London.

Fig 2. top right, *The Cast of Characters* catalogue cover, 1995. Photo: David Cripps. David Cripps. Various private collections.

Fig 3. bottom left, Interior installation shot, 'Fragments of Narrative' exhibition, Wapping Hydraulic Power Station, 2000. Photo: Kate Forrest. Owner of work/ location: n/a.

Fig 4. bottom right, *Prometheus* (1999), 168 × 44 × 36 cm. Photo: Kate Forrest. Owner of work/location: artist's collection.

1993 and 1997 when I was seeking new techniques that would develop the successful but potentially formulaic method of working that I had established during the 1980s and, more importantly, would facilitate a clearer form of expression for my ideas beyond the decorative and ornamental. Although still related in many ways to the work of that period, the pair of figures entitled *The Philadelphia Twins* (Fig 1), made in 1991, was a significant development in which two figures were conceived as one work and given a title that related to narrative and memory. From this piece *The Cast of Characters* grew (Fig 2), drawing on my dream world and referencing my early interest in theatre. The series aimed to establish a discourse with the overlap between personal and universal characterisation through the use of the Jungian idea of the archetype as a collection of inner models which reflect shared behaviour patterns and form the content of the collective unconscious. In this series earlier Classical and Renaissance influences gave way to the study of more archaic cultures and an increasing interest in the significance of archaic artefacts. But my interest in the parallel between psychoanalysis and archaeology only really began in the specially commissioned exhibition *Fragments of Narrative* at Wapping.

The commission was to make a body of work in response to this large industrial site by the Thames (Fig 3). The scale of the space was daunting and challenging. The structure of the main interior echoed a Romanesque church with high windows and columns,

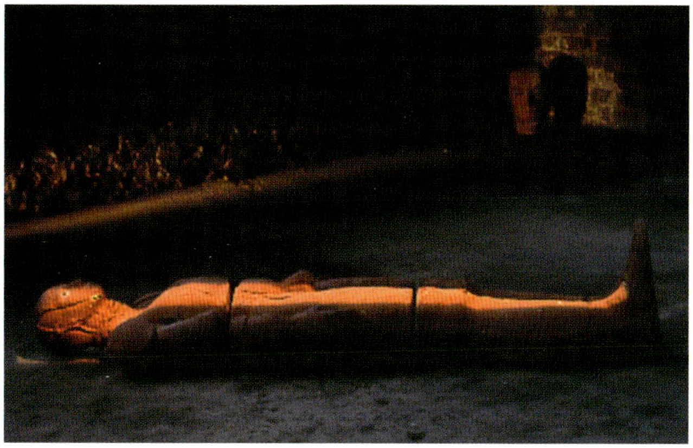

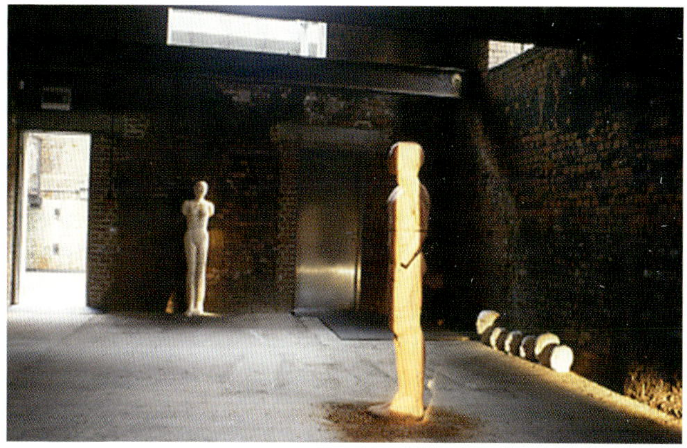

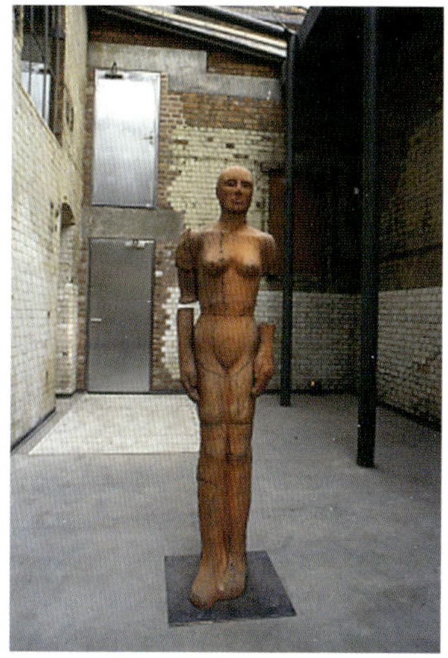

and the whole site was filled with the traces and memories of its previous existence as a place where steam power was generated to animate bridges and lifts. This was my first experience of making work that required a response to a particular site, and it enabled me to broaden out my ideas beyond the personal and subjective.

The outcome included three large wall installations and two groups of ceramic figures. The life-size figures, made either from red brick clay or stoneware painted white to echo the colours of the brick and tiled walls, were inspired by characters from myths of creation such as Prometheus and stories about animate and inanimate beings like the Golem, which connected both to the archetypal language of the material and to the original use of the space as a source of power. *Prometheus* (Fig 4) created the human race out of clay and defied Zeus to bring us the secret of fire. *Golem* (Fig 5) is a legendary figure from fifteenth-century Eastern Europe, a large clay man made by a holy rabbi to help him to save his people from persecution. *Golem* lies on the ground and can only be animated by placing the name of God into his clay mouth.

These early tales of creation are to be found in various cultures. They relate to the basic desire to create an animate body and pre-empt later stories such as Mary Shelley's *Frankenstein* and the replicants from the film *Bladerunner*. Other stories such as 'Pygmalion' and 'Galatea' from Ovid's *Metamorphoses* (Fig 6) develop the theme of animation and illustrate the need to create an embodiment of human desires. Pygmalion preferred to sculpt his ideal rather than confront the sexuality of a real woman, and his wish, granted by Venus, to bring life to his statue demonstrates his need for control in this relationship. A similar theme in reverse occurs in the story of *Olympia* (Fig 7), from the tales by E. T. A. Hoffman, about an idealised puppet who is broken up and destroyed by the man who acquires her when he realises she is merely an animated doll.

In his catalogue essay for this show Edmund de Waal refers to making figures as 'a transgressive activity – it is a role that should belong to the gods', and he continues,

> the need to understand our own creation is profoundly mimetic … in the mimetic making of a figure there is the trace and pulse of the mythic at work, something that is always on the cusp of danger.[1]

Clockwise from top left

Fig 5. *Golem* (1998-9), 186 × 48 × 37 cm. Photo: Kate Forrest. Owner of work/location: artist's collection.

Fig 6. *Red Pygmalion and White Galatea* (1998-9), 170 × 43 × 36 cm and 171 × 40 × 34 cm. Photo: Kate Forrest. Owner of work/location: artist's collection.

Fig 7. *Red Olympia* (1999), 171 × 42 × 35 cm. Photo: Kate Forrest. Owner of work/location: artist's collection.

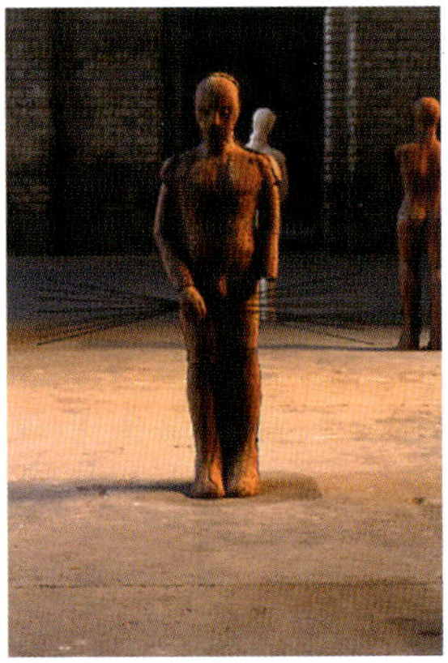

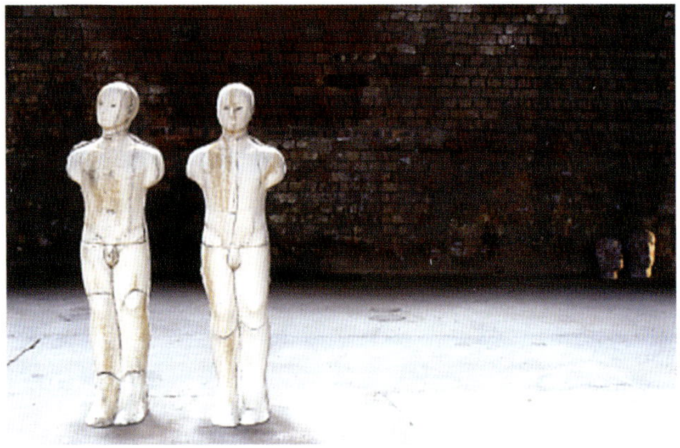

He goes on to suggest that in making figures we make a *doppelganger* and 'it is the compulsion to see that destructive and unsocialised twin, to name it and control it, that can be seen in many of the figurative traditions'. And indeed throughout these narratives there exists an uneasy and potentially threatening relationship between the maker and the creation.

I refer to the second group of smaller figures as *The Helpers*; the name is based on the idea of the Egyptian Shabti who are put in the tomb to take care of certain labours that need to be performed in the afterlife. *Prometheus's Helper* (Fig 8) carries the yarrow stalks for his master with which he will steal the fire from Hephaestus's forge. *The Helpers* includes a pair of twins (Fig 9), a frequent theme in my practice, reflecting various ideas about narcissism and emotional self-sufficiency, the shadow and the unconscious.

Although I had originally envisaged placing the life-sized figures in the main space, in the final display I realised that the scale of the space was emphasised by placing *The Helpers* centre stage so that the small but grown-up people seemed to walk in and out of the vast area as if passing through a piazza (Fig 10). Similarly the claustrophobic atmosphere between the life-sized characters became even more charged when some of them were placed in the smaller spaces beyond (Fig 11).

My approach to the exhibition also included references to archaeological digs, especially since developments of the Wapping project had been held up partly by industrial excavations of subterranean tunnels beneath the building. Two works in particular made reference to this growing interest. *Heads from the Glyptotek* (Fig 12) paid tribute to a collection of archaic artefacts in the eponymous Munich museum. Scattered in corners, gathering dust in rows, they lurked in the dark or hovered on rafters giving the impression that they had been there for a very long time.

Resource – Clay (Fig 13) was composed of a large number of brick-clay fragments mostly made from *The Cast of Characters* moulds that were no longer used to make whole figures. Made partly as a tribute to the people employed to work in the power station, it also referred to the use of fragments as a way of learning, an idea established in the early academies of art where collections of antiquities were used as ideal models for high

Fig 8. left, *Prometheus's Helper* (1999), 111 × 36 × 31 cm excluding steel wands. Photo: Kate Forrest. Owner of work/location: private collection (Australia).

Fig 9. right, *Kalos Thanatos* (1999), 111 × 33 × 29 cm. Photo: Kate Forrest. Owner of work/location: private collection (USA).

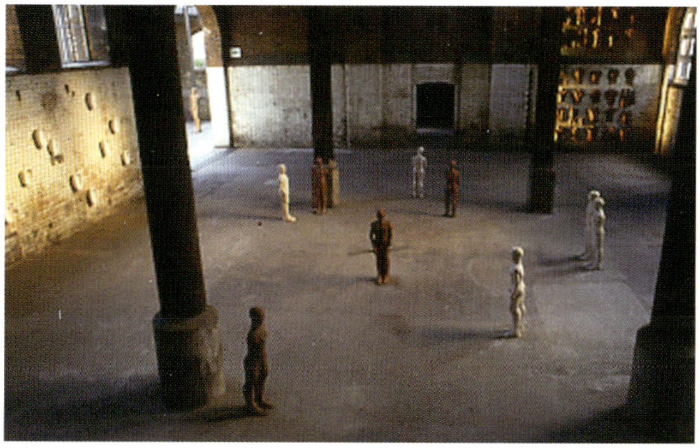

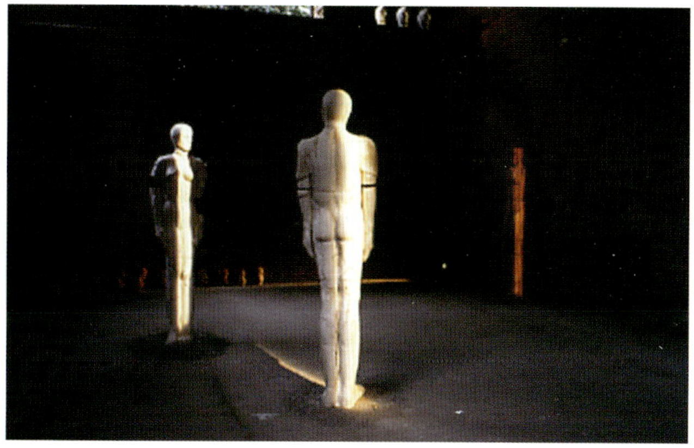

levels of aesthetic attainment. In eighteenth-century Europe these surviving fragments of antique sculpture were collected and preserved and they had a powerful influence on the eighteenth-century imagination by suggesting what was lost or lacking.

In Linda Nochlins's essay *The Body in Pieces* [2] she proposes the fragment as a metaphor for modernity, as artists turned to partial representation as a way of dealing with the lost relationship to the heroic age of antiquity, at a time of industrial development and revolution in which the grandness of the past can no longer fit into the frame of the present.

De Waal extends this idea, suggesting 'in the fragment comes an inheritance from the Romantic movement: a feeling that it was impossible to express the totality of an experience through a complete object'. Citing the 'deep vein of iconoclasm within cultures', he goes on to suggest that

> if figures possess power, if figuration is potentially transgressive then iconoclasm can be read as a profound reaction to it. To break a figure or to leave it incomplete is therefore to enter the territory not only of the psychology of destruction, it is also to raise the imagery of the vulnerability of bodies, their intense fragility.[3]

This work was also inspired by the practice of *ex votos*. In ancient Etruscan and Roman cultures gifts were offered to the gods with prayer as a form of healing, in the hope that the body part would take on the ailment of the original. This practice of votive offerings demonstrates a belief in the curative power of mimesis, and the practice continues to exist in many contemporary cultures such as those of Italy and Brazil.

The idea that a representational object can contain the spirit of the original is developed by the anthropologist Michael Taussig in his book *Mimesis and Alterity*.[4] Writing about the figurines which represented white colonialists, carved by the Cuna Indians of Central America in the mid-twentieth century as part of their curing rites, he speaks about the 'magic of mimesis' and how 'the making and existence of the artefact that portrays something gives one power over that which is portrayed'. Behind most of these fragments of narrative there lies the repeated and deep engagement with the power struggles enacted within human relationships as a protection against loss, and in the year or so that followed this exhibition I began to develop a greater focus on the significance in

Fig 10. left, Installation shot, Wapping Hydraulic Power Station, 2000. Photo: Kate Forrest. Owner of work/location: n/a.

Fig 11. right, Installation shot, Wapping Hydraulic Power Station, 2000. Photo: Kate Forrest. Owner of work/location: n/a.

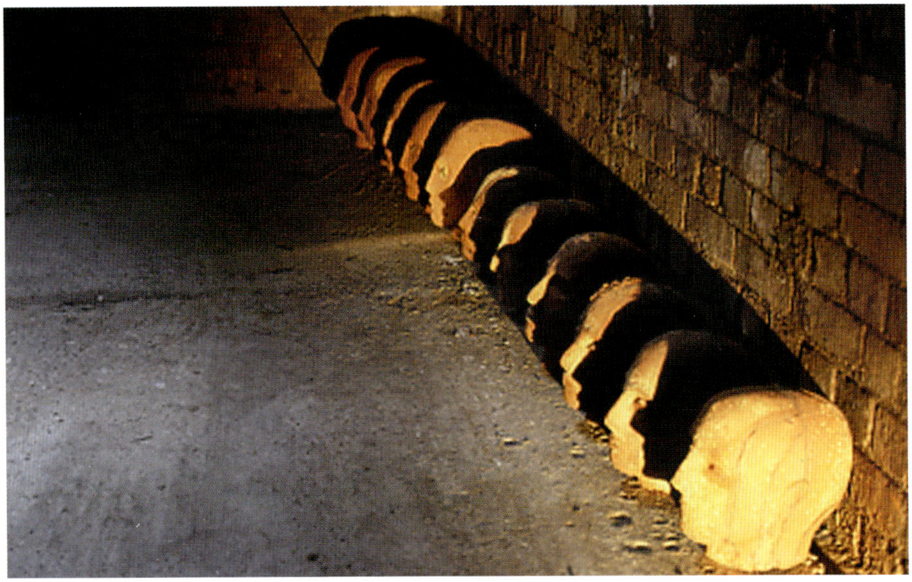

cultural life of archaic artefacts, which in many ways are designed to assist in this process of protection.

As a ceramicist I never experienced a strong connection with the late-twentieth-century contemporary abstract vessel movement or the decorative history of functional pottery, but a growing awareness of the range and meaning of clay artefacts in burial sites presented me with an area of the discipline that carried deep significance. Ceramic artefacts occur in large numbers of graves from many different countries (for example, Mexico, Japan, and China) and were almost certainly carriers of deep meaning in their time. They often formed part of a complex cultural mourning ritual relating to a transitional journey into the afterlife and affirming relationships with the ancestors, which could be vital to the continuity of the society. In contemporary culture these transitional rituals can be seen to have a parallel with psychoanalysis and the need for transformation through that process.

I am attracted to these objects partly because of their age and their worn aesthetic and partly because of their connection to a history about which we know very little. We share a common interest in people from the past, whether our immediate ancestors or people from long ago, because we need continuity. This is demonstrated by the popularity of exhibitions about past cultures and the current interest in archaeology, a discipline that has undergone many changes since it developed from early natural history into a more disciplined science.

The word 'archaeology' comes from the Greek *arkhaiologica*, meaning 'discourse about ancient things', and in first-century Greece archaeologists were actually a category of actors who re-created ancient legends on stage through dramatic mimes. Today archaeology is about studying human past through material traces of it that have survived, though only a tiny fraction of these traces exist and only a minute proportion of them are

Fig 12. *Heads from the Glyptotek* (1998-2000). Each head is approximately 20-33 cm. Photo: Kate Forrest. Owner of work/location: various private collections.

correctly identified or interpreted. As many archaeologists will confirm, they really only uncover the tip of the iceberg.

But its popularity and fascination is historic and enduring. During the sixteenth to eighteenth centuries this interest was the domain of antiquarians and natural historians who collected large numbers of objects, both natural and man made, and placed them in a setting of display referred to as a *Wunderkammer* or cabinet of curiosities. The *Wunderkammer* offered a microcosm of the world within a defined space. It had a creative quality, presenting diverse objects which inspired wonder and stimulated creative thought in what James Putnam has described as a 'quest to explore the rational and the irrational'.[5] A *Wunderkammer*, he writes, was 'a very private and devotional space specially created with the profound belief that nature was linked with art'. These rooms pre-empted our contemporary museums, and the treasure hunters can be seen as the forerunners of modern archaeologists.

But despite our need to fill the gaps in history, what we invariably get is an incomplete picture, an episode, a glimpse – and it is this fragmentary nature of the narrative that I find so fascinating. Despite a need to find solutions it's the half-known story that is ultimately more intellectually stimulating and challenging.

My interest in this incomplete narrative connects directly to psychoanalysis. In *Archaeology and Modernity* Julian Thomas describes how the historical emergence of archaeology was connected with the development of the structural thought of late modernity, whilst providing a metaphor through which that thought could articulate itself. This was particularly evident in the case of Sigmund Freud. Freud was an avid collector of antiquities and compared his practice to that of an archaeologist, clearing away debris to reveal the hidden treasures of the past. Thomas writes:

> it is clear that Freud took his own metaphor quite seriously and believed the unconscious to be literally stratified, the deeper layers of the psychic apparatus relating both to the early experiences of the person and the prehistoric experiences of the human race.[6]

Thomas points out that archaeology evokes 'notions of the repressed, the lost and the forgotten and of the drama of discovery which are often spatialised in terms of the relationship between depth and surface'. He suggests that this dichotomy developed out of a post-Reformation concern for human interiority and other separations, such as above and below, inside and outside, which contributed to modern thought. Archaeology, Thomas argues,

> has found itself with the burden of being a source of many of the metaphors through which the modern imagination has sought to understand the world. For our culture it is firmly connected with a movement from the present to the past, from superficiality to profundity, from individual to the mythic, from the known to the mysterious.

He considers this to be counterproductive for archaeologists, who seek to demonstrate that the 'remains of the past are all around us', but it goes some way to explaining the contemporary fascination for the discipline.

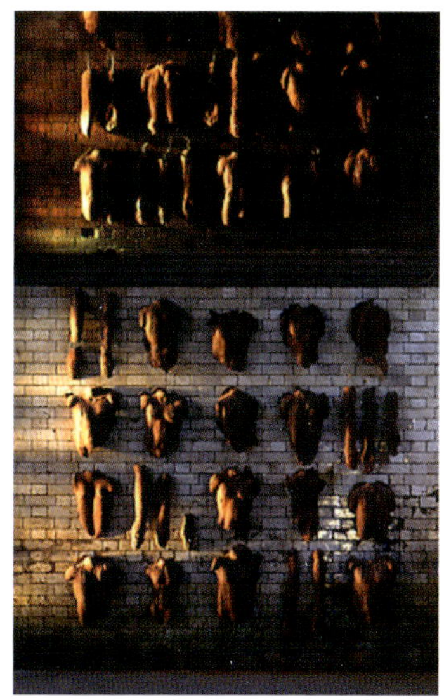

Fig 13. *Resource – Clay* (1995-9), 490 × 260 × 30 cm. Photo: Kate Forrest. Owner of work/location: various private collections.

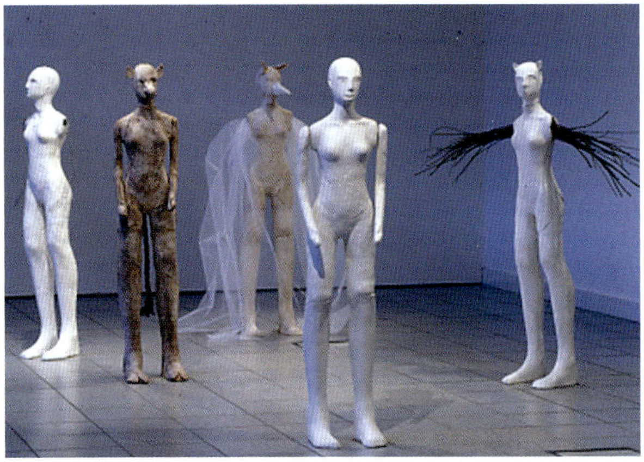

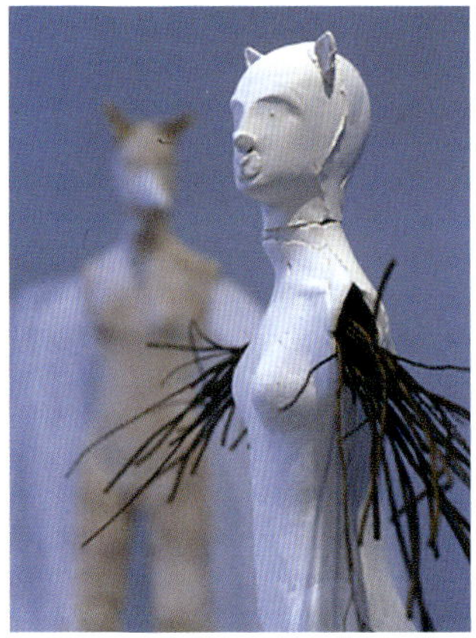

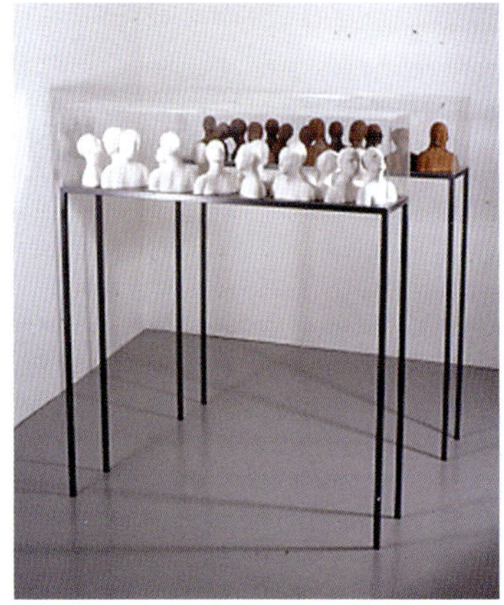

Writing in 1995 for the Tate Gallery's end of millenium exhibition, *Rites of Passage*, curator Stuart Morgan[7] quotes the anthropologist Arnold van Gennep, who proposed that important rites of passage in society are defined by three stages. The first is one of separation from normal daily life, the second is being on a limen or a threshold in a transitional space, and finally the third stage is reintegration into society at a different level. The liminal stage is a vital part of a ritual journey that results in transformation.

In the use of the mould – a positive object containing negative space that can be read as symbolic of the liminal stage – and the technique of casting and press moulding to produce repeated objects, my clay practice embodies transformation, and my most recent series is developing under the broad title *Between the Dog and the Wolf*, which refers to this transitional threshold and is a translation of the French phrase for twilight when the safety of daylight gives way to the unknown forces of the night.

In a work in progress group, *Entre Chien et Loup* (Figs 14 and 15), a metamorphoses or transformation begins to be played out as the female figures manifest change through stance and the sprouting growth of animal features. These are the first five of several, cast from the same mould, and my intention is to develop a crowd or a herd as the human takes on the attributes of the animal as a way of relating to the world at large and as a metaphor for growth and change.

In making this work I am exploring the boundary between our rational and instinctive selves as well as an interest in zoomorphic representation. Alun Graves writes about this piece: 'the suggestion that dark forces are at work is evident yet there is also a playfulness in the group, something magical and dreamlike',[8] and the work is clearly influenced by my recent studies at the Petrie Museum of Egyptian Archaeology of a culture in which the animal world played a hugely significant role.

Drawing on the practices of taxonomy and conservation that accompany museum culture, the vitrine, for example, can magically transform the most humble or mundane object into something special, unique, and attractive. The objects are preserved and contained, set aside, frozen in time, and we the viewers are voyeurs, unable to touch or engage with them except at one remove. In my work *The Problem of Communication* (Figs 16

Fig 14. left, *Entre Chien et Loup* (2003-), 129 × c.25 × 25 cm each figure plus extensions.Photo: Philip Sayer. Owner of work/location: artist's collection.

Fig 15. middle, *Entre Chien et Loup*. (detail). Photo: Philip Sayer. Owner of work/location: artist's collection.

Fig 16. right, *The Problem of Communication* (2003), 174 × 150 × 35 cm each section.Photo: Kate Forrest. Owner of work/location: artists collection.

and 17) I am using the vitrine to comment on my observation of human relationships at both a personal and universal level. Here the frustrations of communication that often seem to be deliberately acted out between us are expressed and emphasised as poignant misunderstanding. The ceramic heads come from four moulds that refer to our basic similarities and essential differences but all vary in expression and finish, emphasising the sameness and difference within humanity. The vitrine encases and protects them. It separates them from the viewer but the eye-level display allows an attempt at engagement.

Another recent work, *Ex Votos* (Figs 18 and 19), from the series *Between the Dog and the Wolf*, resembles an archaeological dig or a burial site. Shards, those pottery fragments that provide archaeologists with scraps of information about the past, fill up the male and female heads with information, history, and memories. These shards come from previous artworks of my own that have been rejected or damaged. The broken fragment of fired clay was once part of a whole form that has been lost, yet the fired fragment remains indestructible and permanent. Each head is documented with a number in reference to museum classification systems, and some numbers are prefixed by dollar and yen signs to demonstrate their timeless, priceless status.

Referring to both the embodied gift as a way of finding redemption and to the recent discipline of archaeology that developed from the practice of natural historians and antiquarians, the wall relief entitled *Insignificance* (Fig 20) developed from an earlier work at Wapping, *The Transformers*. In *Insignificance* the bodies are laid out like a map or a dig, reflecting the power and indifference of the natural landscape. The formal relationship refers to the fifteenth-century transi-tombs in which an ornamental representation of the aristocratic deceased is echoed by the cadaver below, reminding the viewer of physical mortality, to which even kings and princesses must succumb.

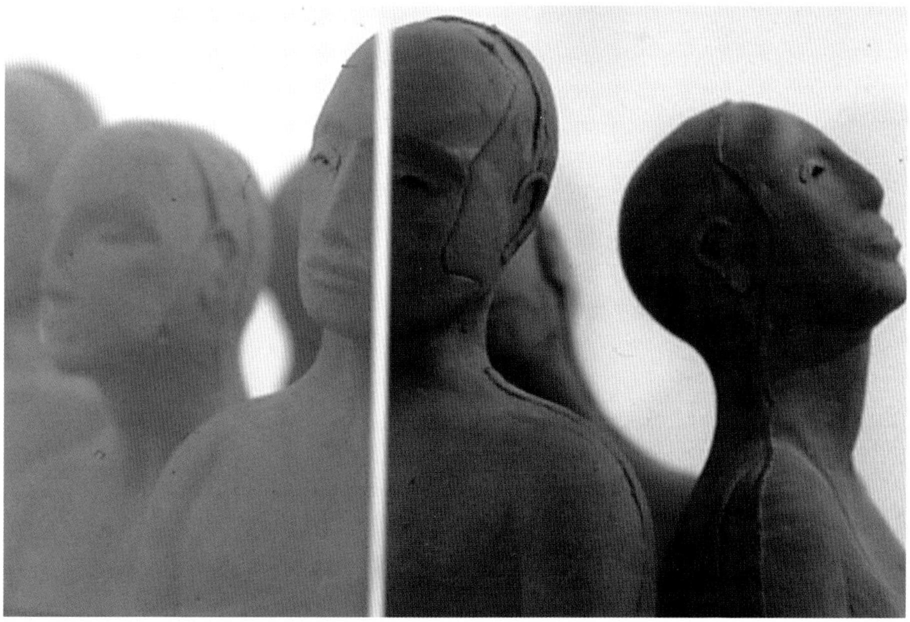

Fig 17. *The Problem of Communication* (detail). Photo: Philip Sayer. Owner of work/ location: artists collection.

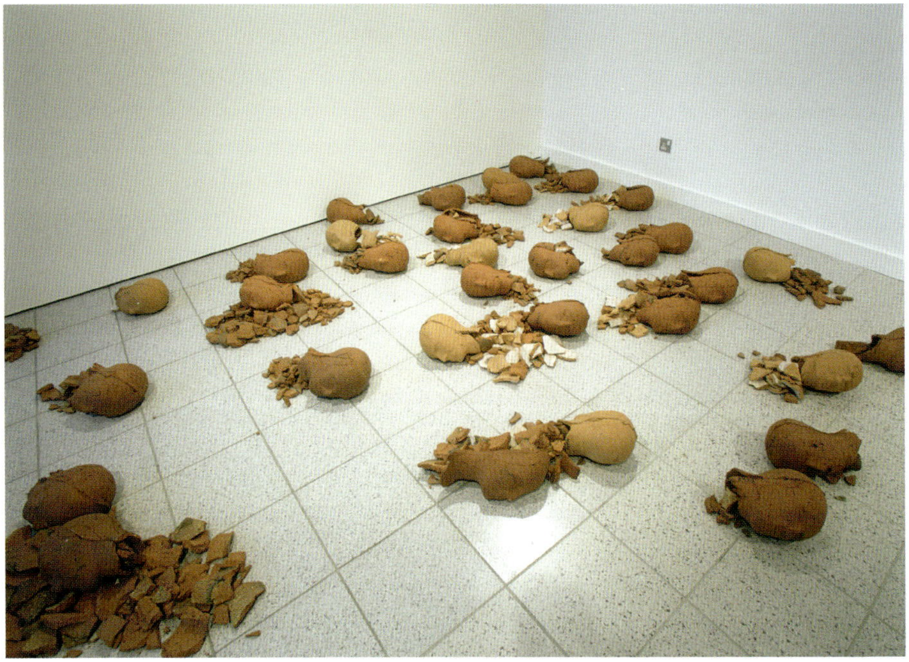

At the same time the hanging body parts make reference both to the practice of *ex votos* and to ancient fragments as a source of knowledge, and this mix of nature and learning offers hope. In her review about the work in progress exhibition of this work, Babette Martini writes that my figures

> become more like 'essays' on a particular experience, they no longer only look incomplete but they are incomplete or unfinished in the same sense that man keeps developing, even over centuries, adjusting mind and body to new environments and challenges. Thus the fragmented figure becomes a sign for healing and in a sense the disjointed body regains completeness, the limbs become re-attached.[9]

I am fundamentally a maker of things first and a theorist second. Making objects requires skill and time, and so I do not deeply engage with the demanding level of theoretical discourse that informs many areas of art practice. Perhaps I can compare myself with Baudelaire's *flaneur*. I wander through the world of theory and pick up scraps which may be useful to me as a way of extending and developing my practice.

Through archaeology I am exploring a connection with aspects of ceramic history and imbuing my practice with a level of meaning through psychoanalysis. My interest in the archaic objects that were used in rites of passage connects to contemporary ideas of transformation and individuation through psychoanalytic process.

Fig 18. *Ex Votos,* 2003-2004, dimensions variable. Photo: Philip Sayer. Owner of work/location: artists collection.

Because my work is both formed and informed by the ability of the mould to receive an imprint and the interface between negative mould and positive artefact can be seen as

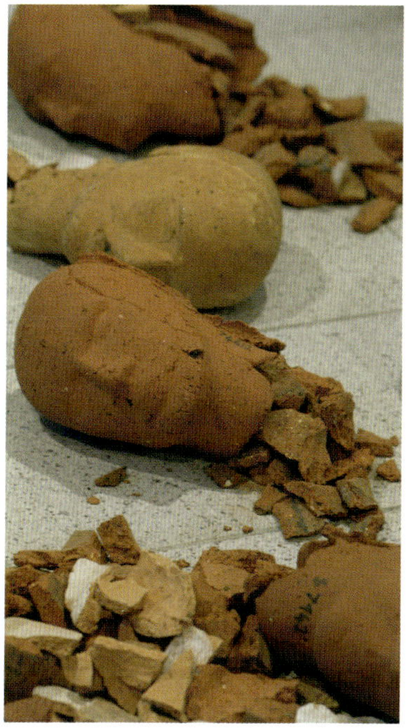

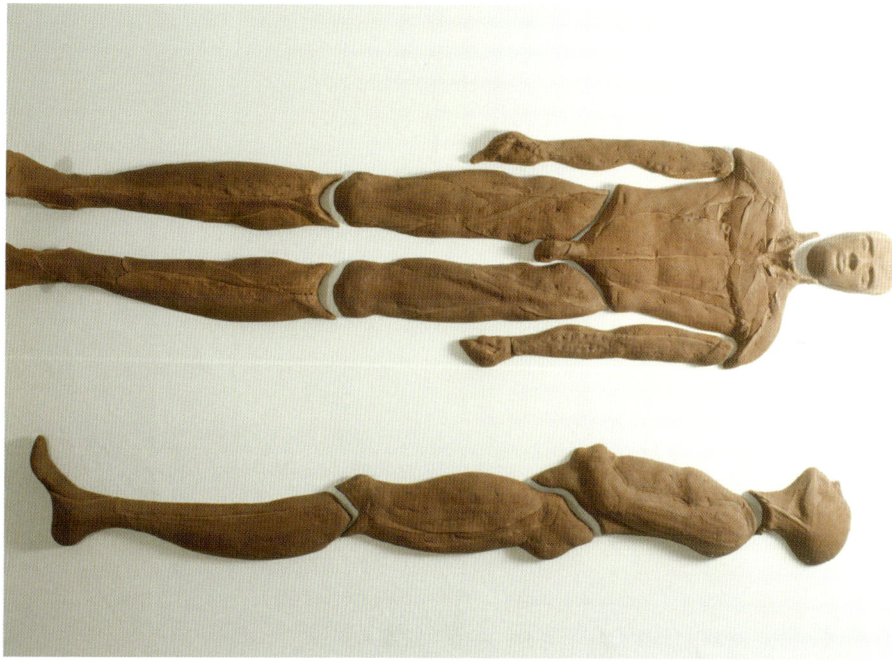

a symbol of liminal space, and because I use historic artefacts that are embodiments of ancient social rites as references, I am suggesting that the objects I create can be seen as embodiments of transition and transformation.

It also seems appropriate that I work in a medium that is not only a transformative material involving the process of firing but also one that occupies a transitional position within contemporary visual culture.

Fig 19. left, *Ex Votos* (detail). Photo: Philip Sayer. Owner of work/location: artist's collection.

Fig 20. right, *Insignificance* (2003-4), 196 × 90 × 20 cm. Photo: Kate Forrest. Owner of work/location: artists collection.

Notes

1 Edmund de Waal, 'Return to your dust: figuration as transgression', in *Christie Brown: Fragments of Narrative*, catalogue for the exhibition at Wapping Hydraulic Power Station, London, 2000.
2 Linda Nochlin, *The Body in Pieces* (London: Thames and Hudson, 1994).
3 de Waal, 'Return to your dust'.
4 Michael Taussig, *Mimesis and Alterity* (London and New York: Routledge, 1993).
5 James Putnam, *Art and Artefact: the Museum as Medium* (London: Thames and Hudson, 2001).
6 Julian Thomas, *Archaeology and Modernity* (London and New York: Routledge, 2004).
7 Stuart Morgan, *Rites of Passage* (London: Tate Gallery, 1995).
8 Alun Graves, exhibition review, *Ceramic Review*, May/June (2005).
9 Babette Martini, 'Between the dog and the wolf', *Interpreting Ceramics*, 5 (2004). http://www interpretingceramics.com/issue005/dogandwolf.htm

The 'Fragmented Figure' conference at Cardiff School of Art and Design in July 2005 was cross-disciplinary and insights and knowledge were shared across the two days of the conference by speakers from a wide variety of subject areas. Opening the conference, Dr Eugene Dwyer of Kenyon College, Ohio, USA, combined perspectives from both archaeology and art history to reflect on the way that the narrative of Pompeii has taken shape in the modern period through the exhibiting of the body casts of its victims. All the papers from the conference are still available to read online in Issue 8 of *Interpreting Ceramics*, originally published in 2006.

From Fragments to Icons: Stages in the Making and Exhibiting of the Casts of Pompeian Victims, 1863–1888

Eugene Dwyer

In retrospect, we can indeed look back upon the introduction of the Pompeian casts in 1863 as the invention of a new art form. From our vantage point a century and a half later, the process can be seen as having several distinct stages of technical achievement and corresponding stages of popular reception. The process started with the 'discovery' that impressions left in the soil by the bodies of Pompeian victims could be cast in gesso. Six imperfect specimens were made during the decade following the discovery. Study, exhibition, and commercial exploitation of the casts ensued, with other experimental agenda paralleling the search for technical improvements in the casting process. In 1875 a new museum opened, with the casts featured as chief exhibits. By this time, due to a number of related factors, the casts had achieved the status of works of art.

A view of the interior of the Pompeii Museum taken around 1890 speaks volumes about the nature and purpose of the famous casts of victims made on the site of Pompeii and exhibited there since 1863 (Fig 1). The objects on display – casts of bodies, wine storage jars and other pots, architectural revetments – were all considered important enough to keep, but not artistic or precious enough to send to the Naples Museum with the rest of the loot. Yet there is undeniable artistry in the casts, and the other items as well, and many a traveller has taken home a photograph or a postcard of the bodies as the most memorable image of a visit to Pompeii.

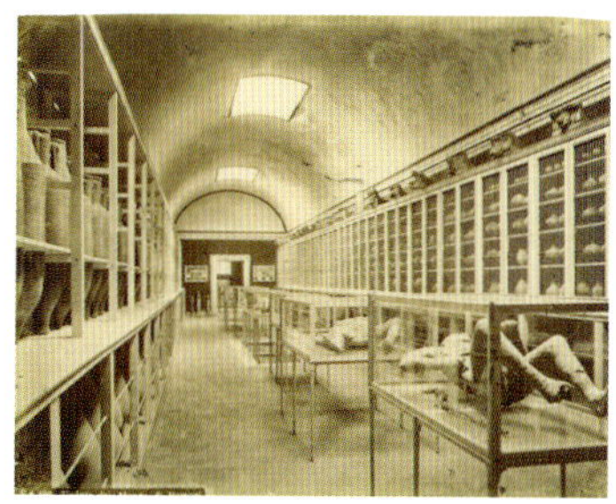

Fig 1. Interior of Pompeii Museum. Photo: Roberto Rive, c.1880. Collection of author.

What precisely are the casts – are they archaeological artefacts, or are they works of art? The casts are the products of both natural ceramic process and artistic intervention. The layer of hardened ash that surrounds and retains the impressions of organic forms in the so-called 'surge layers' of Pompeii's volcanic fill arrived as a cloud of superheated and

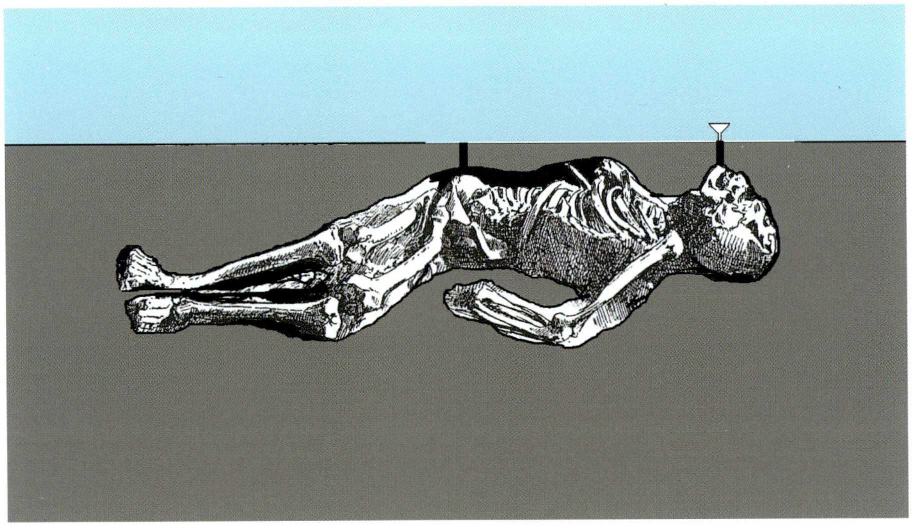

oxygen-depleted gas. The gasified material, which later hardened as mud, covered all as it swept from the direction of Vesuvius southward over Pompeii. It encapsulated those who were attempting to flee atop the nearly three metres of cinders that had been deposited in an earlier phase of the eruption, and it even penetrated the ruined houses to entomb those who were still sheltering within.

Pompeii's unique conditions make it possible to cast in gesso the impressions of the bodies of some of the victims trapped in the layer of hardened ash (Fig 2). To do so successfully, however, requires the eyes of Lynceus (who could see things concealed beneath the earth) or the imagination of Michelangelo (who could see forms present in the matrix). For once the earth surrounding the impression has been removed, the form is gone as well.[1] At the first appearance of a cavity in the mud, gesso must be introduced. After the gesso has been allowed to harden, the resulting cast must be exhumed and the adhering mud – which formed the original impression – carefully removed: a destructive process that permits no corrections. Every casting contains the element of surprise, since it cannot be known beforehand what forms will emerge when the surrounding ash has been removed – whether the figure will be complete or the impression of forms will be lost due to imperfections or anomalies in the original burial. Although a gesso cast of the complete body was the ideal, no 'un-fragmented figure' was ever made by this process at Pompeii.

The history of cast making at Pompeii is a history of lost opportunities and destroyed evidence. More than a hundred years of digging took place before the first cast was made. In that time at least six hundred skeletons had been unearthed and the bones either collected or discarded depending on the policy at the time. In some noteworthy early cases, impressions of the flesh and of clothing in the hardened ash that surrounded the bodies were noted, and some bits of volcanic mud, like that forming the breast of a young woman, had even been taken to the museum in Naples. Plaster casts of inanimate objects had been made as early as the 1770s, and some attempts had been made as early as 1831 to cast human figures in whole or in part, but apparently without success.[2]

Fig 2. Diagram of *in situ* casting process. Drawing by author.

In 1863, in the effort to preserve the archaeological record, the director of the excavations Giuseppe Fiorelli succeeded in making casts of four whole figures. These casts showed the victims' clothing and permitted a much better forensic examination, and were an immediate success. For a period of about ten years Fiorelli treated his casts as archaeological evidence, showing them to visiting archaeologists, anthropologists, physicians, and the like. But Fiorelli, who was an even better administrator and promoter of the excavations than a scientist, was also aware from the beginning of the casts' potential to draw visitors to Pompeii. Around 1873 he conceived the idea of a museum with the casts as principal works of art. This was an idea almost as stunning as his 'discovery' of the first casts themselves.

Despite their celebrity, however, the casts continued to be a feature exclusive to Pompeii. Only in the anniversary year of 1979 did two of the casts – or reproductions of them – venture forth in the famous blockbuster exhibition, *Pompeii, AD 79*. Only in 2003 did the casts reach Naples and subsequent museum venues in the exhibition *Tales from an Eruption*. By that time, however, the casts' claim to legitimacy as works of art had been established by artists like Allan McCollum, as evidenced by his work based on the casts, *The Dog from Pompeii* (1991).[3]

Given the fanfare with which the new discovery was announced to the world in 1863, and the seeming ubiquity of casts in popular impressions of Pompeii, it is not generally appreciated that the number of casts is finite, and that their appearance at Pompeii was gradual. Six were made in the decade between 1863 and 1872, and it was another fifteen years before a dozen had been accumulated – enough, as it were, for a celebration. In retrospect, we can indeed look back upon the introduction of the Pompeian casts as the invention of a new art form. From our vantage point a century and a half later, the process can be seen as having several distinct stages of technical achievement and corresponding stages of popular reception.[4]

The first stage: discovery

Like the 'primitive' or archaic phase of a style as defined by the art historian Heinrich Wölfflin, the first stage in the invention and reception of the casts held all of the potential of the ensuing periods, but was apt to be somewhat confused in its methods, both from a technical point of view and a museological one. The first stage corresponds to the first decade, 1863–72, when the casts were primarily intended as scientific documentation, and only secondarily as exhibition material. It began with the dramatic discovery of the technical process that first made the imprints of the victims visible to the eyes of archaeologists and tourists. If we are to believe later accounts, at the beginning of 1863 Fiorelli instructed his workmen to cease digging at the first sign of any cavity in the layer of volcanic ash that lay atop the approximately two metres of pumice laid down in the early stages of the volcano's eruption. We may assume that previous, unrecorded experience prepared the director for events on 3 February, when just such a cavity presented itself.[5] As reported, Fiorelli himself used a pair of iron tongs to extract the bones of a skeleton from the cavity, and then filled – or had someone else fill – the cavity with liquid gesso. On the following day the skeleton – or the form (*impronta*) – was unburied and freed of

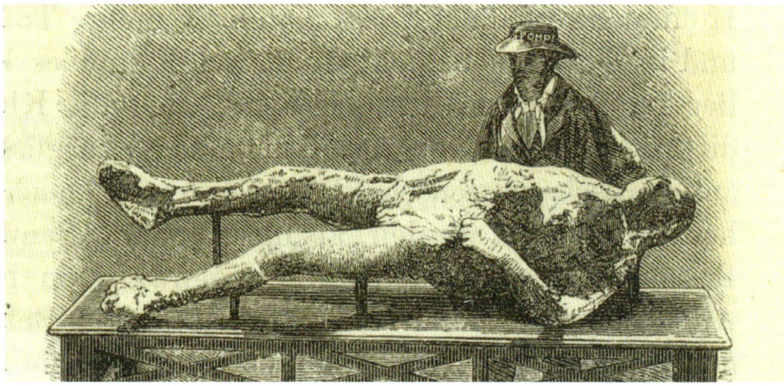

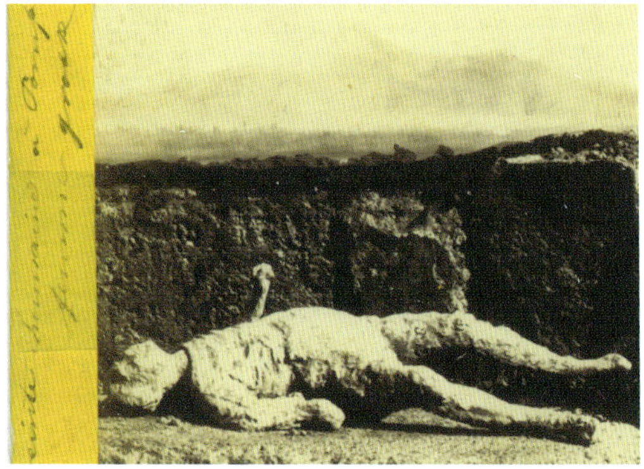

the surrounding ash. The result was a male figure, almost entirely preserved, with traces of his clothing. The giant size of the man – over six feet – and his military bearing impressed those who examined him at the time and those who viewed him during his subsequent exhibitions (Fig 3). William Dean Howells, who saw the cast not long after it had been excavated, admired him for his Stoic calm.[6] In sharp contrast is the attitude of the woman who was found nearby. Mark Twain wrote:

> The woman had her hands spread wide apart, as if in mortal terror. And I imagined I could still trace upon her shapeless face something of the expression of wild despair that distorted it when the heavens rained fire in these streets so many ages ago.[7] (Fig 4).

Together with the other casts from the same location, made within days of each other, these casts were removed from the spot for protection from the elements and installed in the re-named 'House of the Cadavers of Gesso'. It was there that Howells saw them: 'The guide takes you aside from the street into the house where they lie, and a dreadful shadow drops upon your heart as you enter their presence.'[8] There is no doubt that the macabre sight was exploited by Fiorelli both to draw tourists to Pompeii and to enhance his own reputation.

The fame of the casts spread immediately by newspaper accounts, and by the graphic media of engraving and photography. The authentication of the victims' fate provided by the casts was so ideally suited to the new medium of photography that, in the words of a writer in the *Photographic News* for September 1868,

> it is difficult to divest the mind of the idea that they [the photographs of the casts] are not the works of some ancient photographer who plied his lens and camera after the eruption ceased, so forcibly do they carry the mind back to the time and place of the awful immurement of both a town and its people.[9]

While the casts were impressive and horrific when viewed from a distance, closer inspection revealed many imperfections in the casting process. The early photographs and the wood engravings made after them were quite limited in their selection of views. Closer examination through the objective lens of a later photographer reveals that the casts were seriously flawed to begin with, or that they had deteriorated significantly over a period of about twenty to

Fig 3. left, The first Pompeian cast ('Victim Number 1'). Metal-cut book illustration, after photo: Giorgio Sommer. After J. Overbeck, *Pompeji*, 2nd ed. (Leipzig, 1866).

Fig 4. right, Cast of a woman ('Victim Number 4'). Stereo-card photograph by Michele Amodio, 1863. Collection of author.

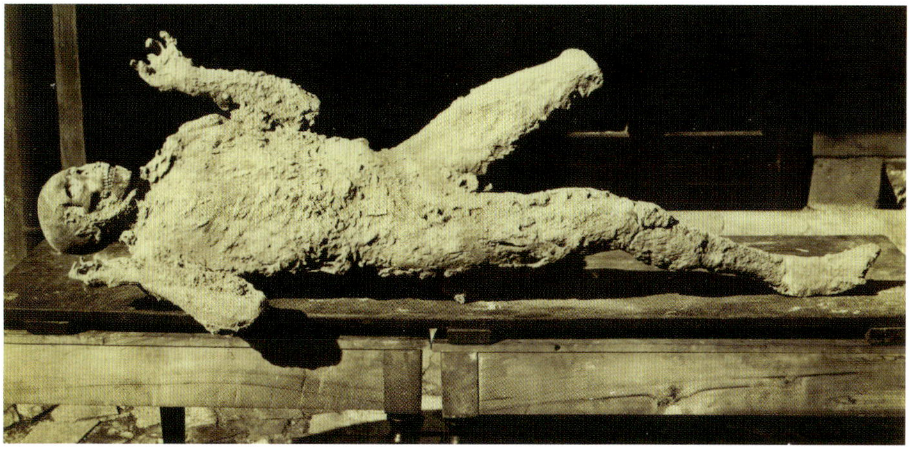

twenty-five years. Each of the six casts produced during this first period must be described as fragmented. At least part of the effect that the casts had upon contemporary visitors was certainly due to the grim surfacing of the underlying skeletons, as in this startling image from 1868 (Fig 5). The victim's body was actually found face down, but has been arranged for the camera in the more dramatic supine position. Even without the archaeologists, this cast – seen here in a trophy-shot, and compared with the earlier convention of viewing skeletons – added a new chapter in the history of the grotesque.

The second stage: unity and the formation of icons

During the second decade the technical difficulties attending the making of casts were better understood, and a select number of successful castings of nearly perfect – unfragmented – figures resulted in an iconic series of images such as the *Sleeping Man* (Figs 6 and 7), the *Watchdog* or chained dog (Fig 8), and the universally admired *Body of a Young Woman*. By the 1880s the individual casts had become favourite subjects of photographers, leading to a kind of iconography of the casts. Prominent commercial photographers like Michele Amodio and Giorgio Sommer offered a stock of photographs of Pompeian subjects, among them the popular casts, in formats ranging from the diminutive *carte de visite* to large eleven-by-fourteen-inch prints. It was possible to purchase made-to-order albums, and many albums of the period contain a selection of photos of the casts.

The emergence of a market for photographs was accompanied by a change in the exhibition of the casts. Around 1873 Fiorelli began to plan a museum on the site of Pompeii. This became a reality in 1875, when the casts were moved from the houses where they had previously been kept. The new museum was less grim than the houses because it was better lighted, but it gave the distinct impression of a morgue. The casts in their glass cases literally held centre stage. In spite of the grim appearance of the place, the opportunity that it presented for closer study of the casts seems certainly to have contributed to the formation of a new canon of showpieces: archaeological artefacts as works of art. Fiorelli's original casts of the 1860s occupied glass cases of their own,

Fig 5. Cast of a man ('Victim Number 5'). Photo: Giorgio Sommer, 1868. Collection of author.

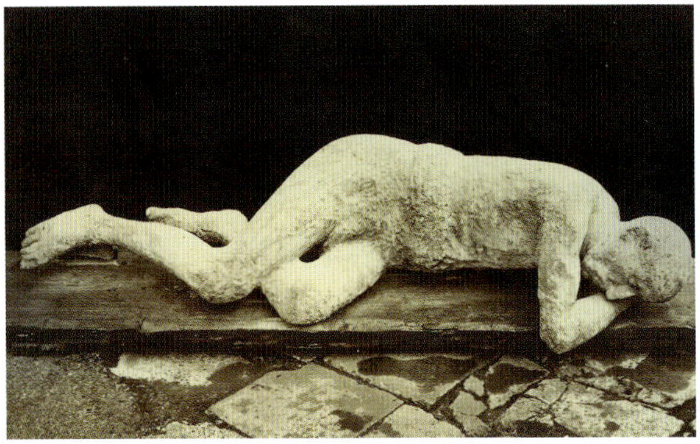

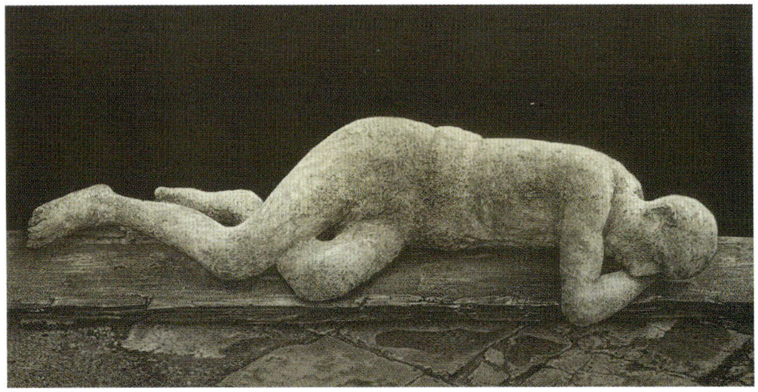

along with more complete casts made during the 1870s and 1880s. I refer to the latter as 'icons' because, owing to their striking attitudes, to the success of their castings and the photogenic quality of the subjects, these particular victims together account for the greatest number of illustrated postcards and book illustrations among the casts. As frequently reproduced images from Pompeii, they have taken their place alongside the *Dancing Faun*, *Narcissus* and other famous works of painting and sculpture from Pompeii. The *Sleeping Man*, found in 1873, was universally admired, being selected for the first photogravure-printed plate in the third edition of Overbeck's monograph on Pompeii published in 1875. In Fiorelli's words, the man, having sought refuge in a vacant spot just inside the city gate, 'sensing that he was being suffocated by the volcanic gases, and that he was losing his strength … lay down on the ground and there fell calmly into his eternal sleep'.[10] Its popularity extended to the masses of visitors to the city and its new museum. An anonymous visitor's comment, written on the back of a postcard of the *Sleeping Man*, about 1900, reveals much about the search for works suitable for exhibition: 'There are several such in the museum at Pompeii, including a child and a dog in terrible contortions. But this is the most complete and perfectly preserved. It is much less agonizing than some of the others.' Giorgio Sommer's photograph, made between the time of his discovery in 1873 and his transfer to the museum in 1875, shows him 'asleep' in the courtyard of the Archaeological School of Pompeii (where the cast of 1868 had been photographed). A photograph made after the move to the museum shows him to be less relaxed when viewed from above.

In the following year, 1874, the *Watchdog* was cast. Like the *Sleeping Man*, the dog is a spectacular technical achievement, though contrasted by his agonised attitude. The watchdog had been held to the door by his chain and thus was prevented from escaping. The form is so complete that the means by which the gesso was introduced into the impression is nowhere to be seen in photographs.

In 1875 the impressions of a man and a woman were found within the city, in the vicinity of one of the northern gates to Pompeii. Giorgio Sommer's photograph shows them side by side on pavement, perhaps that in the courtyard of the Archaeological School. The woman lies face down, and appears to have buried her face in her dress, leaving only her waistband in place. In another Sommer photograph she lies face down upon a board draped in black cloth and is viewed from the prospect of someone standing over

Fig 6. left, Cast of *Sleeping Man* ('Victim Number 7'). Photo: Roberto Rive, 1873. Collection of author.

Fig 7. right, Cast of *Sleeping Man* ('Victim Number 7'). Photo-engraved book illustration, after photo by Roberto Rive. After J. Overbeck, *Pompeji*, 3rd ed. (Leipzig, 1875).

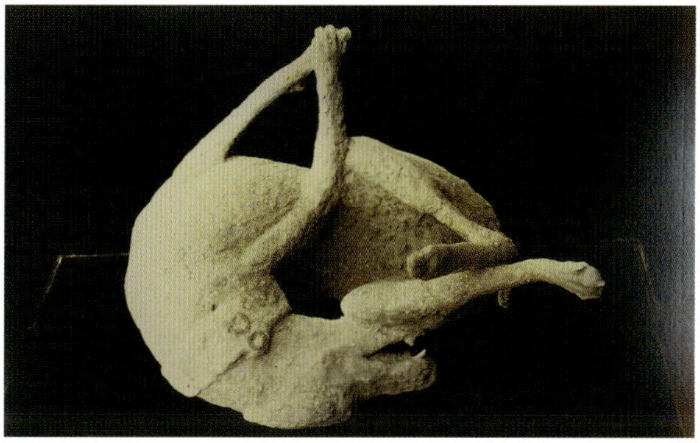

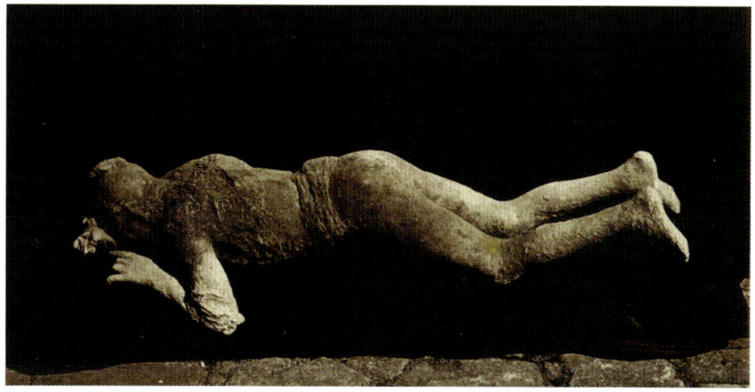

her (Fig 9). Her removal to the museum permitted photographers to treat her figure in a manner that was both more objective and more revealing (Fig 10).[11] A fourth icon emerged in 1882, when the body of a child, perhaps a boy of about ten, was found together with the arm of his mother who had once held him (Fig 11). Unlike the other casts in this series, this cast was part of a group of two figures, one of which could not be cast. Because the mother lay in the layer of stones, her cast was not successful, but the full figure of the boy – who may have been unable to walk by himself – was successfully cast. He is shown here as he appeared in the *Illustrated London News* for 1882, engraved after a photograph submitted to the paper by an English resident of Naples (Fig 12).[12] He took his place in the museum as a pendant to the *Watchdog*, on the opposite side of the door. By 1888 the number of casts in the museum had reached an even dozen – not much to show for twenty-five years of trying, but several of them had already become quite famous. The culmination of the second stage came with the production in 1888, on the occasion of a visit by Kaiser Wilhelm II, of a series of twelve reductions of the first dozen victims by the Neapolitan sculptor Achille d'Orsi. When the prospect of a state visit from the German emperor Wilhelm II arose, someone in Rome, perhaps Fiorelli himself, had the idea of presenting the royal visitor with a set of reproductions of the Pompeian casts, and d'Orsi was hired to make them. He advised making half-scale reductions in terracotta, which might then be cast in gesso. He worked on them in August and September so they would be ready for the emperor to examine beside the originals during his visit in October. D'Orsi's copies were apparently a success – and, incidentally, demonstrated the artistic side of the undertaking. They were subsequently shipped to Berlin, each with its own specially made glass case. In Berlin the casts were given permanent exhibition space in their own room in the Antiquarium on the second floor of the Altesmuseum. (It is presumed they were destroyed during the Second World War.)

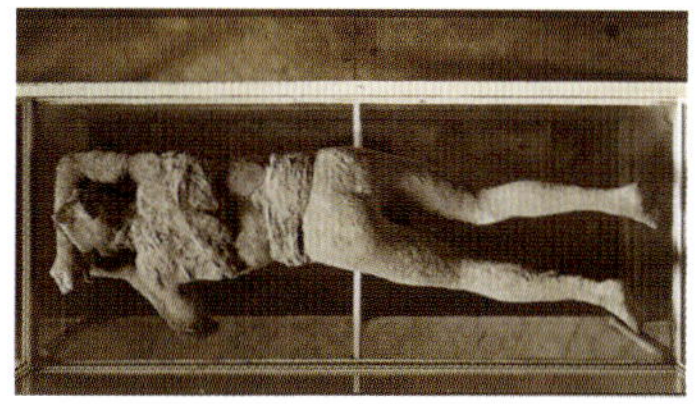

Clockwise from top left

Fig 8. Cast of *Watchdog*. Photo: Giorgio Sommer, 1875. Collection of author.

Fig 9. Cast of a young woman ('Victim Number 10'). Photo: Giorgio Sommer, 1875. Collection of author.

Fig 10. Cast of a young woman ('Victim Number 10'). Photo: Giacomo Brogi, c.1875. Collection of author.

The third stage: context and multiplicity

By 1889 the Pompeian museum had run out of space in which to absorb new casts. A photograph of the museum taken in the 1890s shows casts from 1889 in cases stacked one atop the other, creating a bizarre effect.[13] In some ways the progress of the excavations and the remodelling of the museum necessitated by continued progress had little effect upon the newly attained icon status of the casts. The *Sleeping Man*, the

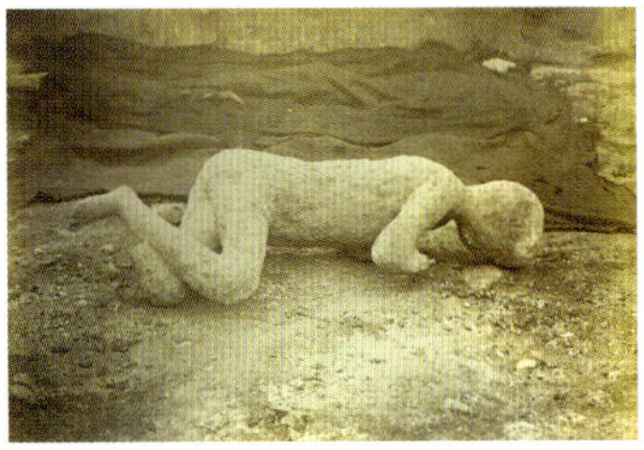

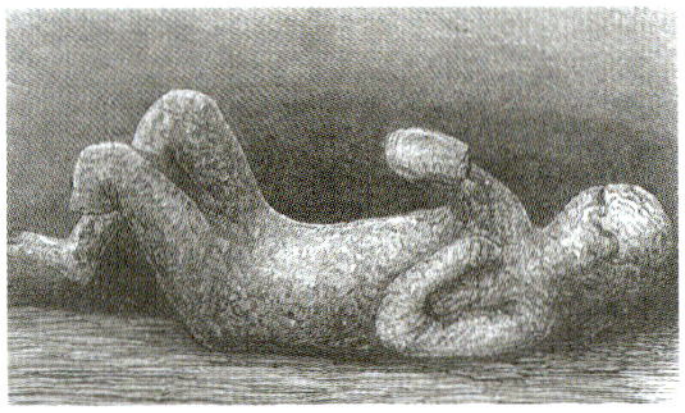

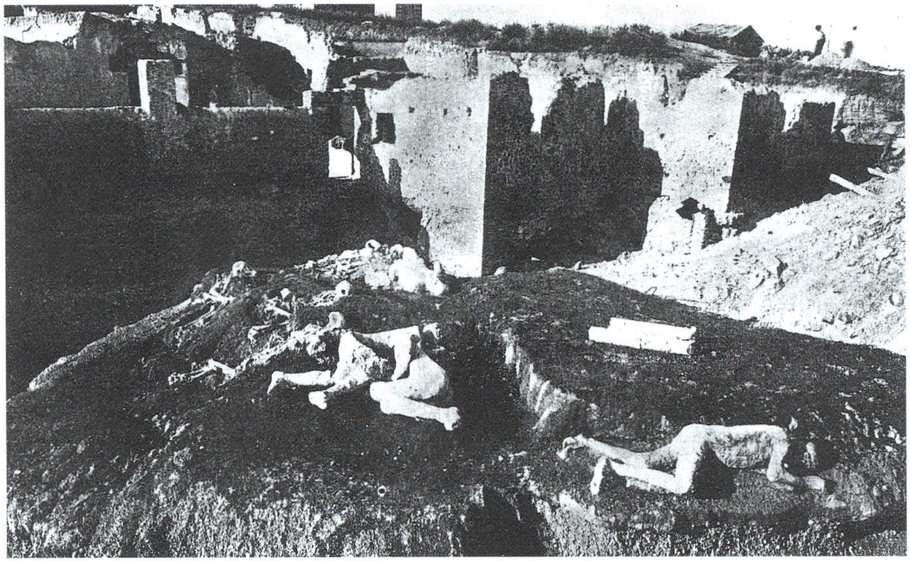

Watchdog, and the *Body of a Young Woman* continued to sell postcards and to draw visitors to the site.

A third stage in the development of the casts occurred when the excavators – and the photographers – began to develop the potentials of contextualised groupings, noted as early as 1863 but, for technical reasons, left undeveloped by the excavators.[14] Emphasising groups, however, meant taking attention away from the individual bodies and so the third stage may appear to be distinctly 'post-classical' in the production of iconic images. This third stage in the history of the Pompeian casts saw the appearance of site-specific casts – and the return of (or the refusal to exclude) fragments. In this grouping from 1914 some fine casts are to be seen together with a larger number of skeletons in a photographic ensemble, which seems to have served the purpose of final record (Fig 13). In any event, the only cast made subsequent to the 1880s to achieve the status of an icon is the *Crouching Man* found by Maiuri near the Grand Palestra in the 1930s.[15]

A brief survey of the history of the early casts, 1863–88, shows a rapid development in technical proficiency, the introduction of a new medium – photography – that was to have drastic consequences, and a radical shift in popular taste which led to the acceptance of the display of human remains in a scientific context. It appears that the intent of Fiorelli and his colleagues was at first scientific rather than artistic. During the first decade of their existence, Fiorelli's casts led a dual and somewhat compromised life as objects of study among selected visitors and as objects of curiosity for most of the others, like William Dean Howells. A second phase followed the first, dating from around 1873, when Fiorelli began to develop his ideas for an on-site museum at the Pompeii excavations. Casts made between 1873 and 1888 were more consciously made as works of art intended for exhibition. When the museum was filled to capacity after three excellent casts were made in 1889, it again became necessary to re-evaluate the nature of the casts, and they once again became archaeological artefacts.

Fig 11. top, Cast of a boy ('Victim Number 11'). Photo: Giorgio Sommer, 1882. Collection of author.

Fig 12. bottom, Cast of a boy ('Victim Number 11'). Metal-cut illustration. After *Illustrated London News* (11 March 1882).

Fig 13. right, Group of casts in an excavation at Pompeii, 1914. After *Notizie degli scavi*, 1914.

Notes

1 Various terms have been used to describe the different properties of the matrix. The hardened ashes of the 'surge and flow' layers are often described simply as 'mud' (Italian: *fango*). For example, 'cavity' (Italian: *vuoto*) may denote the impression (or *impronta*) of the victim's flesh formed at the time of the eruption, but surviving only as an empty shell.

2 The first human casts did not happen accidentally, but were preceded by a series of unsuccessful castings. As early as 1831 an attempt had been made to cast the body of a woman found in the House of the Faun in plaster of Paris, but without success. The idea surfaced again in 1861 with the discovery of a woman whose jewellery box and clothing had left perfect impressions in the mud. See Austen Henry Layard in *London Quarterly Review* (American edition), 115 (1864), pp. 161–80, esp. p. 180.

3 The sculptures of George Segal are frequently compared with the casts from Pompeii.

4 Three successive stages bear an uncanny similarity to J. J. Winckelmann's characterisation of three phases of ancient art as successively embodying the *necessary*, the *beautiful*, and the *superfluous*. See J. J. Winckelmann, *The History of Ancient Art*, trans. G. Henry Lodge (New York: Ungar, 1968), vol. 1, p. 29 (1,1,1).

5 At the beginning of 1863 the director of the Pompeii excavations Giuseppe Fiorelli was intent upon consolidating into one contiguous block all of the sites that had previously been dug within the circuit wall of Pompeii. In early February Fiorelli had his workers digging previously unexcavated ground at the intersection of two narrow streets in an area of the city known to be devoid of wealthy houses.

6 'The man in the last struggle has thrown himself upon his back, and taken his doom sturdily – there is a sublime calm in his rigid figure.' Although this cast was repeatedly described and documented, it seems that it no longer exists.

7 Mark Twain, *The Innocents Abroad* (1867), chapter 31.

8 William Dean Howells, *Italian Journeys* (Marlboro, VT: Marlboro Press, 1988), pp. 67–8.

9 J. Werge, 'Photography and the Immured Pompeians', *Photographic News* (4 September 1868), p. 427. The passage is cited in Adam D. Weinberg, *The Photographs of Giorgio Sommer* (Rochester, NY: Visual Studies Workshop, 1981–2), pp. 31–2. My thanks to Dan Younger for directing me to this valuable study.

10 Giuseppe Fiorelli, *Descrizione di Pompei* (Naples, 1875), pp. 452–3.

11 Amazingly, her nudity does not seem to have offended visitors to the museum, as this card, sent by her father to a young lady of Glasgow, bears witness. The overhead photograph never achieved much popularity, but it offered a better look at critical details, such as the manner in which the victim has wrapped her dress over (and perhaps around) her head in an effort to protect herself from the suffocating ashes and fumes.

12 'A Child of Pompeii', *Illustrated London News*, 80:2236 (11 March 1883), p. 228 (figure) and p. 230.

13 Anderson 26540. The casts of 1863 seem to have been moved out of the museum at this time in order to accommodate the casts of 1889.

14 The group of two women that emerged from a single casting in February 1863 is the most notable example to stimulate discussion of the psychological connection between individual figures. To some extent, all four of the figures cast in 1863 had been treated as a group by guides and by some authors. Of course, groups of skeletons had already by that time been appreciated for their collective fate.

15 The most famous group of victims consisted of eighteen adults, mostly women, and a child found in the cellar of the Villa of Diomedes in the eighteenth century. This story can be found in all of the guidebooks. More recently, A. Maiuri has written eloquently and memorably about the group of fugitives found in the 'Garden of the Fugitives' in the excavations near Porta Nocera in the 1950s. See A. Maiuri, 'Le vittime di Porta Nocera', in G. Clemente (ed.), *Pompei ed Ercolano fra case ed abitanti* (Florence: Giunti Gruppo Editoriale, 1998), pp. 83–8.

Many artists who have taken up the challenge of working with the figure have adopted a strategy of representing parts of the body rather than the body as a whole. Fragments are offered instead of the whole body with an implication that this is a more authentic expression of the predicament of the artist and also of his/her contemporary audience. This was a key theme of the 'Fragmented Figure' conference held at Cardiff School of Art and Design in July 2005 and it was one that was explored in a particularly poignant and affecting way in the following essay on the work of Robert Arneson. The author, Mary Drach McInnes, is Professor of Art History at the School of Art and Design, New York State College of Ceramics at Alfred University, USA. All the papers from the conference are still available to read online in Issue 8 of *Interpreting Ceramics*, originally published in 2006.

Interpreting Ceramics

Selected Essays

Visualizing Mortality: Robert Arneson's *Chemo* Portraits

Mary Drach McInnes

> *My body is infested with worms,*
> *my skin is cracked and discharging.*
> (Job 7:5)[1]

Beginning a talk on Arneson with a biblical passage is, at best, unorthodox. He was not personally religious, and his professional reputation lies in the profane. Yet in his final months Robert Arneson created two self-portraits – *Chemo I* (1992) and *Chemo 2* (1992) – depicting himself as a contemporary Job. They are startling portraits of affliction and despair. These terracotta busts offer us memorable images of rupture: torn skin, twisted organs, and tormented expression.

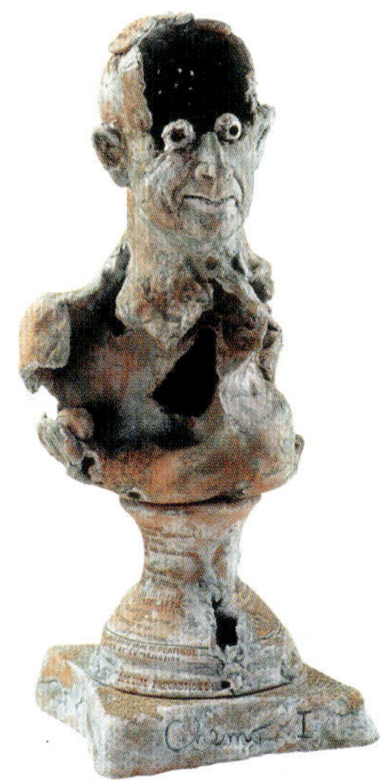

Fig 1. Front view: Robert Arneson, *Chemo 1* (1992), glazed ceramic, 47 × 21 × 19 in. (119.38 × 53.34 × 48.26 cm), San Francisco Museum of Modern Art, 98.514, purchased through a grant from the Koret Foundation, a gift from Christine and Frank Currie, and the Accessions Committee Fund, © Estate of Robert Arneson/DACS, London/VAGA, New York 2012. Photo: Alo Zanetta.

Arneson's vision of mortality is a record of his own long struggle with cancer. After almost two decades of 'managing' cancer, he began a gruelling course of chemotherapy treatment. Shortly thereafter he created the *Chemo* portraits, recording the deterioration of his body ravaged by disease and, ironically, by its treatment. The radical deformation and fragmentation of these self-portraits lie in direct conflict with traditional sculptural conventions. All qualities of classicism – order and restraint, clarity and austerity – are banished. In their place we are given the drama of the scream and the high rhetoric of pain.

In confronting his affliction the artist departed from convention and his own celebrated 'funk' vocabulary.[2] With the *Chemo* portraits, Arneson aggressively roamed outside the perimeters of figurative sculpture into the fields of modern painting and medical literature.[3] In particular, there are correspondences with Francis Bacon's portraiture. Arneson's intense interest in Bacon, especially the painter's anatomical disintegration and psychological escape of the body, seems to have provided the ceramic sculptor with a new set of ideas for portraying mortality.

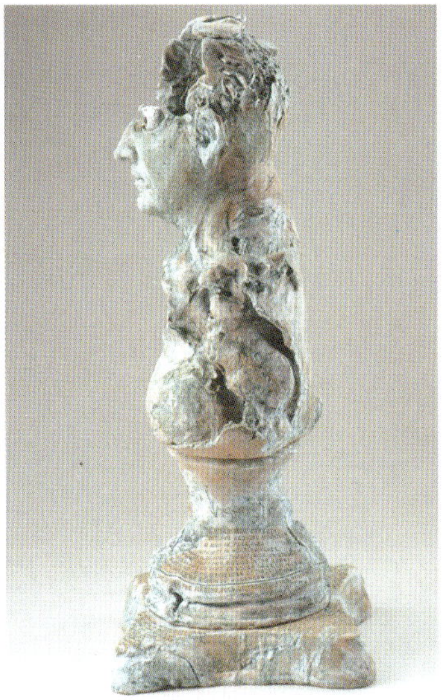

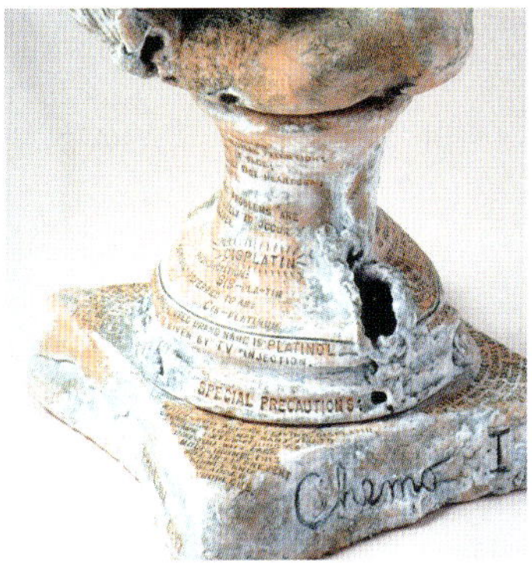

Fig 2. Side view: Robert Arneson, *Chemo 1* (1992), glazed ceramic, 47 × 21 × 19 in. (119.38 × 53.34 × 48.26 cm), San Francisco Museum of Modern Art, 98.514, purchased through a grant from the Koret Foundation, a gift from Christine and Frank Currie, and the Accessions Committee Fund, © Estate of Robert Arneson/DACS, London/VAGA, New York 2012. Photo: Alo Zanetta.

Fig 3. Detail of base: Robert Arneson, *Chemo 1* (1992), San Francisco Museum of Modern Art, 98.514, purchased through a grant from the Koret Foundation, a gift from Christine and Frank Currie, and the Accessions Committee Fund, © Estate of Robert Arneson/DACS, London/VAGA, New York 2012. Photo: Alo Zanetta.

Portraiture, its nature and limitations, is a central concern for Arneson in these late sculptures. In *Chemo I* and *Chemo 2* the artist uses language to augment his attack on the portrait. Text plays an important part in the artist's sculptures, and the 1992 self-portraits display a type of vocabulary that is new in his work. *Chemo I* and *Chemo 2* are each encircled with text sequences drawn from his cancer treatment. These stamped, fractured lines effectively extend the formal fragmentation of the figure and break the conceit of mimetic representation.

Arneson's dismantling of representation is seen in the *Chemo* sculptures. Like his other self-portraits these busts began with casts of his head, which endow the work with an initial mimetic quality. Those familiar with Arneson's self-portraits instantly recognise the artist's features.[4] Even those new to this body of work sense the particularity of the fleshy nose, the distinctiveness of the chin. The features are specific and represent an actual person. Mimesis, however, is immediately compromised here by a breaking-apart and a tearing-down of the body. Arneson gives us an open, flayed torso. In place of clarity we have formal chaos; in place of moral elevation we have the baseness of physical decay.

Arneson's deformation of the figure pulls us into a new emotive reality.[5] In *Chemo 2* the artist depicts himself contorted in pain. His neck curves in convulsion, his head is thrown back and lies horizontally on the spine.[6] The sealed eyes give a sense of profound exhaustion; the mouth is open in agony. We sense pain escaping the body. Other openings – in the base of the neck and in the chest – are cut into the body adding to the frantic release.

Material, bodily violence abounds in the *Chemo* portraits. Clay, or flesh, is not merely cut or broken, but ripped apart. The entire identity of the body is compromised. The back is ribbed in alternating lumps and hollows; the shoulder is amputated; the chest cavity is opened, exposing a twisting, folded spinal column. The surface forms a new topography of pain, a geography defined by the dry pitting and muddy abrasion of terracotta. A mouldy film of white and irradiated green on the surface adds to the palpable physical decay. The 'exhilarated despair' of the *Chemo* portraits is indebted to Francis Bacon's material assault on portraiture.[7]

Arneson's engagement with Bacon is witnessed in the number of images that the sculptor made of the British painter. Beginning in the early 1980s Arneson did a series of portraits ranging from drawings, masks, and a large sculpture entitled *A Likeness of Francis B.* (1981). The maquettes of this work, like Arneson's other depictions of artists (Pollock, Picasso and Duchamp, for example), are a combination of homage and caricature. Three maquettes from 1981 show the artist's close attention to Bacon's paintings. Commenting on Arneson's use of pedestals in his *Model for 'A Likeness of Francis B.'* and *Model for 'Francis Bacon'*, Signe Mayfield finds that each 'wittily condenses Bacon's foreshortened, windowless rooms into a base detail'.[8] There is also a deformation of form and a wilful play of colour across the body, imitating the painter's own methods. Arneson transformed his own sculptural practice by carefully appropriating Bacon's pictorial strategies of representation.

Francis Bacon's distortion of the portrait and its overwhelming assault on our senses are the hallmarks of his work. In any number of images we see the painter's play with representation, his disruption of mimesis through jarring colour, displaced form and unconventional space. His formal liberties are evident in the pigmented screens that break down his subject's face, while the subject itself seems to secrete its own dense shadow. While Bacon's formal slippage moves away from mimesis, the effect of his distortion invokes an intense emotional response from us. In place of documentation we receive an unsettling psychological reality beneath the material surface.

Bacon (and later Arneson) used distortion to get closer to the 'real' appearance of his subject. As the scholar Ernst Van Alphen observes, the painter insisted on the seemingly paradoxical need for distortion to both move away from a stereotypical representation and to move toward a more precise documentation.[9] Bacon's remarks in his interview with David Sylvester detail this very act:

> FB: What I want to do is to distort the thing far beyond the appearance, but in the distortion to bring it back to a recording of the appearance.
>
> DS: Are you saying that painting is almost a way of bringing somebody back, that the process of painting is almost like the process of recalling?
>
> FB: I am saying it.[10]

Van Alphen, citing this exchange, remarks: 'Bacon talks about his portrayals as conflicts between the artificiality of representation and the resistance of the model to that artificiality.'[11] In this battle between subject and representation, fragmentation is the inevitable outcome.

Bacon's paintings deny the conceptual unity and formal cohesion of mimesis. His subjects are marked by a distinctive erosion of the boundary between the figure's interior and exterior. His signature elision of facial planes, where one plane glides over another, allows us to look onto, around and through the face. Similarly, his use of shadows – strong, flat, negative shapes that float beside recognisable features – disrupts traditional modelling of the human figure.

Bacon's figures also devolve taxonomically, visually sliding from 'human' to 'creature' to 'meat'. In *Three Studies for a Crucifixion* (1962) we scan the triptych (one of the artist's favourite formats) and read this shift from man to carcass.[12] The two figures on the left, while distorted, maintain their essential human identity. That is, we discern 'head', 'eyes', 'nose' and 'mouth'. This identity is compromised as we visually move to the central section. Here a grotesque figure reclines on a divan. The body is a set of rhythmic black lines splattered with paint, defying any definition. The grizzly head hovers over this formlessness. This bloodied figure transitions to a hanging carcass on the far right. In the final panel a flayed form hangs from the ceiling, its vertebrae exposed and its haunches red with blood. In this painting Bacon's subject shifts identity from portraiture to genre to still life.

Similarly, Arneson's self-portraits shift identity from the organic to the inorganic. The body's skin becomes a vast topography in which the surface changes from cracked to pitted, while the external membrane is pulled open to reveal internal organs or empty caverns. The chest is cracked open for our inspection. Thus, the broken carapace of *Chemo I* evokes caves and plateaus; the torn stomach of *Chemo 2* connotes rotten fruit.

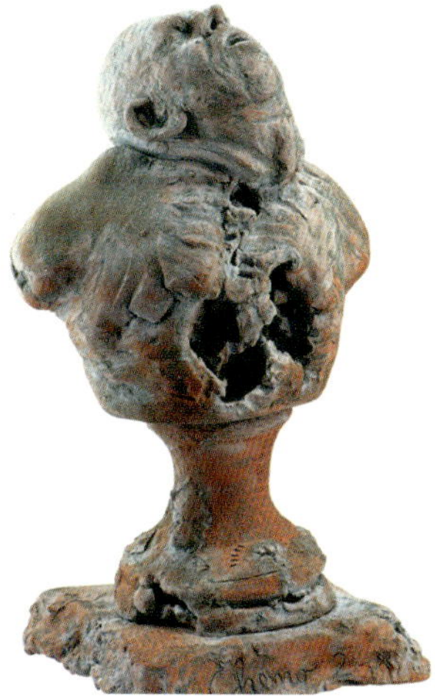

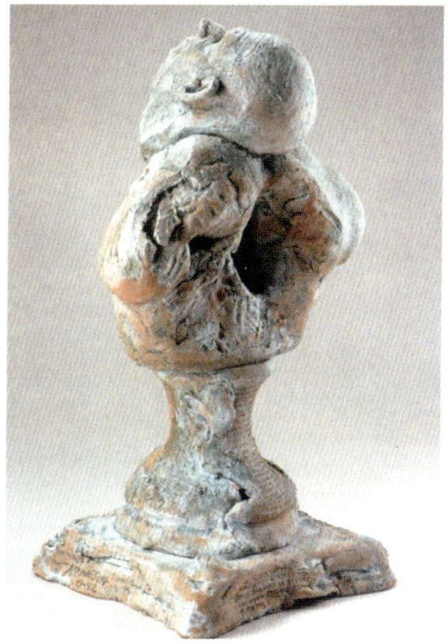

Fig 4. Front view: Robert Arneson, *Chemo 2* (1992), glazed ceramic, 40.5 × 24 × 21 in. (102.87 × 60.96 × 53.43 cm), San Francisco Museum of Modern Art, 98.515, purchased through a gift of Phyllis Wattis and a gift of Sandra Shannonhouse, © Estate of Robert Arneson/DACS, London/ VAGA, New York 2012. Photo: Alo Zanetta.

Fig 5. Back view: Robert Arneson, *Chemo 2* (1992) (and details), glazed ceramic, 40.5 × 24 × 21 in. (102.87 × 60.96 × 53.34 cm), San Francisco Museum of Modern Art, 98.515, purchased through a gift of Phyllis Wattis and a gift of Sandra Shannonhouse, © Estate of Robert Arneson/DACS, London/ VAGA, New York 2012. Photo: Alo Zanetta.

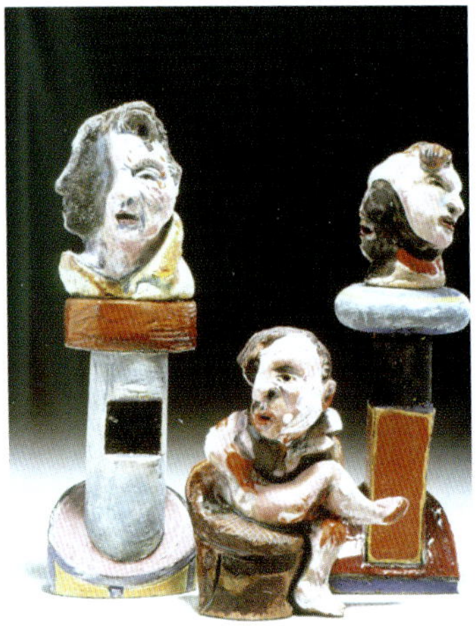

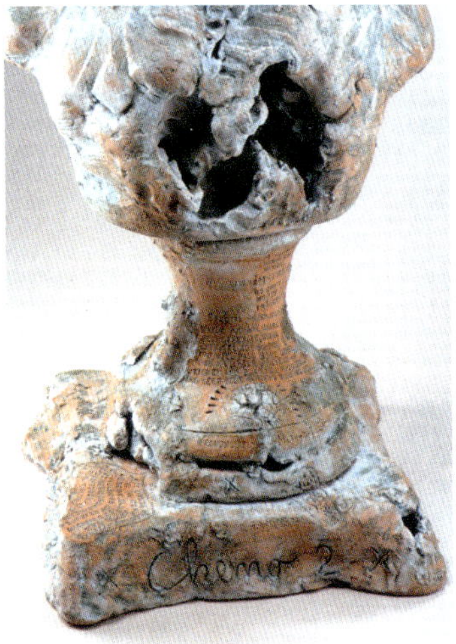

Fig 6. Robert Arneson, from left to right: *Model for 'A Likeness of Francis B.'*, glazed ceramic, 10.5 × 3.5 × 2 in.; *Model for 'Francis Bacon'*, glazed ceramic, 10 × 3.25 × 2.5 in.; *Model for 'Francis Bacon'*, glazed ceramic, 6 × 5 × 2.5 in., © Estate of Robert Arneson/Licensed by VAGA, New York, NY. Photo: M. Lee Fatherree.

Fig 7. Detail of base: Robert Arneson, *Chemo 2*, San Francisco Museum of Modern Art, 98.515, purchased through a gift of Phyllis Wattis and a gift of Sandra Shannonhouse, © Estate of Robert Arneson/DACS, London/VAGA, New York 2012. Photo: Alo Zanetta.

The human identity – as in Bacon's *Crucifixion* – is compromised. This metamorphic quality is apparent on the back as well. Here the artist aggressively manipulates the clay, his fingers dragging vertically across the skull and then down the torso as the vertebrae shift and form rivulets. Again we lose the human subject. Instead of portraiture we have landscape.[13] Parched ground and pitted earth, rivulets of clay and fissures of baked earth, replace 'man'. In Arneson's work the materiality of the surface becomes the critical text. At this moment, material is elemental. The portrait evolves from clay into being, then devolves back to material. This strategy uses clay's inherent malleability and its biblical associations with creation and death.

To this primal language of materiality the artist adds the contemporary lexicon of pharmacology. One of the critical aspects of both *Chemo* portraits is Arneson's use of text to complement his manipulation of clay. Encircling the lower bust and base of the self-portraits are broken text sequences naming medicines and pronunciations, special warnings and precautions, possible side effects and emergency procedures.[14] Typical of the stamped text is the section at the base of *Chemo 2*. Outlined in a floating 'thought balloon', it states, in fragmented form, the following:

DO NOT DRINK ALCOHOL
WHILE USING THIS MEDICINE.
ALCOHOL CAN INCREASE
THE RISK OF LIVER
PROBLEMS. SIDE EFFECTS
NEEDING IMMEDIATE
MEDICAL ATTENTION:
BLACK, TARRY STOOLS;
BLOODY VOMIT; DIARRHEA;
SORES IN MOUTH AND
ON LIPS; STOMACH PAIN.
SIDE EFFECTS
NEEDING MEDICAL
ATTENTION AS SOON
AS POSSIBLE: FEVER,
CHILLS, OR SORE
THROAT; UNUSUAL
BLEEDING OR BRUISING;
BLOOD IN URINE; BLURRED
VISION; CONFUSION; CON-
VULSIONS OR SEIZURES;
COUGH; DARK URINE; DIZZINESS;
DROWSINESS; HEADACHES; JOINT PAIN;
SHORTNESS OF BREATH; SWELLING OF
FEET OR LOWER LEGS;
UNUSUAL TIREDNESS OR WEAKNESS;
YELLOWING OF EYES
AND SKIN

The dispassionate yet imperative language of the medical establishment (familiar to all of us who have read a prescription bottle) dramatically underscores the daily, impersonal brutality of chemotherapy. Arneson creates a schism between the objective cautionary text and the subjective torn topography of his self-portraits. The text highlights the mortal irony of the cure destroying the body. But what does it really tell us of Arneson's own affliction, the decay of his own body? Ultimately, this litany of side-effects tells us little. When confronted with narrating the reality of pain, language is simply impoverished. The very poverty of language underlies Arneson's portrayal of mortality. This 'shattering' of language in the face of pain is the particular interest of anthropologist Elaine Scarry. In *The Body in Pain* Scarry theorises that pain, unlike any other sensation, has no referential content – it is simply without an object outside of itself. Pain 'is not *of* or *for* anything … more than any other phenomenon, [it] resists objectification in language'.[15] Pain is not only resistant to language, it actively destroys it. This view is echoed by Virginia Woolf in her 1930 essay entitled 'On being ill'. Here she wryly notes the inability of language to communicate even simple physical phenomena: 'English, which can express the thoughts of Hamlet and the tragedy of Lear, has no words for the shiver and the headache.'[16] Language, concludes Woolf, 'runs dry' in the face of pain.

Arneson's text passages reveal the inability of language to adequately describe a prolonged, debilitating, terminal disease. He forces upon us a new text for pain, one that is grounded in the materiality of clay and that embraces the abject and, at times, the comic. In *Chemo I* the language is a mixture of the grotesque and the farcical. Like its cousin, this self-portrait offers us an astounding inversion of interior and exterior: the front bulges out and rips open, the side erodes and deposits clay, the back undulates and forms rivulets, the base cracks and opens large fault lines. In the midst of this deformation is the grizzly and near-comic handling of the head. The cranium is cut open around the eyes – the glossy, glassy eyes are preposterously pinned to the cheekbone, appearing like bad props in a horror show. When we look inside the cranium we see it repeatedly pierced. Visual puns abound: 'hole in the head', 'mind like a sieve', 'riddled with cancer'. Arneson's funk vocabulary makes a brief yet potent contribution.

The contemporary sculptor's material rhetoric seems anticipated by Virginia Woolf. She imagines someone taking a lump of sound and fashioning a new language, one startlingly close to Arneson's ceramic formlessness:

> [T]aking … pain in one hand, and a lump of pure sound in the other (as perhaps the people of Babel did in the beginning), so to crush them together that a brand new word in the end drops out. Probably it will be something laughable … Yet it is not only a new language that we need, more primitive, more sensual, more obscene, but a new hierarchy of passion; love must be disposed in favour of a temperature of 104; jealousy give place to the pangs of sciatica.[17]

Further, she suggests that the English will not take the necessary liberties with language, but help may come from the Americans, 'whose genius is so much happier in the making of new words than in the disposition of the old'.[18] The ironic smile of *Chemo I* suggests that Arneson accepted the task.

In place of the 'babble' of language or the clarity of mimetic representation, Arneson creates a new rhetoric in the clay itself. The artist's manipulation of clay – using its essential malleability – creates a responsive text that refers directly to the body's breakdown. In fragmenting the body, in breaking down the tissue, in compromising the membrane, Arneson creates a language of pain, a way of visualising mortality.

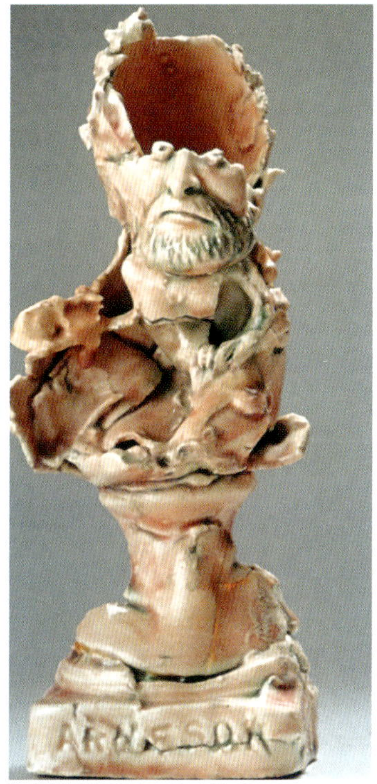

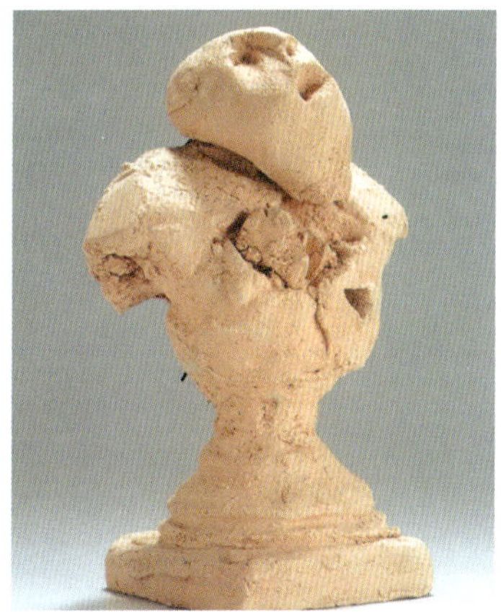

Fig 8. Robert Arneson, *Trophy Bust* (concept for *Chemo 1*) (1978), glazed ceramic, 7.5 × 3 × 3 in., © Estate of Robert Arneson/Licensed by VAGA, New York, NY. Photo: M. Lee Fatherree.

Fig 9. Robert Arneson, *Trophy Bust* (concept for *Chemo 2*) (1984), ceramic, 6 × 4 × 2.75 in., © Estate of Robert Arneson/Licensed by VAGA, New York, NY. Photo: M. Lee Fatherree.

Notes

1 *New English Bible* (New York: Oxford University Press and Cambridge University Press), quoted in James Elkins, *Pictures of the Body: Pain and Metamorphosis* (Stanford: Stanford University Press, 1999), p. 108n.
2 Arneson, as leader of the California-based movement called 'funk', made a name for himself through a series of sculptures – toilets and toasters – that mocked both fine art and the field of ceramic art. His work is marked by an overtly crude voice and transgressive vulgarity. For an overview of the artist's œuvre, see Neal Benezra, *Robert Arneson, a Retrospective* (Des Moines: Des Moines Art Center, 1986), and Gary Garrels, *Robert Arneson, Self Reflections* (San Francisco: San Francisco Museum of Modern Art, 1997).
3 For *Chemo I* Arneson went back to a small study, *Trophy Bust* (1978). This glazed ceramic maquette features the torn skull and convoluted chest cavity of the 1992 self-portrait.
4 This genre formed the mainstay of the artist's prolific production. More than half of his over two thousand works were in the form of self-portraits.
5 I am indebted to the writings of Ernst Van Alphen on Francis Bacon for his reading of that painter's intentions and, more broadly, to the writings of Michel Leiris on this artist.
6 According to his widow, Sandra Shannonhouse, Arneson drew this image from a Second World War photograph, brought back from Europe by her family, of allies freeing Jews from the concentration camps (author's interview with Sandra Shannonhouse, April 2005).
7 Leiris ends his text on Bacon describing the painter's work with this Nietzschean formula. See Michel Leiris, *Francis Bacon, Full Face and Profile* (New York: Rizzoli, 1983), p. 47.
8 Signe Mayfield, 'Big idea: the maquettes of Robert Arneson' in *Big Idea: the Maquettes of Robert Arneson* (Palo Alto: Palo Alto Cultural Center, 2002), pp. 31–2.
9 Ernst Van Alphen, 'The portrait's dispersal: concepts of representation and subjectivity in contemporary portraiture', in Joanna Woodall (ed.), *Portraiture: Facing the Subject* (Manchester: Manchester University Press, 1996), p. 246.
10 *Ibid.*
11 *Ibid.*
12 See www.guggenheimcollection.org/site/artist_work_md_10_1_2_3.html.
13 In both *Chemo* portraits, the portrait is further compromised by Arneson's unconventional manipulation of the base. In place of the traditional separation of 'figure' and 'pedestal' Arneson links these two elements formally through a dissolution of bodily parts that extends down and over the base. Further, Arneson uses text that spills out from its perimeter of the base and into the regions of the body. This further complicates our reading of the 'bust'.
14 According to his widow, Arneson took most of the text from a publication of the National Institute of Health entitled *Chemotherapy and You* (author's interview with Sandra Shannonhouse, April 2005).
15 Elaine Scarry, *The Body in Pain: the Making and Unmaking of the World* (Oxford: Oxford University Press, 1985), p. 4.
16 Virginia Woolf, 'On being ill' in *Collected Essays*, vol. 4 (London: Hogarth Press, 1967), p. 194, cited in Scarry, The Body in Pain, p. 4.
17 Woolf, 'On being ill', pp. 194–5.
18 *Ibid.*, p. 194.

Fig 10. Robert Arneson, *Chemo 2*, San Francisco Museum of Modern Art, 98.515, purchased through a gift of Phyllis Wattis and a gift of Sandra Shannonhouse, © Estate of Robert Arneson/DACS, London/VAGA, New York 2012. Photo: Alo Zanetta.

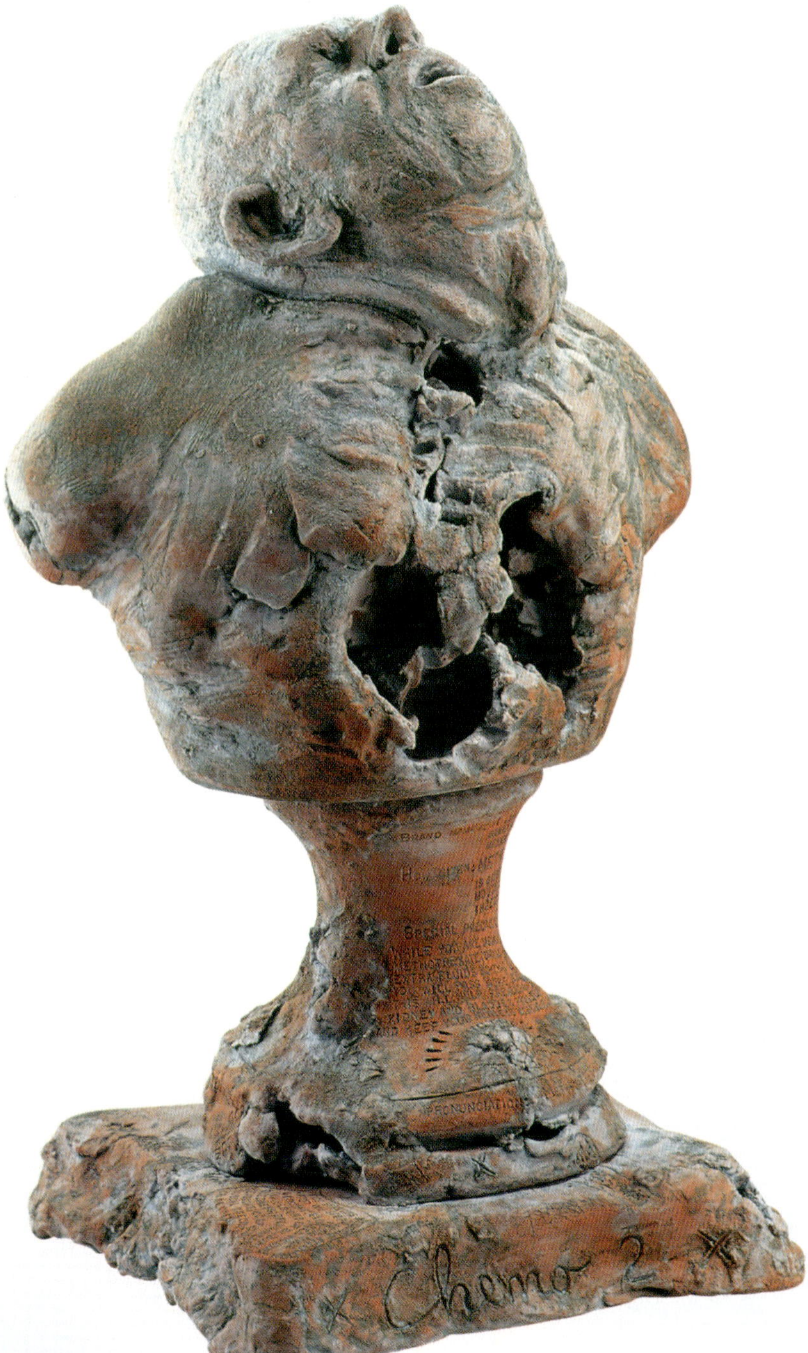

PLATE 50

This chapter was first published in Issue 9 of *Interpreting Ceramics*, which was guest edited by Mary Drach McInnes (New York State College of Ceramics, Alfred University) and titled 'Ceramics: Five Emerging Artists Survey the Field'. The five artists had all been key participants in a College Art Association panel discussion on Contemporary Ceramics (New York, 16 February 2007). In her editorial, McInnes describes Ruhwald's work as 'both physically emphatic, yet conceptually elusive. His sculptures continually remind us of familiar things – their forms recall domestic fixtures; their surfaces resemble plastic objects – yet they are not anything known. His work swings conceptually between the sterility of the white, modernist gallery and the disarray of everyday life.' Anders Ruhwald has been Artist-in-Residence and Head of Department at Cranbrook Academy of Art, Detroit, USA since 2008.

Functional Languages

Anders Ruhwald

I write as a ceramist who is interested in working with the 'thingness' of the ceramic object. My sculptures mediate the domestic sphere – not as the actual everyday item, but as a commentary on that item. The objects mediate this position through debating issues of colour and materiality, context and functionality. Initially, the pieces project a sense of familiarity, yet once this is identified some other element within the objects quickly destabilises this response. Ultimately, the pieces exist in a transitory state – as half-remembered things that seem to be, but yet aren't. They are purposefully open-ended objects that sit in the realm of 'things', but resist the easy fit of the everyday. My work functions as a kind of interior or social sculpture.

Like many ceramic artists, I came to the field through making pottery. It was an important entry point to my work. For the first ten years I worked with clay I made pottery; these functional pots were meant for use. Through this activity, I came to understand the things we surround ourselves with beyond the level of consumption. I got to understand the potential of using functional forms to mediate concerns that lie outside the confines of pure utility. With this realisation my work changed course and I developed an artistic practice, which I still label 'craft', or to be more precise and use my mother tongue, *kunsthåndværk*. *Kunsthåndværk* (literally art-craft) is defined by a studio practice that generates carefully laboured objects formally linked to objects of utility but rarely fulfilling that role practically. *Kunsthåndværk* therefore differs from the English language definition of craft which 'could also take in lots of handwork in industry and surviving vernacular craft' to quote the British craft-historian Tanya Harrod. By labelling my work as such I position it among utilitarian objects at a conceptual level without committing to it practically.[1]

In their editorial to the first volume of *The Journal of Material Culture*, Daniel Miller and Christopher Tilley describe how 'the relationship between persons and things is becoming once again a less dichotomous and more fluid one. The cause of which is generally felt to be the rise of commodities, where … the sheer quantitative increase is such as to constitute a qualitative change in many of our lives.'[2] How this qualitative change has

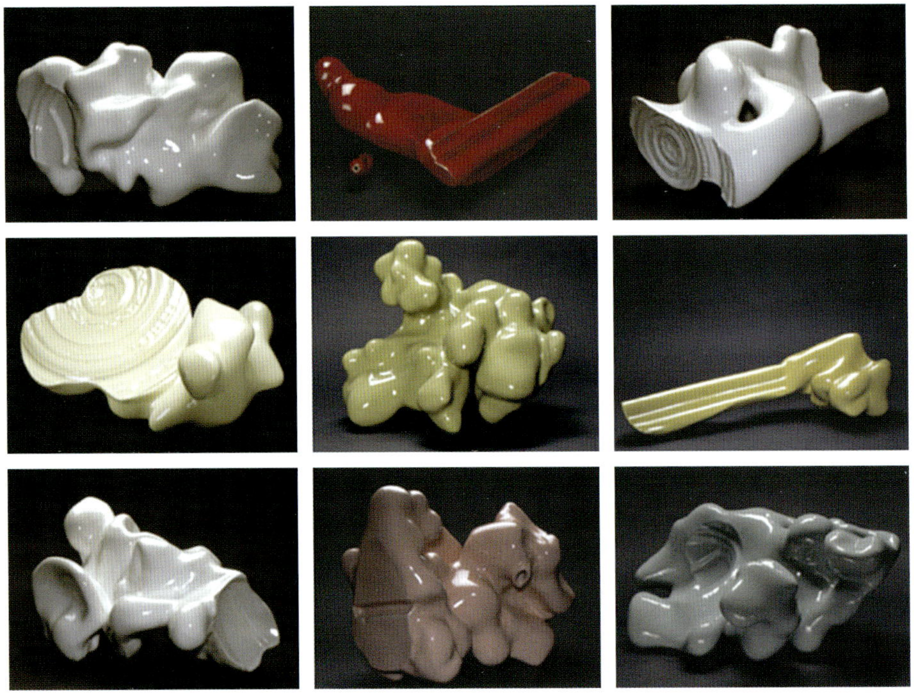

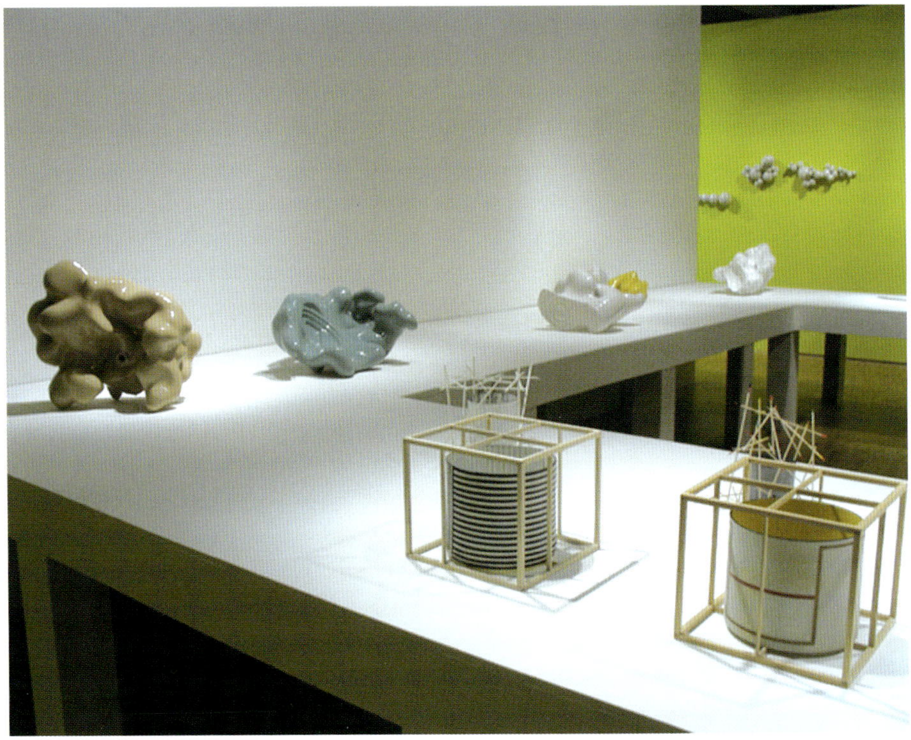

Fig 1. Selected works, 2002–3. Photo: Kira Brandt.

Fig 2. Installation view: *Stuff, Ingenuity and Critique*, Harbourfront Center, Toronto, Canada, 2004. Right and back: Anders Ruhwald. Left and front: Bodil and Cecilie Manz. Photo: Rasmus Koch.

disseminated through society is still an open question and a highly contested area of discussion. But it raises the interesting question of what the relationship between objects and people actually is. This basic query has been at the centre of my artistic investigation over the last several years.

(Fig 1) At the outset, this concern came into form through a series of objects that merge organic constructions referencing the body with fragments of everyday objects. The work implied a fusion between product and organism, surroundings and person, object and body. It set out to question the perceived rigid separation between humanity and our physical environment. If the objects with which we surround ourselves inform human identity to some extent, do they not also influence what we become? Thus the work was a formulation of what happens to common objects when they are assigned symbolic value, and become more than just their physical selves. The essential enquiry was whether human beings and our physical surroundings are transformed in the encounter with each other. Is there a possibility of considering the two becoming a larger entity?

In time, I became frustrated with the conventional presentation of this body of work. The objects existed in the gallery space as traditional sculptural objects, usually placed on white surfaces, detached from the reality they were trying to comment on (Fig 2). People could observe them, but there would be no interaction at the material or practical level. I conspired to establish a body of work that could have a similar relationship to its audience as the utilitarian objects I had made previously.

As this body of work came to its conclusion, I became increasingly interested in investigating the actual objects we surround ourselves with (Fig 3). This desire grew from a drive to try to give the work a literal material presence in the encounter with its audience, a presence closer to how we perceive things in our everyday. Essentially, I was looking for a way of making work that would pertain to the world of things, but not be immediately co-opted by the world of advertised realities and commercially mediated experiences (Fig 4). I was aiming for a body of work that would be understood and read within the world of manmade objects without being submerged in the haze of consumerability. In a sense, I was trying to map out an area of resistance within the world of things. I was looking for a place where we could meet and deal with objects that could present questions of the broader material culture.

Initially, I began this exploration by nominating abstract objects as functional objects or furniture, and placing them in such a way that they establish a physical relationship with the audience (Figs 5 and 6). Certain pieces have balloons inflated into plastic-looking ceramic forms, thus confusing the experience at the material level, while encouraging physical interaction. Other work from this period mimics a functional language; it might appear in some measure to be useful, but resists any clear relation to known categories of objects and thus asks the basic question of what its purpose might be (Fig 7).

My practice evolved into a series of works with a literal function, mostly chairs or stools, which could be sat on (Fig 8). I wanted to break down the distance between the viewer and the objects fully, to have people engage the work in a very direct manner. I was trying to encourage a material reading. What does the work do? How does it stand? What does

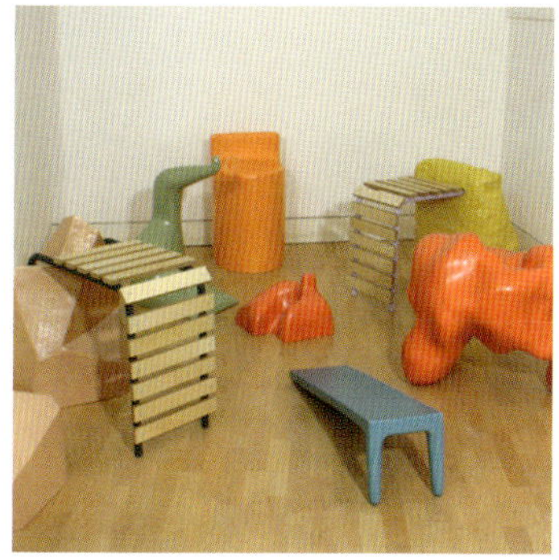

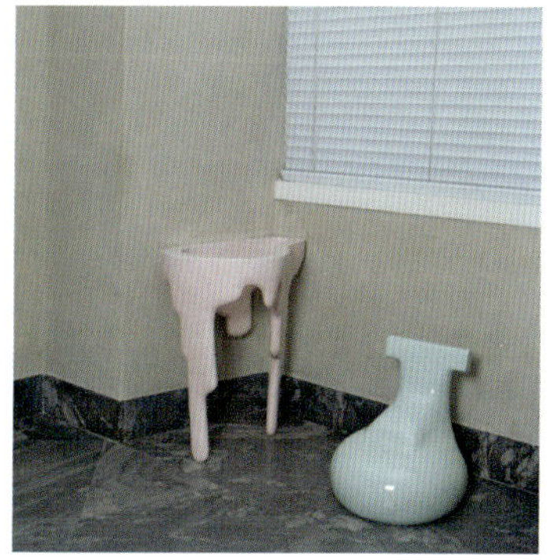

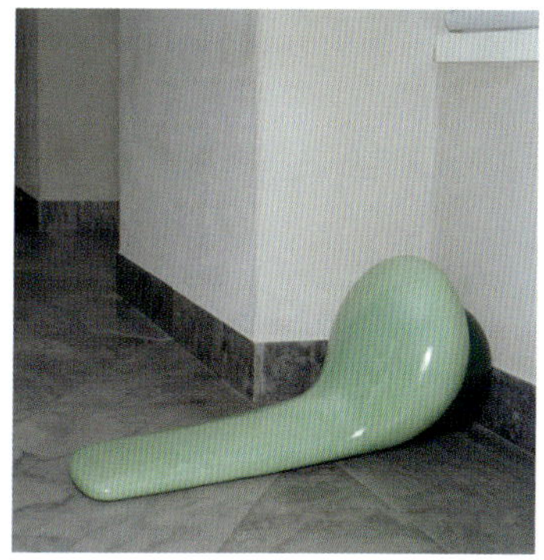

Fig 3. Selected works, 2005. Photo: Anders Ruhwald.

Fig 4. *Social Piece of Furniture*, earthenware (2004), collection of the Norwegian National Museum of Decorative Art, Trondheim, Norway. *Untitled #4* (from the functional series), earthenware (2004), collection of the Swedish National Museum, Stockholm, Sweden. Photo: Kira Brandt.

Fig 5. *Formal piece of Furniture*, earthenware and balloon (2004). Photo: Kira Brandt.

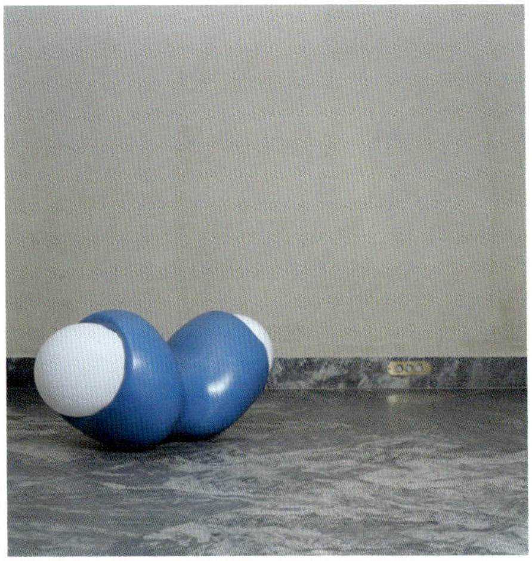

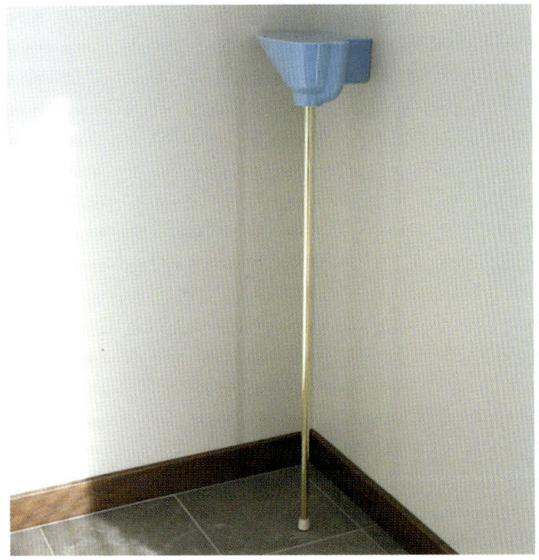

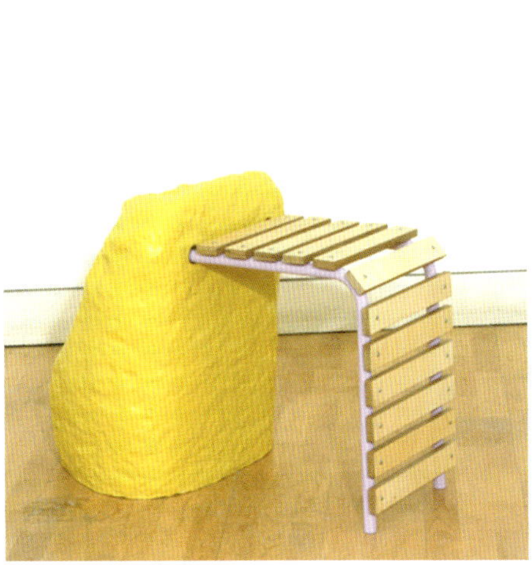

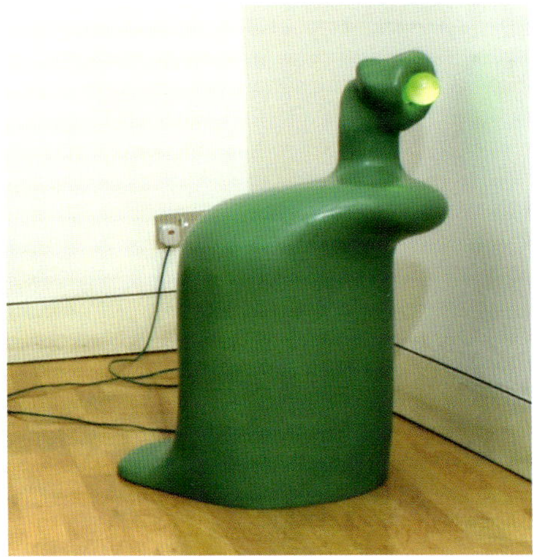

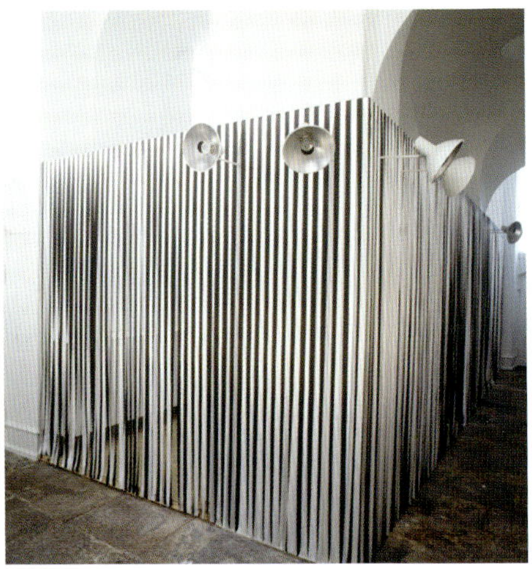

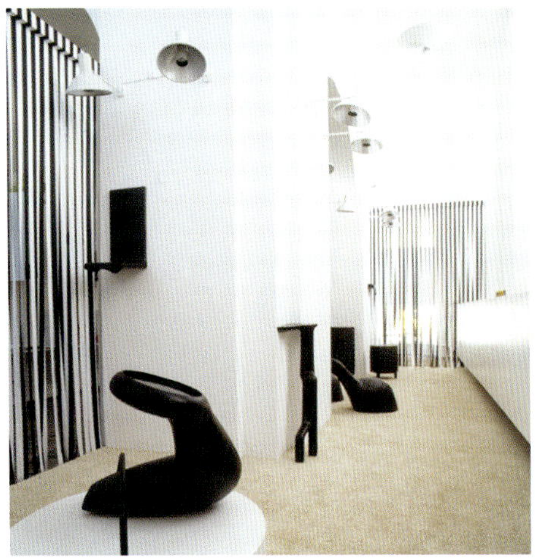

Fig 6. top left, *Piece of Furniture*, earthenware and balloon (2004). Photo: Kira Brandt.

Fig 7. top right, *Social Piece of Furniture #2*, brass, vitreous china and rubber (2005). Made during an Art/Industry residency at the Kohler Factory. Photo: Art/Industry- Kohler.

Fig 8. middle left, *Piece of Furniture #2*, earthenware, plywood, iron tubes, rubber and screws (2005). Photo: Anders Ruhwald.

Fig 9. middle right, *Stool/Lamp*, earthenware, bulb, cord and plug (2004). Photo: Anders Ruhwald.

Fig 10. bottom left, Installation view, *If all man's products were well designed, joy and harmony would emerge eternally triumphant*, Drud & Køppe Gallery, Copenhagen, Denmark, 2007. Photo: Søren Nielsen.

Fig 11. bottom right, Installation view, *If all man's products were well designed, joy and harmony would emerge eternally triumphant*, Drud & Køppe Gallery, Copenhagen, Denmark, 2007. Photo: Søren Nielsen.

it feel like? (Fig 9) But with no fixed relationship to other objects in the world, this reading could remain open. And so I was searching for an engagement with the work, one that would parallel how we experience the things we live with everyday.

A body of work that was completed for a 2007 exhibition in Copenhagen was titled *If all man's products were well designed, joy and harmony would emerge eternally triumphant*. The show consisted of fourteen works, all black, installed in the gallery so as to reference a domestic interior (Figs 10 and 11). To accentuate this look, a white carpet covered a section of the gallery floor. Along the edges of this carpet strips of black and white satin ribbons were hung from the ceiling, creating a ten-foot wall around the carpet enclosing it fully. The show took its form loosely from a reproduction of Kandinsky's *Picture II*, an installation and painting from his *Pictures at an Exhibition* made to accompany a performance of the Mussorgsky orchestral piece of the same name. Kandinsky's intention behind this installation was to create three-dimensional paintings that would be released from the confines of the canvas and become real. I wanted to make a play on this intention by loosely referencing Kandinsky's composition to create a context for the work in the form of a stage.

To enter the exhibition space the audience had to walk through this wall of satin in order to see the actual pieces. The striped wall established a room within a room, a space where the rest of the gallery was constantly present visually and audibly, while creating a sense of intimacy at the same time. The stage was a space that consciously felt mocked up, yet established a familiar setting that could contextualise the work within the material world. Inside this curtain the viewer encountered a variety of objects, which could be interpreted as functional. To establish a focus on the purpose and meaning of the objects, the same black glaze had been applied to all the work, thus bringing it together while emphasising the variations in placement and form. The installation design allowed the work to be experienced as several tableaux. Each invited comparison to a common domestic setting.

In the seminal book, *The Meaning of Things, Domestic Objects and the Self*, Mihaly Csikszentmihalyi and Eugene Rochberg-Halton illustrate how domestic objects reflect the owner's self (Fig 12).

> The objects of the household represent, at least potentially, the endogenous being of the owner. Although one has little control over the things encountered outside the home, household objects are chosen and could be freely discarded if they produce too much conflict with the self. Thus household objects constitute an ecology of signs that reflects as well as shapes the pattern of the owner's self.[3]

The implication of a domestic setting thus activates a situation that potentially opens up a reading of the work where we engage with the objects at a one-to-one level (Fig 13). The potential of identification in the context of usability, whether implied or real, gives way for a reading of the work different than the one we would have in a traditional exhibition environment. I was looking for something akin to the situation we have when we experience the home of another for the first time. But in this situation certain objects would have the potential for a reading as functional items, recognisable without suggesting any specific purpose (Fig 14). Others seem more ambiguous, clearly belonging

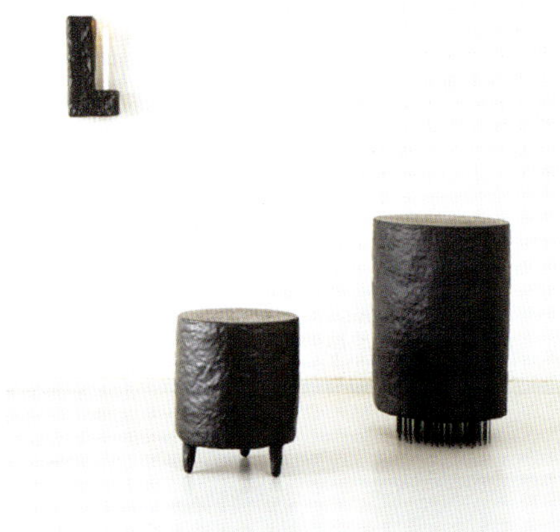

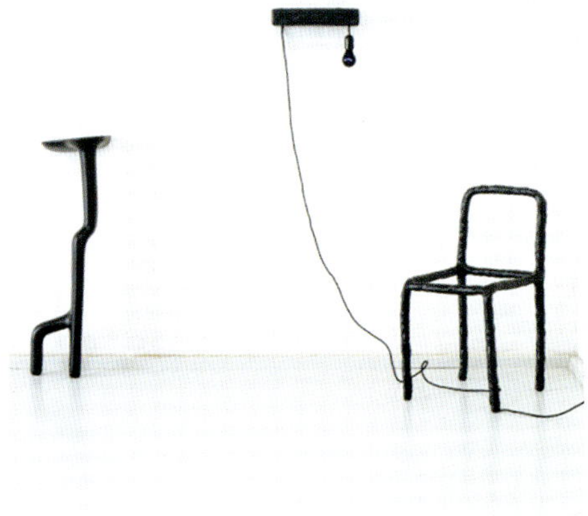

to the world of things but not fitting in to any specific categories. It is not an easy read and purposely one that does not add up. Some of the objects are in conflict with each other formally, while others destabilise themselves by ambiguity.

My work negotiates the space between the essential and the pragmatic object (Fig 15). It clearly references functionality, while at the same time resists its utilitarian potential for a cerebral engagement. It exists as an extension of the category of functional objects, but does so without achieving the basic requirement of any functional object, namely to fulfil a practical purpose. The space of this work is not the space that sculpture traditionally occupies; these objects should not be understood as autonomous works that point towards a definite meaning. Instead they suggest a functional potential and relate to objects that already exist yet defy to be read in a singular manner. I consciously seek out this state of ambiguity when I make the work in the studio. It is an important mediator for the underlying discussion of our relationships to objects and how they inflict on our life. The ambiguity is a means to create a space in which the viewer can approach and meet the work without necessarily having to understand the artist's intention. My work therefore sits within the trajectory of craft or *kunsthåndværk*, being objects that speak about everyday objects, while simultaneously debating and commenting on our relationship with them. The work is paired with the viewer's understanding of the rest of the material world, and has no prescribed conclusion.

Fig 12. left, *Candleholder*, glazed earthenware, candle (2006). *Three legged stool*, glazed earthenware (2006). *127 legged table*, glazed earthenware, painted steel (2006). Photo: Søren Nielsen.

Fig 13. right, *Social Piece of Furniture #5*, glazed earthenware (2006). *Shelf/lamp*, glazed earthenware, cord, bulb, plug (2006). *Beginning/ending*, glazed earthenware (2006). Photo: Søren Nielsen.

Notes

1 Tanya Harrod, 'House-trained objects: Notes towards writing an alternative history of Modern Art', in Colin Pinter (ed.), *Contemporary Art and the Home* (Oxford and New York: Berg, 2002), p. 63.
2 Daniel Miller and Christopher Tilley, 'Editorial', *The Journal of Material Culture*, 1 (1996).
3 Mihaly Csikszentmihalyi and Eugene Rochberg-Halton, *The Meaning of Things* (Cambridge: Cambridge University Press, 1981), p. 20.

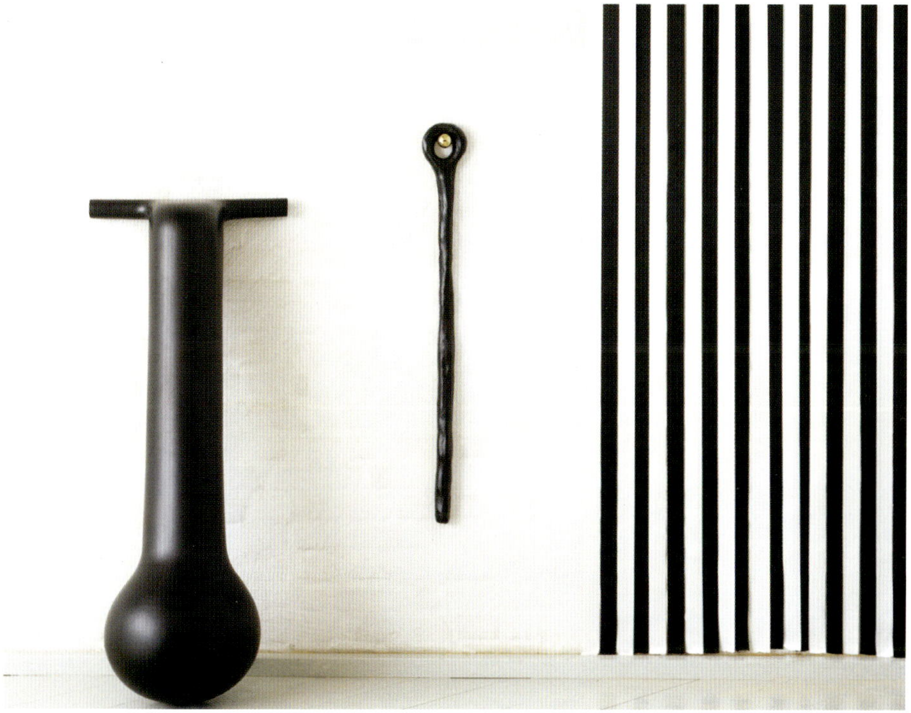

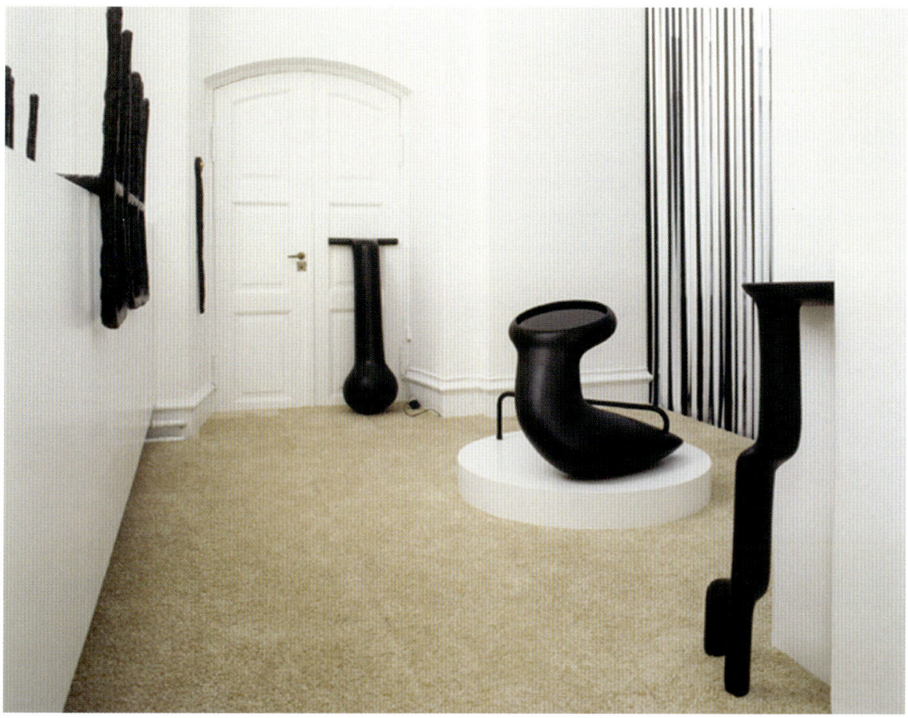

Fig 14. *Untitled #7* (from the functional series), glazed earthenware (2006). *Untitled #8* (from the functional series), glazed earthenware (2006). Photo: Søren Nielsen.

Fig 15. Installation view, *If all man's products were well designed, joy and harmony would emerge eternally triumphant*, Drud & Køppe Gallery, Copenhagen, Denmark, 2007. Photo: Søren Nielsen.

Through the life of one artist, this chapter explores how Zulu politics and history are embedded within artists' ceramic expression. Elizabeth Perrill documents the ways in which Azolina MaMncube Ngema has created distinct styles of ceramic production for various audiences – local Zulu, white South African, and international buyers – and the ways in which Indigenous Knowledge Systems are utilised within all of these ceramic lines. Additionally, an eye-catching borrowing from Zulu beadwork within MaMncube's œuvre is brought to light for the first time. Perrill is Assistant Professor of African Art History, Department of Art, University of North Carolina at Greensboro. The chapter draws heavily on her doctoral research; since she completed her PhD, she has published extensively on Zulu ceramics and curated several exhibitions. A version of the text was given as a presentation at 'Traditional Women Potters: Old Forms and New Markets', a symposium convened by Moira Vincentelli at Aberystwyth University, Wales, in 2007. Papers from the symposium were published in Issue 10 of *Interpreting Ceramics*, which was edited by Vincentelli.

Interpreting Ceramics

Selected Essays

Indigenous Knowledge Systems (IKS) & Zulu Ceramic Arts: Azolina MaMncube Ngema, One Woman's Story

Elizabeth Perrill

> I source these artists in the rural areas and want to promote their work for it[s] aesthetic beauty, authenticity and cultural uniqueness, in order that the potters may achieve greater rewards for their skills. However, my dilemma lies in whether I should help economically empower these artists or keep their skills and expertise to myself in order to preserve their indigenous knowledge.[1]

This excerpt is drawn from Juliet Armstrong's 'Zulu pottery', *Indilinga: African Journal of Indigenous Knowledge Systems*, 2005, and captures the anxieties scholars struggle with when they begin to acknowledge the deep implications their action or in-action can have on the standard of living and artistic practices of the individuals with whom they work. Armstrong's article represents one of the first forays into explicitly Indigenous Knowledge Systems (IKS) discourse by scholars working on Zulu ceramics, and the first arts-focused article to be published in *Indilinga*, an IKS journal predominantly concerned with agriculture, medicine, educational policies and intellectual property rights.

When Armstrong speaks above of 'preserv[ing] their indigenous knowledge', she is referring to the attempt to protect artists through isolation from a trend she describes as threatening to 'bastardise' Zulu ceramics.[2] Her concern is that 'ill-informed dealers are dictating to these women' styles that stray from the types of *izinkamba* (s. *ukhamba*) used in some Zulu homes.[3] The most common type of *izinkamba* Armstrong refers to are nearly spherical vessels of a type incised or decorated with raised bumps (generally referred to as

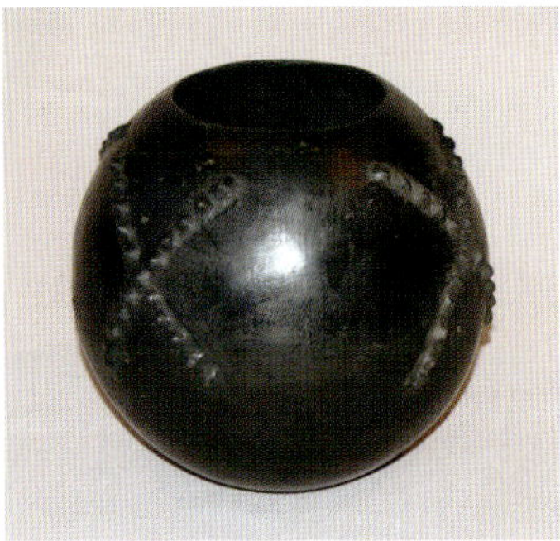

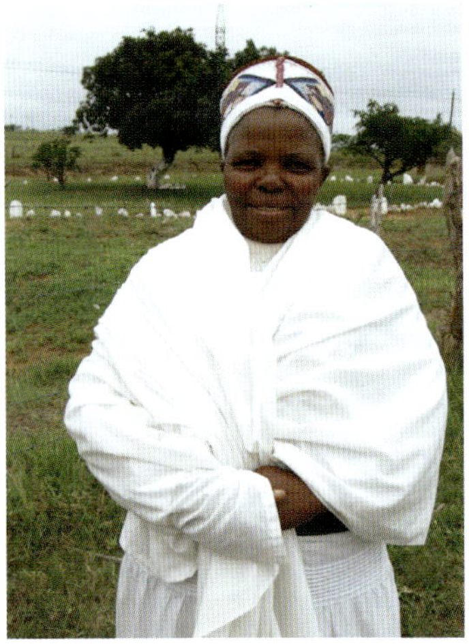

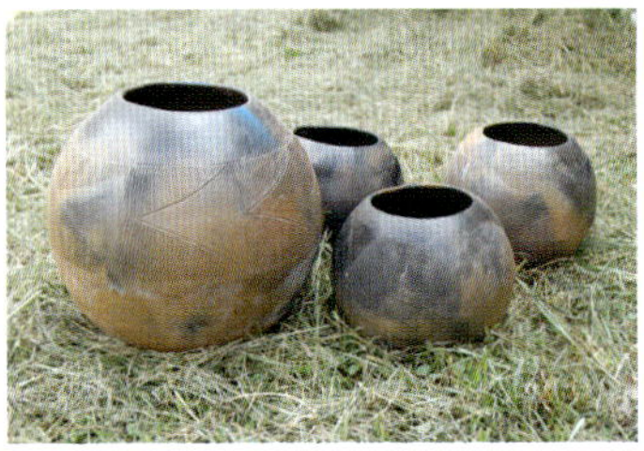

Fig 1. Azolina MaMcube Ngema, *ukhamba*, clay with *amasumpa, ukufusa* and wax finish, 2006.

Fig 2. Azolina MaMcube Ngema dressed for a Shembe worship service. An open-air Shembe church, a worship circle denoted by white stones, can be seen in the background.

Fig 3. Azolina MaMcube Ngema. Unblackened *izinkamba* with incised decoration created for King Bhekizulu College art courses, 2006.

amasumpa), burnished at the leather-hard stage, blackened with a second *ukufusa* firing, and polished with cow fat or waxes[4] (Fig 1). Thus, it is with extreme irony that a pot of a type that Armstrong discusses in her 2005 article as 'bastardised', un-blackened with a very atypically wide neck and 'Chinese-influenced' ringed handles,[5] is one of the only images on the *Indilinga* IKS journal website.[6]

The reality is that material and aesthetic innovations made by individual artists/creators are tied to historical and economic changes; broad historical flows influence IKSs. To think of an IKS as unchanging is just as false as claiming that traditions are static, an assumption that thankfully has been challenged and defeated in the past twenty years of anthropological and art historical writing. Artists utilise Indigenous Knowledge in KwaZulu-Natal in artworks that appear to 'break' with 'traditional' Zulu forms and use IKSs to inform their innovative designs. Despite assumptions that they are isolated, rural Zulu-speaking artists are all participants in a non-monolithic, dynamic and contemporary Zulu-ness, replete with formalised schooling, cell phones, and development initiatives, as well as darker trends of migrant labour, violence and economic depression.

Azolina MaMncube Ngema: ceramic lines, life lines

The life of Azolina MaMncube Ngema (Fig 2) brings together some of the more complex historical twists and turns that have shaped localised, national and international appreciation of Zulu *izinkamba*, also known as *utshwala* ceramics or Zulu beer pots.[7] MaMncube's career and ceramic styles reveal some ways in which artists encapsulate moments within their life histories in their artistic production. Ceramic traditions that rely upon a blend of indigenous and contemporary input defy labels such as 'bastardised' as it is used above. MaMncube's life history and the ceramic styles she associates with key moments in her biography poignantly bring out dramatic moments within the last fifty years of South African history. What is considered to be one of the most 'traditional' of women's art forms provides the medium for this talented ceramist to express her contemporary life experiences, inspirations and aspirations.

Documented as Azolina Mncunu, Aselina Mbatha and Azolinah Mbatha in various publications,[8] Mncube's work was featured in the Royal Academy of Arts 1996 catalogue *Africa: The Art of a Continent* with no name attribution.[9] Additionally, I have identified an *ukhamba*, with an undulating raised design and subtly bottom-heavy form, that is nearly identical to the one shown in *Africa: The Art of a Continent* and strikingly similar to the one attributed under the surname Mbatha. This vessel was published anonymously in *Ubuntu: Arts et Cultures d'Afrique du Sud*, an exhibition and catalogue organised by the Réunion des Musées Nationaux of France in 2002.[10] I would confidently attribute this vessel to Mncube. It is held in the private collection of the artist Karel Nel in Johannesburg, and is most likely of a similar vintage to the *Africa: Art of a Continent* one and a ceramic vessel held in the Tatham Art Gallery published in the 1998 *Ubumba* Zulu ceramics catalogue. The simultaneous erasure of Azolina MaMncube Ngema's name and showcasing of her talents in international venues was rumoured in the South African ceramics community for years. The *Africa: Art of a Continent* publication was finally acknowledged within a footnote in Frank Jolles's 2005 article,

'The origins of the twentieth century Zulu beer vessel styles',[11] although Mncube is still documented as Azolinah Mbatha within this publication. For an example of this style before blackening see Fig 4.

During eighteen months of doctoral research in KwaZulu-Natal, I spent several weeks speaking with MaMncube. During 2006 and 2007 interviews, MaMncube identified several distinct styles or lines of ceramic vessels in her production:

- blackened *izinkamba* with ridges or *amasumpa* (Fig 1)
- unblackened *izinkamba* with incised decorations (Fig 3)
- painted *izinkamba* that utilise a network of incised patterns as the base of the design (Fig 5)
- vertically ovoid vases and flower pots with incised or pinched decorations (Fig 6)
- figural sculptures (Fig 7)

Each of these lines caters to a specific audience, and MaMncube's marketing, targeted at varied clientele, reflects similar efforts by many Zulu ceramists to diversify their works and make a living from their art.

Royal ceramics or *abelungu* wares?

The examples of Mncube's work illustrated within *Africa: The Art of a Continent* and *Ubuntu: Arts et Cultures d'Afrique du Sud* fall within the style of *izinkamba* that Mncube has stated, on several occasions, she keeps on hand in case *abelungu* (white people) stop by her home. At least, she attempted to have three or four works of this particular style in her home whenever possible up until she was forced to move from her residence near Nongoma, KwaZulu-Natal due to a violent attack in March of 2007, but this is a point to which we will return.

MaMncube pointed out that the *abelungu*-preferred style of vessel consists of *izinkamba*, spherical drinking pots, that are blackened, often bearing raised *amasumpa* decorations, have no lip, are burnished and are subsequently polished with 'natural' substances. What constitutes 'natural' will be discussed below and is highly enmeshed with the question of whose ideals this style was originally created for and, moreover, for whom the style continues. I would like to unpack just a few of the qualities defined by Mncube and some of the life experiences that she associates with these aesthetic traits.

Azolina MaMncube Ngema is a woman who enjoys telling stories, entertaining and educating others with her oral narratives. Other Zulu potters who interacted with MaMncube during a business-skills workshop held in Durban in May of 2007 agreed that she is extremely skilled at crafting yarns, jokes and anecdotes.[12] During both formal interviews and informal discussions of her work MaMncube associates specific life experiences and periods in her career with the *abelungu*-preferred pots.

MaMncube skips back and forth between a formalised analysis of *amasumpa*-bearing works and references to the sporadic moments between 1965 to the 1990s, during which foreign visitors visited her home, purchased works, and asked her to travel with them abroad. These narratives she repeats over and over, particularly a story of when two white

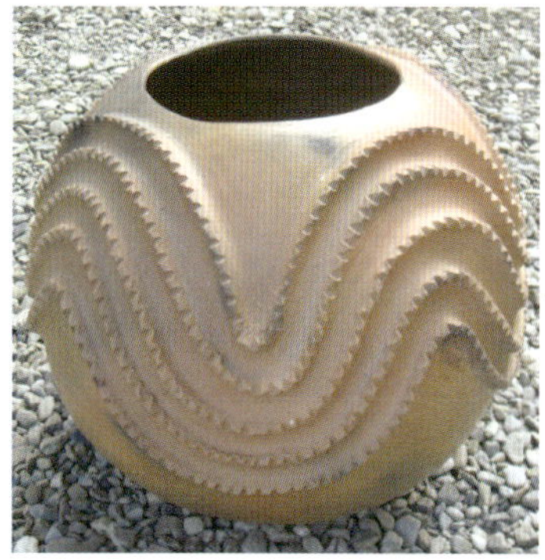

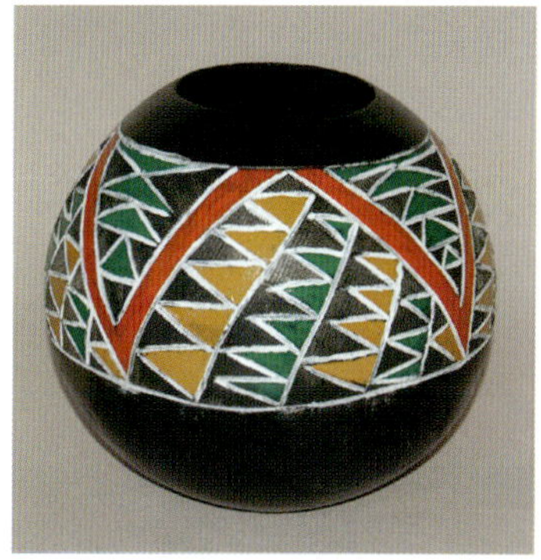

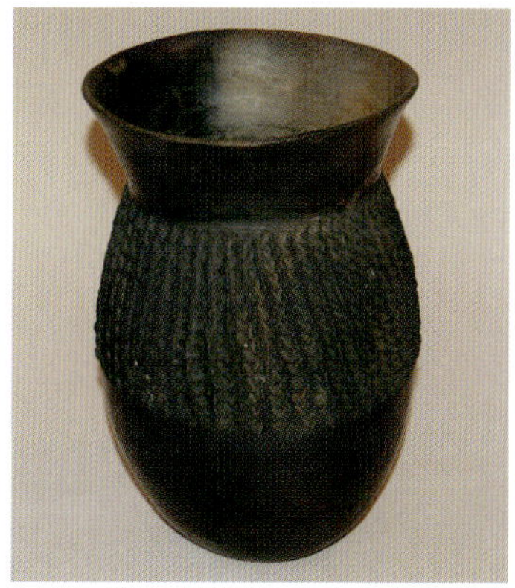

Fig 4. Azolina MaMcube Ngema. *Izinkamba* with undulating parallel bands of decoration before blackening.

Fig 5. Azolina MaMcube Ngema. *Ukhamba* decorated with enamel paints, 2006.

Fig 6. Azolina MaMcube Ngema. Ovoid vase with pinched design, 2006.

men wanted her to travel abroad with them, which corresponds directly with one of the heights of the sales in 'traditional' and anonymous Zulu ceramics in the 1980s.[13]

Collectors and scholars of Zulu ceramics have acknowledged that blackened works bearing *amasumpa* have historically been a more prestigious type of ceramic ware, sometimes associated with Zulu royalty.[14] Indeed, the frontispiece of the most influential exhibition catalogue of Zulu ceramics published to date, *Ubumba*, shows King Dinizulu's wives and *amasumpa* wares.[15] However, for Mncube and many others, the continuation of this style is integrally linked to another type of high-paying patron – white, *abelungu*, scholars and collectors.

MaMncube and at least a dozen other Zulu-speaking ceramists have described to me how the time-intensive process of using applied decorations is simply too costly in terms of temporal outlay to waste at the prices most local buyers can afford. At eighty to one hundred rand, or roughly six to seven British pounds/twelve US dollars at the time of her interviews, finely burnished, *amasumpa*-bearing drinking vessels were outside the financial reach of local buyers. Instead, *abelungu*, a new set of social or economic elite, constitute a contemporary clientele. *Amasumpa*-bearing ceramics are associated with a romanticised past of Zulu royalty for collectors. This is an idealised past that these works share with many African ceramics traded on a commercial scale outside of their local area of production and associated with what have been assumed to be anonymous 'traditional' artists. Within Ruth Phillips and Christopher Steiner's now foundational text, *Unpacking Culture: Art and Commodity in Colonial and Postcolonial Worlds*, multiple authors concur that within sculptural, masking, beading and weaponry collecting crazes 'curators and collectors were frequently either unaware of … or chose to suppress' the fact that works

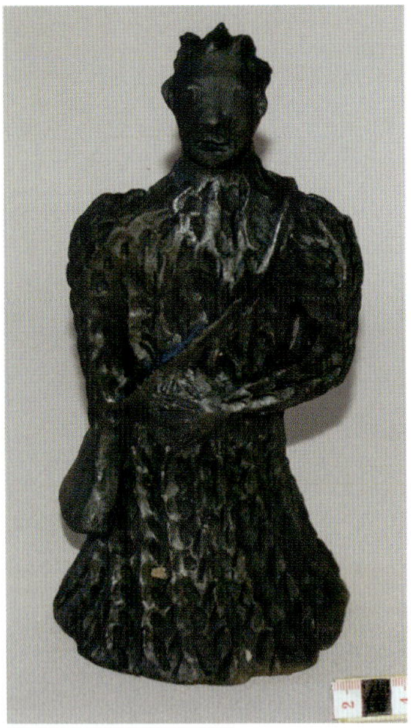

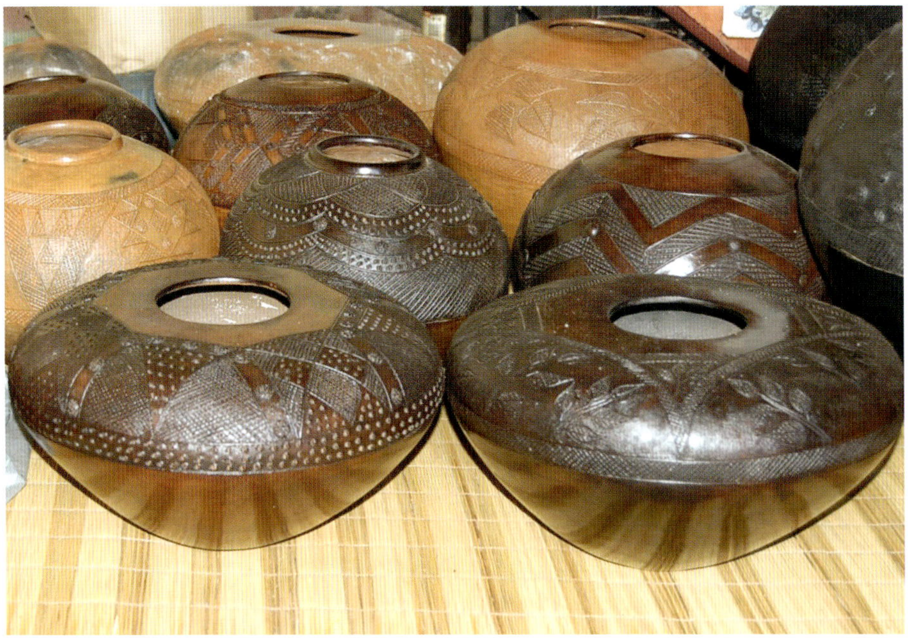

Fig 7. above, Azolina MaMcube Ngema. Figure of a woman with purse. Pinched decoration, 2006.

Fig 8. right, Buzephi Magwaza. Group of ceramics all polished with various types of shoe-polish, 2006.

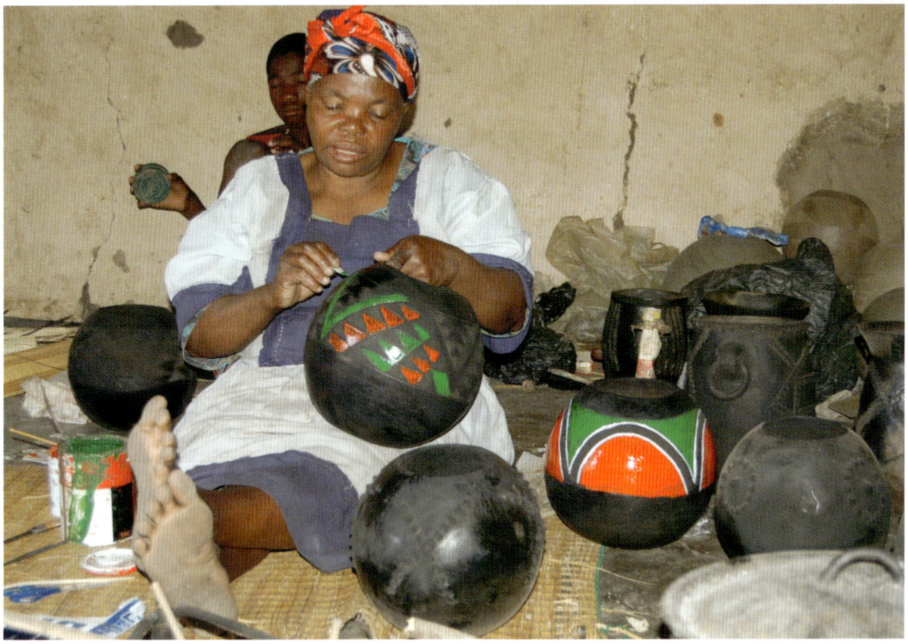

were commercially produced replicas.[16] This similar wilful ignorance seems to be the case within the collection of Mncube's works during the rush to collect 'older' Zulu ceramics from the 1970s to the 1990s.[17]

Mncube does not produce commercial replicas *per se*, but her works have been portrayed as idealised museum examples of Zulu *utshwala* ceramics. The value placed on collecting works of antiquity and owning a piece of this idealised past would certainly explain why MaMncube's works in *Africa: The Art of a Continent* 'lost' their provenance somewhere *en route* to publication. This loss of attribution would increase their value and prestige.[18] To say they were created by a woman who is still alive and, up until 2007, capable of producing works very similar to those published for a price of six to seven British pounds/twelve US dollars would, at that time, decrease the works' prestige and commodity value.

The positive response MaMncube has had when presenting these *amasumpa*-bearing pieces to *abelungu* audiences at ceramic workshops and exhibitions has made white consumers her target audience for these vessels, and this audience does affect the works' material aesthetics. That norms of antiquity are associated with these works does not escape MaMncube's keen observations. In particular, she has emphasised that she knows that *abelungu* customers do not want shoe polish to be used on this style.

Shoe or boot polish is commonly used by many contemporary Zulu ceramists during a final, post-firing polish, even within local communities when works will be produced for drinking. But, MaMncube has noted at gallery openings and during visits to her home that lifting and sniffing pots is part of routine *abelungu* evaluations of ceramics. She describes a humorous moment at a gallery opening where artists had been demonstrating in the

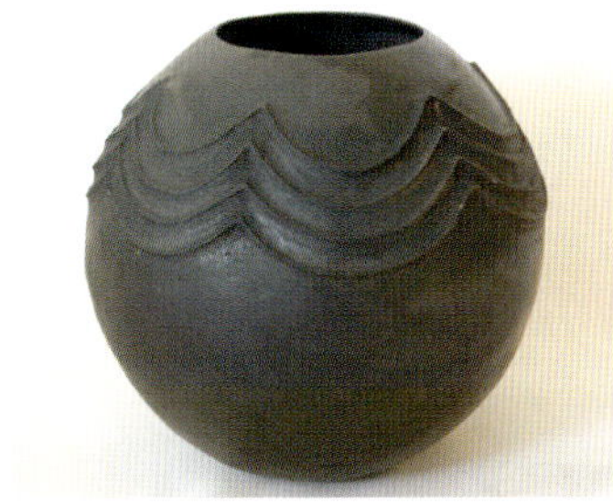

Fig 9. above, Azolina MaMcube Ngema. Ridged ukhamba blackened work polished with candle wax, 2006.

Fig 10. above left, Azolina MaMcube Ngema, in her Nongoma home painting ceramics, 2006.

exhibition venue and, after completing almost all of the steps in the ceramic process, a back room was used as the site for applying shoe polish prior to taking works into the final venue for the ceramic exhibition and sale. The preference for 'natural' polishes and the categorisation of shoe polish as an unnatural and negative aesthetic choice is something that MaMncube has certainly noticed.

> Mncube: Ayi angisawasebenzisi
> No, I don't use it [cow fat] anymore.
> Sibiya: Kodwa ususebenzisa upoloshi
> But you still use shoe polish?
> Mncube: Bathi abelungu abawufuni upolishi
> The white people said they don't like shoe polish.
> Perrill: Manje ususebenzisani?
> Now what do you use?
> Mncube: Ngisebenzisa ikhandlela ngoba u Julia wathi asingawufaki upolishi phambu kwabelungu
> I am using candles because Julia [Mncube's name for Juliet Armstrong] said that we should not put on shoe polish before/in front of the white people.[19]

Mncube explains the various problems with shoe polish and cow fat and later goes on to emphasise that they both smell strongly. Some ceramics she sells for external consumption simply remain un-blackened, a style of work that saves her the work of the *ukufusa* second firing and avoids any concerns that ceramic works might smell like shoe polish. Creating non-blackened works presents one quick solution to this problem, and holds the extra appeal to some of capturing flame marks on their surface, a feature valued by some collectors (Fig 3).

However, many *abelungu* buyers will not accept un-blackened *izinkamba*. There is a substantial amount of scholarship mentioning the importance of having blackened pots to honour one's ancestors, as black has been aesthetically linked as a cool colour that pleases Zulu ancestral spirits. Additionally, Zulu ceramists and ceramic customers confirm that *amadlozi*, the ancestors, enjoy a black pot.[20] Thus, an un-blackened pot is seen as non-traditional by many buyers, both Zulu and non-Zulu.

Additionally, MaMncube has observed white buyers' concepts of what is 'clean' and their dislike of the way the carbonised surface of pots that have been blackened by the historically older process of a second *ukufusa* firing comes off on one's hands if *izinkamba* are polished with *ifutha*, cow fat. To satisfy *abelungu* buyers' conceptions of a 'traditional,' 'natural' and 'clean' finish MaMncube uses clear candle wax on her blackened works. Odourless and much less likely to come off on one's hands, candle wax represents the perfect compromise to satisfy her affluent audience's selectively historical and hygienically informed aesthetics.

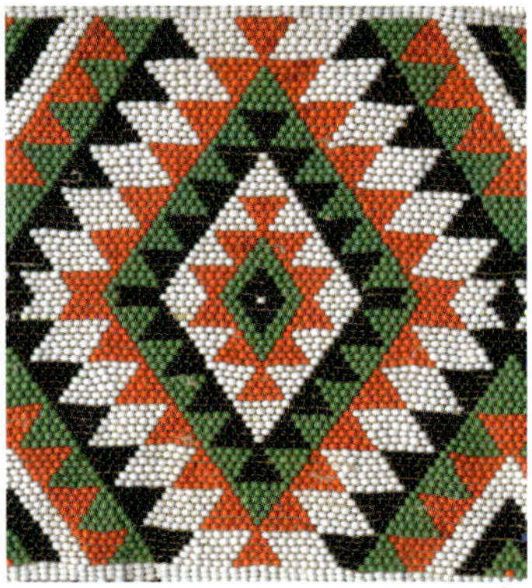

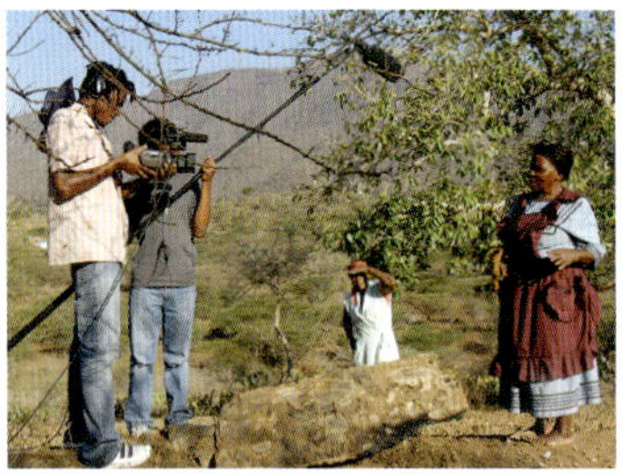

Fig 11. Detail of Nongoma beadwork apron, ca. 1960, worn by married men and unmarried women. Photo: Gary van Wyk/ axisgallery.com.

Fig 12. Azolina MaMcube Ngema & 12am Productions film crew, rural KwaZulu-Natal, South Africa, 2007.

All photos: Elizabeth Perrill unless otherwise stated.

Painted pots: local prestige and aesthetics

Another line of more 'high-end' ceramics produced by MaMncube consists of her painted ceramic wares (Fig 5). She is very pointed about the fact that these are high-end works for local consumers, produced on commission. As with the work bearing *amasumpa*, the time involved in painting the triangular or more freeform designs she has developed dictates that these works sell at a higher price.

MaMncube first saw the use of paint on ceramic wares in Johannesburg while travelling to see her husband, who was working as a migrant mine-labourer. The style that she created just after this experience has a great deal of resonance with her local audience, and the way in which Mncube has created a hybridised decorative style certainly is participating in an indigenous system of aesthetic knowledge.

As part of a social structure tied to the migrant labour system, Mncube was one of many women who were banned from visiting husbands in South Africa's mines. Despite the risks, Mncube illicitly stayed with her husband for several weeks. Although she has no recollection of the precise date of this journey, it is likely that MaMncube visited Johannesburg sometime between 1986 and 1990. During this period, regulations had loosened and space was freeing up in the workers' hostels popular with Nongoma miners.[21]

When she returned home, MaMncube began producing painted ceramics with her own distinctive style. Most often this consists of a grid-work of red, green and white triangles set off against a blackened background. The pattern is pointedly similar to Nongoma style beadwork (Fig 8, compare with Fig 5). Mncube developed this new decorative style with an obvious visual appeal to local aesthetic preferences.[22] It is important to note that the 1980s and 1990s, when MaMncube was first making these pots, was a time of extremely violent faction fighting and increased Zulu nationalism. Traditional dress was often used during this period as a visual signifier of political unity and mobilisation. Nongoma, Mncube's home, was a stronghold of Zulu-nationalism and a powerhouse within urban South African workers' hostels. The leadership in workers' hostels would often romanticise rural homelands and use them as a basis for urban solidarity.[23] Mncube's borrowing of regional beadwork designs fit in with the desire for regionalised Zulu-ness to be displayed in the regalia that would accompany life events, such as weddings, coming-of-age ceremonies or funerals.

Mncube is a businesswoman adapting to different markets and accommodating aesthetic desires within the bounds of her own expressive style. Her painted wares retain and build upon the Indigenous Knowledge System of Zulu ceramic production and localised, Nongoma-area aesthetic preferences of pattern and colour combinations. She also knows that painting ceramics with enamel paint is considered by many to be a Sotho or BaSotho tradition.[24] MaMncube emphasised that she had never shown these works to *abelungu*. However, she is always evasive when asked if this was a deliberate move or a coincidence, simply the product of works not being on hand because they are consistently commissioned and retrieved by local consumers with little time to sit around Mncube's home. The question remains: Did she keep these wares away from her *abelungu* customers to focus their attention on her *amasumpa* wares and hide what outsiders might see as less 'traditional' works, or was it just happenstance?

My own role as a scholar is in no way neutral. After seeing my interest in her style of painting, MaMncube stated she would now show these works to the *abelungu*. I explained that my interest is informed by my preoccupation with the history of Zulu migrant labour that Mncube associates with this style. We discussed at length together, and with Nathi Gumede, the curator of the KwaZulu-Natal Society for the Arts Gallery, at a business-skills meeting held in Durban in May of 2007, the ways in which the promotion of an art form often has a great deal to do with the story one tells around the piece.

Moulding self-image: indigenous and *abelungu* value systems

The concept of self-presentation and promotion is loaded with political implications in KwaZulu-Natal, where education and ethnic affiliations have been steeped in political connotations before, during and after apartheid. Azolina MaMncube Ngema has learned, during ceramic workshops[25] and through her own astute observations, the importance of being seen as an artist who is interested in creativity and able to understand audience desires.

> Bathi le eMaritzburg la safunda khona masenza izinto ezidayisayo sizenze zihlukahlukane ngoba kuzokwenzeka kufika abelungu noma abantu bezothenga, Mhlampe lo omunye akaluthandi lolu uzoluthanda loluya, yikho siwahlukanisa ama-design, ukuze umuntu akwazi ukuxhoshwa izinkamba ezihlukene aze alubone aluthandayo.
>
> *They said at the course at [Pieter]maritzburg that when we make things that we are going to sell, we need to diversify them, because white people [abelungu] or black people [abantu] who come to buy the pots have different tastes. One might like something that the other does not like, which is why we separate our designs, so that our customers have a variety to choose from and are guaranteed to find what they like.*

A final category of the 'separate designs' MaMncube has created is her line of sculpted figures and vase forms, on which she uses pinched decorative textures that do not appear on her *izinkamba*. Both of these ceramic lines fall well outside of the realm of *izinkamba* or *utshwala* vessels, but they are definitely wares that Mncube uses to define herself as artistic and contemporary to both buyers supplying local shops targeted at Zulu-speaking audiences and *abelungu* visitors.

Virginia Ndwandwe runs a small shop selling goods for decorating local homes near Nongoma that is supported by local government initiatives. She carries vases similar to the style mentioned above by Armstrong and depicted on the *Indilinga* IKS journal website. In the following excerpt she discusses the vases Mncube creates that she was hoping to stock at her shop (example in Fig 6).

> Mabaso: Manje lezi zinkamba okade uzikhomba. Abantu bayazithanda noma …?
> Now the pots you were pointing to [vases]. Do people like them or …?
> Ndwandwe: Bayazithanda ngoba amavasi.
> They love them because they are vases.
> Perrill: Zingenisile?
> Are they in fashion?
> Mncube: Ngamavasi
> They are vases.

> Ndwandwe: Angithi zingamavasi bazifaka izimbali bese bezibeka kuma wall unit. They are vases and they [local consumers] put flowers in them and display them in their wall units.

Ndwandwe responds to the question of whether these works are fashionable by saying they are presented on Zulu-speaking consumers' wall units. To anyone familiar with township or rural life in KwaZulu-Natal this is a resounding, 'Yes!' Wall units are where televisions, radios, decorative knick-knacks, clocks, enlargements of family photos, and school diplomas are proudly displayed. The markers of affluence and life events in a family, particularly electronics and photos or documents from matriculations, weddings and coming of age ceremonies, signify success within this very dynamic Zulu cultural practice. Both tradition and contemporaneity are celebrated on wall units. The production of ceramic vases for flowers is a way MaMncube caters to this contemporary fashion.

On the other hand, it is around her small figurines of men holding *izinkamba* or women with contemporary handbags that Mncube builds a narrative of artistic creativity (Fig 7). When discussing these figurines MaMncube often says that she dreams or simply comes up with these ceramic forms from her imagination. She is adamant that no one tells her how to make these figures. Something that has struck me as important in her narrative style is Mncube's repeated discussion of learning ceramics first in formalised school education as she works on or evaluates her figural works. While working on the piece in Fig 6, Mncube said the following:

> Isona isikole sokuqala lana isasifundisa amantombazane nabafana abadala, isikole samaRoma, izingane eziningi lana zazingafundi kwaba yasona isikole sokuqala … Mina ngafunda ngayeka ngoba ubaba wami washona sekuwumama yedwa ngase ngiyayeka, kodwa okusho ukuthi lokhu engakufundiswa esikoleni ngakubamba … Noma sifunde kancane imisebenzi esayifundayo esikoleni yasiphumelelisa, ngoba mina ngasuka lapho ngaba nenqondo ehlakaniphileyo.
>
> *It was the first school in the area where both boys and girls attended, it was a Roman Catholic school, lots of people here were not educated … I left school because my father passed away and my mother was left alone, so I was forced to leave school, but all that I learned from school I still apply it now … Although we did not study a lot, the little things we have made us to be prosperous, it made my mind to start reasoning things around/made me clever.*

Although she does not refer to ceramics directly, Mncube mentions the 'reasoning' or 'cleverness' that she associates with the wide variety of ceramic work she has developed. She also tends to reassert this as a difference between herself and other ceramists from the Nongoma region.

Formalised schooling connotes a great deal of prestige for MaMncube. Her style of narration when explaining her figurines is also often re-emphasised when she sends a child off to her sleeping room to bring back the image of her and 'Julia' (the source of this pseudonym for Juliet Armstrong comes from the misprinted label below the image, 'Asolinah & Julia'). This labelled photograph acts as Mncube's document of her time with the famous ceramic lecturer during workshops held at the University of

KwaZulu-Natal. At workshops Mncube recalls being asked to prove she was a ceramist by drawing her designs, and how she was able to recall and illustrate more designs than any other attendee.[26]

The viewing of her photograph from the University of KwaZulu-Natal has become linked in her narratives to her early school experiences at the KwaDenge Catholic School in approximately the mid-to-late 1940s.[27] These two institutional experiences have affirmed her creativity in terms of what she calls 'cleverness', which she associates with the diversity of her forms and designs. Despite their distance from one another temporally, both institutional experiences are repeated in narrative structures Mncube has developed in reference to her figurines.

Yet, formalised education constitutes only one component of Mncube's self-presentation as a creative individual. She also frequently discusses the indigenous system of dreaming about one's inspirations and discusses the older women who come to her in dreams to give guidance and premonitions. These dreams inspired her to create ceramic figurines, inform her of new clay sources, and let her know of upcoming visits from influential clients. When I had tried to call and failed to reach her, prior to one of my visits, MaMncube teased me by saying she is never surprised when *abelungu* appear at her house, even if they do not call ahead via cell phone.

> Khona kunomsebenzi omkhulu makuyiso isiphiwo, angike ngithi nje wena njengoba usebenza lomsebenzi fanele ucele ukuthi kube yisiphiwo sakho ungaqheli kuwo. Uyabona uma usebenze into kufanele uyicelele uzimisele. Mina ngiyaye ngenze utshwala ngicele ngibonge ngikhulume nabadala. Wena uphike ngokubonela mina uphike nje ngokwenza kuyaphela, ngiphupha kuqala uma labelungu bezofika, ngesikhathi bezofika ngatshela intombazane yami ukuthi kunabelungu bazofika.ngiyaphupha ebusuku mbezoza nabantu ngibabone, ngibona umlungu ngibone nabantu mangilele. Kunenyoni ehlala phezu kwendlu makukhona ozayo, ithi 'sawubona sawubona' noma kanjani kuba khona ofikayo.
>
> *There is great potential in this type of work if you have the talent and passion for it, take you [Nozipho] for instance you do the same work [arts] right? You need to ask the ancestors to sustain your talent and not turn your back on it. When you are doing a job you must excel in it and constantly ask for guidance from your ancestors. I myself make Zulu beer and thank my ancestors and also ask for guidance. When people are going to come here I see it in a dream first when the white people were coming, I told my daughter in the morning that they were coming, I really dream at night, whenever someone will come to me. There is also a bird that sits at the top of the roof and makes noises, it calls, 'hello, hello' when there will be a visitor.*

Mncube follows instructions given in her dreams and, prior to her recent move from the Nongoma area, she had three separate clay sources, one of which she discovered in 2005 after dreaming of an older woman who guided her to this new source. These stories are deeply ingrained in IKSs. The links to ancestral spirits are a point of curiosity and added value for Zulu speakers and non-Zulu speakers alike.[28] I have seen individuals of both linguistic/cultural backgrounds enwrapped by Mncube's narratives of dreaming, ancestral guidance and creativity.

Conclusion

Certainly, claims of 'authenticity' versus 'bastardisation' create a false dichotomy that falls away when we consider MaMncube's complex inspirations. Indigenous Knowledge Systems encourage her innovations and creativity – she dreams of figural ceramics and creative designs. MaMncube also uses her insight into collectors' concerns to create 'traditional', 'natural' and 'clean' *amasumpa* wares. Detailed research brings to light the subtleties of the contemporary philosophical and cultural knowledge systems from which Azolina MaMncube Ngema draws. The give-and-take between that which is 'traditional' and that which is 'imported', the preservation and/or modification within each of Mncube's ceramic lines, makes dichotomous thinking much less useful when trying to understand her creativity and self-presentation.

In his April 2005 speech to the National Heritage Council Transformation Conference, South Africa's Minister of Arts and Culture laid out a definition of 'Intangible Cultural Heritage', which incorporates Indigenous Knowledge Systems. He stated:

> The intangible cultural heritage, popularly known as 'Living Heritage' of South Africa, which manifests itself in: Orature, Oral History, Performance, Ritual, Popular Memory, Skills and Techniques, Indigenous Knowledge Systems, predates the imperial and colonial era. Despite the passage of time, elements of it still are the lived experience of the various communities. They have been preserved in the manner in which these communities deal with birth, the coming of age, maturity, marriage, old age and death. These ways of doing things have provided people with the survival strategies to deal with poverty and destitution, how to create stability and have instructed them how to co-exist with other communities.

The minister's comments struck me at first as troubling. He all too comfortably juxtaposes 'living heritage' as predating 'the imperial and colonial era' with an inventorying of familiar anthropological litanies of 'birth, coming of age, maturity, marriage, old age and death.' The essentialism implied is a bit shocking, for certainly Indigenous Knowledge Systems also help individuals negotiate political power struggles, develop their own styles of using cell phones and the internet, and can be incorporated into complex systems of individual creativity. Nevertheless, after presenting a much earlier version of this paper at the University of KwaZulu-Natal, I returned to his statement and was intrigued by the minister's closing line that IKSs help individuals 'create stability' and 'co-exist with other communities'.

My doctoral research, now completed, was a specialised network study that historicised the rise of particular Zulu ceramists to relative fame within South African and international ceramic markets. As such, I was attempting to understand constantly transforming norms of communicative action and aesthetics. To pin down indigineity in MaMncube's work is tricky. Historically referential *amasumpa* wares created today for mostly white audiences, the painted wares made on commission for local weddings and sculptures inspired by ancestral dreams are all derived from Indigenous Knowledge Systems. The economic exchange value placed on each style of ceramic work is in the end tied to consumers' Knowledge Systems, their level of affluence, and to the aesthetic 'traditions,' histories, inspirations and aesthetic preferences they want to support through their purchasing power.

Between 2001 and 2006 MaMncube collaborated with Reeves Gumede, Wilbur Force Shamase and Jannie Van Heerden at the Bhekizulu College in Nongoma, South Africa. She became the instructor for the ceramic component of students' arts studies in a programme that Van Heerden, senior subject adviser for arts and crafts in the KwaZulu-Natal Education Department, implemented to encourage support of indigenous arts throughout the KwaZulu-Natal school system.[29] This instructorship was one step towards ensuring Zulu-speaking students value the transforming Indigenous Knowledge Systems that are a basis of inspiration and creativity for ceramists in rural KwaZulu-Natal.

One of the students involved in this project, Nozipho Zulu, travelled in 2007 with me to Nongoma to visit her instructor MaMncube on her way home during a school break. Zulu had recently won the top prize for a third-year arts student at the Durban University of Technology in 2005 for her portfolio of work which included welding, casting, painting, drawing and ceramics.[30] By incorporating MaMncube's instruction into the curriculum, the teaching at the Bhekizulu College provided Nozipho Zulu with the proper context to appreciate the deep connotations associated with Zulu ceramic arts. Zulu was given the chance to start from a foundation that values the complexity of local artistic creation and in 2010 she began work as the Development Officer for the non-profit African Art Centre in Durban, one of the major institutions promoting and supporting IKS artists in the province of KwaZulu-Natal.

In the end, all of the works in MaMncube's *œuvre* are infused with some level of IKS knowledge. Her acknowledgment of her multiple audiences and hybridised ceramics could, in the words of the Minister of Arts and Culture, be seen as her particular style of 'creat[ing] stability' and 'co-exist[ing] with other communities'. Mncube would often mention during my early visits that she saw on the television that people were not always kind to tourists, and that she wanted to try and be as welcoming as possible. Yet, the balancing act she performed between satisfying internal and external audiences was destroyed by the reverberating effects of local poverty. On 28 February 2007 Azolina MaMncube Ngema was, at the age of seventy, shot point-blank several times in the abdomen and right arm. This professionally commissioned attempted murder was carried out at her home in Nongoma.

As an independent woman with moderate economic success MaMncube was the target of violence, a type of event that is surprisingly common within a nation that ranked fourth out of sixty-two nations evaluated in the International Crime Victimisation Survey 1989–2000. As this, and other statistics report, women are often vulnerable to violent crime, a situation that is only exacerbated by economic depression.[31] MaMncube miraculously survived this attack and has found support in the community of ceramists and scholars who have played some role in her life for the past several decades: members of the Nala family of potters, Juliet Armstrong of the University of KwaZulu-Natal, Jannie Van Heerden the senior subject adviser for arts and crafts in the KwaZulu-Natal Education Department, Wilbur Force Shamase of the Bhekizulu College in Nongoma, and myself. Her son helped her relocate to a different region of the province, but Mncube is fearful of returning to her home and the life she built near Nongoma, KwaZulu-Natal and is struggling to collect her old-age pensions and the government grants she relied on to support the three orphaned children in her care.

In the midst of this violence it is difficult to continue discussions of indigenous or non-indigenous aesthetics, cultures, or indeed value systems. The Arts and Culture Minister's claim that indigenous knowledge has created

> ways of doing things [that] have provided people with the survival strategies to deal with poverty and destitution, how to create stability and have instructed them how to co-exist with other communities …

rings a bit false when the ceramist whose work was held up as an ideal in a publication like *Africa: The Art of a Continent* has found, despite her attempts to create stability and survival strategies, that the vulnerability of a widow living with young orphans outweighs community involvement and IKSs that should respect a woman of such advanced age.

These are not issues that art historians and ceramists often confront within their research, but I cannot help but close with these tragic events in one gifted artist's life. MaMncube's life history has encapsulated so many historical moments in South African history, the unfolding history of formal education systems, migratory labour, the liberal fascination with indigeneity and arts, and now the violent flux that is experienced by urban and rural South Africans and occasionally pours into the broadsheets of the rest of the world.

Certainly, the concepts of economic empowerment versus protection of indigenous knowledge that Juliet Armstrong brought up within her 2005 quotation at the beginning of this article takes on a *double entendre* given recent events. Due to familial jealousy one of the famous Nala family of Zulu potters was also shot and killed in 2006. The violence of contemporary South Africa is impacting rurally based women, not just urbanites. It may certainly be that the attention and moderate success brought to artists by arts communities is a liability in the midst of economically depressed areas. Indeed, MaMncube has been denied one of the basic human rights provided for under the progressive South African Constitution. Section 12.1.c reads: 'Everyone has the right to freedom and security of person, which includes the right to be free from all forms of violence from either public or private sources.'[32]

As tourism and the arts become more and more important in non-G8 or 'developing' nations, stability is not necessarily ensured for those who, against the odds, find financial success. MaMncube is nothing if not a woman of amazing spirit and determination. She has built upon a contemporary ceramic tradition to find a way to *live* and create in the midst of dramatic times. Yet, who can protect 'Living Heritage', when economic depression and violence can bring murder to the homes of women who do not consistently have running water, electricity, or the security of one of South Africa's constitutional rights, the freedom from violence?

Acknowledgements

I would like to give thanks to Azolina MaMncube Ngema, Virginia Ndwandwe, Jannie Van Heerden, Bill Itter, and Nozipho Zulu for their time and insightful discussions during interviews cited within this chapter. I am indebted to my research assistants Sibusisiwe Nxele, Sithabile Cele, Nothando Sibiya, and my colleague Muziwandile Hadebe for their insight and instruction within both linguistic and cultural understanding. Many thanks to Moira Vincentelli for her academic support and excellent editorship of the original article.

Note

1 Juliet Armstrong, 'Zulu pottery', *Indilinga: African Journal of Indigenous Knowledge Systems: A Cross-pollination and Critique*, 4:1 (2005).
2 *Ibid.*, p. 344.
3 *Ibid.*, p. 343.
4 Juliet Armstrong, 'Asumpa in ceramics', *The Mechanisms of Power: eleventh Annual conference of the South African Association of Art Historians* (Johannesburg: University of the Witwatersrand, 1995), p. 81 (spelling as in original publication used here); Juliette Y. Armstrong, 'The tourist potters at Mtunzini,' *Negotiating Identities: Proceedings of the 14th Annual Conference of the South African Association of Art Historians* (Johannesburg: UNISA, 1998), p. 4 (spelling as in original publication used here); Armstrong, 'Zulu pottery', p. 343–4; Juliet Armstrong and Ian Calder, 'Traditional Zulu pottery', *Zulu Treasures: of Kings and Commoners: A celebration of the material culture of the Zulu people. Amagugu KaZulu: Amakhosi Nabantukazana: umgubho wezinto ezihambisana namasiko amaZulu* (Pietermaritzburg: KwaZulu Cutural Museums and Local History Museums, 1996).
5 Armstrong, 'Zulu pottery', p. 343.
6 As of this chapter's time of writing, the *Indilinga* website was available at www.indilinga.org.za and the image mentioned is featured on the left side of the site template.
7 Throughout this essay I refer to Azolina MaMncube Ngema as MaMncube or Mncube. The title MaMncube follows Zulu norms of respect known as *ukuhlonipha*, in which a woman is referred to by her maiden name and the prefix Ma, meaning mother, but also goes beyond a woman's motherhood and marks her familial origin. Alternately, my use of Mncube is borrowing from the scholarly and art world style of showing respect by referring to artists by their surname.
8 Brendan Bell and Ian Calder (eds), *Ubumba: Aspects of Indigenous Ceramics in KwaZulu-Natal* (Pietermaritzburg: Albany Print, 1998), p. 29, p. 126; Frank Jolles, 'Zulu beer vessels', *Spuren des Regenbogens: Kunst und Leben im Sudlichen Afrika* (Linz: Arnoldsche, 2001), p. 317; Frank Jolles, 'The origins of the twentieth century Zulu beer vessel styles', *Southern African Humanities*, 17 (2005), p. 105.

9 Images of these works can be found within Tom Phillips (ed.), *Africa: the Art of a Continent* (New York: Prestel, 1999), p. 221.
10 Images of this work can be found in, Hélène Joubert, *Ubuntu: Arts et cultures d'Afrique du Sud* (Paris: Réunion des Musées Nationaux, 2002), pp. 244–5.
11 Jolles, 'The origins of the twentieth century Zulu beer vessel styles', p. 105.
12 *Ukucwebezela: To Shine Exhibition Business-Skills Workshop*, Durban, South Africa, 9 May 2007.
13 Bill Itter, personal conversation, 5 April 2007 – on the height of sales.
14 Armstrong, 'Asumpa in ceramics', p. 81; Sandra Klopper, 'The Art of Zulu Speakers in Northern Natal Zululand; an Investigation of the History of Beadwork, Carving and Dress from Shaka to Inkatha', (PhD thesis, University of Witwatersrand, 1992); Carolee Kennedy, *The Art and Material Culture of the Zulu-Speaking Peoples* (Los Angeles: UCLA Museum of Cultural History, 1978).
15 Brendan Bell and Ian Calder (eds), *Ubumba*, frontispiece.
16 Ruth Phillips and Christopher Steiner, *Unpacking Culture: Art and Commodity in Colonial and Postcolonial Worlds* (Berkeley, Los Angeles and London: University of California Press, 1999), p. 10.
17 Jolles, 'Zulu Beer Vessels', p. 105.
18 *Ibid.* and Phillips and Steiner, *Unpacking Culture*, pp. 9–11.
19 Interpreters and translators who worked on the excerpts included in this article: Nothando Sibiya, Sibusisiwe Nxele, Nozipho Zulu, Nomusa Mabaso and Muziwandile Hadebe. All excerpts are from interviews conducted between 2005 and 2007; full details can be provided upon request.
20 Mncube states that, if there is no blackened pot at hand, a non-blackened pot can be used to present *utshwala*, sorghum beer, to *amadlozi*.
21 Ari Sitas, 'The new tribalism: hostels and violence', *Journal of Southern African Studies*, 22:2 (1996), p. 242.
22 Jean Morris and Eleanor Preston-Whyte, *Speaking with Beads: Zulu Arts from Southern Africa* (New York: Thames and Hudson, 1994), pp. 33, 44, 50 and 51.
23 Thembisa Waetjen, *Workers and Warriors: Masculinity and the struggle for nation in South Africa* (Cape Town: Compress & University of Illinois Press, 2004), pp. 96–7; Sitas, 'The new tribalism,' p. 247.
24 Within text distinguishing cultural typologies of ceramics it has been mentioned that Sotho wares historically used red ochre and black graphite to enhance etched designs (Walter W. Battiss, *et al.*, *The Art of Africa* (Pietermaritzburg: Shuter and Shooter, 1958). p. 91.) Painting on wares is likely an extension of this historical design work and similar innovations made in the incorporation of paint into Sotho/BaSotho wall painting. In the attribution of historical artworks from this region 'a Zulu label obscures the conflation of divergent Northern Nguni groups which constituted the regional confederacy dominated by the Zulu' (Gary Van Wyk, 'Convulsions of the canon: "convention, context, change" at the University of Witwatersrand Art Galleries', *African Arts*, 27:4 (1994), p. 65).
25 Mncube has attended at least one of the University of Natal workshops held at the University of Natal, Pietermaritzburg in 2003 and 2004 under the organisation of Juliet Armstrong. Within her accounts of this workshop Mncube recalls visiting museums, attending a gallery opening, and interacting with scholars and patrons of ceramic arts (informal discussions, 29 September and 16–18 November 2006 and 5 June 2007).
26 Personal interview, 18 November 2006; Nothando Sibiya, interpreter and translator.
27 Personal interview, 28 September 2006; Stabile Cele, interpreter; Nomusa Mabaso, translator.
28 Additionally, Mncube will often sneeze and mutter under her breath in a formalised style that insinuates ancestral inspiration within Zulu styles of expression. These mannerisms are instantly identified by many Zulu-speakers.
29 Van Heerden, personal interview, 13 October 2006.
30 Nozipho Zulu, personal interview, 28 November 2006.
31 Ann Alvazzi del Frate, Jan J. M. van Dijk, John van Kesteren and Patricia Mayhew, *International Crime Victimization Survey 1989–2000*, first ICPSR version (Ann Arbor, Michigan: ICVS International Working Group, 2003).
32 South African Government information website. Bill of Rights page, www.info.gov.za/documents/constitution/1996/96cons2.htm. Accessed 26 June 2007.

Richard Carlton is visiting Fellow in Archaeology at Newcastle University, UK, and a professional archaeologist with a research interest in the archaeology of the Ottoman-Austrian borderlands of Bosnia-Croatia and modern pottery production in the Western Balkans. Having been taught to make pottery whilst carrying out ethnographic research, the author continues to add to the future archaeological record by making and selling pottery each summer in southern Dalmatia and Herzegovina. A shorter version of this article first appeared in Issue 10 of *Interpreting Ceramics* in 2008. The issue was edited by Moira Vincentelli and focused on the theme of Gender and World Ceramics.

Interpreting Ceramics

Selected Essays

Re-evaluating the Role of Women in West Balkan Pottery-making Traditions

Richard Carlton

This paper focuses upon the role of women in the various modes of pottery making recorded in the Western Balkans, particularly the area of the former Yugoslavia where it has long been noted that women potters have been largely confined to domestic production, producing mainly for the household rather than for sale. Just why this should be the case, given the diversity of pottery-making technologies in this region and the existence of female potters in commercial industries elsewhere around the Mediterranean, remains somewhat obscure but is explored below.

The fieldwork research upon which the present paper is based has been undertaken by the author since the 1980s, beginning with a long-term, ethno-archaeological study of the potters on the island of Iž in North Dalmatia,[1] and continuing with visits to all the surviving potters of Bosnia, Croatia and western Serbia, as well as fieldwork in other parts of the Balkans and elsewhere. The initial focus on production techniques amongst potters using the hand-wheel has changed over to time to include parallel pottery-making traditions and to consider the role of the (mainly female) consumer in determining the forms and fabrics produced. In addition to the author's fieldwork, a wide range of published reports have been accessed which add geographical and temporal depth to the range of examples used in the study.[2]

Traditions of pottery making in the West Balkans

The recorded modern pottery-making traditions of the Western Balkans are amongst the most diverse in Europe, having developed by a process of invention, invasion and local adaptation into a proliferation of forms fully reflective of the long and complex history, not to mention present ethnic diversity, of the region. The usual way of rationalising this enormous variety is to select for purposes of classification a single, easily observable

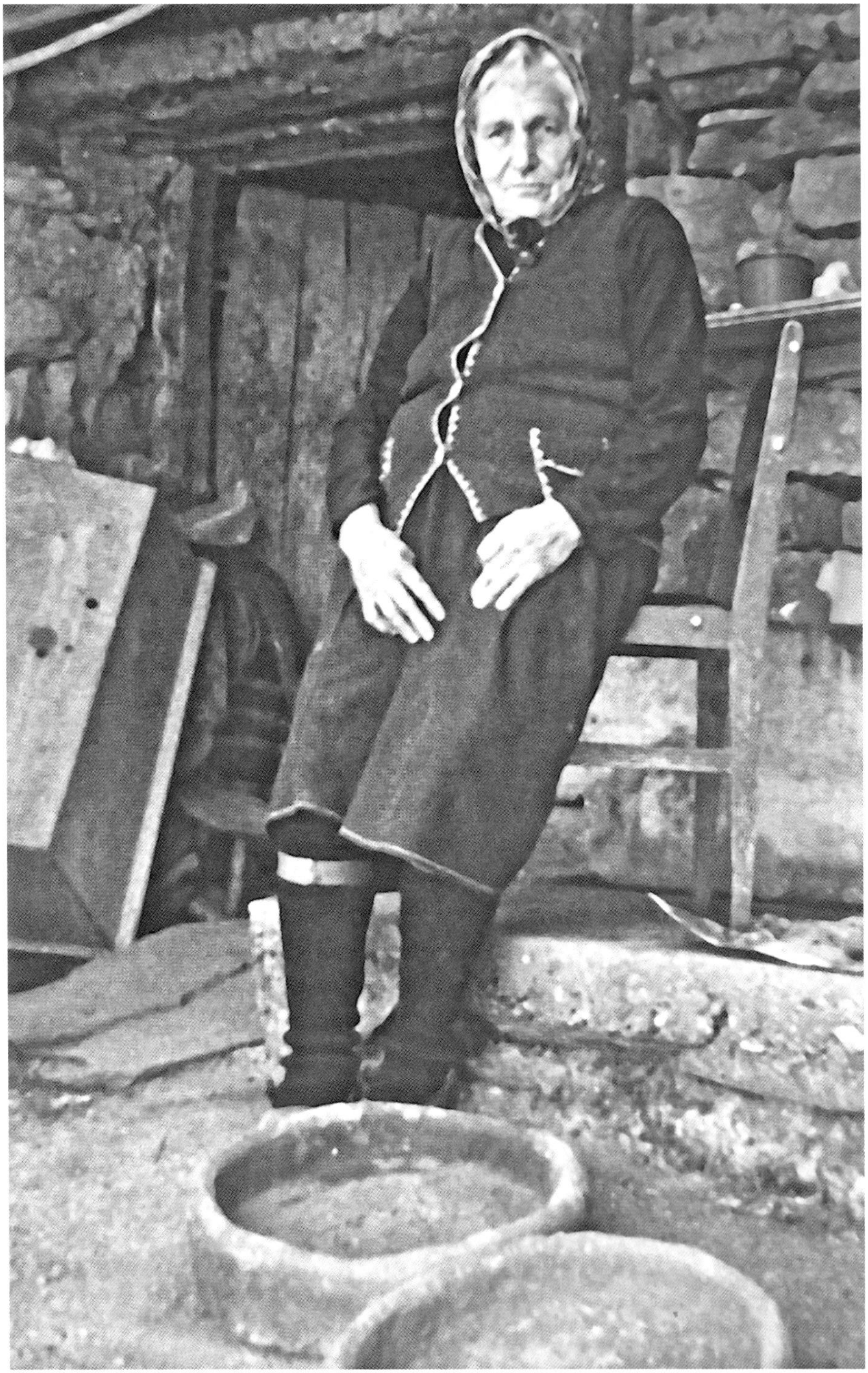

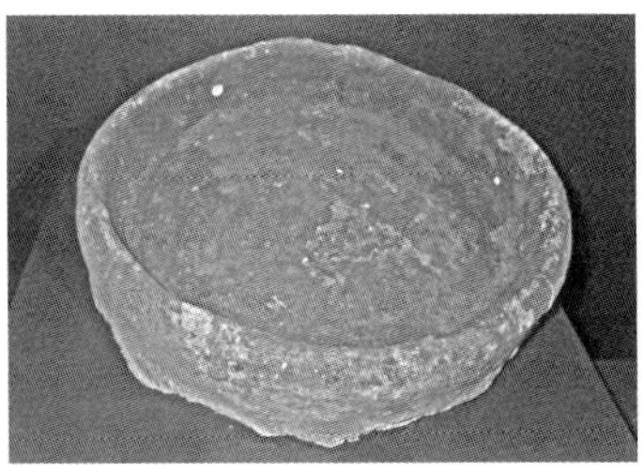

Fig 1. right, Desanka Antić of Gostuša, Stara Planina region of eastern Serbia, with her bread-making pans, or *crepulje*. Photo: Aca Djordjević, in B. Djordjević, *Three Facets of Traditional Pottery Making in Serbia*, 2011.

Fig 2. above, Bread-making pan from Gostuša, Stara Planina region of eastern Serbia, in the collection of the National Museum, Belgrade.

characteristic, exemplified by Tomić's division of pottery-making industries in Serbia according to their use of hand-wheel, foot-wheel or non-wheel technologies.[3]

Pottery making using non-wheel technology

Female potters were formerly best represented within the non-wheel technological tradition; indeed Tomić[4] refers to this tradition as *ženska keramika* (female pottery), although notes several villages in Kosovo, Serbia and Slavonia where it was practiced by men. Most of the locations where women were the principal or only potters were in highland areas where open-hearth cooking remained in use longer than elsewhere, such as in southern and eastern Serbia, western Macedonia and northern Albania. The main products of female potters were shallow dishes, or bread-making pans (Figs 1 and 2) known as *crepulja* (sing.),[5] baking covers or portable bread-ovens known as *vršnik* (sing.), and truncated cones, *topka* (sing.), used to support *crepulje* over the open hearth. The manufacture of baking covers and supports seems to have been largely abandoned by the beginning of the twentieth century, although Tomić reports the continued use of the former until the 1960s amongst the highland Vlachs of the Negotinska Krajina (Serbian, Romanian and Bulgarian border region), some 250 km east of Belgrade.[6] The manufacture by women of *crepulje* was also largely abandoned by the mid-twentieth century, but it seems that widespread knowledge of manufacturing techniques has persisted until the present, along with sporadic production.[7] Such pottery-making traditions were known at Konavle in southern Dalmatia,[8] but were mainly located further east, in Montenegro,[9] Albania,[10] the Rhodope Mountains of northern Greece and southern Bulgaria,[11] northern Bulgaria,[12] Macedonia,[13] southern Serbia,[14] Kosovo[15] and probably, although not mentioned by Butura,[16] also in highland Romania.[17]

The traditional practices used by women to make bread-making pans and associated pots varied according to differences in raw materials as well as the long periods of relative cultural isolation experienced by different groups of makers.[18] Production was generally carried out to satisfy domestic needs between late spring and early autumn, and was often carried out by women as a group activity, sometimes connected to church or other village festivals. The clay, sometimes from more than one source, was excavated from local sources and prepared by drying, crushing, cleaning and rehydrating after being spread out on flat surfaces. After rehydrating, one of a variety of organic or, less commonly, inorganic tempering materials were added by treading – animal hair, straw, chaff and dung were all common additions – with the women rhythmically moving around the clay heap, periodically turning it and treading with one foot. Clay paste thus produced by a group of women would then be divided between those capable of forming the pans. The forming process, often on a wooden board, involved pinching or drawing the clay from the centre of a flat base to form the sides, and was usually completed without adding a separate roll of clay to the incipient walls, which generally measure between 3–5 cm thick and 7–13 cm high.[19] The vessels were then self-slipped by smoothing over with wet hands, or coated with a slip of mud or dung, before drying using methods suited to the clay paste and environmental conditions, after which the unfired vessels were ready for immediate use. Thus, their first use was the beginning of their firing, or a continuation of the manufacturing process. In practice, this meant

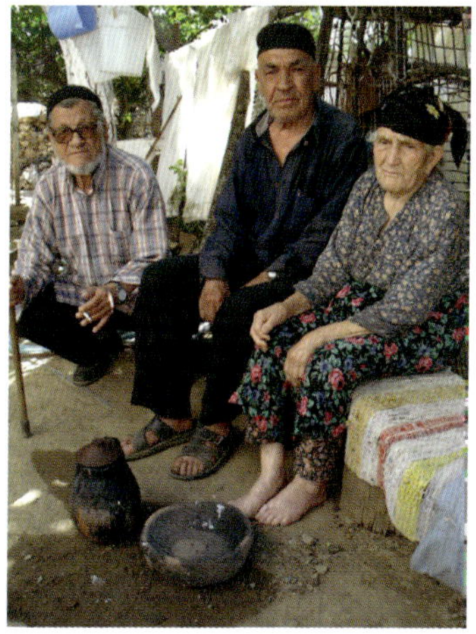

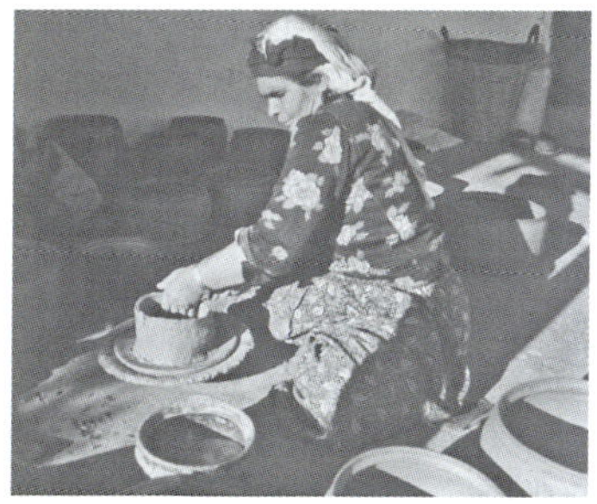

Fig 3. A potter photographed with male relatives at Bashiboz, Macedonia in 2010. Photo: G. Nikolov.

Fig 4. Potter at Gokeyup in western Turkey, photographed in 1989.

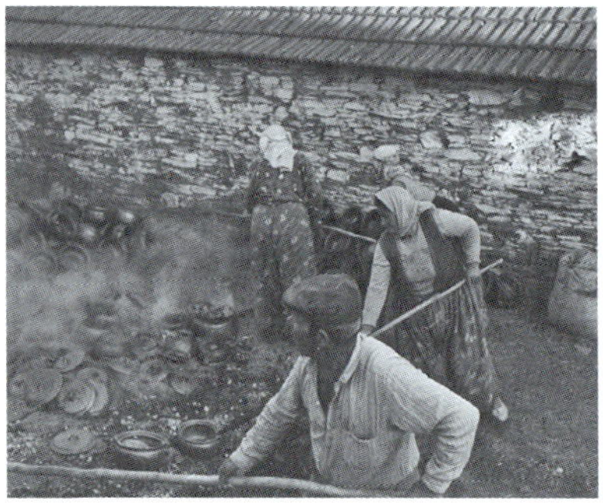

Fig 5. Women and men bonfire-firing pots at Gokeyup in western Turkey, photographed in 1989.

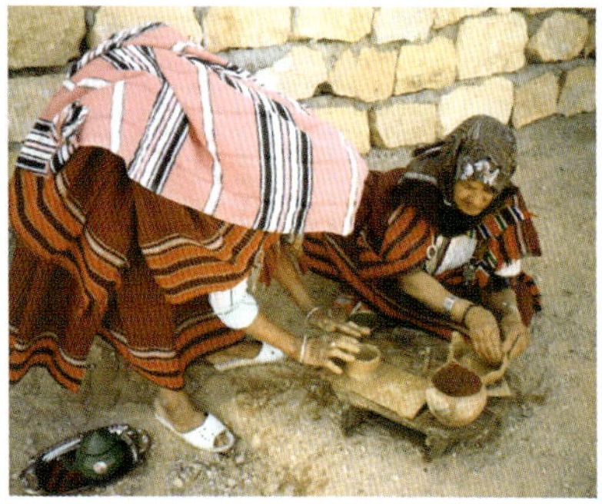

Fig 6. Berber potters in southern Tunisia, photographed in 1994.

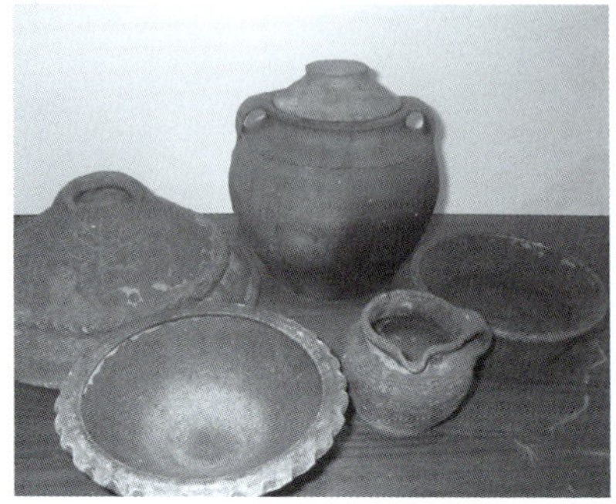

Fig 7. The range of cooking pots produced at Ularica, northern Bosnia, in 1988.

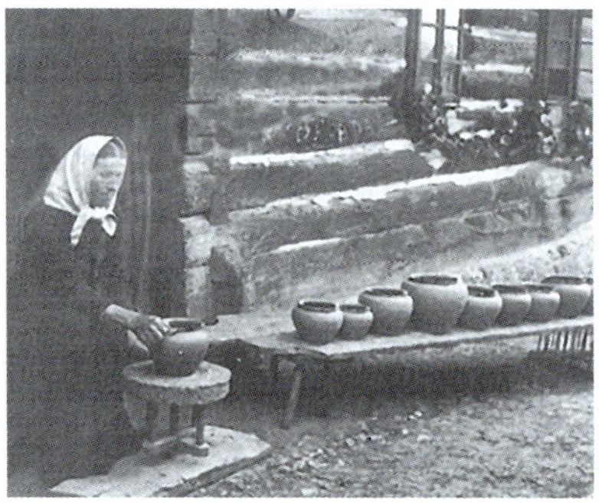

Fig 8. Marija Medić photographed at Grič, western Slovenia around 1930 (Karlovšek 1951).

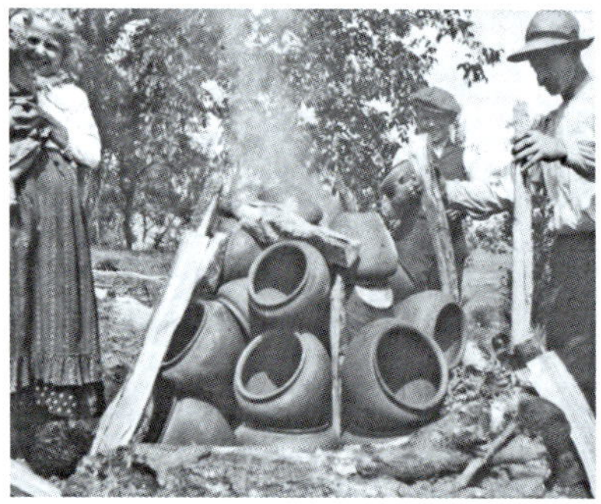

Fig 9. Firing pottery at Grič in the Bela Krajina district of Slovenia c.1900 (photograph supplied by Anton Starc).

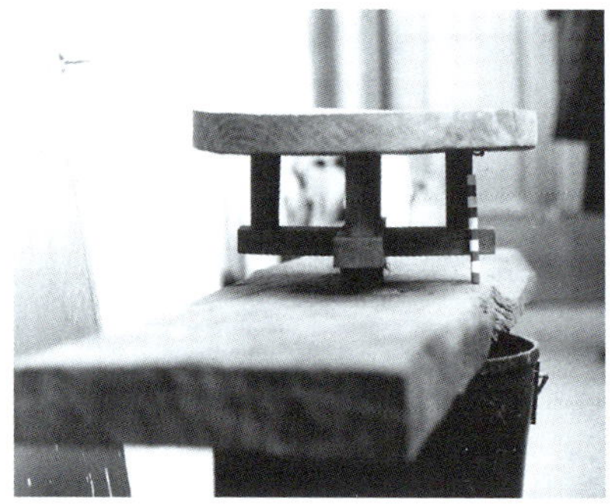

Fig 10. Hand-wheel used by Marija Medić photographed at Grič.

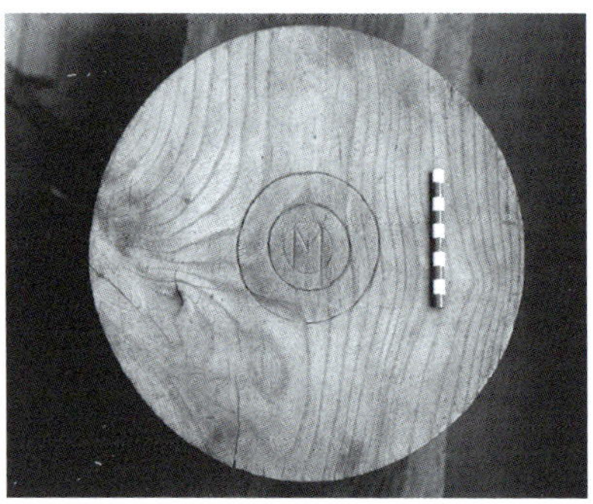

Fig 11. Working surface of the hand-wheel used by Marija Medić, showing her personal mark cut into the wood, which transfers itself to the base of vessels and serves as an identifier.

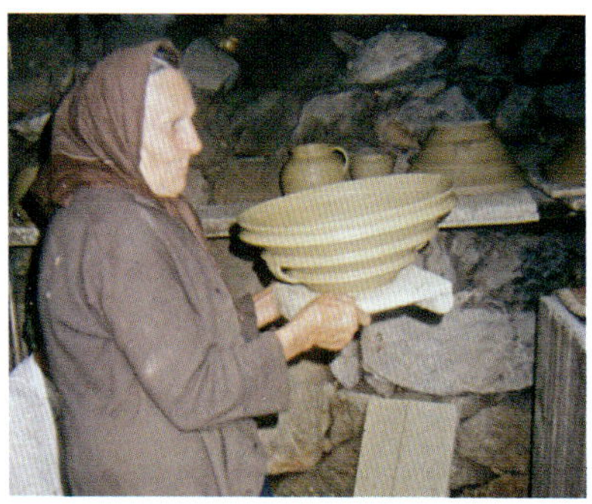

Fig 12. Ana Arbanas carrying a bread-oven from the wheel at Kaluđerovac, Croatia in 1990.

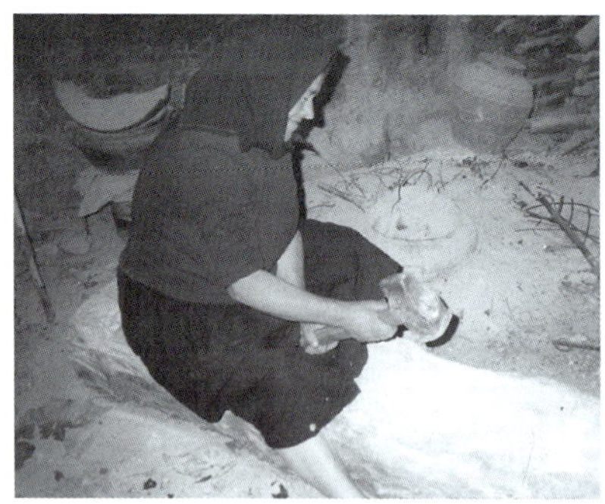

Fig 13. Anđe Knežević of Potravlje breaking calcite in a wooden trough.

that most vessels were only partially fired at best,[20] even after sustained periods of use, accounting for the rarity of these artefacts from archaeologically excavated contexts.

Most of the pots produced by women in this way were for the personal use of the potters themselves, though Tomić[21] notes some instances when it was carried out for profit. Onuzi reports that in Albania, as well as the widespread production of unfired bread pans in '*a considerable number of villages*',[22] a rather different tradition of female production existed in the village of German,[23] where women made single-handled jars, as well as *çerep* and *saç*, often coated with red slip and all fully fired before use. In Macedonia, as late as 2010, Nikolov discovered a survivor of an apparently similar tradition within the mountainous, Turkish-speaking community of Bashiboz[24] (Fig 3). The techniques, particularly the firing methods used here, are similar to those reported elsewhere in Europe and the Mediterranean region, as at Gokeyup near Salihli in western Turkey[25] (Figs 4 and 5), amongst the Berbers of North Africa[26] (Fig 6) and as far north as the Scottish Highlands.[27]

In some places, as in the micro-region of Rajevići south of Novi Pazar in the former Sandžak region of southern Serbia, domestic pottery making by women took place alongside (and, indeed, outlived) commercial coarse-ware production by men using hand-wheel technology. Indeed, Djordjević (following Filipović)[28] notes that in some locations the wives of foot-wheel potters in southern Serbia would make bread-making pans. This suggests that the pottery was not merely utilitarian, and that its production and use also involved symbolic meanings for women which appear almost entirely absent amongst male producers in the Western Balkans. Vincentelli proposes that the activity of pottery making by women is itself intimately connected with female identity and, by implication, that it does not perform the same role for men where it is a male-dominated activity.[29] Djordjević summarises the numerous rituals, customs and taboos associated with female production of bread-making pans in the West Balkans.[30] These seem to have survived longest in Bulgaria and Macedonia, but ethnographic accounts also suggest that they were formerly present in Serbia as well, covering issues such as ritual chanting during manufacture, specific times for clay digging and pan making, ritual purity associated with reproduction (e.g. pregnant women excluded from making) and the rule of odd numbers (e.g. bringing clay from three sites, treading it three times, making an uneven number of pans by an uneven number of women, etc.). Kalmeta cites symbolic reasons associated with the making and use of such pans for the survival of a localised female pottery-making tradition at Konavle, near Dubrovnik; elsewhere, Holleyman cites similar reasons for the survival of the Scottish 'craggan' tradition.[31]

Commercial, rather than domestic, production on the scale noted amongst women potters in Anatolia and Berber-populated parts of North Africa (see above) was carried out in the Western Balkans using non-wheel technology only by men, mainly in parts of Kosovo/south Serbia, Macedonia and Slavonia.[32] The production sequence was similar to the above, but greater quantities of raw materials were required, with inorganic tempering agents prevalent, forming techniques more standardised, pots generally larger, and firing done in open fires separate from kitchen hearths,[33] thereby ensuring that the quality of the finished product was more consistent. The same applied to potters using non-wheel technologies who worked in the Vojvodina until the First World War[34] and in neighbouring

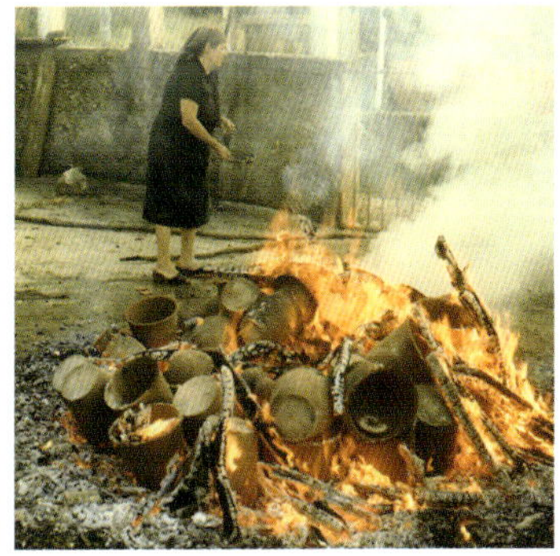

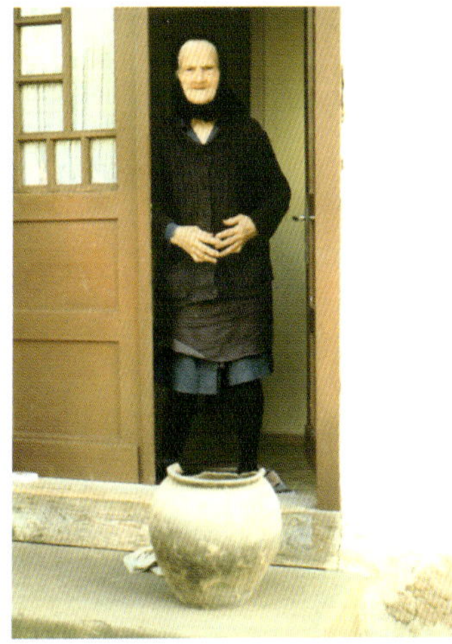

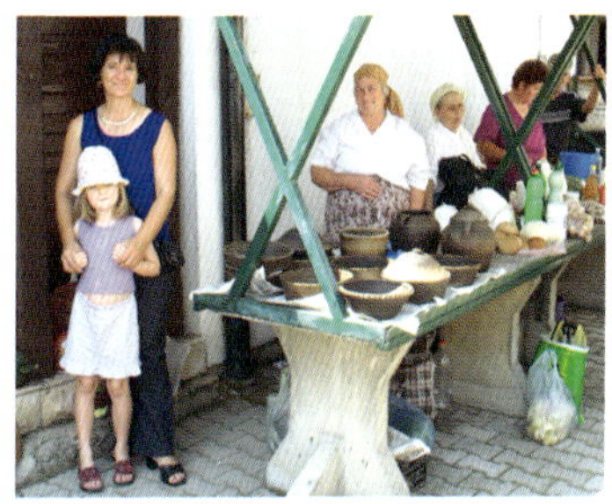

Fig 14. Anđe Kneževic of Potravlje firing pots made by her husband, Jure, in 1995.

Fig 15. Ana Tkalčević of Liplje, Croatia, who sold pots on long trips by horse and cart in Croatia and Bosnia, photographed in 1998.

Fig 16. The wife of the potter, Stjepan Bejić of Ularica, selling pots at Tešanj Market, northern Bosnia, in 2002.

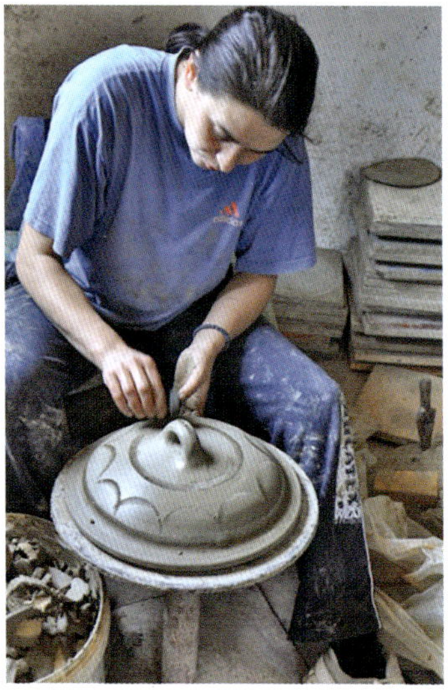

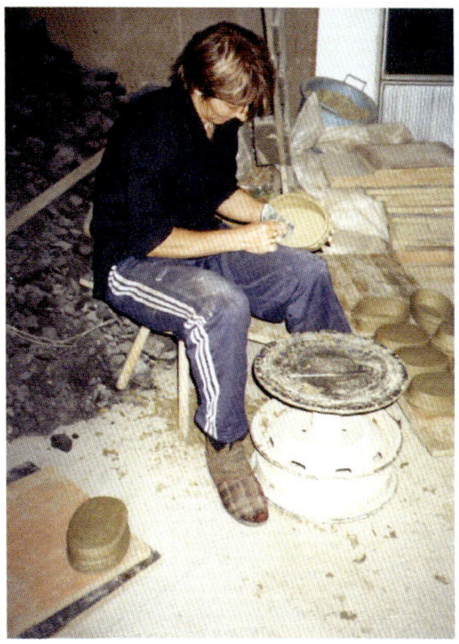

Slavonia, near Slavonska Požega, until 1962. Lechner's exemplary ethnographic description of the latter reveals all stages of production (including the use of moulds for forming bread ovens) to be highly standardised and output high.[35]

Pottery making using hand-wheel technology

Pottery making using the hand-wheel is practised mainly in central and western Bosnia-Herzegovina, southern Croatia, and western Serbia. It is characterised by the use of a wheel rotating upon a fixed, upwardly pointed pivot and operated entirely, or almost entirely, by hand. A great deal of regional and sub-regional variation occurs at all stages in the production process, from the morphology and size of wheels to the nature of firing process, but fabrics are usually coarse, generally calcite-tempered, and firing is usually by means of an open fire, though sometimes in single or double-chambered kilns. Types of pottery produced vary from place to place, but are mainly baking, cooking and storage wares rather than decorative or tablewares (see Fig 7).

Almost all hand-wheel potters were male peasants who depended partially upon pottery for their livelihood, but regarded themselves primarily as farmers. Most of the few remaining potters continue to conform to this broad pattern. The only recorded cases of communities where female potters traditionally predominated were at Grič in southern Slovenia, where production finally died out in the 1950s (although large-scale commercial production had ceased much earlier) (Figs 8–11) and Rakalj on the Dalmatian Primorje where women potters formed the vessels but were assisted by men in paste preparation and firing.[36] Elsewhere, individual female potters are recorded only as exceptions: Popovic records that a woman at Donji Rujani in north-east Hercegovina continued the work of her deceased husband out of economic necessity;[37] Rajković records that a female potter at Donji Dobrkovići in east Hercegovina produced small vessels, '*faster than her father*';[38] and this author was informed at Veselići in 1993 that one of the last potters at Goli Vrh in west Croatia was a deaf, mute woman.[39] At Zlakusa in western Serbia, Djordjević (pers. com.) reports that a single woman, Tadijana Sunjevarić, formerly made pots 'in secret' – implying some kind of taboo against female potters using the wheel, and reflecting a situation common throughout the wider region. These few cases in Croatia, Hercegovina and Serbia[40] suggest that formerly, single (widowed or unmarried) women turned to pottery making only out of dire economic necessity, and seemingly in opposition to mainstream cultural expectations. It is notable, however, that although women tended not to be involved in raw materials procurement and forming, they were (and are) often involved in clay processing, removal of pots from the wheel (Fig 12), drying and firing, as well as buying, selling and, most conspicuously, domestic use (see Figs 13–16). Within the last decade or so, Djordjević (pers. com.) reports that at Zlakusa more women have begun to learn the skills of pottery making and are now accepted as potters. One of these women, Danica Sunjevarić (granddaughter of the aforementioned Tadijana), has become as proficient as any of the male potters (Fig 17), while others, such as Dragica Sunjevarić (Fig 18), continue to be involved mainly as assistants to male relatives (*op. cit.*).

Fig 17. The potter Danica Sunjevarić of Zlakusa, western Serbia. Photo: Aca Djordjević.

Fig 18. Dragica Sunjevarić at Zlakusa, in 2007. Photo: Aca Djordjević.

In the context of the use of pottery, it is worth reasserting the close relationship between the process of manufacture and use, which, as noted above, are most inseparable in the production of 'female' bread pans, which become (partially) fired only when they are first put to use on the open hearth. However, other vessels, particularly low-fired cooking pots made by hand-wheel potters, also change in appearance and physical character due to repeated use, notably by absorbing fat and oil which become part of the fabric of the vessel and can, in time, form a desirable 'non-stick' surface coating. Thus, the process of use continues to modify the vessel; arguably, the production process instigated by male potters is continued by female users. It should also be pointed out that women, as the primary consumers of pots, have traditionally been mainly responsible for the 'quality control' mechanisms imposed on hand-wheel (and other professional) potters, impacting through their purchasing decisions upon the forms and fabrics of pots produced (Fig 19). Thus, as in Vrkašić in north-west Bosnia, prospective buyers chose from up to three distinct fabrics, with those tempered entirely with calcite being considerably more expensive than those tempered entirely with sand or with a mixture of sand and calcite. The preference of a significant proportion of female customer-consumers for calcite-tempered vessels may have prolonged the use of calcite by potters who, without that constraint, might rather have used more readily available and easily prepared materials such as sand.

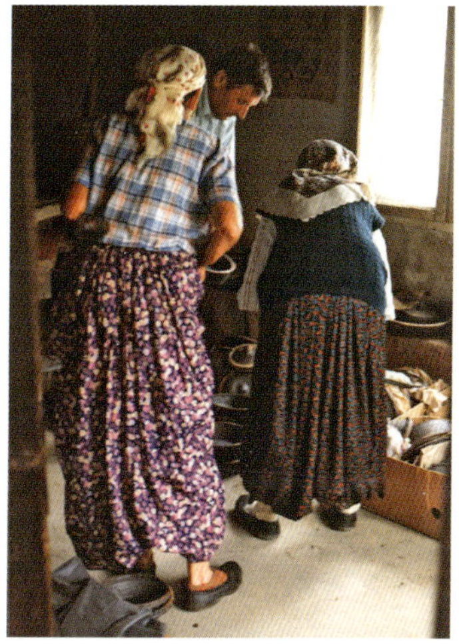

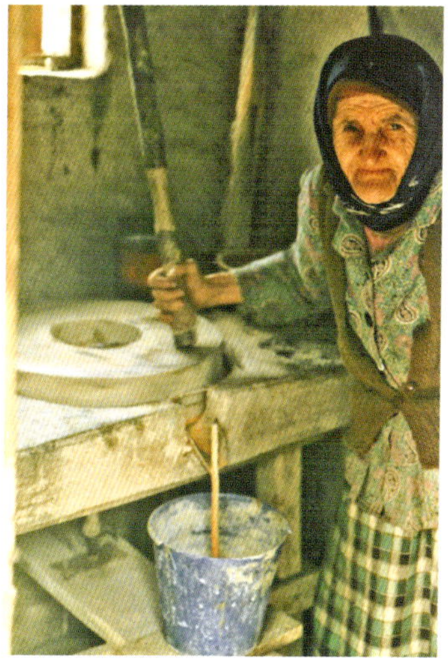

Pottery making using foot-wheel technology

The term 'foot-wheel' normally refers to a wheel constituted from an upper working platform and lower fly-wheel which rotates within a fixed bearing below the fly-wheel. It was, and to some extent still is, used exclusively in some areas throughout modern Serbia and the Vojvodina[41] and parts of Kosovo,[42] west and central Macedonia,[43] north Croatia,[44] Slovenia except the Bela Krajina-Ribnica valley areas[45] and in Bosnian urban centres.[46] Foot-wheel technology is always accompanied by the use of updraught or through-draft kilns and associated with male potters, many of whom operate in urban environments where, lacking connections with the land, they seek to derive most or all of their income from pottery. The universal use of kilns carries a number of implications for foot-wheel potters, including increased costs in time, materials and space, and the ability to produce stronger, glazed products. Where production continues to be based around the household, rather than removed to detached workshops, women tend to be involved in the production process. At Rastoki in northern Croatia, for example, women were responsible for preparing the clay paste and supplying pre-formed balls of clay to male potters at the wheel.[47] Elsewhere, notably in Bulgaria and Romania, pottery formed by men was often decorated by women (see Figs 20–22). In such cases, as at Oboga and Romana in southern Romania, traditionally each woman (or family group) is said to have had her own recognisable decorative style. Finally, it is important to note that the majority of pots offered for sale at markets and fairs throughout the Western Balkans were sold by women; in the case of pots produced on the foot-wheel these would be close female relatives of the potters (Fig 23). This is significant because it places women, as principal consumers and sellers of pots, in a pivotal position to influence the forms and fabrics of vessels produced.

Explaining the absence of female potters

As noted above, in south-east Europe and the wider Mediterranean region, pottery making by women was largely restricted to part-time work in the domestic context, using

Fig 19. Discerning female customers purchasing from the potter Ibrahim Delić at Malešići, northern Bosnia in 1999.

Fig 20. The wife of a potter grinding lead glaze at Oboga, southern Romania in 2002.

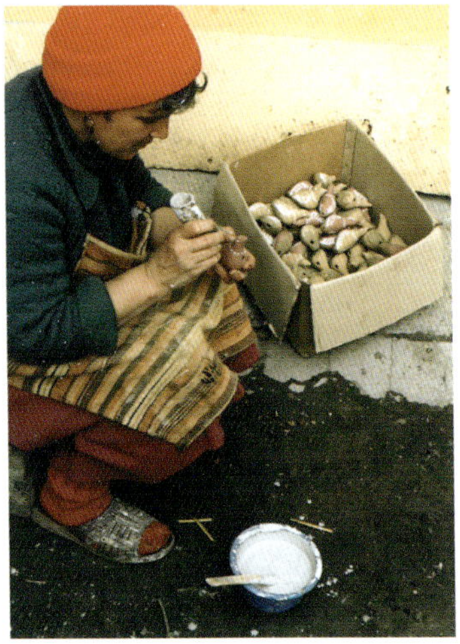

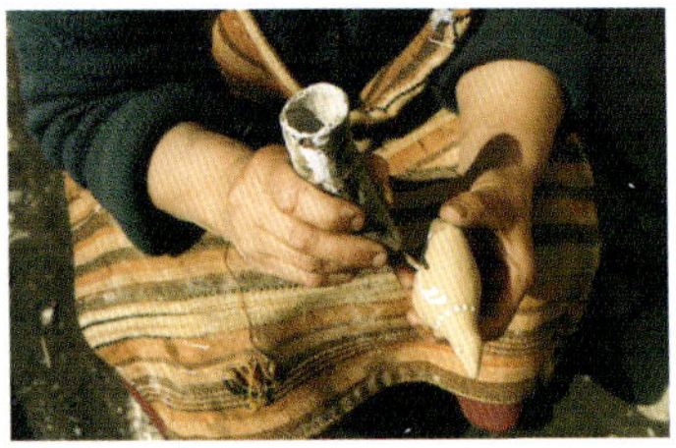

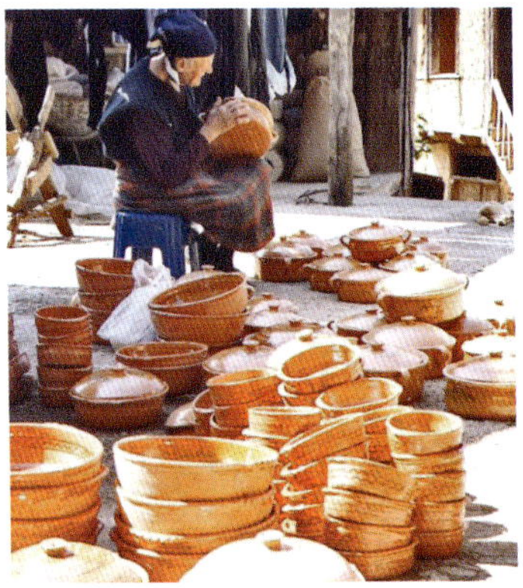

few tools and producing for home use or limited sale, although some exceptions have been noted. Large-scale professional concerns are usually the preserve of men; exclusively so when they involve the use of foot-wheels. Traditions involving the use of hand-wheels occupy the middle ground, in gender terms, with both male and female potters represented. Thus, both male and female potters were recorded by Soviet ethnographers in the area between Belarus and the Northern Carpathians,[48] male hand-wheel potters work near Vila Real in Portugal and in the Spanish province of Asturias, but in Brittany,[49] Cyprus[50] and the villages of Moveros and Pereruela in the north of Spain, female potters predominate (see Fig 24).

Using these examples and based on the strong universal tendency for women potters to be associated with the simplest forms of portable, usually non-wheel technology and part-time or occasional work, it might be expected that women rather than men would be involved in using the highly portable hand-wheel technologies of the West Balkans which are well suited to part-time work in the domestic contexts of peasant communities, where both space and time are limited. Indeed, Peacock arrived at just this conclusion based on the example of Rakalj, which for him appeared to confirm the association between hand-wheel technology and female potters, but is actually rather exceptional.[51]

Why is there such a limited tradition of commercial pottery making practiced by women in the Western Balkans? Certainly, it can not be accounted for by any coherent set of differences between the obligations and aspirations of the (female) peasantry in the Western Balkans compared to northern Spain, the Troodos mountains of Cyprus or central Anatolia, since, although women do make pots commercially in each of those locations, the socio-economic conditions they operate in vary enormously – for example, those in Spain and Cyprus work for themselves or as equal parts of co-operative businesses, while those in Turkey form pots as part of family firms controlled by men. It can certainly be refuted that women lack the strength to carry out the work, as suggested by some male potters; instead, they seem to be checked by a combination of social convention, domestic and agricultural duties. Perhaps we should view the absence of female potters as an emancipation from the drudgery of domestic toil (pottery making is rarely – and even then only partially – viewed as an opportunity for artistic expression). Alternatively, it may be most enlightening to view pottery making as a multi-task activity wherein clay preparation, decoration, firing and selling are just as important as forming. In this respect, women continue to play an important role in activities which can be practiced flexibly, and generally do not require exclusion from farming, child-rearing and cooking – activities to which women in predominantly rural societies are universally bound – for long periods. Thus, in this sense, it could be argued that women in the West Balkans do indeed participate in commercial pottery making, by preparing clay, firing and selling; activities which are as integral to the production process as forming, but which can be practiced more flexibly around the domestic responsibilities to which women in rural environments tend to be bound. Viewed from this perspective, the perceived relative absence of female potters may be more a matter of semantics – i.e. a potter is normally considered to be the one who forms the pots, rather than the one who prepares materials, fires, decorates and sells them – than reality.

Fig 21. The wife of a potter applying slip-trailed decoration at Oboga, southern Romania in 2002.

Fig 22. The wife of a potter applying slip-trailed decoration at Oboga, southern Romania in 2002.

Fig 23. Woman selling pots in a Macedonian market. Photo: G. Nikolov.

Pottery making in the West Balkans is in all respects – socially, spatially and economically – closely tied to the household, with individual production units comprised of individuals working for the exclusive benefit of a single household. Where women are involved exclusively or predominantly in the preparation of hand-built wares, some symbolic element seems to be involved in production, which is lacking when they are part of a family-based team in commercial production. The extent to which women are able to assist with pottery-making activities in such contexts depends upon their obligations to domestic activities and upon the availability of male family members and children as alternative sources of labour. The nature of such assistance is generally regarded as a domestic chore performed within the household context, of no greater or lesser significance than agricultural or domestic tasks.

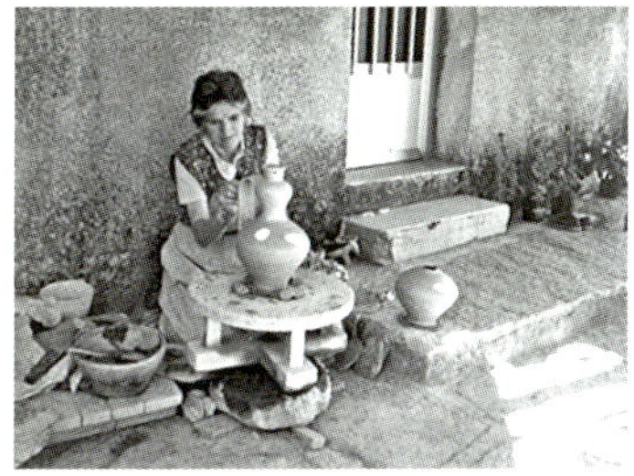

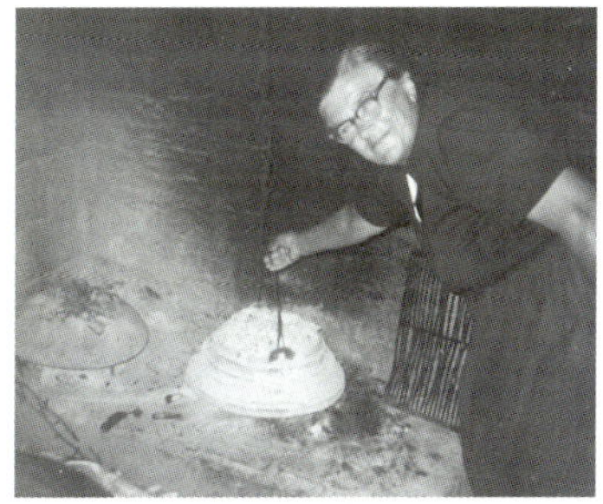

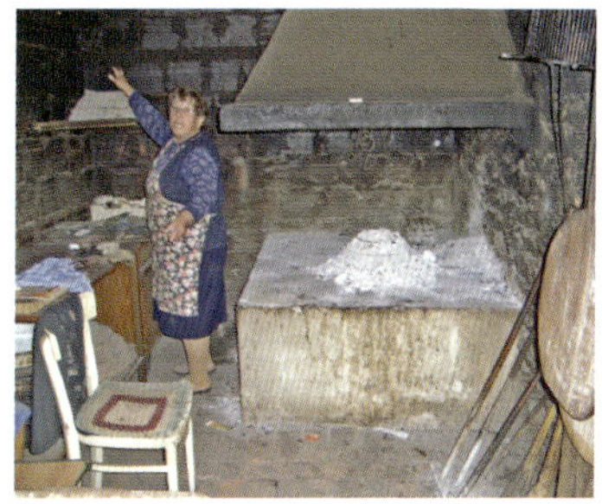

The future of pottery making in the Western Balkans

The wars of Yugoslav succession in the 1990s affected the surviving West Balkan potters, and pottery-making traditions, in different ways. Some potters, such as Meho Begović, the last potter at the once extensive pottery-making centre of Višnjica near Sarajevo, were forced by conflict to stop working and did not survive the war. In contrast, pottery making at Zlakusa in western Serbia, which was outside the war zone but affected by economic sanctions, increased considerably both in numbers of potters and total output as consumers turned to traditional pottery in the absence of reliable power supplies.[52] Others, in Bosnia and Dalmatia, cut off from clay supplies or markets during the war, were forced to cease production during the hostilities but resumed thereafter. These potters found a ready market in the immediate aftermath of the war, since many households wished to replace pots lost or broken during the war, or were forced by circumstance to cook on the open hearth. In 1994 the author accompanied a potter and his wife from recently liberated Potravlje, near Sinj in Dalmatia while they peddled pots in the vicinity of Sinj and Trilj, the pots being bartered for goods rather than money due to the paucity of money in the post-war economy. The exchange was carried out for measures of grain between the potter's wife, who as well as selling also assists with clay preparation and firing, and women in the households visited.

Pottery making during and immediately after the war found an important role in a time of need, as did other aids to self-sufficiency which were accessed from general and localised reservoirs of residual traditional skills, held by memory and tradition within the community and revived to meet demand. However, pottery making since the late 1990s has resumed the decline into which it fell during the middle of the last century, although the few remaining producers still find a market amongst pockets of consumers and, perhaps increasingly, in restaurants selling traditional food, such as meat cooked *ispod peka* or *sač* (under a baking cover, see Figs 25 and 26), or slow-cooked stews such as *Bosanski lonac* (Bosnian pot). The potters of the region have generally been slow to awaken to the potential demand from tourism, nor have they been encouraged to do so by government agencies that appear still to consider pottery an unworthy symbol of a modern nation. However, in Serbia, whilst commercial foot-wheel potters have foundered and now barely exist, the hand-wheel centre of Zlakusa flourishes. This is in no small measure to the efforts of Biljana Djordjević in promoting the potters and their products,[53] but exploits a growing internal and external tourist market and the strong desire of Serbs to maintain domestic

Fig 24. A female potter at Moveros in Northern Spain, photographed in 1987.

Fig 25. Earthenware and metal baking covers photographed at Privlaka near Zadar in 1988.

Fig 26. A Potravlje baking cover in use in 2008 near Nin, near Zadar in Dalmatia.

All photos: Richard Calton unless otherwise stated.

culinary traditions. Zlakusa may provide a model for potential regeneration elsewhere, notably in Bosnia and Croatia, where pottery making in the hand-wheel tradition lingers at four locations and could be reintroduced elsewhere, as well as in Slovenia where efforts are being made to reintroduce it to the village of Grič. Since the culinary traditions and future of the region rests predominantly with women, the future of pottery making is probably also in their hands.

In order to advance traditional pottery and pottery making in the Western Balkans by promoting its importance as a cultural asset – as has been done successfully at Zlakusa in Serbia[54] – a considerable challenge to overcome within wider society and officialdom is to raise the profile of the arts in general, and traditional culture in particular.[55] In Bosnia, a country that has been left culturally battered by recent events and endures continuing nationalist rhetoric,[56] this is a particular problem, since the cultural expressions most likely to be promoted are those with clear ethno-religious affiliations, which pottery lacks. Djordjević's comment, partly based on Filipović's seminal work on female pottery, that the form and production methods of *crepulje*, in particular, can not be related to the ethnicity of the producers is certainly also pertinent to potters working in the hand-wheel tradition.[57] Perhaps because of its relative ubiquitousness, and its association with the 'female' domestic sphere, pottery has not been co-opted as a symbol of ethnicity or nationality in Bosnia-Herzegovina or the wider region and stands, indeed, as a symbol of a deeper, underlying common culture, effectively symbolising unity rather than division. This, together with a general perception of pottery making as a marginal and unclean occupation involving mysterious processes, does little to promote it in the eyes of officialdom. Despite numerous obstacles, however, it should be possible to improve the fortunes of potters in existing and recently extinguished centres of production by promoting the practical benefits and symbolic associations of traditional pottery, stressing its close connection with food production in the domestic context.

The prognosis for the survival of pottery making carried out by, rather than for or at the behest of, women in the Western Balkans seems rather poor, particularly in the absence of a strong modern tradition of studio pottery.[58] Although there is undoubtedly a surviving, albeit already much-diminished knowledge base, domestic pottery production barely survives in the Western Balkans and, although female participation in male-dominated commercial enterprises (e.g. Figs 12, 13 and 20) will continue, even those traditions (with the enigmatic exception of Zlakusa) appear to be dwindling. Pottery making in general and non-wheel work in particular are still considered as 'low culture' and representative of a 'backwards' peasant culture that remains stigmatised in many quarters. However, the resurgence of the hand-wheel tradition at Zlakusa is notable for several reasons, not least because of the greater involvement of women in all aspects of production (e.g. Figs 17 and 18), and because it is buoyed by the continued strength of demand from mainly female consumers. Whether this demand is led by utilitarian or symbolic factors, or a combination of both, is a subject for further research, but gives some cause for optimism and arguably provides a potential key to the regeneration of similar traditions elsewhere. In the meantime, however, the main role of women in the pottery traditions of the region is likely to be in curating and reporting it, a role in which women have gained the ascendency since the middle of the last century, as exemplified recently by Djordjević, Džeko, Onuzi and Randić.[59]

Notes

1 R. J. Carlton, 'Paste and fire: Some comments on the technology of prehistoric pottery in the Western Balkans in the light of ethnoarchaeological research', in D. Georgiou, *The Archaeology of Fire* (London: BAR, 2003), pp. 63–81.

2 It is of some interest to note, with respect to the role of women in the pottery-making traditions of the region, that, since around 1960, the main scholars of pottery making in the region have been women – Onuzi in Albania, Randić/Randić-Barlek in Croatia, and Tomić and Djordjević in Serbia – whereas almost all reports up to the 1950s were produced by men.

3 P. Tomić, *Grnčarstvo u Srbiji* (Beograd: Etnografski Muzej, 1983).

4 P. Tomić, *Narodna Keramika u Jugoslaviji* (Beograd: Etnografski Muzej, 1966), p. 5.

5 *Crepna* in Macedonian; *çerep* in Albanian.

6 Baking covers, usually called *sać* or *peka*, but sometimes by derivatives of *crepulja* (e.g. Črpnja on the island of Iž in North Dalmatia) continue to be made by hand-wheel potters in Bosnia-Herzegovina and Croatia.

7 As late as 2010 Nikolov reported continuing production amongst a remnant Turkish-speaking highland population in eastern Macedonia. G. Nikolov, 'Constructive, reconstructive ethnology opportunity for a dynamic understanding of folk pottery – Macedonian case' (abstract), in B. Djordjević (ed.), *Traditional Pottery Making from the Ethnoarchaeological Point of View: Scientific Research and Safeguarding of Intangible Heritage* (National Museum: Belgrade, 2011) and pers. com.

8 M. Randić-Barlek, *Lončarstvo u Hrvatskoj*, katalog izlozbe, (Zagreb: Etnografski Muzej, 1982), p. 4.

9 J. L. Vukmanovic, 'O izradi crepulja I pečenju hleba u Crmnici (Montenegro)', *Glasnik Ethnografskog Muzeja u Beogradu*, 12 (1937), pp. 133–5.

10 A. Onuzi, 'Mjeshteria e punimit te eneve prej balte ne fshatin Farke (Tirane)', *Etnografia Shqiptare*, 8 (1976), pp. 177–89; A. Onuzi, *Poceria Popullore ne Shqiperi* (Tirana: Akademia e Shkencave e RPS te Shqiperise, Instituti I Kultures Popullore, 1988), pp. 59–63, tabs XXIX–XXXII.

11 N. Efstratiou, 'Production and distribution of ceramic type in Highland Rhodope: an ethnoarchaeological study', *Origini: Preistoria e protostoria delle civilt antiche*, 16 (1992) pp. 311–27; N. Efstratiou, 'Ceramic ethnoarchaeological research in the Balkans: the case of the Rhodope Mountains', abstract for the conference: Traditional Pottery Making from the Ethnoarchaeological Point of View – Scientific Research and Safeguarding of Intangible Heritage, 10–12 June 2011, National Museum, Belgrade.

12 H. Bakarelski, *Etnografia na Bulgaria* (Sofia: Izdatelstvo Nauka i Izkustvo, 1974).

13 Nikolov, 'Constructive, reconstructive ethnology opportunity for a dynamic understanding of folk pottery'.

14 D. Zlatković, 'Izrada crepulja na Staroj Planina', *Etno Kulturovosku Zbornik*, 13 (2009) pp. 73–80.

15 M. C. Filipović, *Zenska Keramika kod Balkanskih Naroda*, SAN, posebna isdanja knjiga CLXXXI (Beograd: Ethnografski Institut knjiga 2, 1951); S. Kullashi, 'Punimi I çerapëve në fshatin Përçevë', *Glasnik Muzeja Kosova*, 13–14 (1984), pp. 415–20; B. Božović, 'Ženska keramika u Bubama (Rogozna)', *Kosovsko-Metohujsku Zbornik*, 3 (2005), pp. 207–12.

16 V. Butura, *Etnografia Poporului Român*, (Cluj-Napoca: Editura Dacia, 1978).

17 B. Djordjević, *Three Facets of Traditional Pottery Making in Serbia* (Belgrade: National Museum, 2011), p. 9.

18 It is not unreasonable to suggest that the modern tradition of female baking-pan production results from a continuity of tradition from the Neolithic period.

19 Djordjević, *Three Facets of Traditional Pottery Making in Serbia*, p. 15.

20 M. C. Filipović, 'Lončarstvo u Kučinu i Džurovu kod Priboja na Limu', *Glasnik Etnografskog Instituta Srpske Akademije Na auka*, 1 (1952), pp. 507–9.

21 Tomić, *Grnčarstvo u Srbiji*, p. 18.

22 Onuzi, *Poceria Popullore ne Shqiperi*, p. 121.

23 *Ibid.*, tabs I and II.
24 Nikolov, 'Constructive, reconstructive ethnology opportunity for a dynamic understanding of folk pottery'.
25 R. J. Carlton, 'An ethnoarchaeological study of hand-wheel pottery industries in Bosnia and Croatia (with notes on shorter visits to Turkey and Spain)', *University of Durham and University of Newcastle upon Tyne Archaeological Reports Series: Archaeological Reports for 1988*, 56–61 (1989), pp. 60–1.
26 R. J. Carlton and A. Rushworth, 'Exploratory archaeological and ethnoarchaeological fieldwork in Southern Tunisia, 1994', *Universities of Durham and Newcastle Archaeological Reports Series: Archaeological Reports for 1993* (1994).
27 G. A. Holleyman, 'Tiree craggans', *Antiquity*, 21 (1947), pp. 105–11; K. Wilson, 'Barvas ware: women potters of Barvas, Isle of Lewis, Outer Hebrides', *Interpreting Ceramics*, 10 (2008).
28 Djordjević, *Three Facets of Traditional Pottery Making in Serbia*, p. 19; Filopović, *Zenska Keramika kod Balkanskih Naroda*.
29 M. Vincentelli, *Women Potters Transforming Traditions* (London: A. & C. Black, 2003).
30 Djordjević, *Three Facets of Traditional Pottery Making in Serbia*, pp. 19–21.
31 Holleyman, 'Tiree craggans', pp. 105–11.
32 Tomić lists the following locations: Djakovica in Kosovo; Kotraža, Vrnjići, Rujište and villages around Pirot and Negotin in Serbia; and Novo Selo, Golo Brdo, Daranovac, Gradište and Cernik in Slavonia. Tomić, *Narodna Keramika u Jugoslaviji*, p. 17.
33 Tomić, *Grnčarstvo u Srbiji*, pp. 18–21.
34 *Ibid.*, p. 20.
35 Z. Lechner, 'Proizvodnja pokljuka u Požeskom Novom Selu', *Posebni Otisak iz Osjeckog Zbornka*, 8 (1962), pp. 255–80.
36 The most recent potters at Rakalj have been male, and it is far from certain that male potters did not take part in vessel forming along with women in the past. However, it is certain that female potters were formerly active there.
37 C. Popović, 'Lončarstvo u Bosni i Hercegovini II', *Glasnik Zemaljskog Muzeja u Sarajevu* (Etnologija), nova serija, 12 (1957), p. 19.
38 S. Rajković, *Lončarstvo Zapadne Hercegovine*, (Mostar: Zavičajni Muzej Hercegovine, 1956), p. 3.
39 One of the photographs published by Onuzi of hand-wheel potters at Farke in central Albania appears to show a female potter, although this has not been verified. Onuzi, *Poceria Popullore ne Shqiperi*, tab. XLI.
40 Randić-Barlek mentions that female potters were also known in similar circumstances in Bosnia, although Kalmeta, in his survey of Bosnian pottery making, came across none. M. Randić-Barlek, *Lončarstvo Ručnoga Kola*, katalog izložbe (Zagreb: Etnografski Muzej, 1990), p. 5; A. Kalmeta, 'O seljačkom lončarstvo u srednjoj i zapadnoj Bosni', *Glasnik Zemaljskog Muzeja u Sarajevu* (Etnologija), nova serija, 9 (1954), p 155.
41 M. Banski, 1975, *Narodna keramika Vojvodine*, katalog izložbe, 'cvet keramike', 1-5 (Aranđelovac: Muzej Aranđelovac, 1975).
42 R. Barisić, *Keramika Kosova i Novog Pazara* (Beograd: Etnografski Muzej u Beogradu, 1989).
43 L. Orr, 'A Macedonian pottery village', *Studio Potter*, 26:1 (1997), pp. 92–4.
44 V. Pinter, 'Lončarstvo u Jerovcu', *Vjesnik Etnografskog Muzeja u Zagrebu*, I (1935), pp. 69–78; L. Kašpar, 'Lončarsko rukotvorstvo u selu Liplje u Gorskom Kotaru', *Vijesti Muzealaca I Konzervatora Hrvatske*, 3/4 (1978), pp. 58–62; L. Kašpar, 'Piročanski pecalbari u Vrginmostu', *Etnološka Tribina*, 2 (1979); B. Uzelac-Bijelić, 'Ni lončari više nisu', *Revija Đakovacki Vezora* (1981), pp. 60–1; Randić-Barlek, *Lončarstvo u Hrvatskoj*, p. 4.
45 J. Karlovšek, 'Lončarstvo na Slovenskom', *Slovenski Etnograf*, 3/4 (1951), pp. 87–111.
46 Carlton, 'An ethnoarchaeological study of hand-wheel pottery industries in Bosnia and Croatia', pp. 56–61.
47 A process observed and filmed by this author in 1990.
48 A. A. Bobrinsky, *Pottery of Eastern Europe: Sources and Methods of Study* (Moscow: Tsetlin, 1978), e.g. p. 41, pp. 126–7, p. 149.

49 L. Franchet, *Ceramique Primitive: Introduction a l'Etude de la Technologie* (Paris: Librairie Paul Geuthner, 1911).
50 G. London, F. Egoumenidou and V. Karageorghis, *Töpferei auf Zypern damals-heute* (Darmstadt: Verlag Philipp von Zabern, 1989); I. Ionas, *Traditional Pottery and Potters in Cyprus: The disappearance of an ancient craft industry in the 19th and 20th centuries*, Birmingham Byzantine and Ottoman Monographs Volume 6 (Farnham: Ashgate, 2000).
51 D. P. S. Peacock, *Pottery in the Roman World: an Ethnoarchaeological Approach* (London: Longman, 1982), p. 19.
52 Indeed, for reasons that are not entirely clear, Zlakusa has continued to grow and develop new technologies during peace time, so that by 2011 the number of active potters there numbered over thirty.
53 Biljana Djordjević is director of the National Museum in Belgrade and became involved at Zlakusa as an ethno-archaeologist, but through her involvement has provided additional support and impetus to the resurgence of pottery making there.
54 Djordjević, *Three Facets of Traditional Pottery Making in Serbia*; and see S. Drndarević, *Zlakusa: Turističko Selo* (Belgrade: Ministarstvo Poljoprivrede Šumarstva i Vodoprivrede, 2010).
55 Unfortunately, Heyl and Gregorin's recent book *Traditional Arts and Crafts of Bosnia-Herzegovina*, by focussing only on the potters of Liješevo and devoting half of the chapter to non-traditional studio potters, tends to reaffirm the perception that only the branches of pottery making perceived as aesthetically 'fine' merit promotion to the wider world. N. Heyl and C. Gregorin, *Traditional Arts and Crafts of Bosnia-Herzegovina*, trans. C. L. Walford (Italy: DITRE, 2005), pp. 96–105.
56 Symbolic of the level of importance attached to ethnography in modern BiH is the current (2011 – early 2012) closure of the National Museum of Archaeology, Ethnography and Natural History; various complicated reasons are behind this, including politics and funding problems, but governmental and societal apathy also plays a part.
57 Djordjević, *Three Facets of Traditional Pottery Making in Serbia*, p. 25.
58 Although see Heyl and Gregorin, *Traditional Arts and Crafts of Bosnia-Herzegovina*, pp. 101–5 for an example of studio pottery absorbing some elements of traditional practice in Bosnia, albeit using non-wheel technology – interestingly, in this context, Vincentelli in *Women Potters Transforming Traditions* notes that although women gained access to the wheel in the last century, principally through the promotion of pottery as art, she feels they are also in the forefront of the reaction against using it.
59 Djordjević, *Three Facets of Traditional Pottery Making in Serbia*; L. Džeko, 'Pottery in Liješevo (Bosnia and Herzegovina) – a living tradition', in Djordjević (ed.), *Traditional Pottery Making from the Ethnoarchaeological Point of View*; Onuzi, *Poceria Popullore ne Shqiperi*, pp. 59–63, Tabs XXIX–XXXII; Randić-Barlek, *Lončarstvo Ručnoga Kola*; M. Randić, 'Svi Lički Lončari', *Etnol. Trib.*, 22:29 (1999); M. Randić, 'The role and position of traditional pottery production in Croatia', in Djordjević (ed.), *Traditional Pottery Making from the Ethnoarchaeological Point of View*.

Acknowledgments

We would like to acknowledge the contributions of all the authors whose work has been published in the *Interpreting Ceramics* electronic journal over the years. We have only been able to include a representative sample in this book and hope that readers will be encouraged to return to the *Interpreting Ceramics* web pages to read more (www.interpretingceramics.com). The members of the editorial committee of the Interpreting Ceramics Research Collaboration are grateful to the universities who have supported our project over the years and to our editorial advisory board members who have acted as peer-reviewers.

Glory Hall has designed *Interpreting Ceramics* from the beginning and we are delighted that she has been able to carry forward the distinctive look of the journal into this selection of essays. The editors would also like to thank colleagues at Wunderkammer Press: Dr Graham McLaren, proof-reader Anna McLaren and image researcher Katherine Hallett. We are particularly grateful to Viv Kenchington for steering the book through to publication.